Teenage Nervous Breakdown

Second Edition

Teenage Nervous Breakdown

Second Edition

Music and Politics in the Post-Elvis Age

DAVID WALLEY

Routledge
Taylor & Francis Group
New York   London

Routledge is an imprint of the
Taylor & Francis Group, an informa business

Published in 2006 by
Routledge
Taylor & Francis Group
270 Madison Avenue
New York, NY 10016

Published in Great Britain by
Routledge
Taylor & Francis Group
2 Park Square
Milton Park, Abingdon
Oxon OX14 4RN

International Standard Book Number-10: 0-415-97857-2 (Softcover)
International Standard Book Number-13: 978-0-415-97857-6 (Softcover)
Library of Congress Card Number 2005057520

Library of Congress Cataloging-in-Publication Data

Walley, David.
    Teenage nervous breakdown : music and politics in the post Elvis age / David Walley. -- [2nd ed.].
        p. cm.
    Includes bibliographical references (p.) and index.
    Contents: "This, here, soon" -- Who stole the bomp (from the bomp sha bomp)? -- Blame it on the sixties -- Boxers or briefs? : music politics in the post-Elvis age -- Play school : you can dress for it, but you can't escape it -- The twinkie defense -- Bad day at internet -- Asking Alice : fighting for the right to party -- Don't touch me there : whatever happened to foreplay? -- White punks on dope : why Camille Paglia is academe's answer to Betty Page -- Da Capo.
    ISBN 0-415-97865-4 -- ISBN 0-415-97857-2 (pbk.)
    1. Music--Social aspects--United States--History--20th century. 2. Popular culture--United States--History--20th century. I. Title.

ML3795.W29 2006
306.4'8420973--dc22   2005057520

Taylor & Francis Group
is the Academic Division of Informa plc.

Visit the Taylor & Francis Web site at
http://www.taylorandfrancis.com

and the Routledge Web site at
http://www.routledge-ny.com

Dedication

To Jim Morrison, Duane Allman, and Vivian Stanshall, but especially Lowell George

TEENAGE NERVOUS BREAKDOWN

some contend that rock and roll
is bad for the body and bad for the soul
bad for the heart, bad for the mind,
bad for the deaf and bad for the blind.
make some men crazy, make them talk like fools
make some men crazy, and then they start to drool.
unscrupulous operators could conceal, could exploit the
   scene,
conditional reflex varies, change the probabilities
it's crazy and raucous at its crack-assed pace,
it's a Pavlov on the human race,
it's a terrible illness, a terrible disgrace,
and it's usually permanent when it takes place.
It's a teenage nervous breakdown,
a nervous teenage breakdown,
it's a teenage nervous,
nervous teenage
teenage nervous
nervous teenage
nnnn-----ah----yes.

Contents

Preface to the First Edition

Somewhere back in the midseventies I chanced upon an essay by Kurt Vonnegut called "Good Missiles, Good Manners, Good Night," wherein he relayed the comments of an Indianapolis luncheon companion with an "upper-class Hoosier" accent who said this:

When you get to be our age, you all of a sudden realize that you were being ruled by the people you went to high school with.... You all of a sudden catch on that life is nothing *but* high school. You make a fool of yourself in high school, then you go in to college and learn how you should have acted in high school, and then you get out into real life, and that turns out to be high school all over again—class officers, cheerleaders, and all.[1]

Of course, he was right, but because it's been happening for a few generations now, most of us have all but ceased to notice it—we are resigned to it in fact. So was I until faced with the prospect of going through adolescence yet again, but through the eyes and feelings of my eldest daughter (11 but going on 16 as kids increasingly seem to be nowadays). This book is as much for my generation as for hers who will, in time, I suppose, wonder about the same thing.

We all know that being a teenager and having to endure high school sucks, and the sooner it's over the better. If this is true, I'm puzzled why we as a nation *willingly* continue to haunt the corridors of rock and roll high school, but now as hostages to a system (and state of mind) that encourages our adolescent selves, needs, desires, fears, and tastes rather than getting on with our lives in the present tense. As a cultural historian, I've devoted most of my adult creative life to being fascinated and intrigued by how we got to this point in our national development. Who really made the dance steps it seems we all have to learn? Even our national political campaigns resemble high school student body politics, some not even as clever. What for newer New Age journalists is that "ultimate" litmus test of character? How the candidates were in high school, especially for elections in this Post-Elvis Age, post-1978.

Why the "Post-Elvis Age," you ask? It was during the career of Elvis Presley from 1954 to 1977 that America and by extension rock and roll music made its mark on the world: as an attitude as well a sonic environment for commerce. "This, Here, Soon" (Chapter 1) will explain when and how this happened by placing it within its historical context.

The essays and philippics in *Teenage Nervous Breakdown* are my attempt to examine the ramifications of this continuing state of affairs by focusing on the many interfaces between music and politics. It will examine how a state of mind that originated in fifties high school culture and peer group morals has been culturally and commercially exploited, and in what ways our lives and our world (including the nature of American democracy) have been altered in the process. While this secular teenage religion with its broad-based multinational and ideological appeal promises to keep us young (in mind and spirit if not in body), it is simultaneously exacting a terrible price. Though the songs of youth (present and past) inform our lives and promote a sense of shared time and history, I've wondered whether it is even real or a collectively homogenized compilation of electronic media nostalgia that has been developed, perfected, and refined over the past 40 years of increasingly wired-in life in this global society. I've been thinking, in short, about time, time and those waves—cultural historians among others are fond of doing that.

Teenage Nervous Breakdown is basically a series of word-jazz rock and roll improvisations and variations on the above themes. I'd like them to be thought of as a jumping-off place, a platform that will provoke further investigations and dialogues about the nature of the beat and rhythm of contemporary American life.

Instead of musical notes arranged in various time signatures, I'm using ideas from historians, economists, social scientists, poets, and rock and rollers too. Each essay has its own individual form and rhythm, but don't be fooled by the "time": "White Punks on Dope" (Chapter 9) for instance, might appear to be an academic essay—it's not, trust me. Some essays have extensive endnotes and structure, others are little more than free form—that's where I'm riffing, taking a solo. "The Book of Head" in "Blame It on the Sixties" (Chapter 3), and most of "Don't Touch Me There" (Chapter 8) are examples of that I suppose.

Relax and enjoy the set.

David G. Walley

York, Maine

Preface to the Second Edition

I have always maintained that thinking is a subversive activity,
so I'm delighted that Routledge agrees with me, and has seen fit
to reissue *Teenage Nervous Breakdown: Music and Politics in
the Post-Elvis Age* to prolong its useful life. My faith in the publishing business restored, not only have they have allowed me
to revisit these essays, but also expand on certain aspects of the
book that the previous introduction didn't cover as well as add a
bonus track that was left out the first time around. Good taste is
timeless they think; and amen to that I reply.

The original preface is a fair representation of my thoughts
when I was 53. And though time keeps on slipping into the future
and I'm 60 with my eldest daughter a junior in art school, high
school is eternal and American culture continues to be manipulated by peer group pressure tactics in advertising that sell all
manner of goods from automobiles to political ideology, though
it seems that less and less people ask themselves why this is
so. When I wrote *TNB* my intention was to question this reality,
because I thought others might want to do the same. Call me a
romantic fool or an old sorehead, which undeniably I am, but
I'm still convinced this is the case.

As it stands, *TNB* is still as much a meditation on American
culture as it is about rock and roll, which commercially and culturally informs us, and though in its past and present state it continues to be the soundtrack of our lives that claims to promote a
sense of shared time and history, I still wonder in a larger sense

whether it is even real, or, as I said seven years ago, a "collectively homogenized compilation of electronic media nostalgia" that has been developed and perfected and refined over the past half century of "nows". Though each essay here stands alone as a variation on this basic theme, and the reader can read them in any order, they're all about establishing a context. And if I may be so bold, in order to fully understand that context, I recommend reading "This, Here, Soon" first since it places the my argument within the context and setting of more than 200 years of American cultural and literary history, just in case anyone thought I made it up for my own amusement.

I have my favorites of course, and as a product of the Sixties, "Blame It on the Sixties" has special relevance especially these days when the United States is governed by those of the "boomer" (boy do I hate that word!) generation who may or may not have inhaled, but who fundamentally misunderstanding what the culture had to teach, nevertheless expropriated the buzz words and concepts for their own use and willfully allowed them to be relentlessly homogenized out of recognition by MTV and the wonderful world of Fashion when they knew better. I'm very fond of "Fragments from 'The Book of Head'", the sub-section from that essay since I worked hard to duplicate the flavor of that time in all its anarchic, illuminating and mind-bending glory — but in a semi-linear fashion of course. I tried to give voice to all cultural, social, and intellectual elements that went into the period, and to show how meanings extended far beyond its own time and stand as a more enduring monument to the period than mini-skirts (though there's nothing wrong with them ... really.)

Fundamentally *TNB* is more about asking questions than providing answers, and I ask plenty of them. I wanted to stir the pot, so to speak, so that the reader might be convinced that it was valid to question the fundamental assumptions they had about American life in this commercial society, as well as assure those who were curious or dissatisfied with the way things were to convince them they weren't alone, that someone out there was listening, someone out there was seeing and feeling their unease.

By the way, *TNB* is a great book for college students who might be ready to question their own reality instead of just downloading it to their iPod too. I've used it as a text to discuss a wide range of socio-cultural issues, and the results have been extraordinary.

The topics run the gamut. Some of these essays are laugh-out-loud funny, some will annoy. Repeated readings, sometimes of single paragraphs in individual essays, will provoke contrary thoughts. Depending on your frame of mind, you might be offended, but I hope not. Politics is discussed in "Boxers or Briefs: Politics in the Post-Elvis Age," which uses the music business as an all-pervasive metaphor, especially that fable "How the Kleptos Lost Their Briefs," a disquisition on the pitfalls of fame in the music business that *Rolling Stone* has yet to explore for their readers. The effects of consumerism on public education are examined in "Play School: You Can Dress for It but You Can't Escape It". [Interestingly enough, the second half of the title I stole from an advertisement I wrote back in the late Seventies for an record (yes! record) for the jazz/rock fusion group Weather Report called, "Heavy Weather".] "White Punks on Dope" is a variation of high school, but set in in higher education, God help them, while "Asking Alice" discusses consumerist fashions in recreational drugs. "Who Stole the Bomp (from the Bomp Sha Bomp)?" delves into the origins of musical consumerism and its effects on the critical establishment, while "Don't Touch Me There: Whatever Happened to Foreplay" engenders gender and possibly sexual consumerism but with a slightly retro approach. "Bad Day at Internet," the bonus track for this updated edition, discusses consumerism in the information age, and though it doesn't go into contemporary technology that changes minute by minute, such as file sharing, Kazaa, iPods and the like, the basic thrust of its arguments still holds, the basic mechanism remains. Instead of penis envy, I suppose technology envy works as a merchandizing tool with the netterati, where geeks have a coolness quotient too.

People have asked me why I didn't provide answers to the mess that we've put ourselves in. But in all honesty, there are no *right* answers, only right questions, and my job is to ask them, and yours is to try to answer them if you can. However, once "This, Here, Soon" is understood, you're on your way, and you'll begin to understand how big and complex this problem is, and why it continues to bedevil the great American unconscious of some of us. It's important to keep in mind that *TNB* is not a destination but a point of departure, a jumping off point, and the free-form essays herein are meant to provoke discussion to establish, not shut down, an interior dialogue while proposing an alternative vision to the flash and dash of packaged reality that surrounds us. Think of these essays, these blasts of light as free-form word jazz, or a very long and intricate jam, a theme with variations where you, the reader, will be given space for your own solo and become part of this ongoing dangling conversation. You'll be surprised where it takes you if you allow yourself the time and space to do so.

Thinking is a subversive activity, but not all subversion is destructive. I hope you agree, so again, eight years later, I invite all of you just to sit back, relax, and enjoy the set.

David Walley
York, Maine

Acknowledgments

I'd like to thank the following people, without whom this book could not have been written:

These people provided inspiration in the past tense: Warren Susman, L. B. Namier, M. Gale Hoffman, and Jacques LeGrande.

These people provided insight and encouragement in the present tense: MacAlister "Mac" Brown; Russell Bostert of Williams College; the staff of Sawyer Library, Williams College, especially Walter Komorowski, a prince among archivists; the staff of Williamstown Public Library; Jim Reed and Bill Leach, savvy historians and good friends; Paul Barrère, who, fresh from the shower, provided me with the lyrics for "Teenage Nervous Breakdown" and Elizabeth George's address; and Michael Ochs for aid and comfort, just like old times.

A special tip of the head to Nigey Lennon for listening to huge chunks of this book over the phone, even if she didn't have a clue of the context and for stepping in as a pinch-hitting editor for "Boxers or Briefs"; to The Galactic Editrix who ran this whole manuscript through her magic fingers while mercilessly chastising me for being a comma murderer; to my rock and roll agent, Joe Regal, a.k.a. Dr. Jazz, who took time he didn't have to fine tune "Blame It on the Sixties" even though he wasn't born then.

Geli, my only wife, and our four children, Sean, KC, Lindsay, and Melissa, I thank for putting up with me being abstracted and "out of it" in the course of this project. I'm sure they're glad to have me back for a while.

Last, I'd like to thank the late Don Gifford, my good friend, mentor, and the unindicted co-conspirator who, over lunch 4 years ago, suggested I stop ranting long enough to actually sit down and write this book. Throughout this project, he has kept me on track and focused. His insights on American cultural history, the Transcendentalists, and Henry James and his crowd, as well as jazz history, have been invaluable. I especially thank him for bringing to my attention Louis Jordan and the Timpani Five. I feel truly blessed to have been able to collaborate with such a scholar. It's been one hell of a ride, hasn't it, Don?

Chapter 1

"This, Here, Soon"[1]

Growing up

it's like the high dive
at camp
you went up one way
and you came down another
you could either dive or jump
but you couldn't go back
        down the ladder,
some kids stood there
all thru lunch
but the counsellor
wouldn't let them climb
        down
and the longer you waited
the harder it got.
I did one of those life saving jumps
the kind with my arms and legs spread
but I still splat the water pretty hard
        it stung.

—Peggy Garrison[2]

The younger generation begins in the womb; before it is three years old,
major industries . . . are vying for its favor. By the time it is in its teens, its
purchasing power is immense; and it has by then developed a social style
of its own, which older generations react to, chiefly with aversion but to
some extent with emulation.

—Gilman Ostrander

1

In the Post-Elvis Age our collective perception of our history as a people and the cultural time of our nation have been fundamentally altered. Both have been held hostage by the corrosive effects of an increasingly celebrity-driven consumerism, itself the result of the cumulative effects of the commercial exploitation of high school peer group dynamics that started in the fifties, whose present market share has, as of this writing, been computed to be a whopping $65 billion per annum. During and after the Age of Elvis, this virulent form of goods-driven, not to mention intellectual, consumerism animated by the rock and roll beat has in turn affected our world to the point where a multinational corporate consciousness has replaced our sense of selves. In a little more than a quarter century, these marketing techniques now sell all manner of goods and services, its reach further extended by music television, which broadcasts its visual equivalent 24 hours a day, 7 days a week—our new Voice of America.

In those epochal years from 1954 to 1977 in which Elvis Presley's and the Beatles' careers bloomed and sputtered, rock and roll had succeeded in transforming our collective character. By the early sixties, adolescence, an uncomfortable waystation on the way to maturity—formerly a matter of age or attitude—had become not only a big business, an infinitely renewable commercial resource, but also a desirable state of being all by itself. At one time it may have been that all you needed was love, but now a credit card or two is more than helpful to pay for the rock and roll dreams that money can buy. Today the economic power of youth has become the principal fuel that powers the great multinational entertainment conglomerates to an extent that even a decade ago was impossible to conceive. This state of affairs didn't happen overnight. These tendencies have been inherent in America's character from its inception—we've just ignored them.

In 1835 when Alexis de Tocqueville, a French aristocrat, wrote *Democracy in America*, he was fascinated by the vitality of a young America and its drive to be a great independent commercial power, although he had some reservations about that goods-oriented *now*. He did not question America's being, its commercial spirit, but he was struck by what it could become as a result:

> ... not that it leads men away from the pursuit of forbidden enjoyments, but that it absorbs them wholly in quest of those which are allowed. By these means, a kind of virtuous materialism may ultimately be established in the world which would not corrupt, but enervate, the soul, and noiselessly unbend the springs of action.[4]

Two decades later while roaming the streets of Brooklyn and Jersey City, Walt Whitman, enamored, enraptured, and lyrically drunk on the fumes of American possibilities, wrote *Democratic Vistas*. Like de Tocqueville, he was aware of his nation's *now*, but still held a consciousness of *then*, of America's immediate past in the age of steam and rails, as well as of its immediate future in the Civil War and the era of the robber barons to come. He faced toward the future that he saw from the vantage point of his epochal poetic *now*:

> America, betaking herself to formative action (as it is about time for more solid achievement, and less windy promise.), must, for her purposes, cease to recognize a theory of character grown of feudal aristocracies, or form'd by merely literary standards, or from any ultramarine, full-dress formulas of culture, polish, caste, &c., enough, and must sternly promulgate her new standard, yet old enough, and accepting the old, the perennial elements, and combining them into groups, unities, appropriate to the modern, the democratic, the west, and to the practical occasions and needs of our own cities, and of the agricultural regions.[5]

Quite obviously, Whitman's Democratic Vistas, his speculations, never envisioned multinational conglomerates built upon the commercial possibilities of adolescent consumers becoming bigger ones with more expensive tastes. Or the economies built upon educating preteen and preschool consumers how to step logically from Power Ranger/Ninja Turtle battle axes to Air

4

Jordans to BMWs in their own consumer-affinity groupings. Who knows what he would have made of the debate that has raged for a quarter century about the cumulative effect on children of sex and violence on TV or in movies? How would he have assessed the advertisers who sponsor and package such shows or the commercials themselves? Or the corrosive effects of commercials on the national mind and on the youth who spend a total of 2 months of waking hours per year alone watching them?[6] Yes, these are modern problems for the modern age that Whitman couldn't have foreseen. Nevertheless, it is remarkable that, despite this apparent weakness of vision to our the modern sensibility, he intuited the path America had taken as well as the crisis it would provoke down the road:

> I say of this tremendous and dominant play of solely materialistic bearings upon current life in the United States, with the result as already seen, accumulating, and reaching far into the future, that they must either be confronted and met by at least an equally subtle and tremendous force-infusion of purposes of spiritualization, for the pure conscience, for genuine aesthetics, and for absolute and primal manliness and womanliness—otherwise our modern civilization, with all its improvements, is in vain, and we are on the road to a destiny, a status, equivalent, in this real world, to that of the fabled damned.[7]

5

Fate of the "fabled damned"? That's one hell of a punishment for straying from the idealistic ethical path he envisioned America should and could follow. But without a map-building childhood or an adolescence free from external commercial manipulation, what other course is available? What you see is what you get now, because America's greatest industry, its major export to the world, is devoted to making products mediated on the *now*-ness of a promised collective mythical future that aims to negate the *then* of the past forever, just as our rock and roll world does.

In the roaring twenties, 60 years after Whitman's *Vistas*, Johan Huizinga, the renowned Dutch medievalist historian, arrived on these shores to an America booming in the aftermath of World War I, a war that had plunged everyone into a bloody, pointless, and destructive frame of *now*—in the words of Ezra Pound "For an old bitch gone in the teeth,/For a botched civilization."[8] Like Whitman and de Tocqueville before him, Huizinga was also impressed by the force of America's militant present-tense living. In a series of collected lectures and observations entitled *America: A Dutch Historian's Vision, From Afar and Near*, he summarized the American experience of "This, Here, Soon" as indicative of its enthusiastic acceptance of life in the present and future tense.

And like de Tocqueville and Whitman, he saw that despite its commercial and social energy there was also another force working on the spirit of America:

> . . . a perpetual tension in America between a passionate idealism and an unrestrainable energy directed to material things. And because the popular mind in America is naive and easily moved emotionally, it often does not observe the contradiction between what the country does and its resounding democratic ideals.[9]

Although the Great Depression of the thirties may have briefly administered a shock to America's consumer appetite, the shock did not last; the industrial boom generated by World War II and its aftermath rocketed America into an unparalleled material prosperity. For some at the dawn of the modern consumer era in the late forties, notably clergymen and scholars like Joseph Harountunian, there was a profound and disquieting moral crisis afoot amidst this explosive, unnatural, and surreal abundance that

> . . . tempts men to be at once fascinated and repelled by the good. It tempts men to pursue goods, and in doing so, to fear the good. The good is in "justice, mercy and peace". It is consistency and integrity, in loving according to truth and right. It inheres in men and not in things. It is other than the goodness of goods and without it, goods are not good. But the machine-made spirit teaches otherwise. It identifies the good with goods and induces men to dread it except as thus identified. It persuades men that there is no good other than goods. Thus men come to dread good as evil and to love evil as good. Thus it is that an apparent good produces evil.[10]

Harountunian's dire remarks may have well suited certain segments of the population to whom consumer culture was still a novelty (and some today), but nearly a half century later, after the Pill, credit cards, microchips, and the Internet, his lofty homiletics seem quaint and arcane to the majority of Americans. For them, the Depression and World War II are as so much black-and-white film footage. And although the machine-made world in which we easily abide is deemed user-friendly, more than ever America's watchwords remain "This, Here, Soon."

Morality in a consumer society? Get real: Goods are goods, they're morally neutral, some are better or worse, and about the only time the question comes up is just about the time you've paid for your car or the warranty has expired and it dies (how do they do that?). Only then do you find out that these days "durable goods" are by definition only supposed to last 3 years. If anything, moral rights have become consumer rights—all we need are tighter lemon laws since everyone's a consumer, no? That's the way we've all been schooled, and that goes to the heart of the matter, as we'll find out.

And despite the fact that our playroom remains continually stocked with an inexhaustible surfeit of goods, there is an undercurrent of discontent, a notion of consequences that comes from the selective art of consumer forget. What do we do when we tire of our goods, our toys? According to Bill Bryson, former expatriate American journalist living in England, we banish them and the *then* they represent to the perennial garage, attic, or hall closet

7

> . . . [which] seem to be always full of yesterday's enthusiasms: golf clubs, scuba diving equipment, tennis rackets, exercise machines, tape recorders, darkroom equipment, objects that once excited their owner and then were replaced by other objects even more shiny and exciting. That is the great seductive thing about America—the people always get what they want, right now, whether it is good for them or not. There is something deeply worrying, and awesomely irresponsible, about this endless self-gratification, this constant appeal to the baser instincts.[11]

Though the *nows* of de Tocqueville and Bryson are separated by more than 150 years, their observations neatly dovetail into each other. The problem they uncover deep within the collective American psyche has come to a critical juncture, this result of living without the presence of a past. In Whitman's time it was common to complain that, compared to Europe, America had no past and no culture of its own. It did; it just wasn't on the order of Sir Walter Scott's *Ivanhoe*—it was different, uniquely American, and Longfellow wrote *Hiawatha* in the attempt to fill that void, as did James Fenimore Cooper with *The Deerslayer*. In this Post-Elvis Age, TV, computers, and rock and roll music are supposed to be equivalents, but what do they say?

Back in the fifties, at the dawn of the modern era of TV, Ernie Kovacs, one of the pioneers in electronically enhanced TV comedy, was quoted as saying, "Don't watch too much TV, it will only rot your mind."[12] He may have been right, but that's not all it's done. While today Ernie Kovacs is hailed for the creation and development of a unique comedic electronic visual vocabulary, he was looked on in his time as a lovable if quirky eccentric. An exception in the so-called Golden Age of Television, he managed to succeed despite, not because of, the possibilities already inherent in the intoxicating mixture of commerce and entertainment. TV exerted its fascination not only on adult Americans of the post-War generation who were comparatively new to it, but also on a bumper crop of children. For preschoolers in the fifties, it was an electronic babysitter to give Mom a break, and when the older school-age children trooped in after school it served as company so that the evening meal could be prepared and on the table at 5:30 when Dad came home. Such diversions included not only *Romper Room* or *Kukla, Fran and Ollie* in the morning but also after school teen dance shows like Dick Clark's *American Bandstand* (and its regional equivalents), which publicized the music of Elvis Presley, Jerry Lee Lewis, and others. Wildly successful of course were Walt Disney's *Mickey Mouse Club* and *The Wonderful World of Disney*, which in 1955 launched not only a theme-park way of life and national merchandising fads but also a media conglomerate lifestyle/ideology of considerable economic and cultural strength that still exists today. During this "Golden Age" an enduring connection was cemented between Mickey Mouse and rock and roll (more on that later), through which merchandizing techniques were developed and refined that would appeal to teenagers and future generations of teenagers as well.

According to Steven Kline, a Canadian media researcher, in his book *Out of the Garden: Toys and Children's Culture in the Age of TV Marketing*, it was in the service of the economic goals of Ronald Reagan's America that in the early eighties the children's TV industry was deregulated so that toy manufacturers were given free rein to produce half-hour cartoon infomercials to sell preschoolers and preteens their character toys. Ever the economic realist, Reagan was just levelling the playing field by expanding the reach of merchandizing practices already in place in the early fifties that had been dealing with young teen baby boomers and their uncommitted money, which now could ensnare preteens and toddlers in a market that was formerly off limits. Preteens are no longer considered passive; their "lifestyle preferences" are not only actively solicited and tracked, but it's also commonplace these days for kids themselves to be consultants and junior art directors for toy companies.

Enough time has passed since the fifties, so there's a closed feedback loop operating under these unifying premises: Habituate children early to the values of the broker's world even though they might not immediately have the direct purchasing power, for eventually when they become teens they'll demand their own goods just like their sisters, brothers, and parents before them. Finally it was possible for younger and younger children to be exploited by larger and larger industries for, as it turns out, bigger and bigger bucks. In the nineties, this seems to be an acceptable situation despite the consequences it has on all of us of whatever age. It's an ironic comment on American life that if you want to find out about children in this shopper's paradise, you ask the marketers and brokers rather than child or adolescent psychologists; anyway, grown-ups are now just bigger kids, aren't they? Still, there's nothing sadder in a growing child's room than last year's hottest toy lying forlorn and abandoned and stuffed into a corner (and if ideas were toys, what then?).

9

Now-America guarantees that ghosts of goods past never interfere with the promise of today's playroom, since they can be unloaded on the world after-market—everything from pesticides to TV reruns of *Seinfeld* (or cluster bombs, land mines, or even jet fighters), there's limitless room for expansion. In *Now*-America there is no time for reflection; the system we've put in place discourages introspection. As we approach the twenty-first century, we hold on not only to our toys but also to the preadolescent attitudes that go with them. In doing so, the brokers of the present without the presence of a past have succeeded in short-circuiting our natural development—effectively changing our national motto from *E Pluribus Unum* to *Whoever Dies with the Most Toys, Wins* in the process so we'll never be without our toys.

How has it happened that although America is a world power we haven't yet managed to graduate from high school? The consumerist addiction that has brought us to this pinnacle of power, which animated our becoming, now inhibits our growth and threatens our survival. This consumerist addiction prevents us from seeing who and what we are by substituting a continuous stream of images of what we should be that arrests our social, cultural, and intellectual development—the signs are everywhere. We are first exposed to this system in high school, to the idea that we have vested rights in consumer society. It is here where we are first encouraged to "keep up" with no critical thought about what we are "keeping up." And to be forever in high school holds us focused on today with no consciousness of yesterday, so there will never be any continuity with tomorrow, with fatal political and cultural consequences.

10

In America today, there is no *then*, only *now*; that's how we Americans defeat and neutralize time, the creator/destroyer. Without a presence of a past, there never will be need for any other time, either. There is no room for history because that was *then*, that's old, and as a nation we think of ourselves forever young, right? "That was then but this is now" is also the mantra for the current generation of twenty-somethings, the first real generation of the Post-Elvis Age who've been brought up in the postmodern, or rather postcultural, age of TV, electronic mail, and MTV buzz clips.

The *now* of this first full generation to truly surf the Virtual Reality Channel has convinced them (and the rest of us) that everything can be mixed, matched, controlled, and downloaded with the click of a mouse, and so by extension, the world offscreen can be altered. The creators of *Now*-America have convinced this generation of the possibility that anything is possible, as long as they cede control of their being and becoming and allow themselves to be completely disconnected from their individual *nows*. Speaking to (and for) them in specialized, demographically correct, and comforting tones that surround the images of the rock and roll world, the promoters and brokers of *Now*-America humbly and dispassionately perform their services. *Now*-America comforts this ever-renewable market safely inside its self-referential cultural bubble. If it seems there's no longer any reference points, no matter, the kids are already used to it now. As long as the vision looks cool and appears exclusive and readily available from somewhere or someone—preferably downloaded so you don't have to leave home—that's enough.

Unfortunately here's a high price paid for having no *then* in the electronic *now,* for being comfortable within this consumer world of competing brokers. In exchange for this endless parade of goods, services, and lifestyle possibilities, the creators of the *now* have expropriated each generation's singular childhoods and imaginations and successfully converted them into shares of the nostalgia futures market in a blink of the eye.

If *Now*-America had a living concept of its history that wasn't largely defined and characterized by a nostalgia for goods past, perhaps there wouldn't be the confusion and conflict that alien-ate and fester in the souls of the young and are rapidly becoming *the* issues in our national life as our present affects our future. If America and Americans came to terms with the past in the present, she (and we) wouldn't be so continually astonished and appalled by this crisis, which in one form or other has been with us for 150 years.

11

According to our leading intellectuals, the reason all of us "normal" citizens are frazzled, spooked, and in crisis is that we're having trouble dealing with life in the postmodernist world. Best forget the "crisis of postmodernism" hurting our heads for a moment and check out those rock and roll shoes pinching our feet, if not wearing them out altogether. Our crisis is really the result of living in the Post-Elvis Age, a sociocultural philo-sophical state far more precarious than the "end of history" that official intellectuals like Francis Fukayama preach when they blame everything culturally entropic on the fall of the Soviet Union. To him, that formerly dark political Other was the prime engine of cultural change whose recent collapse and eclipse has put all the politicians, foundation groupies, and think tank intel-lectuals like himself out of a job and left the rest of us twitching. And because we've lost Mother Russia as the schoolyard bully figure to oppose, that's why we're dozing and drooling, as if we've been blinded by the light—maybe Fukayama's boys are, but not the rest of us. They could just as easily have turned on the pop media to find something closer to home whose effects are more pandemic. Whether he and they want to acknowledge it or not, many of his under-60 colleagues who were born into, during, and soon-to-be-after Age of Elvis get as much, or perhaps more, of their intellectual sustenance and world view from the word, music, and philosophy of the Grateful Dead (or Nirvana, Oasis, Madonna, or any one-hit wonder group on the charts) as they do from contemplating the geopolitical strategies of Bismarck, Prince Metternich, Tallyrand, Suleiman the Magnificent, or Henry Kissinger, for that matter.

For many cultural conservatives, especially Allan Bloom and William Bennett, rock and roll is the bête noir, the great beast that is the cause of the end of history as they know it. For Bloom, rock and roll stirs children's sexuality toward a Dionysian frenzy:

> It acknowledges the first emanations of children's emerging sensuality and addresses them seriously, eliciting them and legitimating them, not as little sprouts that must be carefully tended in order to grow into gorgeous flowers, but as the real thing. Rock given children on a silver platter, with all the public authority of the entertainment industry, is everything their parents used to tell them they had to wait until they grew up and would understand later.[13]

12

So nu? This is not a great revelation; everyone knows in America that sex sells everything, not just music. Nor does anyone have to wait very long in this consumer world for the "next thing" to make us cool and with it to please our adolescent selves. Likewise, his description of the rock and roll child as a monster could easily apply to American society in general,

> … whose body throbs with orgasmic rhythms; whose feelings are made articulate in hymns to joy of onanism or the killing of parents; whose ambition is to win fame and wealth in imitating the drag-queen who makes the music. In short, life is made into a nonstop, commercially prepackaged masturbatory fantasy.[14]

What Bloom and his intellectual fellow-travelers should have understood is that rock is an *effect* of high school consumerism, not the *cause* of what ails America. The engine of adolescent consumerism makes the beat go on.

While rock and roll developed during the Age of Elvis into a gigantic economic force in its own right, the worlds of Kissinger, Suleiman, Mozart, Aristotle, et al. existed (and had existed) in simultaneously interlocking universes. Although separate, these worlds coexisted more or less in balance if not always in harmony. Since the midseventies and now in the Post-Elvis Age, however, this weave and texture, this complex interlocking cultural universe, has been gradually altered, and that sense of balance has been compromised. And this has less to do with the decline of the Soviet Union and more to do with rock and roll music politics than most official cultural historians and political theorists would like to admit.

In today's rock and roll world, the boundaries between music, politics, and consumerism are indistinct; after a while it hardly registers, save in egregious examples, like most recently the use of the Chambers Brothers' sixties anthem "Time (Has Come Today)," which back then was a call for political and intellectual liberation but now touts life insurance and financial planning to the very group that eschewed such concerns. Truly, the commercial is a consummate exercise in irony that uses that musical emotional hook to nail all those aging baby boomers who now are seriously thinking about a mortality that little concerned them in their paisley-colored youth. Of course, to everyone else not so emotionally involved and a few generations removed, it's just a catchy jingle. Still, it's a potent piece of commerce.

13

Just how permeable the cultural membrane is between the worlds of rock music and politics was demonstrated in 1995 when Jerry Garcia, the lead guitarist of the Grateful Dead, an iconic sixties countercultural institution, passed on. The flood of tributes emanating not only from the usual suspects, pop commentators and the like, but also from the floor of the Senate and the House of Representatives and even higher levels of government was extraordinary.

It was a little short of astonishing to see the Very Venerable Senator Patrick Leahy from Vermont appearing on the TV show *Nightline* the evening of Garcia's death not only to talk about his love for the Dead's music but also to present an informed appreciation of the lifestyle and attitude the Dead's music promoted to kids of all ages. No less astounding was the decision of the Yale-educated governor of Massachusetts, William Weld, the last person one would suspect of being a closet Deadhead, to order all state flags lowered to half-mast in tribute to Jerry's long strange trip (and it *wasn't* even an election year!). Garcia's obituary also appeared in different forms throughout the world, such was the band's impact on the world.

The Age of Elvis had already left a sizeable footprint on American diplomacy when in 1990 Vaclav Havel, president of the Czech Republic and one of the cofounders of the Republic's Velvet Revolution (and a far more committed intellectual than Francis Fukayama) met Frank Zappa, a man whose music and ideas had inspired Czech students in Prague to battle Soviet tanks with rocks in the late sixties. It was said that Soviet secret policemen at the time of the uprising, while beating students during their "interrogations," used to mutter under their breath that they were going to "beat the Zappa" out of them.[15] To some of Havel's generation who survived to become masters of their own political destiny 20 years down the road, Zappa and his music were a vital part of their living contemporary cultural and political history. To acknowledge those contributions, on behalf of the Czech people, Havel decided to appoint Frank as the Czech Republic's representative on matters of trade, culture, and tourism to promote their economic interests abroad. As a gesture to the rock and roll world in which Havel's contemporaries lived, it was fitting and proper, but as they say, no good deed goes unpunished.

Upon hearing about this appointment from the American diplomats in Prague (as well as Zappa's on-the-record comment to Havel that spending even 5 minutes with American vice president Dan Quayle was a colossal waste of time). James Baker, Secretary of State, stepped into the breach to defend America's honor. Dramatically and unexpectedly, Baker made an eleventh-hour stop in Prague on his way to a Bush/Gorbachev summit to notify Havel and his baffled ministers that such an appointment would be considered a grave affront to the United States; if the appointment wasn't rescinded there would be "consequences."[16]

What Havel did not know was that for the Bush Administration (and the Reagan Administration before it), Zappa had consistently been a trouble-maker, a major ideological irritant who not only had the unmitigated audacity to mercilessly criticize and satirize Reagan's involvement with and dependence on the support of the Religious Right, but had also made Baker's wife and other highly connected political spouses targets of ridicule because of their stance on music censorship (more on this elsewhere). Havel in his sublime hippie innocence (and view of cultural politics) had stumbled into a major diplomatic gaffe, the last thing he needed if he wanted to beg economic boons from his Uncle Sam.

What actually transpired behind closed doors has so far not been revealed, but Havel backed down. Zappa's credentials were revoked, and business, one supposes, has gone on as usual ever since. In retrospect, the whole incident was laughable, diplomatic niceties and idiot national pride aside; everyone knew what the story was and who the laugh was really on. Still, the politics of entertainment and the politics of international diplomacy were as close as they'd ever been before or since, too. Only in America in the Post-Elvis Age would this have been possible.**

15

Judging from the reams of tributes that flowed from the world's press when the King passed to his final reward on August 16, 1977, rock and roll had attained its majority. Elvis had achieved world citizenship right up there with Gandhi, JFK, and the Pope (whichever one had died), and his passing put a power spike into our collective electronic soul. Although in death Elvis may have become a nostalgia piece who died a drug-addled Las

---

* Some stories are too good to be true, and this is one of them. After Teen-age Nervous Breakdown appeared in 1998, I sent a copy to Vaclav Havel, President of the the Czech Republic thinking he'd be amused. I received a letter from one of his associates thanking me but also telling me that there was more to the story which he could not divulge. Through the Freedom of Information Act I queried the State Department to see whether there was any mention of this either in the cables sent between Foggy Bottom and the American Embassy in Prague or amongst the voluminous papers of James Baker. There was none; and the people who did the looking were Zappa fans who actually worked in the State Department archives. Havel did ask Zappa to be his cultural representative, but the reasons he was unasked unfortunately remain secrets locked in diplomatic archives of Vaclev Havel and the Czech republic where there is no Freedom of Information act, and I don't read Czech.

Vegas lounge lizard or, for some, a parody of himself whose own music had little relevance to the world lifestyle he had midwifed, the world he presided over even in exile had become a protean force by itself. Certainly rock and roll has never forgotten the King, for subsequently he has become a focus of a pop mystery cult. Graceland, his Memphis home, is now a shrine-like Lourdes for the faithful—while his life and death have been the subject of numerous popular sensationalist and scholarly academic works and conferences and TV movies. So the rock and roll world continues to expand into every aspect of our lives.

It's a depressing truism that the music of youth (past and present) seems more and more to be a product conceived to appeal as much to the corporate bottom line as it is to the audience whose aural background the music inhabits, to the detriment of both creators and listeners. And we've allowed this to happen, too, have given up the struggle. These days, up-and-coming bands who think that art is stronger than cash are rudely awakened when they learn it costs anywhere from $500 to $1000 per song to break into local, regional, or national charts, according to anonymous industry sources. Cash or digital equipment does the trick for many program directors—hey, that's the business. To hell with love, all you need is cash for that teenage American dream. And we ourselves can never get away from that consumer-nuanced peer group demographic we created in high school; it haunts us, so deeply we no longer know how to get out of the loop.

Chapter 2

Who Stole the Bomp (from the Bomp Sha Bomp)?

One of the most important aspects of post punk dissolution of rock certainties was the replacement of authenticity by artifice as the central concern in critical discourse.

—Simon Frith[1]

Huh?

There's no denying it: Rock and roll criticism has come a long way since the fifties, when the only critical question that mattered was "can you dance to it?" (or make out, you know, "do the do," whatever that happened to be for you when you were young and fresh and fragrant). Forty years down the road in the nineties, dancing has taken a back seat to political content, correctness, and fashion death now that rock criticism has become an arena for respectable high-octane academic politics. Unfortunately, many of these master's essays and Ph.D. dissertations on punk rock and heavy metal—as well as other subcultural divisions—do not focus on the dynamic multicultural universe from whence they all came, but rather huckster the narrow-casted commercial vision that supplanted it. This new academic perspective, according to Ed Ward, a consistently clear-headed writer on music, has taken us all to a place where

> . . . the mystery has been completely taken away from rock and roll, that it has been over-explained, over-analyzed, and, in the process, it has become effectively neutered, incapable of shock and joy . . . that for many "rock artists," the impulse toward fun has been smothered by an increasingly rigidified sense of what is and what isn't acceptable, destroyed by a flock of vultures who won't be sated until the corpse is picked clean, the roll removed from the rock, and every secret, no matter how trivial or irrelevant to the creative act, is laid bare.[2]

How this transformation from a simple background accompaniment of adolescence to a cultural foreground/obsession evolved and when it happened says as much about how the music's emotional meanings have been mutated by the commercial environment as the culture into which it has become its predominant soundtrack. Simply put: In the Post-Elvis Age, rock and roll has effectively changed this country's battle cry of "Give me liberty or give me death" to "Sex, drugs, and rock and roll." Or maybe it could be that the two have become covalent—"Give me liberty, sex, drugs, rock and roll, and death!" (probably in that order)—an even odder state of affairs.

Perhaps the new generation on the (cultural) block and the policeman's chorus of knee-jerk millenarians shrieking in the background are right. Everything appears to be going to hell in a handbasket anyway and the fat lady's obviously going to sing soon, so why bother: Let's party, to hell with it all. Then again, decadence has always been in fashion when a culture can't think of any coherent response to change. Even if this may appear to be so for some, it's instructive to see how we got here and how the larger priorities and values of music and its enjoyment have been over time transformed, if not completely compromised, in the process. The best perspective from which to view this crucial change is from that of the music press/media, which promoted and championed rock and roll, which spoke to and sometimes for its audience before it became a prize for multinational multimedia conglomerates to control if not devour whole. But let's rewind.

Back in the late fifties and into the early sixties, everyone knew rock and roll was about fucking, pure and simple; nobody came right out and said that openly, of course, you just had to read between the lines. Although the official safe Vaseline-smeared vision archtypically disseminated in George Lucas's film *American Graffiti*, said it was all about boys, girls, and parties (it's my party and I'll cry if I want to), it also promoted adolescent angst and alienation. For the rock and roll revivalists, it was primarily about cutting loose with your friends after school or riding up and down the main drag or around and around the town monument in your patched-together jalopy while scouting for the local hot action. (It's not like anyone really knew what to do with it if and when any was found, and weren't the mysteries of adolescent sex far more anecdotal in nature then than they are now?) There were girl groups and doo-wop groups, southern rhythm and blues, plus Elvis and "The Killer," Jerry Lee Lewis, Little Richard, and Fats Domino on Top 40 radio, and the great earth-shaking questions the songs posed were basically on the order of why fools fell in love with the leaders of the pack. Why indeed?

More to the point, rock and roll was part of the background of the fifties American life, a specialized soundtrack for the insular teen subculture of the sock hop and the prom as well as mood music for furtive rec room groupings, or summertime fun, harmless fun. This music for cruising came sluicing out of the Brill Building in New York, the songpluggers heaven, to answer these questions, to stroke teenage libidos, a strictly commercial product from music central just like it always had been since the radio daze of the thirties and forties for older generations. It had no secret meanings, no sociological insights, few cultural subtexts.

Time and those waves kicked in just as machine-made pop music was getting rather boring, formulaic, and safe, and along came the urban folk revival of the early sixties. It was music that filled the maturer needs of a still primarily literate generation of baby boom children who'd just graduated from cruising for burgers in Daddy's new car and were now going off to college, kids whose tastes were developing. Folk music provided an alternative to the Brill Building world, which churned out hit after hit, and the replicant teenage culture of Dick Clark's *American Bandstand* by offering its listeners a less packaged, more authentic American musical experience embodied in the rich folk music traditions of the Appalachians and in the blues from the south side of Chicago and the Mississippi Delta (another way back to rhythm and blues, true). It disseminated visions of not happy commerciality and sociological homogeneity of the post-War fifties but of the cultural values and attitudes of that other America, of disenfranchised minorities, real people with real lives, windows into the true multicultural nature of America. The music also drew from folk forms and traditions not specifically American that stood apart from the official buttoned-down consumerist fifties culture. Magazines like *Sing Out!* sprang up for this audience, publishing song lyrics and music charts for pickers and singers while providing a forum for these artists themselves in which they could air their views, concerns, hopes, and desires.

When the raw blues energy of The Paul Butterfield Blues Band and the electric Bob Dylan merged with the energy of the Beatles and Rolling Stones, rhythm and blues became mixed and matched with the word: machine-made music was supplanted for a time by singer/songwriters and bands for whom all the news was fit to sing. For a moment, it seemed that there was a possibility of creating a multicultural world understanding built around music.*□ (The Beatles' experiments with Indian music spawned a whole raft of imitators and musical side trips as well as an interest in Middle Eastern and African music, which has come back around in the world music scene of today.) For the most part, though, this composite conglomerate music depended on words *and* music reflecting the musical tastes of a college generation that knew its Dostoyevsky, Brecht, Whitman, Vonnegut, and Ginsberg, but were equally at home with the music of Bach and Stravinsky; the boogie-woogie weaves of Professor Longhair, Eubie Blake, and John Lee Hooker; the blues stylings of Bessie Smith and Billie Holiday; and the jazz of Miles Davis, Charlie Parker, and John Coltrane.

For this reason, Bob Dylan's seminal electric albums, *Highway 61 Revisited, Bringing It All Back Home*, and *Blonde on Blonde* still continue to offer nourishment because their literary images were drawn from a much broader and richer cultural palate than from the involuted self-referential pop world. He wasn't speaking *at* his audience as much as *with* them; his morphing of rock and roll with blues/folk effectively inspired other artists and musicians to speak not only to each other in song but also to their audience in a common language: electric music for the body *and* mind.

22

In the early sixties, while television was packaging the "Swinging London"/Carnaby Street/visual-style *zeitgeist* of the British Invasion with TV shows like *Shindig* and *Hullabaloo*, the Brill Building mentality churned out one-shot fanzines devoted to particular mega-hit groups like the Beatles, Rolling Stones, and Monkees and similar packages for lesser-known groups. For the growing preteen market, which wanted to know what was out there to like, there were *Cheetah, Tiger Beat*, and *Hit Parader* magazines, which were highly cost-effective and easy to churn out. Essentially creations of mainstream magazine and newspaper publishers, these small in-house operations were composed

---

* Carlos Santana, lead guitarist of the legendary late-sixties band Santana, is rumored to have said that this happened sometime in the spring of 1970 for about 10 days to 2 weeks. It may have been longer, but not by much.

of an editor, an advertising person, and a few editorial assistants from whom little more was required than their ability to reedit and rewrite canned public relations handouts (press releases, interviews, etc.) into preteen jargon while adequately art directing the fashion spreads, then ship.

Countering these chunks of processed printed cheese was the underground press, which appealed to the politically involved, or at least interested, college folk/blues enthusiasts; papers like the *San Francisco Oracle, East Village Other, Ann Arbor Argus,* and *Chicago Seed* covered radical politics and the anti-War and civil rights movements in all their hues. Textured into more challenging and innovative graphics were also articles on alternative lifestyles (well, not so "alternative" if one was a student of American social history of the Transcendentalists or radical French socialism of the nineteenth century). No paper worth its salt was complete without the freelance book and record reviewers and essayists who spoke to these issues.

From the underground press came music magazines specifically attuned to this same audience that focused on cultural politics. *Down Beat* in the fifties and *Jazz Magazine* in the early sixties (which by the late sixties became *Jazz and Pop*) were for the most part more cerebral, less political in their approach to music criticism. *Crawdaddy, Fusion, Changes, Rock,* and *Rolling Stone* (in its infancy) were magazines in which the official canons of rock criticism originated, the opinions and attitudes of which have become institutionalized in academia today. In its golden age from 1967 to 1972, music criticism produced writers like Greil Marcus, Langdon Winner, Robert Christgau, Robert Palmer, Ed Ward, Jim Miller, David Dalton, Ellen Willis, Robert Soma, Paul Nelson, and Paul Williams. Paul Williams, the founder of *Crawdaddy,* was the quintessential stylist for this new criticism, which mixed personal insights with freely associated literary and musical allusions.

23

In this time and place, for these writers and others like them, rock and roll was not only a window into modern life, but also a place where all kinds of cultural referents were at play, and not all specifically American in nature. Readers were accustomed to and expected a critical style that broadened the periphery of their ignorance. Thus it wasn't surprising in the middle of a discussion of an obscure country music ballad by Warren Smith called "Black Jack David," for instance, to come across a sidebar disquisition about the myth of Orpheus, Celtic mythology, Scottish ballads of the thirteenth century, or the English ballad tradition in the seventeenth century and its embryonic journey into the country music scene of 1966, exactly what Nick Toches did in *Country: The Twisted Roots of Rock 'n' Roll*.[3] No one even breathed hard, since the underlying assumption was that music culture did not exist in a vacuum but was part of a continuum of covalent cultural traditions.

One reason why this was so was that during the era of the Vietnam War and the draft, there was an abundance (a glut?) of grad students in humanities looking for creative outlets. What use was a liberal arts education, they asked themselves, if not to provide tools to understand the society and cultural environment in which they were participating? It's no surprise that many of these first-generation critics were either junior professors looking for a critical outlet or well-read and turned-on master of arts candidates in philosophy, sociology, history, and English doing the draft-dodger rag. It also followed that since most critics and musicians came from the same general educational background, they were also conversant with the same writers, painters, musicians, and philosophies, just like the audiences; music journalism was of a uniformly higher level.

The mind/body split that contaminated the New Left in the late sixties opened up a critical rift between those who viewed the music and its world in a broader interconnected cultural context and a new group of writers who appeared in the pages of Detroit's *Creem* magazine (the late Lester Bangs and Dave Marsh, among others). They viewed music (and virtually everything else) solely from the point of view of Midwestern teen America. The rock and roll world was the created flesh for these latter-day evangelists, these protectors of the Holy Grail of the New Rock Order, and their sworn duty was to keep it free from "foreign" contagion. No analysts need apply, no analysis necessary, thank you. To them and the constituency they represented, rock and roll spoke to *only* American kids in American high schools, working-class kids living working-class lives in the industrial heartland. It wasn't supposed to do anything to your mind except blow it; the only requirement was that it must be fun and could you party-vous? If you did, how stoned did you get? Was it survivable? And would you do it again?

All other approaches were effete, and the "art rock" those overeducated swells wrote about was for sissies, nerds, and dweebs, not red-blooded *American* teenagers. A dependable product that had a dependable effect, rock and roll was a virtual shot of peppermint schnapps with a beer chaser, not some after-dinner drink. It was hard getdown music for boogie and spew, the soundtrack that accompanied real high school life; its sole appeal and focus was the if-you're-not-with-me-you're-against-me universe where peer group rules were the only rules. Neatly sidestepped was the question of how "peers" and peer group were defined. Ironically, these new critics substituted one restrictive and onerous code of behavior for another; presumably it was okay because it was their own (more easily to niche-market, my dear).

The writers who knew better and could write well—like the late Lester Bangs, one of the prime exponents and martyrs to this ideology—purposely "dumbed down" their writing to fit into the new *zeitgeist* of the "doper" mentality, the peer group culture that defined itself in terms of style and the status of consumer goods, whose limited world revolved exclusively around getting loaded and partying. It was the "doper" culture of the seventies that in time transmuted itself into the yuppie culture of the eighties, which defined itself in the same ways but with more expensive goods and designer drugs. What the music did in the present tense was more important than what it had said or was capable of saying within a larger cultural context since there effectively wasn't any, only a series of musical *nows* readily consumed and just as readily discarded until another *now* came along to replace it—fashion incarnate.

As championed by the *Creem* school, this "people's music," which eschewed literate criticism, reflected a basic meat-and-potatoes approach, heavily relying on sheer electric wattage, preferably a 10-foot stack of Marshall amps. The leading proponents for high-energy rock and roll came out of the Midwest:

Iggy Pop, now a grandfather of the punk movement in the nineties,*⊠and the MC5, the ideological poster band for the White Panthers Party (WPP), a self-styled liberation rock and roll collective whose emphasis was more on "party" than *party.* Aside from its flashy graphic sense and a couple of house bands like The Frost and The Up, WPP offered no coherent social programs to speak of (or if it did, no one was never straight enough to carry the programs out). It was brainchild of John Sinclair, a radical community organizer and poet whose only all-purpose ideology was—wait for it, "Sex, drugs, and rock and roll."

Like the Black Panther Party on which it was loosely modeled, the official WPP motto was "All power to the people," despite the fact that the "people" only represented one segment of the population, one taste, and one point of view: rock's version of Socialist Realism. But the MC5 had their 15 minutes of fame before self-destructing. By the early seventies WPP had succeeded in making such a media commotion that the FBI put them on a watch list. Their de facto Minister of Information, Pun Plamandon, even briefly appeared on the Bureau's Most Wanted List, an event that conclusively proved just how out of touch the FBI was during that period. Poor Pun—while fleeing the clutches of the FBI, he was unceremoniously busted for littering in the Upper Michigan Peninsula. So much for revolutionary acts, but that's another story entirely.

When Grand Funk Railroad, a power trio of guitar, bass, and drums, literally blasted out of the Midwest onto the charts, knocking the critical establishment out of their seats with their raw power, the mind/body split between the Midwest and the East and West coast critics was revealed for all to see. Lead guitarist Mark Farner, long on power chords but short on technique, spearheaded the assault, flashily bludgeoning his primarily teenage, male working-class audience into submission on his way up the pop charts.

---

* In 1969 the author asked Jim Osterberg, known now as Iggy Pop, who his favorite composers were. "Carl Orff, Richard Wagner, and Chuck Berry," he replied. His music still sounds like that.

When the critics on the coasts got their hearing back, they were appalled and tried to smother the band in a blanket of bad reviews and scathing commentary. Terry Knight, the band's manager, far more in touch with the ways of the "real" commercial world as it was—not as the critics would have liked it to be— struck back. Craftily, he exploited the issue of the critics' "elitism" by taking out full-page ads in all the major music magazines and music trades that quoted some of the more savage reviews and juxtaposed the concert and record gross sales numbers beside them.[4] His media counterattack neatly deflected the whole issue away from the band toward the critics, using the old high school ploy of "us versus them," normal kids versus stodgy grown-ups. One enterprising writer of the "old school" neatly sidestepped the issue entirely by writing about the audience instead of the band; it was a far more revealing approach for those who were willing to read between the lines, and some did.

Though Grand Funk Railroad eventually receded on the charts, it was obvious that the market spoke with a louder voice; who was buying and in what numbers were far more crucial than analysis. Since the market ruled, critics were persuaded to review the market instead of the music. Maybe "art rock" had become too expensive to manufacture and distribute, to mount for the public, but the short version was that the "people's critics" deemed it too pretentious for the jus' plain folks to digest. The official line here has been disseminated forever after by Ellen Willis, one of the first women writers on rock and roll culture:

> At best [art rock] stimulated a vital and imaginative eclecticism that spread the values of rock and roll even as it diffused and diluted them. At worst it rationalized a form of cultural upward mobility, concerned with achieving the appearance and pretensions of art rather than the reality—the point being to "improve" rock and roll by making it palatable to the upper middle class. Either way it submerged rock and roll in something more amorphous and high-toned called rock.[5]

However it's sliced, diced, and textured these days, the result effectively enshrined the commonly mistaken adolescent notion (though not necessarily restricted to that age group) that *all criticism* was ipso facto negative and "elitist" and so must be avoided at all costs. Any other posture ensured the label of "class traitor," though ironically the best thing about rock and roll up to that time had been that it *didn't* have such restrictive class distinctions and appealed to a broader sociocultural base instead of being circumscribed by the vagaries of teenage taste and fad fashion—"no fun, my babe, no fun," as Iggy Pop might have said. Instead, focusing on the continuities that held culture together, the critics embraced the commerce that manipulated and thrived on apparent cultural discontinuities. Swiftly, the art was excised from the art criticism (that ability to exercise selective discernment), so that music (or film or literature, for that matter) had to fit the specific ideological criteria of the market. To attempt to praise an album with faint damns would only solicit audience incomprehension, getting in the way of the ultimate question: Should I buy it or not?

Thus this market-driven aesthetic forced cultural critics to function as a either record company cheerleaders and publicists at worst or savvy aesthetic handicappers who merely provided consumer guides at best (as Robert Christgau did then and continues to do today). Though it made publisher/industry relations smoother, there was also the chance for abuse on the part of the record companies. Having made a substantial investment with full-page ads on "the next big thing," the companies naturally wanted to maximize their chances of success, regardless of the "aesthetics" involved, as we have previously seen.[6] To be truthful, this made some sort of mutated sense, since this payola scheme, the manipulation of the marketplace by strategic infusions of cash and other goods to influence sales of the product, was what "the biz" had always been about, even when there was comparatively less money at stake. "Look, I'm subsidizing this magazine," the companies said in so many words, "at least cut us some slack," just like large advertisers in major magazines do today (or what newspaper editors say to rein in their arts critics from teeing off on marginal or questionable products when advertising revenues are at stake). And of course the consumer/listener was the loser in this scheme, though no one said so at the time.

Still it would be false to characterize all industry/critic relationships this way, for within the system there was a core of publicists and company people who relied on critics with integrity who weren't just whores out for whatever goodies and access they could get; the publicists depended on the occasional reality check missing in their personal work environment, too. It was an anticipated treat for this minority to spend some part of their day, over lunch preferably, talking to someone who had a working brain with an informed opinion attached, who thought of the music business within a larger context than just the old commercial in/out.

As for those good game players, this system worked just fine, and those who came along, went along, and after a while, one did get the feeling that he or she was doing God's work (whatever that work happened to be and whatever was Number 1 on the charts). One could eventually be convinced after a while, like John Rockwell, former rock critic at *The New York Times*, that "commercial success doesn't so much attest to quality as corroborate it; if you like something the millions like, their general enthusiasm adds resonance to your private enthusiasm, certifying its universality."[7]

The downside of this happy new little reformulated world was that eventually critics felt like they were in a caucus race. No matter how hard they worked, they were always behind, snowed under by the product to be reviewed, analyzed, and pigeonholed. If one perchance took a break, the backlog was a killer. It was not unheard of for critics, while nibbling free hors d'oeuvres at record company functions in the major markets and cities, to informally compare notes on the latest releases and collectively broker a consensus about the groups. If one was hip to the dance, one could just see the ripple effect from these unofficial rating sessions in various newspapers and music magazines in reviews that reflected similar approaches and sometimes even used the same adjectives. One writer of the author's acquaintance dealt with the release glut by simply taking whatever recordings had come in the morning's mail, putting them all on automatic changer, and going about her business—cleaning, filing, researching, making phone calls, whatever. If she stopped what she was doing, she'd replay the cut; if she liked the cut, she'd replay the whole side, and if that went well, she'd review the album. The remainder she'd either archive to her collection, save for her friends who liked "that kind" of music, or leave in a pile by the door for anyone who came over to paw through and sell for a buck a pop. Some days she made a buck.

Being privy to all kinds of inside information because of special access to the managers, artists, or prerelease test pressings posed even tougher burdens for critics. Living in a state of cultural fast-forward 3 to 5 months ahead of the general record-buying public made critics cynical and isolated them from their audience. After a while, like it or not, instead of being commentators on the business, they became an integral part of it themselves, and that world weariness inevitably leaked into the writing, killing spontaneity. It was way too much of a good thing.

Of course, inside access could produce other ethical dilemmas: Critic Patricia Kennealy, the editor of *Jazz and Pop*, not only had a torrid love affair but actually married Jim Morrison of the Doors. Once their romance had begun, she found it increasingly impossible to write objectively about the group without using her inside knowledge or letting anyone know she had it (or was having him). To compensate, she became rather harsh in her public reviews of the group, going so far as to lecture the Lizard King in print on his understanding of Wordsworth's *Preface to the Lyrical Ballads*—Morrison had published some of his desultory poetry and, like the editor herself, had, as the song goes, "been through all F. Scott Fitzgerald's books." Was this not part of his poetic education, she reasoned? (Admittedly this could only have happened back then, since these days the words of Wordsworth are probably used as doorstops, if at all, by the general rock audience.)

Apart from the violation of their privacy, general knowledge of this affair within the music business would have proved not only problematic to Morrison (marrying a critic may be a novel way to get good notices, but it would not have been smiled upon in many quarters even then) but disastrous to Kennealy's own credibility as an objective journalist, though such ethical dilemmas are of little import today, precisely because the boundaries between news and publicity are either indistinct or nonexistent: A rock critic and rock star engaging in the same situation these days would certainly find themselves voluptuously spread all over the gossip pages and, equally certain, would be thrilled to bits to be there.

Twenty-eight years ago, it was a different story: To navigate around and through this quandary. Kennealy enlisted the help of a good friend, a former lover, to act as her escort, her "beard" at public functions, encouraging inquiring minds to think that she was otherwise engaged and effectively enabling her to carry on her relationship with the Lizard King while he had some modicum of personal privacy out of the public eye.[8] (The Morrisons were by no means the only transprofessional couple that rock and roll hath joined together and even conflict of interest could not put asunder—then as now, bedfellows make strange politics.)

Some critics crossed completely over the line, like Jon Landau, who became Bruce Springsteen's producer and manager in the seventies, but while he was doing so, he never wrote about the Boss for the press. Others formed their own bands, like R. Meltzer's Soft White Underbelly, or Robert Palmer's Insect Trust. Some became record producers, forswearing criticism entirely. Those within record companies wrote under other names, and the band played on.

By the midseventies, those who survived the cut eventually reached the point where the thrill was gone. They had become bored with business as usual, and who could blame them—it was getting to be the Disco Age after all. And boredom, as any reader of philosopher Søren Kierkegaard, the true Melancholy Dane, knows well, leads to a pack of trouble (basic riff: God was bored so He created Adam; Adam was bored so Eve was created for him; then Adam and Eve were bored ensemble so Cain and Abel were created for them both; and so on down the line). The critics (who'd learned their lessons from the Grand Funk debacle a few years before), instead of trashing the music that was making pots and pots of money for the industry, decided to create their own counterrevolution if only as a way to reassert their authority and promote their own canon—their favorite New York and Los Angeles underground bands that the industry had ignored. (The invention of the Seattle-based Grunge scene is a more recent example.)

As had happened a decade earlier, the English music scene, that bellwether for trends and a constant font of inspiration, if not fashion sense, came to the rescue with the punk rock movement,[9] a music and a performance style that expressed rage against the disco movement, raging inflation, and massive unemployment among working-class youth. Its raw, in-your-face style in expressing its rage—its very artlessness, in fact—appealed not only to the predominantly middle-class musicians who made up the strictly uncommercial New York and Los Angeles underground music scenes but also to critics looking for a good meaty critical hook.

English punk's celebration of unconsciousness, with its emphasis on hard drug, alcohol, and amphetamine use by musicians and audiences alike and wretched excesses in general (puking and spitting on the audience in particular), as well as the air of riot and physical danger that enveloped performances, was just the kind of style outrage that would bust open the smug plasticity of the disco world. It was hoped that punk would make music honest and authentic again—and cut a piece of the consumer pie for the bands involved, of course. Though no Americans had a clue as to what it felt like to be an unemployed working-class youth in England faced with truly no hope, the next best thing, they reasoned, if only perhaps to show some cultural solidarity, was to expropriate the performance style of the English working-class bands, along with their slang and dress, which was being hyped by the English fashion press.

Though it made a big media splash in New York and Los Angeles for a time, punk was a commercial failure, an imitation of reality with virtually no substance to it other than as a fashion statement. When inevitably funneled through music culture magazines from *Rolling Stone* on down into the great teenage heartland of America, an imitation of an imitation of reality, punk had its second life. As an urban legend, it was enthusiastically translated and reduced down to a style of dress and an attitude, like being a "hippie" or "jock" a behavioral shorthand armor plate that kids used to navigate through the teenage wasteland of American high school life.

Having been characterized as a radical cultural text for the forever after, punk in its time was little more than an attempt by a small group of artists and musicians to dominate the music scene and to substitute for the prevailing commercial sense one of their own liking. That the punk movement has today achieved a mythic state in the minds of cultural historians not only shows ignorance of what the music business was about then and continues to be about now but also overlooks how teenagers view music as a vehicle for their own self-expression, a temporary expedient that confuses style with substance in today's world, yet another example of adolescence's need to be different and shocking for the sake of being different and shocking.

"It wasn't political," stated Legs McNeil, the editor of *Punk* magazine 20 years later. "I mean, maybe that is political. I mean the great thing about punk was that it had no political agenda. It was about real freedom, personal freedom. It was also about doing anything that's gonna offend a grown-up. Just being as offensive as possible. Which seemed delightful, just euphoric."[10] Punk wasn't a statement of working-class solidarity either.

> ... it was about advocating kids to not wait to be told what to do, but live for themselves, it was about trying to get people to use their imaginations again, it was about not being perfect, it was about saying it was okay to be amateurish and funny, that real creativity came out of making a mess, it was about working with what you got in front of you and turning everything embarrassing, awful and stupid in your life to your advantage.[11]

There was nothing revolutionary about this position, and if the truth be known, whoever has somehow survived being an adolescent can attest to similar feelings whatever age or era. McNeil is exercising his 20/20 hindsight now that middle age is staring him in the face. He was also neither a musician nor an artist but a clubbie/observer. The real artists checked out of punk as rapidly as they had checked into it. Far from being some kind of radical restatement, the punk movement was a conservative return to the traditional needs of youth to be different at any cost, purely for the sake of being different. A further extension of the *Creem* school ethos 5 years later, it was a mannered self-conscious turning-away from any realization of the limitless possibilities of what music could be and do, not for one segment of the population but for everyone. In truth, punk was a second-generation imitation of the pop art scene that Andy Warhol mined, but it was based on a distorted reflection absorbed into mainstream American culture, there to be consumed by the middle-class suburban teenagers for whom it was intended.

By the end of the seventies, in a little over a decade, what had been music for people of all ages had been turned into exclusively the music of youth, one more market that fluctuates every 2 to 4 years. This was due to the law of generations, which was succinctly described by the historian Gilbert Ostrander:

> The younger generation is at all times simultaneously appearing on the field and moving off the field and trying to stay on the field while turning into something else. No sooner have the rules of the game been officially explained by the younger generation, than another game is discovered to be in progress on the same field under different rules by a somewhat different younger generation.[12]

So it goes in the music business these days. The rock and roll world is no longer the property of just one particular group of teenagers from a specific time and place; it is a pliant metaphor that every succeeding generation uses as it sees fit for its own needs. Though it speaks in many rhythms, it no longer does so in a common tongue, for each *now* has a specialized constituency with its media organs and consumer goods, its own sociology and secret handshakes. Who controls the generations and speaks for them has given rise to bloody turf wars within the halls of academe.

While these battles rage, the common context in which all these musics speak to each other and to us has been irretrievably lost. This loss has lead to a remarkable form of cultural myopia where the rock and roll world has become all there is, a realm where Michael Jackson's sexual proclivities, or lack of same, or Madonna's status as a pop icon are considered news to be treated seriously by public media and academia instead of the public relations ploys they are, where fashion is news and news is fashionable. More's the pity because rock and roll's alternative vision was potentially far more all-encompassing, less exclusive, and less frightening than the specter of losing status in high school—which seems to the preoccupation of most Americans, if we believe our media. This myopia not only is diminishing our collective sense of self but is well on the way to devouring

the world in which we live. Our focus has been narrowed, as Ed
Ward has observed with ample justification:

> Hey, the poets of our time are poets, not rock lyricists; the musicians
> who will leave the mark are musicians, not rock musicians; the story-
> tellers of our time are writing fiction and journalism, not rock criticism;
> the important artists of our time are artists, not rock artists. If their
> lives or works of art touch rock and roll, well and good, and damn near
> unavoidable, but please don't confuse cause and effect, form and con-
> tent, or structure and meaning. There's a big wide world out there—
> don't you want to know about it?[13]

Who Stole the Bomp from the Bomp Sha Bomp? We did,
and all because we've allowed ourselves to be convinced that
the music that inhabits our lives is no longer a forum for larger
issues, but exists as hostage to youthful nostalgia, an extraordinarily useful commercial tool.

Chapter 3

Blame It on the Sixties

"The style of your own time is always invisible," and if it's not, it's fake.[1]

Headache

When I first heard the song "Revolution" by the Beatles in 1969, I never thought 20 years later it would be used to sell sneakers. I suppose one shouldn't be shocked at progress, at an evolution natural in this commercial society, though it does seem a perverse example of an environmentally friendly method of recycling outdated cultural resources. Yet even if the commercial totally decontextualized the song, it didn't seem to tick off anyone—save for a few old sixties soreheads—and for the most part, it was just another Nike campaign that came and went.

Perhaps.

At the same time, virtually no one seems to have remarked on how smoothly and seamlessly hip-hop and rap, the current generation's style and fashion, have made a similar transition to the commercial sphere, their *zeitgeist* speedily adapted and expropriated to sell everything from jeans to kid's toys. Perhaps music might not mean the same thing to this generation or have the same cultural significance as rock and roll did in the sixties, or more to the point, unlike those old soreheads, maybe this generation is just more accepting of the peculiarly American truism that whatever starts out "on the corner" will eventually wind up selling something and cash in on it. Isn't it a potent testament to the continued power of the American dream that even the casualties of it "buy in"?

"It's just a song, isn't it?" asks the new generation in the process of struggling to define itself. Anyway, what do those sixties guys have to complain about? Aren't the sixties back big time, even if it's a caricature? Mini-skirts are vogue, the acid/X rave scene is happening, just like the psychedelic days of yore, man. It's sex, drugs, and rock and roll and over again, or still—MTV broadcasts rock and roll videos and news 24 hours a day and has its own shopping network and even a Washington correspondent; isn't that what it was all about?

Everybody's socially conscious—there's even an environmentally safe automobile antifreeze on the market, something that won't harm the environment or the dog if it happens to lap it up. And haven't all those sixties therapies been validated and mainstreamed in the nineties? Shiatsu, acupuncture, rolphing, past life regression therapy, and vitamin therapies of all kinds are listed right there in the *Yellow Pages*. What you don't find in the catalogues you can test-drive at New Age conventions in any large regional mall these days; check the Internet for times and places, everybody's doing it now. What did Wavy Gravy, that archetypal sixties Merry Prankster say at the 30th anniversary of the 1964 Free Speech Movement in Berkeley, California? "The nineties are the sixties reversed?" Numerologically speaking, he may be right, but there's more to it than that, much more.

For some, a highly tangible and significant sign of the domination of sixties' ideology in the nineties was the 1992 election of William Jefferson Clinton as the 41st President of the United States, a man who, during the presidential campaign, admitted that as a college student not only did he protest against the war and legally avoid the draft, but he also experimented with drugs. Clinton quickly qualified this revelation by adding that although he may have smoked a little dope in college, like everyone else of his generation, he "did not inhale," which seemed to make matters all right again—or perhaps slightly worse, as though he tried it yet didn't try it.* Currently an innergenerational in-joke,

---

* Historical note: When Bill Clinton was at Oxford, hashish was the drug of choice because it was cost-effective and plentiful; marijuana wasn't widely available, and if it was, it was prohibitively expensive. Hash was ingested by either smoking it in a pipe or mixing crumbles of it with loose cigarette tobacco; the mixture was rolled into a spliff (a hashish joint made up of anywhere from three to six cigarette papers and held together with a cardboard mouthpiece, itself a work of art). However it was consumed, the smoke was harsh. If one inhaled it like a regular cigarette, one ran the risk of coughing oneself silly. Instead one developed the technique of swallowing amounts

that kind of public confession would have been unthinkable a mere decade ago when a highly (sorry!) qualified candidate for the Reagan Supreme Court was rejected because of a similar youthful folly at Harvard Law.

Clinton's election parallels what has come to cap the full ascendence to power in colleges and universities of many former anti-War activists (careerists and opportunists alike) who survived and were influenced by the issues of those times. For the ultraleft politically correct fringe the revolution hasn't gone far enough, while from the point of view of knee-jerk old woman conservative critics, most prominently Allan Bloom, far too much damage has already been done. For him, these radicals' dubious "contributions" have the faint odor of a self-promoting nostalgia, the consequence of finally coming to terms with "growing up," itself a self-serving rationalization for becoming another kind of invidious "establishment," rigid as the one they'd hoped to overthrow when they were mere children. "What remains," Bloom acidly observes,

> is a certain self-promotion by people who took part in it all, now in their forties, having come to terms with the "establishment" but dispersing a nostalgic essence in the media, where, of course, many of them are flourishing, admitting that it was unreal but asserting that it was a moment of significance.[2]

I suspect that even Allan Bloom knew in his heart of hearts that the sixties was no mere "moment of significance" in the order of things or else he wouldn't have fulminated about the legacies of the sixties so eloquently and passionately in his book, *The Closing of the American Mind*. But as the title of Simone Signoret's biography suggests, "Nostalgia just ain't what it used to be," not only for conservatives like Bloom but also for sixties apologists like Todd Gitlin and boosters, who have expropriated the exter-

---

in small gulps, i.e., *not inhaling*, as everyone who survived the sixties in some form or other knows well. Thus the line "did not inhale" doesn't mean that he was squeamish and not really there with it, though more to the point, it would be far more unusual for anyone of that generation *not* to have inhaled at least once for curiosity's sake, which was the point lost in the translation. To be sure, it just wasn't the act as much as what went on "inside" during the act. All heads weren't created equal. Stay tuned.

nal trappings elaborated in brief here. Both sides seemed to have ignored the era's abundant and transcendent inner essences, rituals, and maps that made that time if not unique, then at least historically resonant with echoes of earlier periods in American cultural history.

According to Fred Davis, a sociologist who has studied the phenomenon, contemporary history itself is in danger of becoming a victim of nostalgia, which he defines as

> one of the means—or better, one of the more readily accessible psychological lenses—we employ in the never ending work of constructing, maintaining, and reconstructing our identities ... it can be thought of as a kind of telephoto lens on life which, while it magnifies and prettifies some segments of our past, simultaneously blurs and grays other segments, typically those closer to us in time.[3]

Contemporary cultural history is continually being filtered through the fast-forward world of fashion and commerce, where, in its search for the new in the old, nothing appears to be what it is or indeed was, where all is product. To Davis, nostalgia's function is that it

> mediates the selection, distillation, refinement, and integration of these scenes, events, personalities, attitudes, and practices from the past that make an identifiable generation of what would otherwise remain a featureless demographic cohort, eg. the Edwardians, the jazz age generation, the children of the depression, the silent generation and the turned-on generation.[4]

Since there is this continual need for new product in this hyped-up system, "the very objects of collective nostalgia are in themselves media creations from the recent past. In other words, in their ceaseless search for new marketable objects of nostalgia, the media now do little but devour themselves."[5] Consequently, Americans are never sure what they are being nostalgic about because the ideas themselves are always being rewritten and reinterpreted to suit the "myopia of the moment" dictated by fashion. Is the American past akin to an antique chair, table, rug, or armoire, at least 100 years old according to the dictionary, or to an Andy Warhol "collectible" cookie jar, a bit of manufactured kitsch from the forties or fifties? Or does it lie in the idealized never-never realm of classical Greece, as Allan Bloom and his cohorts believe, in a past can be only imperfectly grasped through its reinterpreted texts?

Or none of the above? For what we propose to do here, as anthropologist Clifford Geertz suggests, is instead of "looking *behind* the interfering glosses that connect us [looking] *through* them."[6] When we do, it appears that the sixties has become a casualty, homogenized out of recognition and Cheesewhizzed by market forces and media.

True, the surface manifestations—sex, drugs, and rock and roll, protest and mini-skirts—are with us still and were noted by news media then, but there was far more going on that has been effectively ignored and/or misreported because it didn't suit the needs of hot copy[7]—but then again, some things change little. Davis's full court field theory to the contrary, the sixties was not another "featureless demographic cohort," for demographers have noted that its greatest impact came with the explosion of students in high school. In the 1930s the ratio of 14- to 17-year-olds in high school had passed 50%, by the 1950s that number had risen to 73% (when the term "teenager" was coined), and by the mid-sixties, all but 5% of the teenage population was in high school.

When college was factored in and the age when one normally entered the workplace was pushed up to 21 or 22, this indicated, according to Landon Y. Jones in *Great Expectations*, that "America's largest generation was growing up in an age-segregated universe, cut off from outside society and … bound together by their own prolonged adolescence."[8] But it wasn't just the numbers as much as what could be done with them—and what was.

Indeed, before one starts blaming the sixties for the supposed mess it has made of the nineties—what with the welfare crisis, the vicious gender battles in the political correctness arena, the rise of AIDS, affirmative action, the overregulation of the environment, drive-by shootings, and youth running wild in the streets (a continuing saga, as any social historian knows)—it would be well to determine just exactly what comprised that decade. What visions, illuminations, epiphanies, insights, what dialectical discussions were bubbling underneath the surface of this outsized adolescent population that the media began to promote? We need therefore to explore, in the Melvilleian sense, the "whiteness of the whale" that was the sixties and that exists now only in fashion-directed memory. And if it's all about nostalgia, let's at least attempt to be nostalgic about the right things, about Beatniks and Heads,* hippies and dopers (prototypical yuppies with a lower grade of goods), for that was what it was all about during those 20 years from the midfifties to the early seventies. Although everyone eventually went on the trip, like Pablo's Magic Circus in Hermann Hesse's *Steppenwolf*, it was "For Madmen Only. Not for Everybody. Price of Admission Your Mind." Come. Let's go.

Fragments from "the Book of Head"

44

"Heads" were primarily a literate, enlightened, and informed elite who saw a higher spiritual reality beyond the annual homecoming game of fifties team America while they were spectators in it. They kept a low profile, were almost invisible except that they read for a variety of experience: *Steppenwolf, The Brothers Karamazov, Waiting for Godot, On the Road, The Waste Land, Howl*: young and old in the tradition pieced the cultural mosaic together. "Beats" suffered and strived in the shadows of *The Lonely Crowd* and *The Organization Man*. The distance between Beats and Heads was incalculable: Heads assimilated all their information moving into, not away from, the world, without the uniform: the black turtleneck and all that jazz.

---

* The term "Head" is used in that peculiarly sixties sense to mean one who had assimilated the spoken, sung, and seen (i.e., the great art and ideas of all our times) and who understood that cosmic dance and laughter, and with that awareness, acted on what one found in those altered states of consciousness. After having absorbed the lessons from all those archetypal visions of morality, philosophy, and cosmology, heads tried to live their lives accordingly in the belief that this life is but a transition into the next, that the wheel of karma turns for all whether they know it or not. And if one is truly aware of all those things, one had no choice *except* to act on what one knew, because *not acting* on that (having reached that level of awareness to see all those things) meant returning to the wheel to try to get it right next time instead of evolving to a Being of Light.

Beat.

Beats were cool cynics who sneered at the agency schnorrers chained to the monotonous beat of the 8:30 from Bridgeport. You couldn't be cool and dig on your work—that's lame, man. The only thing the Beats dug was their alienation, which they deified. Beats embraced jazz and abstract expressionism; to get the most out of jazz you had to be cool, detached, uninvolved. Digging mystical abstract expressionism was like listening to Bird, 'Trane, or Miles—interiors that lead to other interiors'.

Beats hiply and coolly manifested their lifestyle as if their appearance and attitude alone would blow the Squares away (like post '67 counterculture and subsequent stylistic permutations thereafter). Heads were interior but aware, Beats were exterior and insular. Jazz and folk. Jazz is a metaphor on a metaphor of black alienation. Folk blues is the story of that alienation itself, the struggle, a musical social history. Beats talked too much, reacting against psychoanalysis by becoming their own walking traumas. Heads saw Beat angst as self-limiting and self-imposed and probed their own universal unconscious.

45

Heads explored interior spaces freely, constrained by no intellectual viewpoint, open to a multiplicity. Intellectual eclectics, they viewed knowledge as a totality of information, a joyous cosmology, a synthesis used to understand *the universe*, by knowing what things are composed of, motivated by, influenced by. Only when you begin to see the totality of knowledge can you transcend your environment.

Head. Either you were or you weren't. You could spot them on the street since they possessed an inner animation, their brains radiated energy. Heads were not cool—cool was a hipster affectation. Cool was the Beat form of transcendence; but it was pure selfishness, a self-image, an attitude you struck, a pose. Hipsters and Beats were forever concerned about their cool, it was their religion—like Pynchon's Stencil in *V,* whose motto was "Keep cool but care," only the Beats never did care. To be cool with yourself meant being largely uninvolved with the world at large. Heads were never uninvolved: Though they may have possessed cool heads, it was their manner.

Heads integrated realities—POP. Like Claes Oldenburg's plastic hamburgers. Getting to the marrow of an experience: POP. Reality is made up of contradictions, trompe l'oeil, slapstick, Marx Brothers, surrealistic moments. Time is funny, not your individual place in it. Your perspective makes it funny, in time *intime*. Plastic lipstick holders, plastic food—the perfect commercial object, the perfect commercial—POP.

America is one big commercial wasteland, T. S. Eliot without the footnotes. The Beats called it the Square Life; solipsistic Steppenwolves, they fled on the road, to North Beach, Greenwich Village, Seattle, come on, let's go, they said. Beats thought if they ignored time it would cease to exist; the gray fifties would vanish like cigarette haze in the Five Spot. Heads knew it wouldn't. Why run? One builds and lives within an ever-expanding continuum; besides, awareness is immanent for everyone, in time. America was waiting for awareness, had been since its creation.

Head consciousness was self-reflexive and universal, while the Beats deified the addict. Heroin was the ultimate Beat trip, a chemically induced existentialism, and the junkie was Christ crucified and grooving on celestial oblivion of smack. The Square Life could be shut out for good that way. Get back, get under, get out of it; later for that they said. No wonder Bird lived in Beatsville.

Drugs were not a necessary part of the Head cosmology, though they later assumed preeminence when Head culture was debased, brokered as a commodity, media-eclipsed to "hippie." Drugs were an aid to attaining and integrating knowledge, one way to build up experience, but not the only way. (Timothy Leary, the High Priest of LSD, was a psychedelic salesman who sold out into street time, snake oil for the soul.) Drugs that expanded the consciousness instead of insulating it were prized and revered—grass, hashish, psychedelics didn't take you "out of it" but "into it." Heads felt that people who depended on depressants (tranquilizers, barbiturates, heroin, or alcohol) were inferior, low energy, their priorities and human potentialities limited because they preferred oblivion to enlightenment.

Drugs 100 years ago were heady metaphors, a peculiar kind of gateway for Zenos Clark, a friend of William James, whose letter was quoted in his *Varieties of Religious Experience*:

So the present is already a foregone conclusion, and I am ever too late to understand it. But at the moment of recovery from anesthetics [ether], just then, before starting on life, I catch, so to speak, a glimpse of my heels, a glimpse of the eternal process just in the act of starting. The truth is that we travel on a journey that was accomplished before we set out; and the real end of philosophy is accomplished, not when we arrive at, but when we remain in, our destination (being already there)—which may occur vicariously in this life when we cease our intellectual questioning.[9]

They were still doing that, catching "a glimpse" into the forties, although mescaline, not ether, provided the charge, just as Aldous Huxley wrote in 1954 in *The Doors of Perception* for a continuous transcendent metaphor. In the sixties LSD was another expanding intellectual metaphor that forced you to keep your mind pliant whereby those trips and mental excursions will take you all sorts of places you want to go. Knowledge is what it's all about, Alfie. Timeslides cause cosmic laughter where Harry Haller becomes The Outsider, Pablo's Magic Theater presents the possibilities of the untrammeled mind; you can get "out of it" but you never get "away from it."

The funniest thing Abbie Hoffman ever said was, "The only dope worth shooting is Nixon." He wasn't far from wrong. Drugs in America, drugs and America, had been part and parcel of the psychic landscape for more than 100 years for better or worse, a patent medicine prime ingredient. Cocaine and marijuana were big in the twenties. Jazz and tea, stick, reefer all went together in the Beat scene. The hipster smoked pot to dig on his alienation, to enjoy his cool jazz. Some people burned themselves out, some people didn't; it was just there, Harry M. Anslinger, Federal Bureau of Narcotics Commissioner from the thirties to the fifties, declared marijuana "the destroyer of youth" and banned its over-the-counter sale. Like the "Noble Experiment," Prohibition, the ban encouraged organized crime and mass civil disobedience. By banning all "bad" drugs and controlling information on them, the government thought it would be able to keep people in line.

Couched in crude racist and sexist iconography, the fifties anti-drug campaign made no distinction between pushers and dealers. It was more than mere linguistics; the difference spanned and encapsulated cultures. Pushers were capitalists personified, in it for the money; their clients were addicted. In truth, dealers were folk heroes to the developing Head culture, an integral part of the community they served, not outlaws. The drugs they sold were consciousness-expanding and nonaddictive. They linked communities together with input and communications. Unlike the oblivion sellers in William S. Burroughs' *Naked Lunch* who'd peddle baby powder or Saniflush, only one step ahead of the police, psychedelic dealers were concerned about their friends and the purity of their goods. Dealers never sold LSD to people they didn't like or trust. They'd say, "What are you going to use this for and where are you going to use it, and with whom?" Long ago and far, far away.

With or without drugs Heads sought a cross-cultural eco-logical intellectual overview, where ecology was the study of the natural interdependence of systems, a basic organizing principle. For instance, to the Head it naturally made no sense to manufacture an automobile that fell apart in 2 years. It was more economical in the long run to produce a low-mainte-nance, high-performance vehicle. Though a highly reasonable position, this attitude/outlook was also highly subversive to the American businessmen, the promise of GE's All-Electric Kitchen as sold by future President Ronald Reagan on TV's *Death Valley Days*. Instead of a state of dependence, Heads strove to develop themselves to the highest self-actualizing state possible. It was a foregone conclusion: Heads were enemies of the state; was there any doubt of it?

Freedom was the constant. Free your mind—everyone has civil rights, all races and creeds, individuals as well as nations (collections of interconnected communities, social polities); lunchcounter sit-ins, freedom rides for voter registration, or Ban the Bomb marches all encompassed similar aims. Civil rights went along with civic duty and individual responsibility to participate in the decisions of government as well as a collective responsibility by which American democracy allegedly maintained itself. Thus, the war in Vietnam was a massive and disgraceful violation of the civil rights of the individuals in country and out, just as representative of the state of the union as the bus burnings in Americus, Georgia.

The publication of *The Pentagon Papers* brought home for all to see the realization that Dr. Strangelove, Henry Kissinger, and Harry M. Anslinger were one and the same, that civil rights also included freedom from being willfully and consciously misinformed by one's government about everything from drug toxicity to environmental damage, the fruits of the new American Way ("Plastics," The Graduate was advised). *Voila!* Plastic people, plastic culture. Beats accepted it all placidly, dropped out, tried the old end-around play while Heads did not; they dropped in, had to, no choice. The only way to go was straight ahead, to confront the Frankenstein monster that had been or was being created for teenage America.

Against the aural background of Tin Pan Alley, teenage ditties and made-for-order products for the burgeoning, assiduously cultivated, and statistic-driven new market were contrary and countervailing trends. A conscious search for authenticity, for roots, for an authentic indigenous organic cultural referent that spoke to the nascent sense of community, polity, and civil rights was brewing. The early-sixties urban folk revival was a natural springboard for these ideals, the resurgence of humanism in an inhuman era overshadowed by the threat nuclear warfare. Pete Seeger (with or without the Weavers), Ewan McCall, Jean Redpath, Cisco Houston, the Greenbriar Boys—all spurred the reexamination of those marginalized and crushed by Team America like the American hobo and the rural poor of Appalachia. Their songs raised questions about social issues that had been overlooked. For them and other troubadours, the essential American experience was Delta or Chicago-style electric blues, Muddy Waters or Nathan Beauregard, the music of the rural and urban disenfranchised, not the Tin Pan Alley product of Sinatra, Pattie Page, the Andrews Sisters, Perry Como. Time had come to take back control of the module of Spaceship America.

In 1963, along came the Beatles with an insistent electric energy that eventually fused with the American folk scene. Along went Bob Dylan, Simon and Garfunkel, and a host of other young folk performers, and the folk rock crossover—blues for white people to spread the word. Head consciousness flowered in its syncopated earthy rhythms and rhymes cobbled from the reading of Whitman, Dylan Thomas, and Joyce in music that produced literate multidimensional insights on and about time, all kinds.

Art time: Allen Kaprow. Art is a series of events that involve the spectator, an environment you can manipulate and freely pass through. The war in Vietnam was a blunder that turned into a happening that got out of control. Thank you again, Doctor Strangelove.

Understanding Media was the treatise of the age, the ultimate obviousness and obliviousness. McLuhan and Quentin Fiore demonstrated the results of image retention time. In 1966, hippies were the result of *Understanding Media*. In 1968, Yippies were the result of the understanding of *Understanding Media*, an imitation of an imitation of a reality that had been expressly manufactured. Andy Warhol in his pungent commercial cynicism transformed commercial soup cans into natural art statements by drawing the eye from the sublime to the ridiculousness of American culture. Camp/pop becomes Batman!, *Your Hit Parade* becomes *Shindig* and *Hullabaloo*, spangles a-go-go.

Head time has echoes forward and backward, like Antonioni's movie *Blow Up*, where when you dissolve reality you rediscover it anew where it's least expected, in random artifice like random photos. Reality is a chance photograph that becomes greater than the meaning of your life. You blow it up, eventually to become both the photo and the lab technician who creates it.

Head consciousness with Beatles/folk input becomes mod—Mary Quant, Twiggy, mini-skirts, Richard Lester's *The Knack*. Sets change and images flicker. People dance in strobe lights: syncopated movement images frozen while LBJ "wars" on poverty, a spectacular misnomer, and simultaneously escalates the war. Teach-ins on college campuses focus contemporary time on historical imperatives ignoring human nature in statistical manipulations. Fuck the war. What's the difference between *The Man from U.N.C.L.E.* Maxwell Smart, and the CIA? (Not much, even now.) Traditional notions of "straight" historical time broke down, and a generation broke away.

Free the Indianapolis 500.

Media changes man by total immersion. Take Garroway's *Wide, Wide World,* mix with Murrow's *Person to Person,* multiply television sets as babysitters, and add Walter Cronkite. Media now makes artificial communities founded on media artifacts, TV trivia, flared, smoothed, wrinkle-free time, the all-nourishing manna.

McLuhan Oramus.

Truth? What can that be? It's relative, isn't it? said those drowning in a sea of commercial artifactual time. When you become the truth, or what you think the truth is, history and time become material for an eternal cartoon, just like R. Crumb Reality later in the decade said in reply.

51

Mister Goodbar says, "Go fuck yourself. Do it today!"

Right.

And if you're into truth, you're into movement ("the perfection of memory consisting, it would seem/in the never-to-be-completed," as Amy Clampitt wrote in her poem "Dancers Exercising"[10]), you must go back to history. You unearth it, rediscover it, relive it, you confront the evil therein (as well as the joy), which, though it can't be accepted, is acknowledged as omnipresent despite the governmental Anslingerian imperative that's it's bad for you to know. Time (and history) is a continuous show spanning aeons since cave was crack. Through consciousness of history (and time) you experience the continuum and shift inside from time to time, play with pieces of time, spaces in time you are or will be part of. Music is timeless, head music fused time signatures together, like a 12-tone serial version of "In the Midnight Hour" or a 4/4 Magnificat. The background music of your life some days could be *Parsival* or "Ain't Misbehaving," a Zuni war chant or a monkey chant from Bali.

Watching Everett Dirksen filibuster back in the sixties was no better or different than reading that older blusterer Cicero's *Against Cataline*. Politics continues to be entertainment, unfortunately. LBJ, Kennedy, Nixon, Cleon, Augustus, Justinian the Great, political time is always the same old time—who's to choose? The dude with that brunette looker you saw flashing down Sunset Strip or Park Avenue in the white Mercedes 450 used to be a regular at Maeceanus' house, remember?

Hiya Quintus.

Time (and history) is a weird parade. You're in it. It's happening.

So let's bring back Aristophanes.

He hasn't left.

Exactly, and here you are again.

Whether it's the slave markets or the baths or some concatenation of the two, it shouldn't be such a large mental reach. Naturally to describe that place you have to invent a new language or twist the possibilities—like E. E. Cummings, Gertrude Stein, and James Joyce—of the one you have. When you expand the peripheries of your ignorance to find knowledge, language extends with it. Young Robert Zimmermann (Bob Dylan) extended the language of pop music, mixing Kierkegaard, Beckett, Patchen, and Robert Frost with street-fighting man and made it to Highway 61, where God said to Abraham, "Kill me a son," and Abe said, "God, you must be putting me on," and he (along with the rest of the generation) grooved to the sounds of Little T. S. Eliot and the Imperials. If all knowledge is continuous as understanding, use different forms of language, pictures, sound. Transliterate the image. A good light show is better than LSD if you're really there. Heads opened themselves to the vision of the simultaneity of the heavenly spheres, better than a McLuhanesque Madison Avenue celluloid joke.

Who's to choose?

Heads believed in a human and humane nation-state of mind that transcended borders and political systems, that broke down all ideologies because it was stronger and more direct, that would, they hoped, finally destroy the myth that a man does not live by ideology alone, but rather by a human integrity that broke through and reordered ideologies. Heads believed in the idea of humankind over U.S.A., that the only thing that should be exploited is human potential, not avarice, greed, fear, and its stepchildren war, famine, pestilence, and prejudice. So how did this "land of the free and home of the brave" come to be known as The Home Shopping Network?

If you believe people have energy, then it's possible to want to exorcise the Pentagon of evil spirits and raise it off the ground, or even stop the war with street theater, or believe in magic. It's such a cartoon, this TV world. Turn off the sound and put on a Stones record, ferchrissakes.

53

This is your time, good time, bad time. You can get thrown in the hole or put yourself there. Your house is your castle, your prison, your body too, but your soul is immortal. It's all free time, old used time, time that is public domain. Heads check out the time before they play within it, and here's what happened when they did.

The Fragmented Head

I say that our New World democracy, however great a success in uplift-ing the masses out of their sloughs, in materialistic development, producers, and in a certain highly deceptive superficial popular intel-lectuality, is, so far, an almost complete failure in its social aspects, and in really grand religious, moral, literary, and aesthetic results.

Walt Whitman, *Democratic Vistas*[11]

Conspiracy? We couldn't even agree on where to go to lunch.

Attributed to Abbie Hoffman during the Chicago 7 Trial

Only those ignorant of the sweep and texture of American history would attempt to pigeonhole the protest movement and the allied social activism that grew out of the sixties as mere exercises of youthful folly, the consequences of a demographic hiccough; to the contrary, protest—not violence—is as American as apple pie, and it has been woven into the texture of the American experience since the Boston Tea Party. But unlike the Boston Tea Party, the anti-War movement encompassed a far broader racial, social, and gender spectrum: men and women, young and old, rich and poor, black and white, World War II vets and war resisters, Quakers, Catholics, Jews, Protestants, Evangelicals, Atheists, clergymen, and politicians (though only a few and not until the wind was blowing favorably). That wave of discontent that exploded onto the pages of newspapers and cathode ray tubes in the late sixties had been bubbling in the minds of artists, philosophers, and social critics for over 100 years. What was unique in a sense was that the concerns for civil rights, the nature of representative democracy, all commingled into a metaphor of the war in Southeast Asia. Indeed the war wasn't a cause of the sixties; it was a symptom of what had been wrong with the country since the end of World War II. One hundred years or so ago, here's how Walt Whitman so eloquently described the ferment of American nation/spirit in *Democratic Vistas*:

> The problem, as it seems to me, presented to the New World, is, under permanent law and order, and after preserving cohesion, (ensemble-Individuality,) at all hazards, to vitalize man's free play of special Personalism, recognizing in it something that calls ever more to be considered, fed, and adopted as the substratum for the best that belongs to us, (government indeed is for it) including the new esthetics of our future.[12]

The silent vigils, sit-ins, and mass marches were all attempts to put into practice that Whitmanesque idea of "ensemble/individuality," to refocus on fundamental American values that had been lost in the post-World War II/Cold War economic abundance of the fifties. Far from being unpatriotic and anti-American, the variegated protest movement was motivated by "the best that belongs to us." It wasn't just "our war," as war had skipped every other generation in twentieth-century America, nor merely a *realpolitik* exercise in the Cold War chess game of international relations as the government cynically and antiseptically framed and packaged it: It was *the* defining metaphor, a bald-faced cynical manipulation and perversion of the American spirit that Whitman, Emerson, Thoreau, and other writers invoked when they spoke *to* and *for*, not *at*, the American soul.

The war in Vietnam merely exacerbated tensions already bubbling in America at home and served as a "bait-and-switch" technique to keep Americans from understanding and confronting the questions that Johnson's Great Society had imperfectly dealt with. Why were we fighting other people's wars of liberation and sending all this military aid when our own country was in need of it, when there was so much to do in health, education, and the welfare of our citizens? Was our stated commitment to freedom and democracy only for export?

Really, it's just business, forget that other stuff, said the military-industrial complex, which, when the layers of obfuscation and self-serving rhetoric were peeled away and its corporate reports were scrutinized by peace activist historians and economists, was revealed to be the engine that motored the American economy and had been motoring it since the end of World War II. The interlocking lattice of companies that fed the machine turned out to be immense—everyone was directly or indirectly involved. All of which eventually gave new meaning to the aphorism coined by George Orwell in *1984* that "War is peace," which in the sixties itself was further extended in Kurt Von-negut's *Cat's Cradle* to "Truth is lies," which was transmogrified into a popular demo placard/slogan of the time: "War is good business, invest your son." Is there a linkage between civil rights and the War? Why was war the only economic engine that could run America? Was the War also an arm of domestic social policy? Was that really possible? Why? This seems wrong, we protest.

What are you guys, un-American? the authorities wanted to know. What's wrong with providing well-paying jobs and full employment for citizens—that's what we're supposed to do, isn't it? Isn't that why our economic system is the envy of the world?

In reality, the government was saying that being profligate with American human and material resources really benefits the average citizen, that human beings were a disposable element that the post-World War II "peace" created, that investing in the future productivity of American citizens was of less marginal utility than smart bombs, napalm, and chemical defoliants. If Johnson had waged his "war" on poverty with the same single-minded allocation of resources that were expended in South Vietnam, poverty would have been eliminated. There was some kind of cracked logic at work that motivated the government to "protect" foreign civil rights while its own citizens weren't fully enfranchised—not cost-effective enough, eh? The war in Vietnam may have seemed to be good for business, but whose?

Question Authority? Which authority? Whose? The one that demonstrates mastery and competence? The one that looks out for the interests of *all* our citizens? Or only those who have a financial stake in the exercise? Question Authority? You bet your ass we do, replied the mothers and fathers, sons, daughters, grandfathers, grandmothers, the freedom marchers black and white, young and old who were starting to get the message. Why accept answers to our questions that are couched in dehumanizing technical jargon, whose meaning changes monthly (or weekly), an authority, which, when finally ratted out by the press through the leak of *The Pentagon Papers*, prosecutes the leaker to deflect criticism. Instead of answering your questions, we'll make *you* the enemy and thereby suppress all those embarrassing questions for which we have no good answers nor indeed adequate ones and avoid answering at all costs. "Question Authority" may have been a popular lapel button (now a collectible for sixties trivia specialists), but it was also one of the generation's defining ideologies that allied itself firmly with its past. What began with doubts about America's involvement in Vietnam inevitably had to end up in the total examination of the essential nature of the character of American democracy itself.

Unfortunately, as the sixties came to an end, the symbolism of Question Authority became debased and ultimately lost its meaty metaphorical resonances. Taking the query out of the "ensemble/individuality" arena, counterculture youth spokesmen reduced it to a generational question of style of "Don't Trust Anyone over 30," a wiseass comeback and advertising gimmick that conclusively shut down the intergenerational dialogue about the nature of America that the War had finally opened up. It was a catchphrase coined by youth spokesman who were way over 30 themselves.[13]

It took almost 5 years for public protest to reach the point where Lyndon Johnson declined to run for a second full term as president in 1968. It was a bumper year of public conflict asterisked by the deaths of Martin Luther King and Robert Kennedy and the riots in the ghetto streets of Newark, Los Angeles, Chicago, Atlanta, and Cleveland. That summer in Chicago at the Democratic National Convention, the Chicago police rioted, beating and terrorizing protestors and delegates alike on national network television.

Though the images of "war" in America were brought to the heartland and a street theater action was turned into nightly news broadcasts, in the long run it proved to be a gigantic miscalculation, since it gave authorities ample cause to employ their monopoly of force. But by then, the Movement was already imploding, rent apart by the conflicting political and social agendas that spilled chaotically onto the streets of Chicago and into Grant Park.

57

Though more people than ever demonstrated against the war and its ranks swelled in Chicago's aftermath, the mood of the demonstrations had shifted. Underneath now percolated a climate of random violence that wasn't there before, when the metaphor had been more pliant, general in its scope, and timeless in its appeal. Violence began to displace nonviolence as a general mode of action for the Movement. Peace became in a sense a finite commodity, meaning different things for different groups, a means to achieve individual agendas.

Sectarian factionalism dominated large organizational meetings where each group had its own unique agenda that had to be addressed. The war in Vietnam was really the war on poverty, racism, sexism of all kinds, persuasions, proclivities, a War of Liberation that was beginning to unfold in various forms in board rooms, offices, factories, classrooms, and courthouses throughout the land. For the far left it may have seemed to be "total assault on the culture," but no one any longer agreed on its tactics or its targets; we had met the enemy and it *was* us.[14]

The Movement, a loose confederation of like-minded people at best, was atomized into its components, the varieties of socialism, communism (Russian, Chinese, and Cuban variations), and anarchism, civil rights and gender issues. There were Maoists, Trotskyites (who ran the office), and hardline Stalinists at odds with hardcore pacifists and gay rights activists. Everyone seemed to have his own shock troops in place to "liberate the community from the oppressor"—the full spectrum, from the Black Panthers, the extremist element of the civil rights movement, to the Hispanic Brown Berets to the WPP of Ann Arbor, Michigan, who believed in the power of sex, drugs, and rock and roll (preferably together) to knock it all loose. In New York City, even mental patients had their own Liberation League and storefront office.

Totally committed to violence was the Weather Underground, a group of the best and brightest, so elite one had to have a Triple-A Dun & Bradstreet rating to be a member (close, just kidding). Eventually they blew up their New York City townhouse/clubhouse with most of their leadership inside while assembling a homemade dynamite bomb. They were so far in the vanguard they never consulted anyone, preferring to issue press releases before and communiqués after the bombs went off. But their exception only proved the rule since everyone demanded his or her own unique piece of the action, while Whitman's idea of ensemble/individuality, which had somehow unified and energized the factions, was engulfed. Me, what about me?, they all cried.

But what had happened to *us?*

The Rolling Stones song "Street-Fighting Man," which in some small way had typified the protester's attitude in Chicago in 1968, by 1972 had in Miami Beach, Florida, been transformed. In Loomis Park (temporarily renamed People's Park for the duration) off Lower Collins Avenue, a staging area from which the Movement gathered in all its rainbow hues, one could now pick up at the green candy-striped party tent (more appropriate for a country club wedding) an official revolutionary songbook from Students for a Democratic Society (SDS). Progressive Labor Party organizers wore not Army surplus fatigues, but bright red T-shirts emblazoned with the slogan "Smash the State." Perhaps as an

exercise in irony, they'd expropriated a popular soda commercial jingle to use in its war against America: "I'd like to teach the
world to sing in perfect Mandarin/With Uncle Ho and Chairman
Mao, Fidel and Madame Binh/Revolution, It's the Real Thing."
The Mickey Mouse Club closing theme was no less usefully par-
odied: "Now it's time to say goodbye to all the bourgeoisie, etc."
It wasn't ironic; it was pathetic and a little sad, too.

It was also here in front of this very same tent with these
very same revolutionaries and the whole world watching (well
it seemed to be, with so many cameras) that the late Allen Ginsberg, spiritual descendant of Walt Whitman, author of the Beat
paean *Howl* and Movement peacecreep-in-residence, lost his
temper when being told by the red shirts that "all art which
doesn't serve the Revolution is counterproductive." In the same
tones that he had chanted "AH" to any group or camera who
would have him, he chanted "Fuck SDS, Fuck you, SDS, Fuck
you, fuck you, fuck you" in anger and disgust. It was a shocking
deviation from the script the organizers had put together, with
even more disastrous results than 4 years before when chaos
had reigned in the streets of Chicago.[15]

59

But in truth, it was only the media who cared now, for whose
benefit the protests were staged, since for all intents and purposes the Movement had been overshadowed by the phenomenon known as the counterculture, whose attitudes and style
an upcoming generation of youth inherited from their brothers and sisters, a club that included everyone under 30 whose
distinguishing characteristics were a love and allegiance to sex,
drugs, and rock and roll but that trivialized its import. No one
really cared who Ho Chi Minh, Hermann Hesse, Samuel Beckett, Allan Watts, or even Walt Whitman was anymore, since no
one seemed to have any more time to read at the big party, now
that Nixon was withdrawing troops and the boys were coming
home. Considering the forces that were and had been at work, it
was inevitable that the music America listened to would be over-
whelmed, drowning out the discourse that had been the cause
of Whitman's essay *Democratic Vistas* almost a century earlier.
Indeed, there was music in the air, mostly cash registers in this
Brave New World, one that Walt Whitman had warily understood

well enough from his nineteenth-century viewpoint, but would have disowned if alive then.

Question Authority? Whose? Not ours.

Shards

> It would be ironic if, at a time when many of the old institutions of adolescence are in manifest decline, spokesmen for the counterculture succeeded in creating a more sophisticated if no less pernicious version of adolescence, one that sanctions the isolation of youth from adult roles not because such roles "tempt" or "corrupt" the young but because they fail to provide scope for freedom and spontaneity.

Joseph Kett[16]

> It just became something that was necessary. Really as a young person, it became socially necessary.

Kip Cohen, manager of Fillmore East, on the counterculture[17]

60

By the summer of 1967, baptized forever after by the national news media as "The Summer of Love," the music of counterculture had already suffocated that feeling of ensemble/individuality that embodied both head culture and the coalition of forces represented by the anti-War movement. Growing in intensity for the previous year and a half, it had been primarily framed and publicized by the major media (newspapers, television, radio) with varying degrees of truth and insight as an urban or college town phenomenon. *Time, Life, Look, Newsweek, The Saturday Evening Post*—all supplied the colorful pictorials, analysis, and spin for everyone who lived outside the urban centers, where all "the action" was taking place.

Those urban and college enclaves were served by their own media, collectively known as the underground press, with all manner of alternative ideas on health and education, plus poetry and, of course, rock and roll concert and record reviews, the latter of which proved to be its undoing in the end. With varying degrees of effectiveness and candor, what came to be known as the underground press printed, unlike some of their establish- ment colleagues, not only all the news that was fit to sing about the War but all related activities: protests, vigils, etc. New York City had the *East Village Other* and *Rat*; Boston, *The Phoenix*; Los Angeles, the *LA Free Press*; San Francisco, *The Oracle*, as the *Berkeley Barb* and *Bay Area Guardian*. There were papers as well in Austin, Texas, Atlanta, Georgia, and all points in between.

While counterculture was being brokered to the youth under 30, as a "lifestyle" engendered by the sacred triad of sex, drugs, and rock and roll, the historical, literate, and timeless concepts that formerly underpinned it all (as well as the indigenous folk origins of the music) were unceremoniously jettisoned, substituted by the vagaries of a fashion-mediated peer group pressure tactically exploited by various interested parties, especially (but not limited to) the music business. Floundering in the early sixties, it had been revivified by the popularity of folk rock and the English pop invasion of the Beatles, the Stones, and others, as well as the sounds of psychedelia emanating from San Francisco and Los Angeles. It was here that the so-called counterculture made its most visible economic effect, so that by the late sixties there was no record company worth its name that didn't have on its payroll at least a few long-haired "company freaks," former political activists or underground music journalists involved in the various aspects and mechanics of the business, from advertising to promotion to the development of new artists and repertoire.

61

By 1968 rock and revolution had become inextricably linked in the public mind, or at least with the record-buying public mind, as a youth fashion statement, which came to be typified by a Columbia Records ad campaign designed by Jim Fouratt. A former actor and social activist in San Francisco's Haight Ash-bury in the midsixties as well as an associate of Dr. Timothy Leary, Fouratt conceived of a print ad campaign that prominently featured a picture of a group of hippies in a jail holding pen under the tag line, "The Man Can't Bust Our Music." Cool, huh?

There was some kind of logic to all of this: the media freaks, a new elite, working on the inside of multimillion-dollar corporations to subvert corporate America and effect cultural change. Though at the time it seemed like an ideal gig with free typewriters, phones, mail, photocopying, and associated promotional goodies and etceteras, one had to walk a fine line to justify having all those perks and to maintain one's credibility—if only to oneself. Anyway, it was only a matter of time before one would have to work on something that really sucked but that the company had spent a pile on, when the "revolutionary" agent in place on the inside teetered on the edge or fell off. Some did, some didn't, but it was fun while it lasted—a hell of an education in the ways of the world for those who tried to serve two masters and then found that they were serving only Mammon.

If one views the music business of that time as a full field metaphor for how contemporary cultural ideas were transacted, brokered, and subtly (or not so subtly) changed by the commercial environment, it's easier to understand the mechanism by which the loosely defined head culture became the visibly fashionable counterculture, which in turn led to the "Me Generation" discoquaalude shuffle of the seventies and its punk antithesis, to the cocaine-fueled "yuppie" vogueing of the eighties, and eventually to the jacked-in hip-hop information superhighway boogie of the nineties.

More to the point, the commodification process has informed and driven American cultural life since the middle of the nineteenth century, of which the McLuhanesque sixties electric/psychedelic variant was the result. It's what William Leach, in *Land of Desire*, a cultural history of department stores and their merchandizing techniques, characterized as "the cult of the new," which "readily subverted whatever custom, value, or folk idea came within its reach."[18] In essence this happened when head culture was commercially reinvented and brokered as counterculture a process that continues unabated and is rarely commented upon today. To Jim Morrison of the Doors, music may have been your only friend until the end in the late sixties, but there was all that time before the Apocalypse that had to be filled with "product." It was here the underground press and the culture it was to represent in some small way went adrift and aground.

In the beginning, it made good business sense. In exchange for record company support through full-, half-, or quarter-page ads, underground newspaper publishers were able to upgrade and expand the coverage of peace-related events, while the critics' low-paying wages were effectively subsidized by free records, concert tickets, and club tabs. This in turn fed the record business merchandizing machine. (They would have done it in any case without the other perks, but the perks helped.) Living in a state of cultural fast-forward, months ahead of the wave and surfeited with all kinds of "inside information," the critics themselves became estranged from their own audience. The more they became an integral part of the brokerage business, the more cynical they became about their audience. And instead of being content to be merely reporters, they became active players in the commercial dance themselves, using their position to search out newer and newer trends to exploit for their own critical self-aggrandizement, to become celebrities themselves within an increasingly celebrity-driven subculture.

When the music was transcendent and vital, rock critics in the underground press easily maintained their integrity and wrote inspiring prose; but when the music was not so good, or egregiously awful, it was a harder job, because the record companies still expected—nay, demanded—uncritical support in exchange for their advertising revenues. Publishers as best as they could tried to explain the situation with varying degrees of success. Though this unstated quid pro quo between publisher and advertiser may have been an old dance for the establishment media book, movie, and music critics from time immemorial (as is currently unofficially practiced by major newspapers of record), it was a shocking wake-up call to these new kids who thought every one ought to play by their rules. Some papers who tried to buck the system folded because they lost their financial base, while others—like *Rolling Stone*, which had other sources of revenue and a solid demographic base—hung tough until the record companies themselves backed down and some kind of modus vivendi was negotiated. Some critics joined record companies, others quit to be replaced by more pliant, less fastidious souls who were in it for the perks just like any other art-promotion job. Though it may not have been a pretty sight, it was the way of the world, then as now.

All was made immeasurably easier by Nixon's strategy of gradually ending the War, which removed the underground press's political and social vitality, substituting for it issues of style—hence the birth of the disgusting term "lifestyle"—which were all that remained. In a few short years, the protest of the American Way, which was running amok in Southeast Asia and throughout the world, had ironically (to the old heads) become a *commercial* celebration. One 4-year high school generation's introspection and soul-searching became an entitlement, the right to party for the next's.

By the summer of 1969 there was a certain desperate quality to it that Patricia Kennealy Morrison, editor of *Jazz* and *Pop* magazine, noted at the Woodstock Music and Art Fair ("Three Days of Peace and Music"). Amid the good times she saw ominous signs at the birth of the "Woodstock Nation" that both establishment and counterculture media, in its sanctification of the event, chose to overlook:

> Yes, the kids are beautiful: yes I was Out There with them, and I did see a great deal of beauty. But also I saw thousands upon thousands of walking wounded of this Revolution we all talk so much about; kids who hadn't got faces yet, filled up with drugs they don't know how to make proper use of and only take because the Scene makes it easy. Kids like that hurt me; I feel media guilt, that maybe we who are older and supposed to know better did this to them (they're turning on in elementary schools now ...) before they were ready for it; the kids that try to hitch a ride on your car with a V-sign, then snarl viciousness at you when you tiredly explain you have a full car and can't take any more passengers, the kids who have all the right hip clothes and know all the right words and drop all the right stuff but whose *heads* haven't been affected in the slightest; the kids who have come to this festival and are going to consume vibes and dope and music but what are they going to take home with them? Just as importantly, what have they brought?[19]

And what do they bring today?

The Era of Peace and Love had a short shelf-life indeed, lasting less than 6 months before its antithesis, the antifestival at Altamont, took place. Here, Hell's Angels who'd been hired as security guards for a free concert featuring the Rolling Stones, Grateful Dead, Jefferson Airplane, and others stabbed to death a concertgoer in front of tens of thousands of people.[20] To Kip Cohen, the manager of New York's Fillmore East, a premier East Coast mecca for rock and roll, the Woodstock generation appeared to be nothing more than an aggressive gluttonous audience whose members were far more concerned about how they looked than who they came to hear, whose tastes could be extrapolated from the detritus left at 4 AM for the clean-up crew—Romilar bottles and Trojans under the seats.[21]

Back to business as usual: New audiences demanded newer music, newer trends; paisley prints, granny glasses, and grass gave way to glitter, platform shoes, and speed soon enough. The late sixties saw the emergence of heavy metal music, which, though popular among the adolescent crowd, was in reality hype-driven, showy, and musically bankrupt save as pop sociology—which is how some rock critics framed coverage of the shows when they themselves could no longer deal with these new audiences or their music. Groups like Grand Funk Railroad and Black Sabbath were becoming the rage with younger audiences just coming into their majority.

Those groups gave their audience the vulgarity they demanded. According to Kip Cohen, "everything the audience wants, which is loudness, rudeness, lack of originality."[22] How now? If the members of the underground press wished to retain their authority as viable spokesmen for the culture they were supposed to represent, they had to shift their focus away from the politics of liberation (boring and beside the point to this demanding adolescent world) toward the politics of cultural consumption which was how the Establishment media had promoted and framed head culture to begin with.

Unlike head culture, which attempted to "do away" with goods of all sorts by eschewing the heedless consumption of the American way of life, counterculture reveled in it and was served by an alternative though equally rapacious infrastructure of long-haired dope-smoking retailers, merchandisers, and brokers of "hip capitalism" to service the adolescent needs for play equipment, which the underground press uncovered and exploited. Johan Huizinga in 1936 caught an earlier part of this wave when he observed in his book *In the Shadow of History* that the play attitude of adolescents even then had become a permanent feature of Western culture whose emergence was "facilitated not only by a decreased desire for individual judgement, by the standardizing effect of group organizations providing a set of ready-made opinions, but also by the marvelous development of technical facilities."[23] And that's what electronically altered teenage money did with the sixties in the end.

Indeed, the real import of the sixties was *not* the making of the counterculture, but the selling of it, whereby the concept of Whitman's individuality/ensemble became translated and reduced to terms of "lifestyle choice," with the result that the nineties seems to be composed of a vast sea of passive spectator consumers awash in individuated goods that though insidiously varied, have little real value, a situation that has proved to be spiritually enervating to all who have been touched by it, and that's everyone who's alive now. In the process of blaming the sixties we are blaming ourselves for having lost the vision of America, which, however brief and fragile and imperfect, was nevertheless empowering and transcendent for all. Those who blame the sixties now are distraught and angry, and because the vision of the GE All-Electric Kitchen that Ronald Reagan sold on *Death Valley Days* not only came with a hefty price tag, but didn't (or never did) work—and we're stuck with it anyway. It's easy to blame the sixties rather than try to correct the commercial excesses that continue to inform every aspect of our lives. Blaming won't make the corruption go away; blame just amplifies and highlights its truth.

66

Now that nostalgia is driving history's engine, it's convenient for the left and the right to manipulate times past to their own ends since they can assume no one remembers. They think that images and slogans will suffice because they think they control the imagery now. Blame it on the sixties? The sixties blames them for believing in the lie they collaborated upon, for deluding themselves, for believing in the goodness of goods instead of asking something of the humans who make them.

The sixties in its purest form was a shining historical moment that was supposed to raise consciousness, not deaden it, to focus attention then broaden it from the singular to the universal. It was not meant to be brokered by goods, fashion, or style, which weakened its total effect. It was never supposed to be enumerated by statistical polls of ever-narrowing focus groups and in fact lost its power when it was reduced in such a manner. The sixties was about the freedom to question and arrive at answers and still question more, because The Way was not simply the destination. Only in a closed and dead universe were there invariable and inviolate answers. The true spirit of the sixties, not counterculture or its subsequent peregrinations and material permutations, believed in nonrepresentational living, free of endorsement contracts, where one didn't have to be true to one's high school alma mater.

Blame it on the sixties? Well, the "sixties" blames the left and the right for misapprehending its brief moment of truth, for confusing and then preferring style over substance, and for ultimately evading the questions our children pose when we aren't "us" around them now that they want to know all about it. Bring back the sixties? They haven't gone anywhere. If we no longer can or want to remember those old sorehead democratic vistas we saw for America in the sixties, the kids can start with Walt Whitman. You never know; they could be inspired by him, too.

Chapter 4

Boxers or Briefs?

Music Politics in the Post-Elvis Age

For every jump-suited popstar sipping piña coladas by pools, there are thousands of guys strung out along the of nameless small town desolations getting nickled and dimed to death. Roll that up and smoke it.

—Rodriguez'

It was during the 1992 presidential election on MTV's Town Meeting that the "depth" of the interpenetration between the rock and roll world and politics was reached, when candidate Bill Clinton was asked *that* deadly question: Boxers or briefs, which underwear style did he prefer? Constituencies must be solicited and candidates endure all manner of ritual indignities and abuse from the voters every 4 years, true, but what struck me most was not so much the question's insipid cuteness or the feeble attempt at "cutting-edge" humor—true irony requires an exact sense of history to give it some nuanced weight. Was this query supposed to elicit a knowing nod from generational coreligionists at home: "Hi, look at me, ain't I cool on MTV?" Though for me it sort of lay out there in electronic space like soggy cereal, this smart-ass question produced a ripple of nervous titters from the studio audience that night, and for days thereafter in the popular press.

Big deal, so the question was a slogan lifted from a popular Hanes advertising campaign. But I was puzzled. Was the question more on the lines of "How do you see yourself under your suit of clothes, the suit of clothes we all perforce must wear in our daily lives?" or "What image are you trying to promote with your underwear?" or "What's the first metaphor you put on in the morning to cover yourself?" Is underwear and not what's under the wear the true measure of a politician's inner soul? Are presidents really elected on the basis of a nuanced under-standing of an advertising campaign that turns underwear into an item of competition and style, or does this sort of advertising only have resonance for MTV's target audience? Was this the political face of official music culture now: boxers or briefs?

Were Bush and Clinton supposed to frame their whole debate and discussion of America's future within the parameters of adspeak, which would be framed in the postmortem media wrap-ups as "Taste Great. Less Filling. Voters choose?" That's a far more accurate assessment of the level of understanding and discernment the major political parties expect from the national electorate every few years. What would have happened if the candidates had been hip enough to reply "none of the above," neatly blind-siding the smug little twerp and forcing him to think about other realities besides the brand name one he was contemplating and inhabiting? "That's all you can come up with?" replies the candidate with a twinkle in his eye. When did one's choice in underwear become the be-all and end-all of political wisdom? Maybe I was just thinking too hard; but given the chance, what sort of question would youth have asked 25 years ago when the only forums that belonged to the people were the streets? Times have changed. Stop the sketch.

This all was too "out" to contemplate until I remembered that this debate was sponsored by the *news* division of MTV. What *news?* MTV news consists of equal parts of record company promo hype, rock celebrity gossip, and tidbits about what's in and out in the music world—it's just another network like ABC, NBC, CBS, or Fox. From its humble beginnings as a depository for record company promotional videos, in a little more than a decade MTV now produces sitcoms, game shows, special features, and phony self-promoting award shows. Like its older siblings, MTV also works on cultivating and refining its audience demographics to increase its advertising revenues with commercials for beer, cars, and blemish cream for the Lite beer set. In going for the gold, MTV has much abused the "spirit of rock and roll," especially if they mean the feeling of the pure joy of being that rock and roll music unlocks which has little to do with the "goodness of the goods"; the ownership of cars, lipstick, or credit cards. MTV's just like *Rolling Stone* magazine, its print equivalent, which started off "alternative and outlaw" and gnarly 'round the edges in the late sixties, which now rivals *Esquire* and the *New Yorker* in terms of total feel (if not in content) and in terms of the number of full-color ads for major brand-name merchandise. Since it has become part of the Viacom Communications conglomerate. MTV has had even less to do with music or the spirit of rock and roll and has become more involved in the business until it now basically functions as a junior media executive farm team for the Bigs.

"The spirit of Rock and Roll"—I like that.

What if the MTV Town Meeting audience, instead of being demographically correct, was comprised of people who liked rock and roll in all its forms, commercial and uncommercial; if instead of wiseacres whose brains had been permanently damaged by advertising the audience was composed of real fans well into it—heavy metal fans and hip-hoppers, rude-boys and gang-bangers with a dash of suburban snotnoses—to whom the candidates would have had to exhibit their intergenerational knowledge of musically nuanced behavior. One hell of a test for the MTV demographic, eh?

What if a fanatic biker messenger/bungee jumper with a orange mohawk asked a question on foreign policy which litreffed Henry Kissinger or better Otto von Bismarck on the value of *realpolitik?* Would Bill Clinton have charmingly let slip to some earnest prog-rocker that at Yale law school he was such a big Mothers of Invention/Zappa freak that he had a Phi Krappa Zappa poster on his dorm room wall, or that his wife-to-be ripped it off the wall during a spat, or that when he went to visit President Vaclav Havel of the Czech Republic he brought him a stack of Zappa CDs? What would the voters hypothetically have made of a revelation from either candidate who admitted to a serious jones for Nine Inch Nails, NWA, or ZZ Top, or was an unregenerate C&W fanatic (well, hell, everyone has a soft spot for C&W)? It would be informative to voters to learn just what part music played in the soundtrack of their lives. Had rap lyrics gone too far? Why? Youth wants to know. Answers to these questions would have shown that Bill and George were at least human, provided their answers were honest sound bite McNuggets.

73

Dream on. Walley. The context would have been lost on the MTV crowd the candidates were working that night, consumers for whom reality is nice concept so long as it's correctly packaged. Preposterous? Absolutely. It wasn't a political debate that was going on here anyway, but rather a canny business decision that exploited the division between the generations in which the

MTV corporate ethos so heavily invests. Let's face it, the only people who have no stake at all in resolving the conflict between the generations are the advertisers and the fabricators of generational goods who have the most to lose. It wouldn't do on other levels because MTV understands that most young people (adolescents to early 30s these days) are heavily invested in the fiction that somehow politicians and/or celebrities are not real human beings. It's one thing to know friends of your parents who are cool, and quite another for your parents themselves to be cool and be forced to acknowledge it because, by definition, parents aren't cool. It goes against the creed that only youth are entitled to have any kind of inner life of which music is a vital part. That also wouldn't reveal an admittedly informed understanding of "the enemy" in the either/or, black/white world of the ever-changing *now*, not one bit. Boxers are Briefed?

If MTV *really* embodied the real spirit of rock and roll, they could have dispensed with the Town Meeting entirely, and instead featured a Battle of the Bands with Lee Atwater. George Bush's late campaign manager and a self-styled blues guitar strangler, playing against Clinton staff wanna-be irregulars. Bottom line, whoever put together the most ass-kicking, heart-stopping set of rock and roll would have been declared the winner. And if there had to be candidates at all, have them sucking on humongous bongs while seated at a back table at House of Blues or Hard Rock Cafe, critiquing the set or discussing the nature of the interface between politics and music. Awesome, dude. Twenty-five years ago, heads weren't so totally befuddled by the celebrity of politicians (or the celebrity of themselves for that matter) *not* to ask why we were in Vietnam. In that more naive age, young people were less accepting of corporate culture and wisdom, if only because when the rhetoric of patriotism was stripped away from the Vietnam War, they understood just how it was used to defend the rights of corporate interests to exploit Southeast Asia's natural resources, just like France and Japan had failed to do. So much for neat metaphors. Indeed, it is paradoxical that in the nineties, the spirit of rock and roll that spoke to the best of a generation's aspirations has become a hostage to a corporate culture whose implicit assumptions are just as invidious as the ones that generation attempted with varying degrees of success to overcome, replace, or at least humanize.

These days those connections are harder to pinpoint, hidden as they are within an innerconnected lattice of special interest posturings, PR releases, and media conglomerates.

But what would have happened if instead of employing a cute political affairs celebrity-journalist like Tabatha Soren, MTV brought in Hunter S. Thompson as moderator? Father of Gonzo journalism and author of *Fear and Loathing on the Campaign Trail*, Thompson wrote the archetypal new journalism *ur*-text of drug-tinged political paranoia in the 1972 presidential campaign. Bet that George Bush wouldn't have been as threatened as Saxophone Bill (for whom Hunter Thompson's attitude at one time had a deep generational resonance, maybe more than he'd care to admit in public now). Provided the good doctor was more or less "behaving" himself (however he defined "behavior" and the management agreed), an instructive though dangerous vision would have resulted, raising the level of political discourse a few notches—if the intent of the exercise was to bring rock and rollers of all ages together instead of merely the MTV demographic. In truth, that spectacle would have been too visually ragged to be used for pitching big ticket commercial accounts, which in management's point of view was the ultimate point of the exercise. The rest of us would hope that, true to form, Dr. Thompson would rip through the proceeding like the psychic bull in a china shop we think he'd be and not give a rat's ass whether he looked good on camera on not. *This* would not do at all, nor would it be true to the nature of political discourse in the Post-Elvis Age.

Talk about the devolution of political discourse! Whole universes and countless light-years separate the writing style and mind-set of Hunter Thompson from our own. Our politicians today don't even merit paranoid fear and loathing—instead we treat them like any other contemporary whose opinion we don't like: We flat out disrespect them, to hell with the reasons why. Instead of Thompson's darkly twisted and richly multileveled surrealist universe, the political pundits of left and right have relocated to the parking lot before school or the locker-lined high school hallway. There, while changing classes, they rank on each other: "Hey asshole." "No, you're an asshole." "And you're a fuckhead." "That's *Mister* Fuckhead to you," etc. Is it any wonder that comedian Al Franken's collection of political essays. *Rush*

Limbaugh Is a Big Fat Idiot, has been a recent best-seller in this bravest of new worlds where attitude is the only thing? Breathlessly one awaits his sequel. *Newt Gingrich Is a Big Fat Idiot Too.* Dude, go for it!!

Not to be outdone, the neoconservatives weigh in with their own heavy hitters, represented by a Rush Limbaugh or a P. J. O'Rourke, who view national and international affairs from the comparatively "enlightened" perspective of a beer-besotted frat-rat or know-it-all high school cadet who, joint in hand, from his perch on the sink in the Boys Room, disparages the efforts of the spirit committee (do-gooding, soft-minded liberal Democrats, aging peaceniks and their [ahem] weak-kneed wussy New Age-demented neohippie ecologist spawn) in their efforts to clean up the karma at Screaming Eagle High. A far more formally critical though similar discourse style defines as it distinguishes *The New Republic* from R. Emmett Tyrell's *American Spectator,* or even the editorial overview of *The Wall Street Journal* from *The New York Times.* Which is puzzling because Franken, O'Rourke, and many contemporary commentators on American culture have been exposed to, if they haven't actually been beneficiaries of, Thompson's ground-breaking journalistic methodology and attitude. Instead of using it as a staging area from which to launch more pertinent public forms of political analysis and discourse, in their hands it becomes a tool for finagling power-politics dinner party invitations: in effect, to better buy into the world Thompson illuminated while simultaneously undermining its base assumptions. For the new bosses (who are the same as the old bosses), things are just fine, because the spoils of the game as they've defined it, celebrity and insider status, are far easier to deal with than the responsibilities they'd have moderating a dialogue in which everyone else is included. And while these BMOCs are inside collaborating with the principal, so to speak, we're left loitering in another smelly high school corridor ... again. Celebrity consumerhood makes for stranger bedfellows in the Post-Elvis Age.

Boxers or briefs? It really doesn't make much of a difference to MTV's mindset—they reason it's "our" corporate culture, rock and roll's, or better, MTV's vision of the rock and roll world, as opposed to "theirs" (ConGlomCo Inc.'s). Or so they've successfully

deluded themselves into thinking. Long ago it possibly may
have been true that "The Man Can't Bust Our Music," but there's
no reason why the corporate "we" of MTV can't spin control and
homogenize the spirit if not the effect of rock and roll. No matter
how revolutionary, apposite, faintly or potentially seditious to the
survival the music might be, eventually it becomes just another
transitory celebrity product and lifestyle statement. And like other
entertainment media, MTV dispenses the myth that with "access,"
everyone can be an "insider"—the highest social benefit this
celebrity-driven society confers. To be an insider, all one has to do
is follow the rules of deportment as codified by MTV personalities,
just like high school all over again, or the audiovisual equivalent;
everyone watches TV. Within this smug all-access-backstage-
pass world of celebrity maps, MTV supplies to its consumers a
carbon copy of the Hollywood movie version of celebrity. When
the media spotlight shines out, we all know what to expect and
what is expected from us. Access also peddles supermarket tab-
loids like *The Star* or *The Globe*, the "news/gossip" programs on
E! (Entertainment Channel), *Entertainment Tonight*, and CNN, or
tabloid TV like *Hard Copy, 20/20, Dateline,* and even *60 Minutes.*
MTV's continued success both here and abroad is a testament to
just how right they've been in handicapping the trends of youth.
Though far removed from the original "spirit of rock and roll,"
judging from how rapidly the company has been absorbed into
the larger corporate media maw of ConGlomCo Entertainments,
Inc., it's been a good business decision nonetheless.

If all we're really talking about is consumer choice, the connection between rock music and politics used to be easier to
make; perhaps our definition of goods has been altered over the
past quarter century. It could be safely, if generally, assumed 25
years ago that on some level the kind of politics rock and roll
audiences responded to hinged on a belief in the political and
moral ramifications of understanding, equality, cooperation, and
unity wrapped around a beat that was also great to boogie to. In
1971 that mind-set inspired George Harrison, Bob Dylan, and Eric
Clapton, along with other rock superstars, to sponsor the Concert for Bangladesh, a benefit concert with a subsequent record
album merchandising tie-in that raised more than $300,000 for
Bangladeshi flood relief. The events set the media formula and
standard that paved the way for international music fundraisers

like Live Aid, the Mandala Tributes. Amnesty International's Conspiracy of Hope and Human Rights, and, in the United States, the No-Nukes concerts and Farm Aid benefits, all of which have raised tens of millions of dollars for charity, making rock music fund-raisers a common fixture on the cultural landscape.

Though the publicity build-ups, the good will, and/or cash raised have been awesome, afterwards there always seems to be a dearth of follow-up stories concerning the percentage of total monies that were finally dispersed to the causes. Unfortunately, most people tend to ignore the economics of charity benefits. Celebrities may donate their time, but rarely do they forego the limo to and from the gig or, if from out of town, the plane tickets and associated hotel rooms that come with the package. Even if performance fees are donated or waived, the care and feeding of the rest of the concert support team—stagehands, electricians, video, satellite, and sound technicians/directors—also cost somebody in the end. Feeling good having donated some money to the cause, people move on, and the connection is reinforced that cash donations are a covalent substitute for real-time social commitment—no foul, no blame.

With benefits cropping up seemingly every 3 months, though, once we are habituated to the event structure and the proper response to it, these events start losing their emotional punch and political significance because in the broadest terms, one "good" cause is much like another. Okay, so people are dying somewhere, goes the interior monologue, they're starving in droves, their ecology is in the toilet because of clear-cutting, and they're oppressed as shit, okay, that sucks, here's my money to help fix it, now let's get down and boogie. In a nanosecond, the political cause becomes a petty annoyance. Ignoring the scrolling messages at the bottom of the TV set listing the 1-800 donation numbers, we intently concentrate on the depoliticized entertainment event, the ever-changing mini-drama/soap opera of music business politics in which everyone is alleged to be an insider, as familiar a world to us as watching the Oscars now that Whoopi Goldberg, Billy Crystal, or Robin Williams are the emcees. Once that donation for the T-shirt/CD package is American Expressed, Master-, or Visa-carded, we shift our attention to who shows up, how they look, and who's backing up whom. There are all kinds

of musicians: those who are there just because they like to jam
and party, but not exclusive to Rod Stewart, as well as those, like
certain Hollywood celebrities, whose media political commitment is exquisitely of the moment, who mastered the delicate
knack for being associated with each and every newsworthy
cause du jour. It takes a while to figure out who they are.

We psych ourselves up for that quintessential musical/histori-
cal "moment" every benefit claims it will produce. Perhaps there
will be a "reunion" of an old classic rock band who've gone their
separate ways, but, swallowing their egos and their pride, reunite
for One Night Only to play the good old stuff (largely left until
that closing jam session). "Reunions" of Cream, Led Zeppelin, or
The Who are way up there near the top of that event structure
possibility. (And wouldn't it be cool if some rock and roll New
Age psychic guitarist channeled Kurt Cobain back from his final
reward and the donations skyrocketed, proving the economic
clout—or political commitment—of grunge-rockers to the old
hippies who continue to organize these shows?) If not whole
bands reunited, then it's an elevating thing to witness the resurrection of a supposed "has-been" or enjoy the appearance of
a "mystery" celebrity guaranteed to burn down the house and
take no prisoners—Little Richard, Chuck Berry, Jerry Lee Lewis,
or Bob Dylan can't do that enough. Whether some careers are
resurrected or spectacularly crash and burn makes for riveting
media politics worthy of the combo donation for the T-shirt/CD/
tape. Truth is, some shows raise more money than others and
are as much dependent on the political (or celebrity) correctness of the cause as the number or the celebrity of the musicians
involved.

Though we might prefer to think otherwise, pop music is
politically neutral, its fund/political consciousness-raising capabilities are not the exclusive property of liberal, socialist, or envi-
ronmentalist agendas. There are as many if no less prominent
(and not-so-prominent) pop musicians who support the political
right and the Religious Right. Though not as well-publicized, pop,
rock, and country music artists also raise funds for and/or the
spirits of neo-Nazi skinheads, survivalists, segregationists, and
right-to-life advocates just as handily. So do evangelical Christians in their parallel pop worlds, who have not only their own

rappers and heavy metal gospel maniacs but also a whole supporting universe that music unlocks with its own cable networks, magazines, and fan support groups. And please do not forget the enduring presence within the past 25 years of certain forms of heavy metal music whose adherents give their allegiance (symbolically or actually) to His Satanic Majesty. Old Scratch. As far as this writer knows, however, Lucifer doesn't resort to rock benefits to raise money, much as the Religious Right would like to think; the devil has been around longer than consumerist capitalism.

In the main, rock and roll has been apolitical, a public-access folk medium through which many ideas can be funneled and electrically transmuted, a medium that takes on the protective coloration of anyone happens to be using it—with some notable exceptions. In the mideighties the Reagan Administration theoretically could have staged a series of rock and roll benefits for Contra Aid, though one wonders who would have shown up (as well as who would have said what in the media about whom). I suspect that's because many musicians are either apolitical or liberal, if only because the nature of their work environment encourages them to be so, thus creating a patently absurd, almost virtually unthinkable scenario. So depending on how one looks at it, it was either lucky or very unlucky in terms of the subsequent Iran-Contra hearings that Ronald Reagan's advisors chose to draw financial support from other sources with far deeper pockets than the audience for pop music whose good will, since his days as the governor of California in the seventies, he had never been interested in cultivating in the first place. And playing Jimi Hendrix on his press plane during the 1992 election didn't help Dan Quayle prove to the pool reporters that he was one of the guys and a card-carrying rock and roll fiend either. Even when the fact was generally known, it didn't raise anybody's consciousness very much—especially his.

Boxers in Briefs: a Vogue Pictorial?

The term "erotic politician," which in the sixties was used to describe the ability of a Jim Morrison, Jimi Hendrix, or John Lennon to fuse together sexuality with populist politics (the term was, in fact, coined by Morrison, no mean manipulator himself;

the media pounced on it, as of course he had coolly and deliberately intended them to), in the nineties now extends to music personalities like Madonna, Ru Paul, or The Artist Formerly Known as Prince (TAFKAP for short). Their influence is more evident in the style section of major metropolitan dailies or on the pages of *Vogue, Rolling Stone,* or *Spin* magazines than on the street, which, or so it once was said, belonged to the people (maybe the Internet is its equivalent these days).

Unfortunately, when the impetus for change has come from the streets, as in the case of hip-hop and rap, whatever power that music possessed has been inevitably homogenized, rapidly accessorized, and turned into a commodity by the official style council media in its over-the-counter configuration. With so much information and so little time to digest it all, it's far easier to reduce everything to the gestural shorthand of "lifestyle," politics included. We no longer "live our lives" as much as partake of a certain "lifestyle" that, according to advertising motivational researchers and political pollsters, is supposed to represent who we are and what we believe, which they extrapolate from the quantity and quality of the things we consume. When political ideology is viewed in terms of a lifestyle choice, personal commitments are transitory, easily made and just as easily broken and involving about as much effort as it takes to switch from a Big Mac to a Whopper or to choose a different or more effective antidepressant medication (well, this *is* the nineties). The consequences that result from framing political ideology in terms of competing lifestyle choices may seem negligible, but only because the style councils provide us with a shallow, misinformed sense of what this means for us in the longer run.

81

There's no reason why wanna-be singer/songwriter-turned-mass-murder Charlie Manson shouldn't be added to our short list of erotic politicians along with Michael Jackson and Madonna. Charlie most certainly had an effect on the generation of the sixties with his attempt to use rock's persuasive powers to promote political change, and wasn't he successful (on a microlevel, surely) in selling his followers the concept of the Beatles' *White Album* as apocalyptic text? And speaking of Apocalypse, why not include David Koresh as well? Before founding the Branch Davidian sect, which in a fiery shootout with federal authorities

spectacularly self-destructed on nationwide TV, Koresh as lead
guitarist fronted a merry band of apocalyptic fundamentalist
Christians, whose aim was to harness the power of the gospels
for what he thought was the good of humankind. Koresh was
not unlike John Lennon in that regard, save that Lennon used an
alternative set of gospels for an entirely different end. Deluded
and self-destructive though Koresh or Manson may have been
to their followers and themselves, their use of music shows how
powerful an intellectual intoxicant pop music can be as a force
for political change whether we choose to acknowledge the
veracity of the politics they promote or not.

Though not of the *Vogue* mold (though you never know when
their fashion *zeitgeist* will come back as a runway "lifestyle") and
to Koresh's and Manson's dubious credit, as disturbed as they
were, at least these two decidedly alternative erotic politicians
had pretensions to be cultural revolutionaries, not fashion plates
or strategists attached to the vanguard of the cultural revolution
as the major media style councils see and promote themselves.
Music is primarily fashion-driven these days, they assume; when
we buy the music of Madonna, Michael Jackson, or David Bowie,
or follow the leads of quasi-music personalities like Dennis Rod-
man (the cross-dressing pro basketball player and sometime
MTV personality), instead of being passive consumers we are
active supporters of the cultural revolution whose inside track
they alone are privy to. They've almost convinced us that these
artists—along with socialites, supermodels, clothing designers,
and glitterati of the moment who are also part of the pop music
world—are really sixties-style cultural revolutionaries in dis-
guise, and, at the risk of being shunned as unmutual, uncool, or
backward-looking deluded socialist soreheads, we may as well
just bend over and enjoy it.

They're wrong, of course, and it just shows to go you how
language has also become a function of entertainment culture
over the past 25 years. According to Robert G. Pielke's insight-
ful and cogently argued study of rock and roll music. *You Say
You Want a Revolution: Rock Music in American Culture*, cultural revolutions have six major characteristics: (1) they embody
a fundamental challenge to prevailing values; (2) they are never
rapid; (3) they produce strong counterreactions; (4) they are not

merely political; (5) they are not intrinsically violent; and (6) they tend toward the expansion of individual freedom.[2] By these criteria, few if any of today's style council "cultural revolutionaries" would measure up. It might no longer seem to matter what happens to today's cultural revolutionaries who do.

When politics and music converge in the rock music benefit context, music business politics always leads. For artists, it makes good business sense, since appearing at a high-profile benefit has just as much commercial and career-making potential as having a chart-topping hit—only without the needless expense (or headache) of mounting an expensive promotional tour. For stars between album releases, a judicious benefit appearance is a prime venue in which to premiere new material for a live CD-buying or concert-going audience. Record companies and their executives are equally well served by this system. For the comparatively minimal cost of underwriting a benefit's expenses, they gain the intangible corporate asset of "goodwill," if not for themselves personally, then for the companies they represent, for "bragging rights" if you will.

And here's how it works: The higher profile the cause, the bigger the media hype with a larger audience of potential consumers accruing from the hype and the more potential and eventual consumer interest in new material. However, even a good thing can be taken to extremes in the protean world of rock and roll politics, because exclusive and full-time political commitments can be guaranteed instant career killers once the cause is out of the public eye and ear. This maxim is generally true save for superstars like Bruce Springsteen, Bob Dylan, and a few others whose careers and reputations are secure. Having made more than enough money, and if only as a form of psychic payback, these stars have the leisure to do "the good work" whether it is au courant or not. And thank God they can and do, because contrary to popular belief, record companies cannot and will not make those statements.

Call it the worship of the bottom line, or simply naked self-interest, but from a record company's point of view not all causes are equal, nor are all fights "good." From the public relations standpoint, Blitzbomp Records (not its real name), a large

multinational entertainment conglomerate, may feel all warm
and fuzzy supporting famine relief, or say, a flashy celebrity-stud-
ded benefit for PEN, the international writer's organization that
pressures foreign governments to stop censoring and impris-
oning politically inconvenient writers, because, objectively, the
cause is politically neutral. On the other hand, Blitzbomp will
not be so moved to support any benefit that informs the public about its own artistic censorship or economic exploitation,
which routinely takes place within their own company or the
record industry as a whole; it's simply too close to home, simply not done, everybody knows. Grin and bear it. Indeed, it is
a system every bit as totalitarian and repressive as any Eastern
European or South American dictatorship that keeps artists,
save for the very rich and famous, in perpetual slavery. These
are the true politics of the music business and the business of
music, and it goes like this:

How the Kleptos Lost Their Boxers:
a Cautionary Table

The Kleptos (not their real name) sign with Blitzbomp Records,
a subsidiary of ConGlomCo Entertainment (a.k.a The Company)
for $500,000. Though this might seem like a small fortune for
the band, who have been scuffling for years, it's chump change,
since The Company also signed three other bands for a comparable sum. If one band makes it. Blitzbomp—having played the
law of averages—is still ahead of the curve. In exchange for this
advance against future royalties, the band obligates itself to produce two albums with an option for a third. In effect, the group is
leasing their artistic product, the master recordings, to Blitzbomp,
who will distribute the product to record outlets far and wide.
Only after The Company deducts its operating costs (manufacturing, distribution, promotion) and the standard prearranged
percentage and pays the songwriting royalties and mechanicals
will the band start making money, or so it is assumed.

Sounds good enough, think our boys, who commence acting like the rock and roll warriors they always wanted to be.
Immediately, they upgrade their equipment, perhaps invest in a
new PA system for the road or trade in the van for a good used

touring bus. The lead guitarist drops his current girlfriend for an up-and-coming supermodel, the drummer buys a cherry red BMW, the bass player moves out of the practice room over his parents' two-car garage and into a condo, while the keyboard player finds a dealer in specialized pharmaceuticals who has "better connections." So far, so good.

However, in their haste to sign on the dotted line, the Kleptos neglect to read the fine print and overlook the classic rider buried deep in the contract's boiler plate, which obligates them to use only company facilities for recording, mixing, and mastering. A moot point at the time, until they later realize that company facilities are far more expensive than comparable independent ones. (Next time they'll remember to negotiate a separate advance for recording.)

Green but full of hope, they dutifully head off to the company facility, where instead of recording their songs as quickly and efficiently as possible, having worked everything out before hand, they spend countless expensive hours fiddling with the studio's neat effects, tuning the drums, etc. As quick as you can say jumpingjackflash, they've overshot their recording budget. Not to worry, says the in-house producer, as kind and solicitous as can be, you're our artists and we understand your creative process. You just take as much time as you need and we'll work out the details later, trust us. Oy!

In time, a finely crafted cutting-edge piece of pop emerges: The Company product manager and the promotion department think *Slingshot Rumble* will be a monster hit, and they crank up their star-making machine to promote the single "Positive Pain" on radio and in all the music trade magazines. The costs are hefty, especially the under-the-table monies indie promo men unofficially pay to radio station managers to put the single into regional radio market rotation and onto the industry tip sheets that govern them. Though this tactic is nominally illegal, Blitzbomp knows how the game is played; smaller companies or groups who can't afford the "vig" just don't make it. Payola hasn't died, it's just accounted for under another category in the company books.

And so a company-subsidized national promotional tour is arranged, where the group is packaged as an opening act for The Company headliner. Instead of sleeping in Motel 6s they've graduated to Holiday Inns just like real rock stars. Unfortunately, touring isn't all like what it says in *Rolling Stone*. Once expenses are deducted—hotels, meal money, transportation costs, roady salaries, kickbacks to promoters, legal expenses, etc.—there's little left. In that respect they're in the same position as the Rolling Stones, but instead of having Bud Lite or Aramis paying them for product placement, the Kleptos are shilling for The Company and are already well on the way to becoming indentured servants. Every room service steak or extra bucket of ice the band orders on the road just puts them deeper into the hole. Twenty years ago, it was possible to make money on the road—the corporate presence wasn't as pronounced—but now it has become a necessity. Times change. Meanwhile, oblivious to what's about to happen, the band is pumped, enjoying the rush of that first tour. All is going well: They play to packed houses with enthusiastic audiences. The Company is enthusiastic, and the album is briskly selling in the designated markets where the promo men have worked their green magic. Don't worry, be happy, the regional product managers tell them, and 3 furious months later the tour ends.

When the guys return home, psychically bruised but otherwise intact, they learn that not only are they into The Company for a small fortune for the tour but also that the sales of their first CD have already peaked. Additionally, having spent their advance, there's no reserve to cover the recording costs of their second album, whose deadline is fast approaching. Since they had such good response first time out, they decide to go back on the road to produce an album that not only "duplicates the live excitement" of their first tour but also will be padded out with the songs left off their first release. Though the idea sounded good in their living room, the band doesn't realize just how strenuous the road is, even without the additional pressure of writing and recording new material. This plan hinges on the good graces and financial support of The Company and theoretically could work, but meanwhile, because of the lower-than-expected sales figures, Blitzbomp is having second thoughts and decides to reduce its support—a purely hardball business decision.

In fact and more to the point, The Company's A-team of ace publicists and promo men are otherwise engaged in breaking Fruitboy, a Seattle grunge band with potential, who was signed while the Kleptos were on the road; and so its fate is now in the hands of second stringers, trainees, and interns—swell. Since there's less money to spread around, radio airplay slackens. Without the headliner who brought the fannies into the seats last time around, concert grosses decline or gigs are canceled entirely, because whatever audience does show up is smaller now that the band is drawing on its true fans. While the band is on the road, Blitzbomp becomes gradually less available for instant consults; the road manager's phone calls are not returned or returned late. Within the band itself tensions mount; the back-stage ambience, formerly so exhilarating, now resembles the movie *This Is Spinal Tap*, a tour bus video favorite the first time around, but not nearly as amusing when it's happening in real life—as the Kleptos are finding out.

The smell of failure is palpable, and everyone knows it: Do not resuscitate this group, please. The second album, rushed out in haste and shoddily produced, is deemed by in-house sources such a colossal stiff that no one wants to be associated with it. Adding insult to injury, the critics, who are hot-wired into the Blitzbomp creative matrix and are smelling blood in the water, jump all over *Live and Flaming*, the new release, and the band for "not living up to its potential," a potential that they weren't given enough time to develop. Sink or swim, that's how it works. It's triage time around The Company headquarters on Holly-wood Boulevard, time to pull the plug. The band members aren't even talking to each other. After initial attempts are made to patch things up between the band and The Company, the matter is turned over to the lawyers (hot dog! more bloated fees).

Though the contract can be voided and the group released from its recording obligations, the outstanding debt remains, The Company lawyer sharks inform our lads, who naturally freak out because where are they going to raise that kind of money now since they can't stand the sight of each other? Not to worry, here's the deal. The Company lawyers inform the Kleptos' attor-ney over sushi: Until the debt has been worked off, we'll retain the rights to use the master recordings and administer—for a

87

fee—the royalties, and when the debt has been discharged, we'll return the tapes to whoever owns them. The band's attorney, a real estate specialist working pro bono as a favor to his brother-in-law, the bass player, brings the deal back to the boys, who are so demoralized, angry, and pissed off at each other that they agree with alacrity and sign off on the deal. Collectively, they figure it's about the best they can get, considering that no matter what kind of advance and press they had, they're still relative nobodies. Onward and upward.

Though the band temporarily may be history in the music press, the group continues to be of economic interest to The Company. With temporary legal possession and control of the master recordings, Blitzbomp can do whatever it sees fit to recoup its initial investment, swollen by the band's additional cost over-runs and advances against royalties for the second disastrous and ill-conceived album. Numerous options present themselves: (1) The Company may wholesale the remaining CD stock—for a fraction of the original list price—to independent rack jobbers who service music store and supermarket cut-out bins, clean out their warehouse, and write off the whole thing as a bad investment and move on; (2) or on an in-company budget subsidiary. The Company can repackage the Kleptos on a sampler CD along with other failed bands and sell same at deep discount—with those bands having no creative control over the packaging, cut selection, and even mixing; (3) Blitzbomp can license the masters to other smaller companies who will put out their own package to sell on late night TV—the same creative rules as (3) apply; or (4), sometimes the most prudent and long-term expedient, they can do nothing immediately and wait to see what develops. By letting time and those waves take over and by keeping the album in its backlist catalogue, they can have the money dribble into a special account that, though it can't be directly used by the company (that would be illegal), can produce a tidy collective escrow interest income until it does. Time and those waves work in favor of record companies—why else would they have warehouses full of master tapes of busted bands with unreleased albums? It's possible that after a few years the Kleptos might finally get into the black, but who's going to know unless it's some impossibly ungodly amount of money and their resurrection is just too egregious to ignore? Anyway, the cost of hiring a professional accountant familiar with record business accounting practices to handle the audit are astronomical. By the time he takes his fee, there might not be anything substantial left, live and learn. Heads I win, tails you lose.

But let's say the Kleptos are made of sterner stuff and they sign with another label. Cutting a more equitable and realistic deal with better management and better "chemistry" with the front office, our boys indeed do become bonafide chart busters; it does happen. Or perhaps Brash, our mythical Harvard-MBA moonlighting as the lead guitarist, buys the name of the group from the other members (positive product identification), and with an entirely different personnel plus a horn section makes it big under the same name; same time, next year. If either of these two scenarios eventually present themselves, and the band realizes the potential the original Blitzbomp product manager envisioned but The Company had lacked the patience or vision to see. The Company can theoretically rerelease the original Kleptos material in any form they choose. They can hope there will be some spillover, that at the very least, the rabid fans, or the completists who now fetish the group in all its previous incarnations as a sociological artifact (like the Deadheads who prize how Pigpen played keyboards) will buy all the old stuff just to hear what the band sounded like before it went platinum.

Until that happens, the master recordings of the Kleptos join row upon row, rack upon rack of other master recordings in The Company vaults from bygone days. Like its sister ConGlomCos back in the late forties and fifties. Blitzbomp recorded and distributed many black blues and r & b singers who also never earned out, but who though they are no longer with the label, continue to earn substantial sums in their repackaged configurations as samplers, as "best of" series. Having long ago forsaken the ways of the white folks, those old r & b cats are still out there on the Chitlin' Circuit making ends meet by distributing their own CDs out of the luggage bays of their battered tour buses; meanwhile their old companies thrive. That's some kind of sociocultural statement in itself, and it cuts to the heart and soul of the music business and the culture that supports it.

Boxers in Wal-Mart?

Music journalists love to write about the struggle of rock stars to attain fame, but they rarely bother to examine the creative consequences of getting famous. About as far as they go in that direction is when they're composing the obits of the ones who O.D. on China White heroin or in the course of making editorial asides in a news story about another poor schnook who declared Chapter Eleven six months after his career has peaked and is back on the bar band circuit where he started out so long long ago. Creative politics—if discussed at all—are particularized to specific groups or artists, and rarely are generalizations offered about the nature of the industry as a whole; again it's too close to home. Naturally enough, it's the myths of rock and roll that sell music magazines, not the base truths.

There's a class issue at play: There are *rock stars* and then there are *musicians*, and rarely do their two worlds politically coincide except on stage or in the studio. Within this pleasant prison fiction, rock stars are expected to champion political causes because they're celebrities. Meanwhile, rhythm guitarists, bass players, percussionists, or horn players, the worker bee foot soldiers on whose backs the celebrities stand, the ones who support the rock gods and superstars, are dismissed as virtual nonpersons. We want rock stars and that's what we get, unfortunately. It's better like that, since most musicians are a low-key lot and prefer to keep out of the limelight. With some exceptions, musicians tend to hold liberal or libertarian views if only because they work under all sorts of conditions with all manner of people; to get by to earn a living, they've got to get along. That's the reason professional musicians tend to have "out" senses of humor, why, for instance, David Letterman or Jay Leno, on their late night talk shows, direct all their bad jokes to the band, because the guys have seen and heard it all before. And it really is true: The band sees everything.

Unlike rock stars, musicians have simple needs: (1) they like to play their music and (2) they like to get paid, though they'll play even if they don't get paid. Unscrupulous club owners and managers have exploited this since time immemorial; they know that dedicated musicians will endure the most frightful working conditions just so long as they can express themselves musically and be free for those 15, 45, or 75 minutes on stage. On the other hand, though a rock band may think it's getting paid to musically "tell it like it is" by its fans, once it signs on the dotted line, the record company calls the tune, like it or not. Only in retrospect, after the band becomes part of the music business for a while, does it start to realize just how lucky it was when it was on the outside looking in. Perhaps they learn that those scuffling r & b cats who are no longer actively involved in the system were on to something after all. Even though in their prime these journeymen musicians never made the big time and have been systematically denied their songwriting royalties by the record companies that they served so long and so well, they came away from the whole experience with their creative integrity intact; no mean accomplishment and worth far more than a wall of gold records, a consecutive string of Top 10 hits, or the de rigueur million-dollar beach house that pop music fame buys.

It takes a while for young bands and artists to understand what creative freedom is really all about and that "you've got to suffer to sing the blues." Meanwhile, when music consumers go into a mall music store and are confronted with the racks upon racks of shrink-wrapped CDs, they tend to equate the quantity of merchandise with its quality. Because of this seeming abundance, they think that the musicians and artists who provide them with the soundtracks to their lives create in a perfect world without constraint or censorship of any kind—and of course nothing could be farther from the truth.

In the course of the twentieth century, ragtime, jazz, swing, rock and roll in its infancy, and more recently gangsta rap and hip-hop music have been singled out for artistic censorship by individuals or groups of individuals on behalf of impressionable children or in the name of "family values" and have been subjects for heated political debate on the national, regional, and local levels. Fortunately, free expression of music has been protected under the Constitution's First Amendment, though now it is coming under attack not only from the music industry itself, which is responsible for its production in the first place, but also from the major merchandizing conglomerates who distribute the product. It is an action all the more insidious, because not only is it done in plain sight, but it is also covertly agreed to by the artists themselves. Although the debate about the suitability of hip-hop and gangsta music and lyrics has occupied the discourse of the nineties, the debate was originally framed in its present form in the mideighties when the same issue was raised about heavy metal music.

In 1985, an allegedly bipartisan group of Washington politico wives, who included Susan Baker, the wife of James Baker, Ronald Reagan's State Department head, and Tipper Gore (the vice president's wife and, weirdly enough, a well known bubblegum rock fan), formed the Parents Music Resource Center (PMRC). A lobbying group without dues or members, following the agenda of the Religious Right, the PMRC sent a letter to the president of the Recording Industry of America (RIAA) that accused the industry of exposing youth to "sex, drugs, and the glorification of drugs and alcohol" and proposed that rock and roll records should be rated, though exactly who would do the rating was never specified.

Simultaneously, the PMRC applied pressure on Edward O. Fritts, president of the National Association of Broadcasters, who in turn sent a letter to his members implying that if they broadcast songs with explicit lyrics, they would risk losing their licenses. One of the few musicians to take a public stand on this issue of creative freedom was Frank Zappa. An outspoken rock and classical musician and satirist. Zappa was not only a public critic of the Reagan political agenda but an outspoken critic of the business practices of the music industry as well. For Zappa, the PMRC's public position merely confirmed his own belief "that censorship was turning America into a police state which anyone who'd been listening to his lyrics since the midsixties already knew."[3]

The issue wasn't merely about the content of heavy metal songs, Zappa thought, as much as the radical ideas the music, lyrics, and deportment of the bands conveyed—by which the Reagan White House and the Religious Right (on which its power rested) were threatened. In effect, what this group of well-connected Washington political wives wanted to do was attempt to legislate behavioral norms with a set of implied religious values, which not only violated the Constitution's principle of the separation of church and state but also infringed on free speech. To this end, Zappa mounted a personal campaign where he assailed the PMRC and the agenda of the Religious Right at every and any opportunity, not only from the concert stage, but also on radio and TV talk shows, even including ABC's *Nightline*.[4]

At open hearings held by the Senate Commerce, Technology and Transportation Committee on September 19, 1985, Zappa—along with the unlikely duo of Dee Snyder of the heavy metal band Twisted Sister and John Denver, the country/pop singer of "Rocky Mountain High" fame—testified. Neatly attired in sharp suit and tie, hair neatly combed, Zappa sternly lectured these daughters of moral decency with humor, irony, and intelligence; in a masterful and impassioned performance, he explained how freedom of speech, freedom of religious thought, and the right to due process for composers, performers, and retailers would be imperiled if the PMRC and the major labels went ahead with this sort of legislation.

93

Though no legislation was ever proposed, on November 1, 1985, the RIAA agreed to voluntarily post warning stickers on politically offending albums with the tag "Explicit Lyrics: Parental Advisory." At the time, compliance was never an industrywide norm, and if it was used at all it was merely as a hip merchandising tool. Of course, with a label like "Parental Discretion Advised," every kid looking for something to piss off his or her parents would naturally be drawn to it, just as buying a book stickered with "Banned in Boston," was another red flag for the bored.

Lucky Zappa's no longer around to see how things have turned out for the First Amendment, especially if one chooses to buy CDs from America's Store, Wal-Mart—as many Americans do. Especially for teenagers with limited funds, there's literally no other place, because Wal-Mart has put out of business many smaller music retailers. For these kids especially, Wal-Mart, "America's Store" where the consumer is king, is the last if not the only best hope. Whatta kingdom, for here the PRMC's agenda thrives. Though it may appear like any other mall store music retailer, general market rules don't apply; Wal-Mart has its own private moral universe.

Contrary to popular belief, not all CDs are available there. The ones that are, the ones that are considered to be sitting on the cusp of acceptability, are "modified" to meet the outlet's definition of "family values." Cover art is crafted not to offend, lyric sheets are edited. On the CDs themselves objectionable lyrics (if not entire tracks) are sometimes electronically masked, reversed, or expunged entirely—especially if the material is really objectionable to Wal-Mart executives. Meanwhile, record companies, because they're in such bad shape these days themselves, instead of refusing to distribute their product to Wal-Mart, go along, because the half loaf is loaf enough—especially with all their overhead. The chilling effect percolates down to apprentice rock and roll bands, who, ever anxious to please but without economic clout, will modify their songs just to get into the Wal-Mart bins. If not the band members themselves, then the producer or the manager leans on them. If a group is intent on moving their product and if the record company wants to stay in the good graces of America's Store, they had best comply with their directives[5] where, in essence, greed's the key.

Corporate censorship also plays a role in the publishing business. It is not uncommon for representatives from the big chains like Waldenbooks or Barnes and Noble to sit on editorial boards to advise publishing houses of a manuscript's "saleability factor." If the big chains don't or won't order the book, no matter how good the title or the subject, the book will be rejected, and to hell with the reader and freedom of speech. Censorship isn't dead; it just smells funny.

In the end it all comes down to that old proverb musicians have: "The more they pay you, the less they want you to play." That goes to the heart of the issue, that interface between music and politics, exactly what the MTV Town Meeting wasn't going to allow either its audience or the candidates to examine in depth. Who would have asked the question? Better, who would have had the ears to listen and hear the answer? The way things are heading these days, pretty soon we won't be allowed our own ears at all.

Boxers? Or briefs?

Chapter 5

Play School

You Can Dress for It, But You Can't Escape It

Recently, while channel-surfing late one night. I caught a pretzel commercial whose setting was a high school reunion where the "Nerd/Dweeb/Grind" gets his revenge. Immediately after being harassed and taunted by his Jock nemesis, our Everyman whips out his secret weapon, a box of pretzels, and after eating a handful like Popeye with his spinach, soundly thrashes the big lug in rope climbing and wrestling, thereby impressing the Cheerleader who never gave him a thought years before. "I think it's the pretzels," confides another Nerd as they both watch the happy couple dancing the night away Disco Fever style.

It was a good piece of work, really, an effective commercial vision, one of many in that vein that to an increasing extent makes up the American cultural landscape these days. Without really meaning to I found myself asking why such a scene was used and why it had so much evocative power (it must have been a good one or I wouldn't have thought about it at all). But more to the point, why was this particular vision in one way or another embedded in the American psyche and continually drawn on as background for innumerable movies, sitcoms, and, especially these days, numerous commercials, for an infinite variety of products? I guess there's a lot to mine there if you are looking, or you still care.

It never changes, does it? Set at least a decade or two after the fact, graduates come back to the smelly old gym to reminisce, comparing notes and dancing to a cheesy band. Wassup? Perhaps the Bad Girl had become a madame (or the Cheerleader, which would go against character but be a twist) or married a power politician; the "Most Likely to Succeed" was very rich or doing 10 to 20 for fraud after having done so illegally at the get-go (served him right, we think); or the Jock, having busted his knee and had a few knocks from life, was mortal like everyone else, etc. Think about it—though living in the present, all these "graduates" still seem prisoners of an adolescent past that has overshadowed any life they've had since.

Is there life after high school? If we live in America and watch television commercials, not really.

High school reunions can be traumatic, no doubt about it: We've got to look our best. Some of us go on crash diets, get a new do (a nose job? liposuction?), new clothes, show up in a stretch limo, possibly all of the above if we're *really* paranoid and self-conscious; some Come Out but most regress entirely. If single perhaps we enlist, entice, or even rent the cooperation, services, and companionship of a dream gal/boy toy for the evening (and who hasn't a clue who the players are); if not, we'll pressure, prep, and spiff up our spouses and significant others to lend some moral support. Some of us may even lie about who we are or what we've become (far easier if we've moved out of town, or the state). Old jealousies flair, old boyfriends/girlfriends reconnect, however briefly; the atmosphere is tense and so are we, and the air around the punch bowl is loud and thick with intrigue or it is pretension as we go through entirely too many changes in the course of the evening.

98

And even if we boycott the whole business, deep down inside we feel uneasy: obviously the current neologism, "That was then but this is now" doesn't work really, postmodernism to the contrary.

Why does high school still exert such a grip on our emotions and sense of self even when we're safely out of it? The truth is as Parson Weems said of George Washington and the Cherry Tree, "too true to be doubted": We never leave. Oh we may survive it, barely, perhaps—but it dogs our steps forever. And it's no longer just an American peculiarity; for not only is our country awash with adolescent symbolism, but so are the nations of the world who follow America's lead. Indeed, it is this image of adolescence that informs our behavior as well the world's view of us.

Only Americans seem to have this intense investment in their adolescent selves; the rest of the peoples of the world, despite the pervasive influence of American pop culture, still see themselves as developing individuals within a wider perspective, a larger context, culturally and historically. Somehow other cultures get over their adolescence and their minds seem more historically focused and oriented, which in the words of Johan Huizinga, the Dutch historian, "embody in [their] idea of what is 'modern' and 'contemporary' a far larger section of the past than a mind living in the myopia of the moment."[1]

To the contrary: We seem to have no sense at all of our collective historical past, and if we do, we view it with suspicion if we haven't already rewritten it entirely or had a psychiatrist or therapist do so for us. Locked in the myopia of the moment, our idea of continuity can barely be maintained for a week, much less a decade; just look at how the American media reports international "hot spots" when they are "out of the news" for more than a few weeks. When things blow up again, it always comes as a big surprise to us. Generally speaking, most people of the world never have to contend with the trauma of high school reunions, nor do their rituals really lend themselves to such elaborate commercial exploitation, nor would they conceive of movies like *Peggy Sue Got Married* or *American Graffiti*—and maybe never would. Would a Frenchman or a German even think of writing a book called *What Ever Happened to the Class of '65?* Who would read it? And why?

99

Whence comes this attachment to who we were from the ages of 14 to 18 rather than to what we are, or even who we could become—an attachment so deep that it has become a total world view pervading the very nature of this country's commercial, social, and political interrelationships? Why does this state of expanded adolescence continue to exert such a profound effect on the cultural lives of Americans at the end of the twentieth century, when merely 100 years ago, adolescence and peer group pressure hadn't really been invented and/or commercially exploited and Disney hadn't taken over the world?

Of course high school itself has evolved considerably. What it means today is not what it meant 100 years ago or even 50 years ago, so it's best to define terms, since there are three different kinds of "high school" and adolescent behaviors operative here.

First there is the idea of adolescence and the function of high
school as explored by G. Stanley Hall, a pioneer psychologist
and contemporary of William James and one of the founders of
Clark University; second is how Hall's findings and insights were
imperfectly interpreted and emasculated by schools of education and professional administrators; and finally, there is the high
school of today that administrators have allowed to happen, a
society of consumerism and celebrity that feeds a national culture, a candy-land of jocks, cheerleaders, fashion jeans, and
celebrity journalism all mediated and driven by peer group pressure. Instead of being a rite of passage in an ongoing educational
and emotional process, high school has become a terminal state
of being for many and has made America into a play school.

In 1907 G. Stanley Hall published *Adolescence*, a seminal two-
volume work that straddled the fields of adolescent psychology
and education. The work was encyclopedic in its overview, scru-
pulous in its scholarship; Hall showed himself to be a fearsomely
well-read and erudite advocate of "humanism" in the care and
feeding of the sometimes contrary, testosterone-driven, and,
these days, headbanging/party-hardy teenager of common contemporary literary currency. Hall's view of *pubescesis america-
nus* was more benign and transcendent, less consumer-driven.
To his mind, the adolescent

> awakens to a new world and understands neither it nor himself [where]
> character and personality are taking form, but everything is plastic. Self-
> feeling and ambition are increased, and every trait and faculty is liable to
> exaggeration and excess. It is all a marvelous new birth, and those who
> believe that nothing is so worthy of love, reverence and service as the
> body and soul of youth, and who hold that the best test of every human
> institution is how much it contributes to bring youth to the very fullest
> possible development, may well review themselves and the civilization
> in which we live to see how far it satisfies this supreme test.[2]

For such an individual, a nurturing, empowering educational
system was vitally necessary because "youth needs repose, leisure, art, legends, romance, idealization, in a word humanism, if
it is to enter the kingdom of man well equipped for man's highest
work in the world."[3] Consequently, Hall argued, a new breed of
teacher must emerge who was able to initiate students into the
mysteries of the universe rather than a drillmaster transmitting

information by rote memorization.[4] It was in adolescent youth
that Hall saw the hope of mankind and its traditions:

> Youth when properly understood, will seem to be not only the revealer
> of the past but of the future, for it is simply prophetic of that best part
> of history which is not yet written because it has not yet transpired, of
> the best literature the only criterion of which is that it helps to an ever
> more complete maturity, and of better social organizations, which, like
> everything else, are those that best serve youth.[5]

(On the whole, this seems to be a more elevating alchemic
description of a teacher's function than that of pencil counter,
disciplinarian, or study hall monitor, no? And it's a far more
desirable occupation than being a shuttlecock, bereft of the
authority to teach what and how they know best, in the badmin-
ton match between their union, school administrators, parent/
teacher groups, and politically ambitious school boards, not to
mention the test scorers and their brokers. Maybe it's all that can
be expected in a society that grossly underpays and undervalues
its teachers and their contributions and where students, by and
large, mimicking society's low opinion of their jobs in the "real
world," don't give them any respect either. Compared to the lures
of celebrity, fame, and money, the teacher's life is, well, pale. You
poor sap, they think, can't you do better, can't you make something of yourself and make some *real* money?

To Hall's mind, the high school philosophy that would serve
youth best was one that provided "evolution, not revolution,
grafting and not uprooting, a revival of the best in them in this
best age and not a fanatical running amuck."[6] Though these
thoughts and aspirations still have considerable resonance today
and lip service is paid to his theories (excerpts from his book are
required reading for educational psychology students). *Adolescence* is rarely ever read and studied in its entirety because the
prospect of slogging through 1700 closely reasoned Whitmanesque pages of prose is a daunting prospect. So much the worse
for the state of American education.

It's true that Hall's conception of adolescent education and
adolescents seems a bit idealistic to our modern sensibilities, but
it was positive. However, at the end of the nineteenth and beginning of the twentieth centuries, for intellectually challenged run-

of-the-mill administrators and bureaucrats in the nascent field of education fighting for respect with the disciplines of sociology and psychology, his ideas posed considerable policing and control problems. And as administrators have done from time immemorial when challenged by complex thoughts, they sought to reduce his ideas to technology and "science" that focused largely on mechanics rather than on his underlying philosophy. Hall was horrified at how rote learning and mindless memorization had already disfigured the educational process and how administrators had encouraged and produced teachers whose methodology was to

> dissect large living wholes, which pubescents crave, into elements, which they abhor ... [in a system that involves] logic chopping, formal steps, analysis of processes that should never be analyzed, or overexplanation ... [which blunts] the intuitions, the best thing of youth.... More, it tends to pedantry that shields ignorance from exposure, teaches the art of seeming wise with empty minds, brings complacency that tends to arrest in the teacher, and whips up a modicum of knowledge to deceptive proportions.[7]

If they couldn't blind with brilliance, they'd baffle students with bullshit, no?

It was also Hall's belief that high school should not be *scholiocentric* but *pediocentric*: one taught from the point of view of inspiring students. Teachers were there to facilitate learning and not as tools or guinea pigs for whatever trendy educational philosophy was being pushed by their administrators.

Formerly voluntary, compulsory secondary education by the twenties was mandated for all regardless of abilities or proclivities. Though on the surface a step forward, the overall result for thinkers like historian Richard Hofstader, among others, from the vantage point of the early sixties was that

> secondary school pupils were not merely unselective but also unwilling; they were in high school not because they wanted further study but because the law forced them to go. The burden of obligation shifted accordingly; whereas once the free high school offered a priceless opportunity to those who chose to take it, the school now held a large captive audience that its administrators felt obliged to satisfy ... [resulting in] schools filled with a growing proportion of doubtful, reluctant, or actually hostile pupils.[8]

In truth, Hall's ideas were either imperfectly and shabbily grafted onto the developing system or ignored altogether; high school principals and school boards, instead of being educators, became custodians in the entertainment business, in effect shifting their attention away from those who wanted to learn to those who had little desire. As high school attendance rose in the forties and fifties the idea of a "life adjustment" curriculum to cope with this influx of the willing and the unwilling came into educational vogue, which, according to Hofstader "gear[ed] the educational system more closely to the needs of children who were held to be in some sense uneducable."[9] This gave the definitive boot to Hall's notion that there was a basic body of knowledge upon which *all* students could focus *whatever* their individual gifts. Instead of a positive view of youth, secondary education focused on the negative systemwide assumption that "in a system of mass secondary education, an academically serious training is an impossibility for more than a modest fraction of the student population."[10]

The ensuing result has been disastrous as well as predictable, since the "life adjustment" curriculum was aimed

> not primarily to fit them [high school students] to become a disciplined part of the world of production and competition, ambition and vocation, creativity and analytical thought, but rather to help them learn the ways of the world of consumption and hobbies, of enjoyment and social compliance—*in short to adapt gracefully to the passive and hedonistic style summed up in the significant term adjustment* [emphasis mine].[11]

Considering that the advertising industry had already launched a major effort to define and exploit the burgeoning teenage market of the fifties, this was hardly news. In truth they'd been working for the previous 60 years on ways to commercially exploit the research findings of Progressive educators like G. Stanley Hall and John Dewey, who'd been doing similar studies on adolescent behavior but for less mercenary ends.*

---

* For an extraordinarily detailed, informed, and acutely observed history of merchandizing in America, see William Leach's *Land of Desire: Merchants, Power and the Rise of a New American Culture* (New York: Pantheon Books, 1993).

It's also not surprising that this trend continues today and that a recent study by the National Commission on Time and Learning discovered that high school teachers spend only 41% of their time on academic subjects[12] while the remainder is occupied by nonacademic subjects like drivers' ed, sex education, home economics, self-esteem courses, special interest clubs, study hall, or writing reports on who was accountable to whom for what.

Now we are up to speed, since the modern high school was essentially a creature of the fifties. It was here that the newly discovered economic clout of the teenage market was added to what had been since the twenties an age-segregated universe. When the two converged with the "life adjustment" curriculum, an adolescent consumer kingdom was created. And though the school administrators may have convinced themselves they were following Hall's pediocentric principles, they were in effect opening a marketplace that offered students the freedom to choose what *they wanted* to learn (simultaneously keeping them content and occupied until age 18), not what they should learn, which would have opened them to the educational possibilities of a lifetime. Instead of a place where one learned how to learn, high school became a vocational institution that parents and communities demanded and expected because it was easily quantifiable and utilitarian. Industrial arts students learned industrial arts, college-track learned liberal arts, and so on, though both (all) could have benefited from a knowledge of the other's field. Instead of providing tools to seek answers or lifetime long-term learning strategies, high school promoted (and to a large extent continues to provide now) short-term answers for long-term questions, i.e., how to pass *the test* (college boards, etc.) that gives the appearance of having mastered knowledge. This is a weakness that contemporary colleges are paying dearly for since it takes almost 2 years for high school "graduates" to get up to speed for higher education. As a result, teachers having by default given up the function of being initiators of learning became administrators of entertainment programs if they were lucky, or enforcers of penal colony study halls if they were not.

104

"Twenty years of schooling and they put you on the day shift" may have been an ironical comment voiced by Bob Dylan to the generation of the sixties, but for the temp's life in downsized

America today it has even more validity. College or grad school notwithstanding, the one thing that ties multicultural America together is that everyone goes to high school, and for better or worse, that's where we all learn about the franchise that America now represents to the world. Once safely out of its clutches, unless we are essentially flunking high school with pay in our jobs, the experience tends to be mercifully and quickly forgotten, glossed over and buried, or at the very least protected by a hard mental calculus.

We chuckle about it uneasily when confronted with the inevitable pictorials in periodicals from *People* to *Esquire* to *Rolling Stone*, those grainy yearbook miniatures of the super-jocks, glamourpusses, egregious axe-murderers, former cheerleaders turned stock swindlers, or even billionaire techno-nerds in all their geekiness or glory. Yes, we think to ourselves, even "they" had to endure high school just like the rest of us mortals, the spear carriers, the walk-on players who endured like Faulkner's Dilsey in the background. Seeing them the way they were makes us all feel a little better, but why? When it's all said and done, what did we learn, those of us who haven't totally repressed the whole business?

For students then and now the song remains the same: You can dress for it, but you can't escape it. It's so much a part of our experience that the wry observation "Hollywood is high school with money"[13] is understood by all with a wince of recognition. What is a no-brainer to any kid paradoxically escapes the most articulate and committed educator, to wit: It's not so much what goes on in the classroom that makes high school *high school*, but what goes on before or after school, in the halls changing classes, in the lunch room, in the gym, or out on the ball fields. And as long as there isn't a riot in the hallways and the natives aren't restless, administrators don't want to deal with what comes in to the school as much as the stats for certifying what comes out of it to someone else. Principals and school board members hardly ever change; students do, continually. It's protean world out there, an ever-shifting universe for the average freshmen to see the parade of one's peers, a place previously described by historian Gilbert Ostrander (see Chapter 2), where, "No sooner have the rules of the game been officially explained by the younger generation, than another game is discovered to be in progress on the same field under different rules by a somewhat different younger generation."[14]

And you never catch up to any of it (nor are you supposed to).

It's painful, it bites the big one, if you could die and somehow graduate, that would be fine, too; still, everyone agonizes(ed) over learning the right intricate dance steps and moves. Essentially, it is a period, in the words of E. Z. Friedenberg, "during which a young person learns who he is, and what he really feels. It is the time during which to differentiate himself from his culture, though on the culture's terms."[15] It is also the first universe youth experience outside of the safe confines of home (aside from the toy merchants on TV) and the comparative safety of one teacher and one homeroom. Age-segregated, insular, and self-referential, it is a total universe where one is provided with an identity of a peer group that "takes over where the individual student–school dynamics leave off."[16] In this unforgiving and merciless universe, style is more important than content, and one learns the weight of outward appearance and social rituals that, though extrapolated from mainstream culture, are filtered through the prism of an adolescent angst that completely skews one's perspective; truly it is "the received world experienced as the only world."[17]

And even this would be fine if it were a developmental stage rather than a feedback loop, but it's not, and perhaps here's why:

It is not only the present generation of high school students "moving off the field and trying to stay on the field by turning into something else" who are involved, but also nearly 85% of all Americans who've gone through high school since the fifties, including the original "teenage market" that Madison Avenue exploited, for whom high school is never far away, and our spirit, like Marley's ghost, lingers in the halls nonetheless. As fifties' teenage concerns were serviced by a variety of specialized goods and "our class" moved out of high school into college and eventually into "the real world," we were statistically identified, coded, and tracked, subsequently to be offered more "adult" versions of the same goods that animated our desires and defined

our "coolness" (or lack thereof) back then. It is the same mechanism that has evolved into a powerful and efficient merchandizing machine, the model for how future generations were to be
commercially exploited. Now high school generations, instead of
being considered 4 years long, are only 2 years long, thanks to
sophisticated marketing techniques that have promoted homog-
enization of tastes through overdiversification. What was once a
paradox is now a TV given, for not only are school-age children
and young adults encouraged to keep up, but so are the rest of
us encouraged to maintain the "edge" advertisers tell us we are
in danger of losing. Each successive high school "generation" has
only refined the franchise's nuances; in truth. Ostrander's observation describes one of the mechanisms by which American
markets have been exploited over time.

It's been going on for almost 50 years, from the ubiquitous
Saturday morning cartoon–toy tie-ins to the ever-glamorous
Lite beer MTV teen world of today, so much a part of our consciousness we don't even notice it anymore. It's a given: Whatever styles brew in the hormonal soup of high school eventually
will wind up in *Vogue*. And though definitions of what constitutes
"cool" may change from generation to generation (i.e., every 2
years), we are all led to believe that our need to maintain our
"edge" remains constant. Which is what the franchise has banked
on anyway, and they've succeeded in getting us all by the short
hairs whether we want to admit it or not.

High school has devolved into a climate-controlled social
and cultural environment in which one is encouraged to try
on various off-the-shelf lifestyles (be they costumes, attitudes,
poses, identities, etc.) provided by consumer society. Instead of
a place to develop individual maps, it has become primarily a
place where the collective assimilation of peer values is taught. It
would be a fairer fight, a more transcendent journey, if the maps
came from a variety of sources and age perspectives.

If everything is brokered and judged solely in terms of style
over substance, especially self-knowledge, that's big trouble.
When consumerism is promoted as a quick and painless fix to get
through adolescence, it's disastrous unless everyone is willing to
remain defined by the high school game. And who among us has

not thought how wonderful life would have been if somehow we all managed to avoid it entirely, high school and adolescence?* By this quick palliative the consumerist mind-set legitimizes and promotes early and at a highly impressionable age the rule of the "cult of the new." Students are the priests, while the fashion brokers advertise themselves as the only and preferred authority (or a more seductive one than boring adult retrospective wisdom) for many crucial "teenage" decisions. Thus seamlessly have the brokers neatly harnessed the "myth of progress" to the myth of the "Endless Summer" working up an appealing notion that sells everything from beer, hamburgers, and automobiles to coordinant lifestyles and foreign policies (but that's another matter entirely). While portraying itself to youth as a benign, largely apolitical, neutral public service providing an all-purpose series of maps for guiding youth on its journey to "adulthood," consumerism has actually supplied youth (and the rest of us too) with relative and contradictory maps the meaning of which it controls and that are dependent on the value of its goods alone.

As goods become ideas and students become habituated to the ever-changing panorama of prepackaged images, they become easier to manipulate, and a kind of mindless goods-enforced conformity is elevated and encouraged. In the end, this process runs contrary to the idea that adolescence is a period of "growth and individuation [which] can be fruitful only if a reasonable and increasing degree of integrity is maintained."[18] These days, there is no chance to discover that integrity, since the ideas themselves have none in real time. A spurious kind of integrity is substituted instead, far easier to comprehend and infinitely interchangeable as fancy (and/or fashion) dictates—which superficially appeals to a teenager's desperate need to know. The pace and cost of this kind of change has exacted a heavy price, not only for those in the system now but also for all the rest of us who survived it.

---

* It may be fashionable these days to dismiss the notion of "storm and stress" in adolescent development as irrelevant or old-fashioned, but I suspect those who do don't have any teenagers around the house or haven't really talked to them if they do.

The bottom line, of course, is what novelist, essayist, and humorist Kurt Vonnegut observed more than two decades ago: "that life is nothing *but* high school." And the reason has as much to do with the quality of high school life today as with how the quality of American life has changed or has been atrophied. In truth, we are never far removed from the high school experience because the brokers are constantly reinventing it with television shows like *Welcome Back, Kotter* or *Saved by the Bell* or *Beverly Hills 90210* or movies that range in budget and/or attitude from *Blackboard Jungle* through the films of John Hughes (*Sixteen Candles. The Breakfast Club*). *Fast Times at Ridgemont High*, and *Bill & Ted's Excellent Adventure*, to *Weird Science, Clueless*, and *Romy and Michelle's High School Reunion*. And while those presently in "the big house" chuckle knowingly at exquisitely observed details (the command of contemporary slang, the clothes, etc.), the rest of us wipe our sweaty brows and heave a sigh of relief, as though we're afraid we never really leave, and there's the rub. So—what song remains? Whose was it? Was it real—or Memorex after all?

For us as individuals, retrospective reediting of memory's tapes or nostalgia's healing properties coupled with some semblance of productive post-high school life will perhaps help to assuage those old feelings, and we may succeed at the very least in rewriting the whole business. Perhaps we can exorcise the memory of being in a total environment controlled for the most part by teachers who were marking time and making do or flashbacks of chuckle-headed principals and assistant principals and phys ed teachers who themselves were working out their own high school disappointments on you and yours eternally. (Ain't that the truth?) Then what? How does America deal with its collective tapes? Where do we begin? Whose rules were lodged? Which games did we all learn how to dodge?

Here's what it is: If instead of accepting, making do, or settling for their designated identities as consumers, market makers, and/ or omniscient spectators, high school students lived more within the world instead of out of it in age-segregated and peer-mediated environments, they'd be able to effect real societal change. By living in the present with a presence of the past they would cease to be mere bellwethers for transient consumer preferences whose future identity was to be inevitably homogenized as items on their own nostalgia futures market down the road, a statistical blip. Instead of being a symptom of the problem, the linchpin that eternally ties them and us all into the consumer society, they'd become part of the solution, and we'd all have a chance to break the loop.

As it stands, high school is a far cry from the environment G. Stanley Hall had envisioned for youth (and eventually for all Americans). For students in its grip today there is no time for "repose" amidst the crush of extracurricular activities, while "art, legends, romance, and idealization" are now supplied by ABC/Disney. As for the "kingdom of man"—for which the adolescent should have been "well-equipped for man's highest work in the world"—that has become the art of knowing how and when to buy discount Air Jordans at the mall. Jeez.

Chapter 6

The Twinkie Defense

The defendant is innocent of murder by reason of diminished capacity brought on by eating too many Twinkies.

> —Judicial reason for acquittal of Dan White for the murders of San Francisco Mayor George Moscone and City Supervisor Harvey Milk, 1978

Recently my wife and I attempted our semiannual clean-up/edit of our children's room—more specifically, their toy box caches, which periodically overflow, threatening the sanity and general safety of our home. We have four under the age of 12: two girls, plus twin boys. God love 'em all, so there's an extraordinary amount to rifle through in the short period of time when the children are asleep at a decent hour (*when* is also problematic as those with young children can attest).

If the purge is done ineptly, whatever you throw out, if not decisively hidden, will find its way back inside; if done craftily, by the time they find out they're missing that three-wheeled car that invariably winds up on the staircase to trip you up their attention will be taken up by a new Something That Everyone Everywhere Has—there's always another movie with another burger promotional tie-in that eventually turns up underfoot, stuffed into sofa cushions, or tossed under the seats of the baby-mobile for you to find months later. It appears that in franchise food America, there are endless vistas of disposable plastic gewgaws to look forward to. Glasses with logos are a whole other matter; we've got a cupboard of these "plastic refugees"; though shatter-proof and prone to cloud up after machine washing, they have some-what more utility, though the day is rapidly approaching when that space will be liberated and they too will exit, stage right, into the garbage. It's not that they aren't nice enough, and even use-ful; some of them are even artful. It's just that I don't like being hyped while I'm eating; enough's enough already.

Nevertheless, while our children slept, having crashed early for a change, we diligently and frantically worked our way through the accumulated rubble of promotional toys, the busted and damaged plastic action figures, testaments to our numerous trips to the franchise burgerterias of western Massachusetts, the accumulated receipts from our worship and attendance on the altar of fast food America. It proved an exhaustive and instructive trip down memory lane (of course we had all the videotapes), from *The Little Mermaid* to *Aladdin* to *Beauty and the Beast* to *Batman*, plus there were others that neither of us could identify from *temps perdu*. And so while mucking out my children's Augean stables, it seemed to me at least that the fast food franchise business was no longer even concerned with selling convenience food and had turned into just another outlet for promotional goods, that their true business was to continually add to my children's mythopoetic midden heaps or the plastic refugee closet. In fact there were so many of them it is hard to tell which campaign came with what figure (or maybe all too apparent), and at that point I started thinking about fast food in America, how America eats and goes home, and what.

In 1983 *Blue Highways*, a quirky American road trip travelogue written by William Least Heat Moon, was a national bestseller. A satisfying leisurely read, it was an eye-opening meander into and around the heartland of America, as much about the varieties of roadside food found off the interstate as the individuals he met and places he passed through. In his circumnavigation of the United States, Moon encountered and sampled a variety of culinary experiences in the Great Unknown—some good, some bad, and some inedible—but throughout his odyssey, he followed the Traveling Salesmen's Golden Rule: If in doubt, *cherchez le truckstop diner*. After all, diners don't stay in business long if they don't satisfy the customers. In the course of the book, Moon developed for himself (and his readers) a kind of folk diner taxonomy, a classification system further fine-tuning the maxim: While invariably every diner has a calendar beside or above the cash register, the better ones had two, but the really extraordinary legendary ones had three—for no good reason really, it just was.

Sitting with Moon in the booth at these three-, two-, or one-calendar diners, the reader also waxes nostalgic and wonders how this formerly thriving "counterculture," with its unique regional specialties, pies, cakes, and breakfast specials, has been slowly fading away, smothered and displaced by franchise and mall culture, how even our patterns of eating have altered. The pace of contemporary society doesn't encourage us to linger over coffee and donuts and pie anymore, and the uniquely regional variations of food we used to take for granted are being replaced by the glossy pictures of junk food hamburgers that have displaced the calendars in franchise palaces.

Before the Golden Arches and the interstates, America used to be a land of uniquely regional roadside stands, each with its own spirit, character, and tastes mirrored in the burgers, shakes, hot dogs, hoagies, submarines, sundaes, and the like served. The diners may have been truck stop oases, breakfast clubs, high school hangouts, or morning community coffee klatch stops, and they functioned as community meeting places after the prom, the football or basketball game, or the movies. The service may have been fast or indifferent; the food itself may not have been so great, but the community feeling was there, and that's what counted. (Of course there were those kinds of places where everything was really horrible, including the coffee, but they survived because they were the only place to hang.) The point that Moon was getting at was that what was a matter for individual taste and preference has over time become an interchangeable industrial component.

Once upon a time long ago and far away in America, there used to be a daily social ritual called "dinnertime," still available in grainy electronic simulation and 5-minute video bites in netherworlds of the sitcomland of Nickelodeon, the Nostalgia Channel, or FX. Before we had it "our way" out, dinnertime took place when families sat down to eat the evening meal. Depending on one's age and abilities, everyone pitched in so that at a stated time (5 to 6:30, perhaps) all could sit down to be debriefed and discuss the remains of the day, probably the main time when the family interacted as a unit.

That was superseded by the ritual of the "TV" dinnertime of the late fifties when people sat around the old tube with prepackaged individualized food portions and more or less did (or tried to do) the same thing, depending what was on and who had control of the buttons on the console (or the clicker). Though less labor-intensive for Mom, Sis, Junior, or Dad (if he was trying to

be helpful around the house by scoring a few points and maybe
get lucky with Mom after the kids went to bed), the lowly TV
dinner still required a moderate sense of timing, some personal
attention. With the rise of the two-working-parent family and
the phenomenon of latchkey kids, dinnertime has receded into
memory, replaced by take-out, which may or may not accomplish the same family thing.

However, if we believe the incessant barrage of advertising
(virtually impossible to avoid in any media), modern families
on the go prefer meeting in Burgerland rather than even eating take-out at home because no one can be bothered to cook
(microwaving, or "nuking," counts in this psychology) or clean
up; it's just too time-consuming and tedious, however short
order. "I want it now and I don't want to think about it" is the
prevailing fast food philosophy. Included along with the food,
of course, is the "wholesome family environment," so about the
only thing that these marvelous multicultural oases don't provide are beds (but we all know that's coming). However, even
under the best circumstances the ambiance is harried; what with
all those microwave bells and the pinging of the fry cookers, it
sounds almost like a hospital emergency room, not the place for
more than a refuelling stop. No one lingers as one did in a real
old-fashioned diner, and those who do are the desperate and the
homeless—eat and go, not come and eat, that's what we all do.
But then again, "dining" is not the fast food experience, nor was
it intended to be.

116

If function ultimately supplants form and technology inexorably marches onward, as it seems inexorably and regularly to
be doing, crafty food technologists some day soon will, by dint
of a strong and persuasive advertising campaign, convince us
that even the dubious pleasure of eating in these burgerlands
will be deemed unfashionable. In their incessant selfless struggle
to service their public's fetish for convenience, promoted in its
place will be the far handier, more instantaneous and time-effi-
cient cost-effective expedient of pill-popping; or for people with
more time on their hands, just hooking up the 'ole IV to a designated port; best believe the Internet junkies have that concept
hotwired and already on-line. Soon hamburger midnights with
or without the family will be history, along with all that touchy-

feely family stuff that's freighted with the pitch now too. Nor will anyone cook at home; it will be just a place to crash.

The result of course is that progress will be served while at the same time ethnic, regional, and eventually family cooking traditions and the accompanying lore will be forgotten. Instead of Mom's home cooking, it's Miguel's down the block. Instead of the home being the focal point of family life, it will be the franchise, which will result in more families imploding or self-destructing, and consequently people will get more crazy and alienated from each other than they apparently already are. They won't know why they are, but we who are watching this phenomenon take hold will, won't we? But let's not move too quickly here; rather, let us rest for the moment in this present time and space while that scenario is momentarily unthinkable. Yes, we think to ourselves as we bus our trays and return to our so-called lives, that definitely hit the spot, now what about some real food?

This is not to diss the individually prepared and attention-lavished backyard burger or the odd roadburger Out There. Rather, we are examining those that are mass-produced by the millions or consumed by the sackful. It's an operative consideration to note again that though the former may take a little longer to prepare and serve, you *can* really have it your way instead of theirs. And the trick the franchises have pulled off big time is they've made us (and the world) think that "their way" *is* ours (or yours) through the incessant barrage of advertising. Magnificently and professionally they have succeeded in creating a total universe they control, one that isn't merely confined to what's on the menu either. What does this junk food fascination really say about us? What does this experience promote and project?

We're not talking about other fast food like fast-fried chicken, pizza, barbecued ribs, sushi deluxe, or an overstuffed dripping pita—though all are consumed with relish and are fast enough to be fast food but not the "real thing." There's something ineluctably inalienable and utterly unique about the franchise fastburger—as any true aficionado knows—which is akin to mainlining heavy drugs. It's so sublime, so satisfying, that instantaneous unmistakable hit, the rush that takes place when the stomach's former void is decisively nullified, and temporarily one feels at peace with the world; there can be no equivalent, no substitutions permitted. It's universes away from the feeling that the English have when "peckish" for something to eat—a term way too specific, effete, and delicate, since it implies there's some deliberative process at work that is based on the operant consideration that one has the ability, nay, the leisure, to pick and choose what one wants to eat on the spur of the moment; there's a delicious feeling of discerning indecisiveness in the term, no?

Au contraire—in American burgerspace, instinct prevails; thinking has nothing to do with it, it's a gestural characteristic of Americans that one surrenders enthusiastically and obliviously, inhaling in seeming seconds a junkburger with all the trimmings and fries, washing it all down with the franchise-approved carbonated, flavored water. In the ultimate present tense of "eat," this is all well and good, but (and this is a big *but* for some) somewhere between three-quarters of an hour to an hour and a half later comes the inevitable aftermath, the afterburn, when gastrointestinal juices attempt to decode the latest substance without sustenance one has instinctively and with no malice aforethought (or any thought, for that matter) ingested. As with any archetypical junk food experience, said digestive process will in fits and starts continue throughout the remainder of the day as if to remind us of what our baser instincts have made us do. We always tell ourselves we'll go for the salad next time, but we forget. Anyway, didn't that burger look good?

More to the point, didn't the food pictured over the cash register (or in the TV advert) look mouth-watering, which is what we think we're eating? And it damned well better look good, if we'd spent the millions the burger boys have on food stylists who transform the product to make it look scrumptious after sitting under the hot klieg lights for hours and hours for those product shoots; it's a miracle there's anything even remotely organic left to photograph, but it looks good, and that's the point. (One remarks in passing that the Japanese, when viewing the artful plaster of Paris representations of sushi in the windows of their restaurants, are in no way laboring under the delusion that what they see will be what they'll eat quite in the same way; to them, art is art and eat is eat, though perhaps they're responding to the art in the Golden Arches, who knows?)

Here each time we go into the burgerteria we somehow forget that this is the case and then become disappointed and dispirited when the apparent 6-inch tall delish-looking wonder-burger is less than one and a half, wilted and squashed when unwrapped, but then again the Japanese are still an inscrutable people.

Now everybody can eat American junk food. It's inevitable, the quintessential American franchise experience one no longer needs to be American to enjoy; just ask the ravenous crowds in Moscow, Bejing, or Tokyo who are scarfing down Big Macs and Whoppers in record numbers these days. The former bête noir of fusty leftists. Coca-Cola imperialism has long since been eclipsed, decisively supplanted by burger madness, that international fondness for the American franchise fastburger, a new form of benign multicultural nationalism less socially threatening and, to the modern sensibility, of little consequence.

In World War II, our boys may have promoted Europe's love for Spam, and during the Vietnam era, Coke was it, the Real Thing that taught the world to sing. The "Cola Wars" continue as the Cold War has ended, and for good, one hopes, and now we Americans seem to have it "our way" just like the jingle promises; but whose way is that? In a few short decades since our collective national perspective has "evolved" yet again, today it's an unremarkable fact that in the late fifties when then-Vice President Richard Nixon, a designated point man and "agent of godless imperialism" for the Cold War, went to Russia for his famous "kitchen debate" with Premier Khrushchev, he was simultaneously acting as a middleman for Pepsi Cola to broker distribution rights throughout the mighty Soviet Union.

Cola politics has taken on a greater significance these days, for at a Russian–American summit meeting that coincided with the 50th anniversary of the end of World War II. President Bill Clinton was photographed drinking a Coke (horrors!) instead of a Pepsi brokered in the dark Nixonian past. American political and diplomatic observers were quick to divine this act's significance: A sign of the times of shifting power, they concluded, since Pepsi was a "Republican" drink while Coke was the beverage preferred by Democrats—a pointed observation of questionable veracity if there ever was one, for political historians to divine at some future date. It's probably more the case for Clinton of grabbing what was close, cold, and wet, since mineral water doesn't really hit the spot and liquid potato, unless one is habituated to its taste, doesn't satisfy after a hard day of specifying on the international stage—though it may dull the pain somewhat.

These days, vice presidents don't have the clout they used to have (or maybe never really did) in international affairs, since American fast food multinationals routinely bypass the federal government and deal directly with premiers and finance ministers abroad. Ironically (and this age is big on irony), setting up a bottling plant and a distribution network is a comparatively small investment as opposed to what McDonald's has done in the former Soviet Union. Not only did it provide the architectural blueprints for the Big Mac outlets themselves but also the economic agricultural R & D so that their Russian business partners could be supplied the requisite grade beef and vegetables when their native produce proved too variable, unsuitable, and substandard.

A further irony is that though this simple act of franchise-building commerce may appear on the surface to be less diplomatically pernicious than building another aggressive-looking high-tech listening post in the middle of nowhere, its effect on the host country's national and cultural integrity is far more insidious and pronounced. (Naturally one wonders just how many spooks are working their Russian McJobs under Agency sponsorship, but that's a thought too bizarre to contemplate … for now, isn't it?) But that's what the McDonald's Corporation did (the franchise, not the McSpook interns) with their money, and all so their Big Macs will taste as if they came hot off the griddle in Peoria. Though seen as a contemporary consumer miracle for the postmodern age and yet another indication of how interconnected we all have become, it is also highly paradoxical how much more effective their franchise has been in "winning the Cold War." What Lend/Lease, grain and commodity deals, or the budget-killing Star Wars boondoggle programs failed to achieve, McDonald's and Burger King have done without killing anyone in the process (a debatable sidebar, as any French cultural nationalist will explain). It's really true that though the world may yet have problems swallowing the concept of representative democracy, few countries will refuse the pleasure of an all-beef patty slathered with mustard, ketchup, lettuce, and special sauce for its people, consumers all. How come?

Junk food is not peculiar to America or Americans, God knows; we're not the only people who like finger food or eating on the run. Any international traveler knows the English have their fish and chips, the French their crepes, the Russians their blintzes, the Chinese their noodle stands, the Japanese their yakitori, the Indonesians their satay, the Middle Eastern countries their kebabs and falafel, as well as the South Americans their tacos and burritos, etc. And so we encounter all of them either in mildly spiced forms in mall land or full-strength in ethnic enclaves in any large or medium-sized city. Getting good eats isn't the issue here; exactly what we're really eating is.

So it's great happy business for the burger kings that everyone just everywhere loves their food, but ignored and overlooked in this worldwide feeding frenzy are far larger questions: Is the demand based solely on the product itself or on what the product stands for? What possesses hearty Muscovites to queue for hours just to spend close to a day's salary on something that costs us a fraction of that amount and that we as Americans take for granted (if we take it at all)? Could it be due to the iconographic packaging that subliminally appeals, or is it perhaps yet another example of the truism that you are what you eat, itself some mad blasphemous parody of That Supper where Christ advised his disciples, "Do this in remembrance of me" and the ubiquitous Big Mac is transformed into an alchemic wafer, an edible vehicle for the transubstantiation of life in these United States? If so, are ancillary citizenship rights or privileges of which we are not aware magically appended thereto? Does the appearance of Marlboro T-shirts, Coca-Cola rally caps, or Warner Brothers cartoon jackets also activate such marvelous visions of our "off-the-shelf" lifestyle? Is this junk-food-ization of world culture the mechanism by which democracy is to be promoted and extended? The ultimate Trojan Horse? I mean, why is there really something so overwhelmingly comforting and satisfying, so ineluctably necessary that the junk food experience (save for the small change) remains invariant, so that the burger one eats in Paris, Rome, Kuwait, or London tastes as though it came from right off the interstate in Anymall U.S.A.?

And while attempting to digest our mythburger we have plenty of time to consider just how representative it is of modern life in these United States while simultaneously noting to our astonishment just how prophetic Johan Huizinga's comments on America were in the twenties (see Chapter 1), how he himself may unknowingly have been the patron philosopher of franchises like McDonalds, Wendy's, or Burger King when he characterized the American experience as "This, Here, Soon"— the junkfood mantra. Not only do we expect our burgers (ourselves?) to be instantaneous, filling, and of a known quantity, but we expect the same from every other commodity, from washing machines to cars to Q-tips (and we're habituated to the inevitable merchandizing tie-ins as well, with brand-name iconography on the rally jackets, T-shirts, and baseball caps, too). To have those expectations with consumer goods is one thing, but we get into serious trouble when we do so with social and political ideas by marketing them with the same panache, brio, and industrial efficiency as Whoppers (the metaphorical burger, not the familiar name for prevarications—you know, big lies?).

Every current event seems the stuff of fast food road-burgers these days; we are reminded daily that we live in an in-your-face age where regularly (regular?) diverse sociopathologic miscreants of the criminal, financial, and political kind hide in plain sight. Voyeuristically we look on as they are captured, tried, convicted, and/or exonerated with dismal regularity in expensive show trials. Too shell-shocked or desensitized to care, we become cynical or go into denial as we look for someone to blame, while feeling irresistibly entertained as the titillating stories are regularly turned into movies of the week, some stories whose ashes are barely cold, like the federal botch of the Branch Davidian shoot-out in Waco, Texas, a few years ago. Or the now-mythic O.J. Bronco slow-pursuit convoy on the freeways of Los Angeles, watched by millions coast-to-coast on network and cable TV and invested with exhaustive expository insights delivered in *New Yorker* magazine and *Esquire* with photos by Annie Liebowitz or Richard Avedon, incredible but barely credible events all.

We can see this trend most clearly in the virulent and ultimately self-defeating public debates that surround the issues of feminism, racism, and affirmative action today that spillover from college campuses to talk radio and Internet chat board-rooms. Looking dispassionately at the rhetoric that informs the issues exclusively, one sees that these debates have less to do with the real substance of the issues than a public brawl over who will control the way issues are presented and packaged to the public, whose McSlogan will be used to represent it. In this peculiar sense—in feminism's continuing definitional struggles, for instance—it's not the case of the issues that women have with each other and with men now as much as it is with the com-peting visions women have of themselves. This has ultimately turned feminism's focus into a debate over which advertising agency will be responsible for the campaign and whose artfully crafted photos and identifying captions will be hung over the cash register at the check-out line, in the boudoir, the office, or the voting booth. Soon enough the coded catch phrases take on a life of their own and individuals take a back seat to ideology, which pleases no one really.

Instead of specific knowledge—the antidote that would at least allow if not encourage reflection and informed action—we are swamped with undifferentiated sound bites the collection of which is substituted for informed understanding. And we accept the afterburn that accompanies it, that subtle intellectual indiges-tion that comes from having it "our way," day after day, and we've grown habituated to waking up hungry, ravenous for more.

Fast food is to food as bumper stickers are to political dis-course, and one need not be a Ph.D. in political science or gov-ernment to easily reduce any political campaign, be it for the presidency, state legislator, or school board, to its basic bottom line. It's clear that office seekers could just as well be selling hamburgers as representative democracy, since the pitches are so similar. Many contemporary and modern nuanced political scientists maintain that it's the price one pays for living in our democracy because people are so busy with their own lives that major issues must be reduced to idea Mc-Nuggets to be easily comprehensible and digested. They will further assert, when wax-ing poetic (usually before a national television audience or talk radio call-in shows), that in truth, the "business" of democracy is to provide a kind of consumer satisfaction, that representatives (senators, etc.) are in essence consumer advocate/ombudsman for its citizens; so using the junk food sell is a reasonable and justifiable approach.

Examining how various political programs from affirmative action to budget reform, from environmental conservation to gun control or even to the continuing evolution of the meaning of political correctness are packaged these days, we can see how harmful this is to us all. For cultural critics like Richard Schickel, the use of advertising techniques as a shorthand for informed understanding "ultimately destroys the capacity for subtler, more reflective, and therefore more dangerous confrontations with these issues, indeed with the infinite variety and complexity of our fellow human beings."[1] The "danger" comes in hearing out the other position and perhaps changing or modifying one's own views after one's mind has "been made up." Bigotry and racial stereotypes flourish in such an environment, where brand-name characterization is demanded for all ideas to be comprehensible. Consequently, and more to the point in Schickel's view, we also lose our capacity for abstract thinking and imagination, unless they too are neatly packaged.[2] (A similar criticism has been leveled at MTV and the other music video channels for what they have done to the imaginative component of music itself. In a rather major way, music videos limit the meanings of songs to one "authorized" image instead of allowing the mind to make its own visual connections, its own video that changes with the circumstances and environment; not that the target audience really seems to mind so much watching the radio.)

124

Of course, in 1837 Alexis de Tocqueville nailed it in *Democracy in America* by noting that one of the characteristic wrinkles of American democracy "is not that it leads men away from the pursuit of forbidden enjoyments, but that it absorbs them wholly in quest of *those which are allowed* [emphasis mine]."[3] Like Huizinga's descriptive characterization of America as a land of "This, Here, Soon," it's another covalent term for American junkfood consumerism, burgers and Cokes or tabloid journalism, a far more elegant and polite description of the illusion of having it your way when it's actually theirs.

When this tendency is translated into the mechanics of representative democracy, the purpose of a successful political campaign is to convince an electorate already habituated to instant gratification that they are having it "their way" when they vote for The Candidate, the political equivalent of the menu photoburger that gives us the heartburn later on. However, if the voters are already deciding on muddled homogenized sound bite burgers, the newly elected senator, congressman, assemblyman, etc., is far worse off in believing her or his bumper stickers when the realization hits that in truth the special interests to whom (s)he is beholden, who bankrolled their campaigns in reality have succeeded in having it "their" way—and to hell with the poor schmucks who don't have the money, the ordinary constituents. On the other hand, the incumbents, habituated to the system as it has evolved, already know the drill, grit their teeth, and try to get something done as best they can. Third-party and fourth-party alternatives that occasionally try to reform the system fail, because ultimately the electorate's fascination with and dependence on franchise-style politics is so overwhelming that they are forced into debasing while homogenizing whatever it is they thought they were standing for so everyone can be "for it." Or, on the other hand, as in the case of the recent third-party run by Ross Perot, where a need might be there but a quirky millionaire industrialist as candidate might not be really up to the rigors of the campaign, they bail out and leave supporters in the lurch and adrift with their discontent unfocused save for the vestigial "I Can Fix It" bumper sticker.

"If," in the words of the poet e. e. cummings, "freedom is a breakfastfood," and that's how representative democracy is marketed, is it any wonder that Americans are suffering the fastfood "afterburn," that fewer people are even bothering to vote, or that modern presidents are elected by a little more than a quarter of the registered voters these days? Since the late sixties fast food political techniques have taken over the American electoral process, its methods having become so blatant and transparent that in the presidential election of 1992 between Bill Clinton and George Bush, voters were treated to the spectacle of partisan political managers being interviewed, immediately after the candidate's debate, by learned TV commentators who folded the respective partisan spins into their own "objective" assessments of the candidates' performance. It was almost like taking the word of the racetrack touts and posting the winners from their morning line instead of waiting until after the race was run or interviewing the owners in the *middle* of the race: "The horse has great heart, especially in the back stretch; all things being equal, the filly should win, etc."

This wasn't electoral politics, but PR personality marketing masquerading as news—just another manifestation of that glossy superburger picture over the cash register. In the nineties, the candidates and their campaign manager/handlers don't even bother to hide their strategies from the electorate: it's all out front. No wonder Americans are becoming resigned, distressed, and dispirited. Not only do they tell you what they're going to do and how they're going to do it (which issues, what spin, etc.), but amazingly enough, they go ahead and do it too. And they do it because we've become so depressed that ultimately we let them. Have it your way? Of course, you can. Would you like fries with that?

That's what I was thinking about when I reached the bottom of my eldest daughter's toy bin and extracted a miniature top-hatted Uncle Sam figure. Was that just another promotion for *Troy, New York*, a movie that had come and gone with fries and a shake? Or some sort of federal government promotion for the Fourth of July?

By now it was 3 am and I was tired. Well, perhaps my daughter would tell me where it came from if I happened upon it again. At least I hoped so. On second thought, I pocketed it for my own collection.

Chapter 7

Bad Day at Internet

The present is more frightening than any imaginable future I might dream up. If Marshall McLuhan were alive today he'd have a nervous breakdown.

—William Gibson[1]

<TS: Format the above text as a divider page, followed by a blank>

Nothing to be done. I've come around to that conclusion myself, but I've tried to put it from me, saying, "David, be reasonable, you haven't tried everything," and I resumed the struggle.

By the time you read this essay, everything I'm talking about in terms of computer technology will be obsolete or nearly so.*[⊠] The word-processing program that is more than adequate for my needs (I only use maybe 15% of its capabilities at most) will have undergone two or three new permutations and revisions, which ultimately I will be coerced into buying. The operating system, the traffic cop that monitors this and other programs in

---

* I'm sure you'll note that so much of what I mention here is obsolete, being that I wrote this chapter nine years ago. the points I make here are just as valid now as they were then.

my computer's hard drive, will likewise have undergone more upgrades and refinements. Finally and most essentially, to keep the whole system "on the square" for peak operating efficiency because I'll have replaced the above, not only will I absolutely need a new microprocessor, the accelerator of this information vehicle, but also more RAM (random access memory), which runs the immediate program within the new and improved operating environment. In the computer age as in none other, the consumer/product circle remains unbroken.

By the time you read this essay, (and computer technology is a brilliant consumerist marvel), even the hard drive that contained this essay, the present operating system *and* my other programs — which has more than enough capacity for any future projects I might do with enough resident memory left over to store the collected works of Leo Tolstoy — will also have to be enlarged yet again. Why? It's the nature of the op sys beast, its bureaucratic imperative, its DNA as it were. Coupled to its insatiable appetite, every subsequent upgrade will, like a voracious killer shark, gobble larger and larger portions of my system's resident memory in the name of "progress, speed, and efficiency". And all for me and my work, which is funny because the operating system itself doesn't make me any more creative than I already am. In truth, *I'm* the operating system; in the end it's not the tools that make the man but the quality of the work he produces with them. At least that's what I've always assumed up until now. A nifty-looking typeface or a laser print job may make my manuscript look terrific but it won't change my concepts. It's just like in the music business: A mediocre rock and roll band can go into the best studio with the best producer in the world and still make mediocre music. Oh, it might sound *great,* but it will still be mediocre, a simple awful truth regardless of what the record company PR says to the contrary. Apparently that doesn't hold true in the Information Age; moreso, it's beside the point, and I'd better get used to it.

Only after I've written does the computer's word-processing function really help. It is the editing, the shifting of blocks of text and the ease of re-writing that makes me the proverbial happy hacker/writer. But though ostensibly time-saving, paradoxically I have to be more vigilant in copy-editing because a whole different set of systemic errors occur. Besides the usual mis-keys, there's the danger of word repetition, which happens because I didn't completely cut off the tail of the word skein I'd just edited down or inserted. There are of course the downright usage mistakes like substituting "there" for "their", errors that spell checkers blithely ignore, and so do I if jammed for time. The program makes errors because, I suppose, it can, or I let it, or some combination of the two; every program has its quirks, again having nothing to do with my writing (save for my dyslexic typing errors) but everything to do with the system I choose to write with. On the other hand, because re-writing is a comparative snap, word-processing makes me more nit-picky, more prone to re-writing. It's so easy to be seduced, too easy. Indeed this feature has been an inestimable boon to my marriage, especially when I show my work to my only wife and she makes "a small suggestion or two" when I'm expecting to be patted on my shaggy head as a reward for a job well done, a bonus writers' spouses have been supposed to bestow since time immemorial. In the old days when I was still pounding away on my trusty IBM Selectric II, I used to go ballistic when she pointed out a busted tense, a run-on sentence, a misspelling, the normal stuff. And I'd start screaming at her for pointing it out, for marking up my pristine copy though I was more ticked off with myself because I knew she was right. Of course she was right, but I'd just done it and it took a while to do the "no mistakes" final draft she sees at the end of the day. Hah! These days, I just sprint out to the studio, put the manuscript up on screen, and key in the corrections while the program automatically re-formats and re-paginates the manuscript. Then I hit the print command — GIJANG! — and a few minutes later out spews the corrected copy from my printer like clean pressed laundry, and I'm back in our bedroom. "Is this any better dear?" I ask breathlessly, well-pleased with myself. Of course it is, but that's no longer the point really.

My ambivalence toward the marvels of the new information technology and the mindset it has spawned has less to do with the dialogue I have with my wife and more to do with my attempts to come to grips with my peculiarly American response to the electronic culture that has made these domestic scenes possible. Not only does this new technology or its peculiarly American attitude toward the new technology shape my experience, but also has implications for my future, implications that I have every right to examine and question. Cultural historian Warren Susman, in *Culture as History* (1984) raises questions and proposes approaches that should keep one occupied well into the next century — his is an extraordinary work of historiography. From Susman's historical perspective, my continuing dialogue with and/or diatribe against the current mystery trend is symptomatic of an ongoing series of discussions that has bubbled under the surface of American life since the 1840s.[2] These discussions predate by more than 150 years the current cyber-babble about the implications of the Internet, virtual reality and the like. Back then thinking Americans were concerned about how steam power and the telegraph, that century's information delivery system was transforming life. At that time there was a sense of unease in the air that accompanied those changes, an almost palpable fear of modern civilization that was in part articulated by writers like Nathaniel Hawthorne, Henry David Thoreau, Ralph Waldo Emerson, William Dean Howells, Henry Adams and others. In 1881, this unease was given a name, *American Nervousness*, the title of a best-selling book written by an American physician, George Beard. Considering today's widespread use of mood altering drugs, decaffeinated Prozac and the like to medicate our present century's ills, the title was visionary and prophetic. For Beard, the difference between the "ancient" past and modern times came down to the influence of five elements: the transformatory nature of steam power, the periodical press, the telegraph, the sciences, and the mental power of women[3]. (Feminism has always been a part of the American scene). In the 1890's Beard's findings were further amplified and validated in research done by sociologists*, philosophers, and educationalists at the University of Chicago who discerned another debilitating impact of the new technologies on American society, viz. the gradual disappearance of face-to-face communications, the glue that held the American family together.[4]

---

* Back in the 1890's sociology was not as insular in its concerns as it has become today and included all of what we would call "the social sciences". Its approach and philosophy was much like a parallel branch of the "humanism" that G. Stanley Hall and other scholars practiced (see *Play School*).

Forty years later their findings were further enhanced and refined by Edward Sapir in *The Encyclopedia of Social Sciences* (1930). He articulated a subsequent effect: *because* communications themselves could no longer be kept within desirable bounds, so also literary and artistic values were in danger of being degraded and trivialized. Ask anybody who has ever received an e-mail message or delved into the electronically infinite cyber-babble of the Internet it birthed. Indeed it is a raucous, anarchic wild Westworld frontier populated by a whole host of self-created cyber good and bad guys, black hats, cowboys, Indians and the dance of the just plain folks. For Sapir and the rest of us who are also struggling to find some middle position, some accommodation to this brave new world should be made, for the question comes down to "whether the obvious increase of overt communication is not constantly being corrected ... by the creation of new obstacles to communication. [and] The fear of being too easily understood, in many cases, may be more aptly defined as the fear of being understood by too many — so many, indeed, as to endanger the psychological reality of the image of the enlarged self-confronting the not-self."[5]

Since Sapir's day this creation of and conflict with the media "not-self" has been a pre-eminent subtext for numerous cyberpunk science fiction novels and movies that feature computer technology, prominently among them *Brainstorm* (1983), *Videodrome*(1983), *Blade Runner*(1982), *Lawnmower Man*(1992), or most recently *Strange Days*(1995).* The introduction of virtual reality to the evolution of computer communications technology, the idea that one can not only create but also inhabit discarnate spaces in a computer-generated world, raises the ante some, though in no way diminishes the force of Sapir's observations sixty years ago. It's not just those of us who've opted to permanently move into the cutting-edgeland ozone of the Internet who will be or have been affected either; we all are. And in truth, our perceptions and expectations of promise, "the GE All-Electric kitchen," so to speak, which life in the computer lane is supposed to herald, have soured as a result. From the collec-

---

* In retrospect, it seems worthwhile to mention the *Matrix* trilogy (1999–2003) that is the most recent example of films in this genre. While the plot is flawed, it powerfully dramatized the cyberpunk themes that I mention here.

tive perspective created by movies, advertising, books, and art over the last 25 years at least, our future will be a dark and ominous place. It will be (and perhaps is already turning into), an industrially polluted predatory wasteland inhabited by damaged alienated souls, those happy few already out in cyberspace who are manipulating it for good or ill notwithstanding. The future of business, (my modest enterprise as a writer included), is already here, and though the paper-less office boogie steps are complex, we all know them and they go something like this:

Of course you have to buy the what.sys and the service contract along with a mess of specialty products and then you plug everything into everything else to make a seamless unit you hope. You had all this before with office #1, (the "paper" office?) whose systems were discrete, separate though still technologically interconnected (you were the interface technology). Your office consisted of a desk, a phone, typewriters, file cabinets, but just one additional set of whatever you were shuffling. With the INFORMATION SYSTEM on which your office now depends, you need two or more sets of the same stuff you had before. OK, they say it's better that you can you can shift it digitally and electronically all over creation, to Sri Lanka and back in a few nanoseconds if you choose. For that matter you can even park it all on a hard drive there to save office space. It can be compact enough to carry around with you, or you can have it attached like a polyp. (William Gibson's computer jockey anti-heroes can literally "jack themselves" in to the information matrix if they choose). You can wake up in the morning with it, or use it to sexually stimulate yourself at night no muss, no fuss, (just massive phone bills). Eventually you must have a *hard copy* of some sort, something physically in hand so at least you can remember whatever it was you said or ordered or did the night before if you're at all conscientious.

You just can't have it as backup on the hard drive either, because if you have it on your hard drive, you (your data, and by inference and extension your life) are at risk because something mechanical/electrical could happen to the drive like a freak magnetic storm, a power surge, or outage (and of course you must buy a protection unit for that eventuality, if you're paranoid enough or just being conscientious about your work once again).

Of course, too, the system that runs the drive can crash and frequently does in real life for any sort of stupid reason — nothing
to be done unless you back it all up.

However, the technology of diskettes with which you "back
it all up" is not as advanced as that of hard drives. The diskettes
are just much or more prone to deterioration. (Presently the CD-
ROM appears to be the solution, but when that technology filters
down to the man on the street, and however entropy is temporarily overcome, though having more capacity it will be just as
cantankerous, and prone to more intricate defects. Anyway, once
you've converted everything over, something new will appear,
which will be "better" and which you will buy, and so, and so on
ad infinitum). Again, if you're conscientious (or creatively paranoid enough) your back-up diskettes must be replaced at regular
intervals. You're now buying and collecting and keeping track of
the duplicates themselves prone to errors of transmission instead
of merely storing that carbon copy in the stand-up files.

Even if you have your data on a diskette, you'll need another
what.sys that is *programmed for* your diskette to be able to
read and recover it, fine. What if you don't have a compatible
program, and now the text you typed two years ago is trapped
on the diskette in an obsolete format, and you now find yourself
unable to work with the information? This happens to businesses
more than you might think. What happens if the power cuts out
in mid-transmission, what then? The more you get into the technology of this mindset, the more apparent it becomes that you're
dangerously dependent, at the mercy of the technology that
runs the what.sys onto which you've transferred your data, your
life. So much for the liberating influences of the paper-less office
you were told would save your bacon.

Not just using, but even having a computer inalterably changes
you. And because it's yours, after a while you start acting like
a teenager who's just cobbled together a hot car. You become
obsessed with the need to brag about it because it's so cool and
fast, etc., (and men more than women are prone to this kind of
behavior). It's high school all over again or still: same rules, different things, my dog's better than your dog. Suddenly you're
seventeen years old again hanging out in the parking lot before

school watching the people come and go, talking about cars and trying to appear cool. You used to chat about the weather, the battle of the sexes, sports, or politics, isn't everything going to hell in a hand basket? Now your small talk becomes larded with liberal amounts of techno-babble, which though it shows your coolness quotient to the boys, is guaranteed to put almost everyone including your significant other to sleep. The competitive juices that contribute to driving you crazy doing business in this environment start churning too, unless you're one of those individuals (or network administrators of one of those companies) who just has to have everything the moment it can be had. If not, you're always playing conversational catch-up, and feeling inadequate because you don't have whatever you're supposed to have that they all have when your associates and colleagues rabbet on about their "increased productivity, lower cost, higher benefit-ratios etc.". This is the sort of thing businessmen like to talk about when alone instead of sports (which everyone has given up on anyway). Even if you don't have it all in defense, you learn the jargon much as young men did back in the Fifties who didn't know a Lake pipe from a lifter, but learned so that the hoods who did wouldn't kick the shit out of them and so that they'd blend into the woodwork. This being still the case, either you learn to zip it and moderate your enthusiasms, or you run out of friends. Or you seek the company of other hackers who, I suppose in reality, bore themselves silly even in their protected environment. Thus, your life changes by fits and starts, and imperceptibly it begins to dawn on you that the boon you have sought seems less and less to be a boon when everything else is factored in. Everyone gets to the same page eventually, for no matter how plugged-in you are to the new world order, still there comes a point in time when you realize that no matter how many megs of RAM you're running, how fast your modem, capacious your hard drive, or how many type fonts are loaded up and ready to go, you've still got to have a hard copy, just like you always had. And not only one, with electronic forgeries being a growth industry these days. Instead of the simplicity and good design you were promised, you have wandered into the systems hell of infinite duplication instead.

But come, let's go, let us proceed down this particular garden path. Let's say you've already re-thought your "business

environment," are familiar with the quirks of "information management," and are ready to get out there on the electronic dance
floor. To your chagrin, you find that things have gotten gnarly
out there in the Zone while you were tooling up, or re-tooling
to maintain your edge. Now you have to deal with the Internet
and the World Wide Web, which the vendors have touted as the
answer for everything. Sure it's easy to ship data and graphics,
buy and sell too, but what happens when you send something
to somebody over your trusty modem and what they get isn't
what you sent or is not for him to see because there's a defect in
his office system file manager or in yours, and your data's cor-
rupted? That you won't find out about until much later because it
looks so nice and neat and official (it's laser printed naturally).

Or, worst case scenario, you learn the iron law of technology: the bigger, the faster, the more complex it is, the greater its
capacity for mayhem. In short, technology only amplifies and
encourages human fallibility, and its use becomes the excuse
why things don't work smoothly. A friend of mine related a ster-
ling example of that thinking when he was in charge producing
a CD-ROM containing highly complex actuarial figures for a Fortune 500 insurance conglomerate. The client's Los Angeles representative from whence the data originated, to whom he was
responsible for arranging on the CD, an expensive and tedious
undertaking, never bothered to inform him that what she was
sending was incomplete. It was only at the eleventh hour after
he had already made the defective CD did he discover this. After
producing more than a few useless CDs (which the client paid for
anyway but not the point), he asked her why she never bothered
to check the tapes for data errors *before* she uploaded them to
him. "If I'd known you were going to check, I would have told
you," was her response. Go figure, but this is exactly what happens when people mindlessly abdicate their responsibilities to
machines and systems in the mistaken belief machines can think
for themselves, when they are just being compliant doing only
what they're programmed for, no more no less.

Then you add in the hacker merry pranksters hanging out on
the cyberspace "corner" who are there just to mess with you and
your data because it's fun to break into somebody's house just
to look in their bureaus. Oh it's nothing personal, they do it to

everybody, it's part of the code, the initiation; that's just swell isn't it?. At least in the old days you had a pretty good hunch who was messing with you and why, but now you have to worry about all those electronic bad guys who are playing out the hyper-card version of "Bad Day at Internet" with your precious data, your life. In this new business environment, you're at the mercy of people you don't know, people you can't even see, people you *never* had to deal with before. But OK, you're a masochist, and you're up for it, you've put in that delegated phone line and are ready for the free lunch at Cafe Internet. Having learned the protocols after being ritually singed by the flame artists out there on the Net, you're ready to rumble. Only then do you run into the biggest obstacle, for now you encounter lawyer sharks swimming out there armed with PowerBooks looking for ways to exploit the First Amendment, meaning their right to load up your singular space with advertisements for goods and services you really don't want or need. And they too want a piece of your action, which you thought was free.

You have to admire the lawyers for this, the way they've dealt themselves into your game and are busily occupied with exploiting that good feeling that the free exchange of ideas engenders. In the Sixties they used to say that the streets belonged to the people; in the Nineties, it's the Net that belongs to the people, but that is under assault by the telecom giants who want it all because in America there is no such thing as innovation without commercial exploitation (taxation without representation?). Reach out and touch someone? Right. Here's my credit card number.

Sooner or later that brings in the feds to police it (as if they have any control now), and we all go back to high school, where there's always a kid in every class who brings down the heat on everyone's cool scene. Say some people have a few beers after the game, there's always one who not only has a few more beers to blottos-ville, but then gets into his car and mows down the cheerleading squad or a group of nuns, and you all get the heat and you're grounded forever. Every cyber chat room or bulletin board has someone, a trash-talking smarm, a scam artist selling snake oil, or apprentice terrorist-in-training who abuses the protocols for which eventually everyone pays and a little more freedom is given up for collective security.

So the paper-less office has its sorcerer's apprentice, and while promising yet another "free" frontier it imposes a stiff admission price, just another dealer option that leads to specialization and fragmentation. Instead of opening up the possibilities of the human spirit, it paradoxically limits them, and in the process, we've become the prisoner of forces whose complexity far outstrips our ability to comprehend them and their consequences. It leads us to a kind of technological anhedonia described 100 years ago by William James in *The Varieties of Religious Experience* as one of many types of depression characterized by "mere passive joylessness and dreariness, discouragement, dejection, lack of taste and zest and spring."[6] Post that on the paper-less office bulletin board we say.

Can you blame me if I'm not entirely comfortable with the situation on a general level? On a personal level, it's making me crazy that I've allowed myself to be suckered into this incrementally expensive technological dance. In truth I probably only have myself to blame for being a victim of this contemporary disorder, the *computer inadequataphobia syndrome*, a fear exacerbated by my own feverish perusings of the computer trade magazines that I will be missing out on "something big" if I don't upgrade and take advantage of "what's next". On the other hand, it could easily have a great deal to do with spending protracted periods of time with my computer guru, Dan the Software Man who, who after a few years around me, has become quite the adept at orchestrating my eccentricities, fears, and phobias about my place in the Information Age. Maybe it's *because* of his skillful feeding of my anxieties that I think it's inevitable, that the needs of the system come first, *its* needs, not necessarily *mine*. Despite this reasoning I'm not convinced. This technological break dance I'm engaged in has virtually nothing to do *with me or my work*.

I've been meditating on this idea ever since Dan came over to my studio recently to perform another upgrade miracle on my "system," which to me is nothing more than a super typewriter/filing cabinet. The previous upgrade to the Windows program he "just had to install" a few months back was still primarily being used to play solitaire but no matter. This new installation, he patiently explained, this modem to wire me up to the wonderful world of e-mail and the Internet like the Windows program that preceded it, was for "my own good". He was saying all this with a gleam in his eye as he was deftly and professionally dismantling my electronic helpmate before my eyes and laying it out on my desk like the proverbial patient etherized upon a table: its driver cards and hard drive exposed, its dust cover upended. Apparently the real reason he was being Dr. Kildare, Albert Schweitzer and Mother Thersa combined boiled down to the fact that *he* was tired of playing telephone tag with me, and if I had an e-mail address *he* could get me any time he wanted. Anyway when I got over feeling crazy because he was loading yet another program on my hard drive that I probably wouldn't use, I'd thank him in the end for being connected to the World Wide Web. He was certain of that.

138

But who am I kidding; it's not my system after all, it's his. And even now I am of a few minds about that since I'm still examining the implications of having a computer or the computer having me, the improvement in inter-spousal relationships notwithstanding. It has taken me all this time to figure out that when Dan started me down the path to computing self-sufficiency and converted another computer-phobe to the cause, that he was really on a mission from You Know Who for my soul's salvation. Though he might think that, and I might let him, there's a part of me that remains skeptical, that stands apart watching the whole process and my place in it unfold. Dan should have figured out that if I was a true believer in the new world order, when he did come by for one of our sessions I'd buy everything he had in his briefcase, all the good drugs, the hip programs that are touted to keep me high, happy, productive and addicted. I don't hold it against him that he tries so hard to sell me whatever is the current fancy, for if nothing else, I represent a challenge to his salesman's ego. I guess I do because in fact, I'm rather fond of him, so I'll allow him his delusion that it's his system and that I use it with his sufferance. And well I should since he set me up and has performed all my previous upgrades, and services my machine when it acts up, which ironically enough only seems to happen *just before* he's upgraded me. The whole process is similar to what happens just when you're thinking about investing in a new car, the old one catches on and starts to act up, subtly reinforcing your decision.

Grow up ferchrissakes he tells me. It's not the Fifties or some other comparatively ancient time when one could (and some did) build one's own hi-fi or ham radio set, (or steam engines or electric generators) from the components; no one even bothers to look under the hood of one's car either 'cause it's become so complicated with all their associated anti-pollution devices appended. For that matter who can know what goes behind the dashboard stuffed with microchips. Nevertheless the rationale for how it's all cobbled together is invariant: as night follows day, the least important "bell and whistle" display you thought was neat on the dash seems to incorporate the weakest link in the performance chain of command for the efficient running of your car. And when it blows, so does everything else.

Those hardy hack-it-yourself-ers, those self-styled sports of the culture who on principle "don't read the manual" for macho reasons of hacker *amor propre*, actually spend *more* money and *more* time when waiting on-line for the phone techie to get to them, and still they'll have to go out and buy whatever it is they'll need in the end. It's the same lesson: those who buy deep-cut discount computers and software from Uncle Steve's Discount Store out in mall-land learn when they eschew patronage of their neighborhood store, where prices may not be as "competitive" in the short run. In the long run, the local guy ultimately is a better deal because he'll support whatever you purchase and even throw in the batteries for free. When you bring back your sweet deal to Uncle Steve's, it's possible that the discount package you bought is no longer in stock, so no one remembers how it was supposed to work, or the salesmen that you bought it from is long gone. If not so, the service department is pathetically understaffed and overworked and it will be weeks before they get to you since their warranty only covers their store and you'll have to take a number. The final indignity could be that Uncle Steve is now Uncle Janos, and the store's folded, which leaves you, the thrifty consumer, up the proverbial creek. In the end you may wind up junking that system altogether and buying another one, but's that's another mystery entirely, an entirely disposable one at that. Better to have Mike the Mechanic, or Dan the Software Man, who for $35 to $50 an hour or fractions thereof (not including parts replacement), will pull out the bad whozis, substitute another, reconfigure the what.sys, and in under fifteen minutes (if you're that lucky) have you up and back crunching numbers, words, playing Myst, poker or solitaire.

Before this kind of technology became so indispensable, interchangeable, and commonplace, someone, somewhere at the point of manufacture would have gone over it, if only for the sake of manufacturing integrity, a term that is harder and harder to define. In the era of multinational corporations, every component comes from somewhere else and since manufacturing standards vary as do materials, ultimately fixing the blame when something goes down is almost pointless. So whether the defect was structural or conceptual means little in this consumer culture because we all know there's going to be an upgrade soon that will fix the problem, and that will be on the shelves next week or month, rest assured. And we will buy it.

We might think we're being modern and progressive, but in reality our attitudes are more similar to our 17th and 18th century forbearers who also "... confused the assurance of the bigger and *better* with the purely directional conception of 'further'".[7] Though we pride ourselves on being progressive, pragmatic, post-historical post-modernists, we are being naïve, says the historian Huizinga, when we hold to our belief that "... every new discovery or refinement of existing means must contain the promise of higher value or greater happiness."[8] Additionally we also ignore another basic truth of the Internet Age that has been pointed out by essayist and academic David Ehrenfeld that as a larger percentage of people become involved with manipulating information for the most part of a trivial nature and all in the name of increasing everyone's efficiency,

> fewer people are left to concern themselves with the real goods and services needed for carrying on life... (and) there is a limit to what can be accomplished by increasing the designs and processes, and efficiency may have unexpected and undesirable effects ... (which include) disrupting lives of people and communities and-less obvious-making it easier for us to do the wrong thing. *Our century has been slow to grasp the truth that the efficiency of an action has absolutely nothing to do with its rightness or wrongness.*[9] [authors emphasis]

Despite these misgivings and subconscious rumblings, I genuinely am fond of Dan and though he's endlessly amusing to hang with, it still bugs me that whatever he installs never takes on the

first go-round. His reasons are instructive in light of Ehrenfeld's
observations too: the processor's defective, the software's defective, the installation environment (my studio) isn't static-free, the
electricity's not pure enough, the phone line has too much static
on it and so on. Sometimes in mid-surgery he'll have to go back
to the office for the specialized connector or driver card that's
sitting on his desk and come back a few hours later, that's OK
isn't it? (do I have a choice, Dan?)

It's only a modem ferchrissakes he was mumbling to himself
that evening, how could it be defective just out of the box? Well,
it's no biggie he observed, chump change, he'd installed lots.
Besides going on-line was a snap, as any idiot knew. He griped
as he tried this and that alternative strategy while re-booting the
computer, which groaned and blinked uncomprehendingly. He
was getting mad at me too because *I* (!!) had now made him late
for his next appointment. Did I miss something here? It was then
I asked THAT QUESTION that all civilians tend to ask in situations like this: if this was so easy, why was it so hard for him, of
all people, to install it? Dan hates that question, all those guys do,
can you blame them?

On the other hand, maybe it's me who's causing this Vortex
of the Damned to exist — that's what Dan thinks when he's here.
Or maybe it could be the combination of the three of us: me,
Dan the Software Man and my gray box, and I shouldn't be in
the room when he installs anything in it because the computer
knows and has it out for me, or him, or possibly is just being
post-modern for the halibut. Strangely enough none of this
happens when he's gone, mind, only when it's time for another
upgrade, so perhaps it's the computer's fault because it doesn't
like being a victim of progress either. And how am I going to
deal with a world whose current wisdom maintains that you're
only as good or productive as your last upgrade just like out in
Hollywood with movies?

Why is that I wonder?

Indeed this is what Dan and I argue about constantly even as
he's downloading another program I just "have to have" as he
waxes eloquent on the possibilities of the paper-less office and

Teenage Nervous Breakdown: Music and Politics in the Post-Elvis Age

I try to explain what I mean, but I'm just too tired and let him install it anyway.

Nothing to be done.

Chapter 8

Asking Alice

Fighting for the Right to Party

Here's a riddle, actually a variation on an old studio musician's aphorism: Why is it that if you're working a folk gig, all you'll ever be able to score is pot? The crowd's always pretty mellow, looks like the normal bunch of sixties hippies. As long as it's mushrooms, you really can get anything you want from the same crowd at a Phish or Ratdog concert. Same goes for cocaine, poppers, or downers at the disco, where the seventies style and the retro spirit of *Saturday Night Fever* inhabit those glitzy interiors like flies in amber. At the reggae/ska/dub clubs where the natty dreds hang, jah-filled spliffs abound, while at rap and gangsta concerts, urban and suburban wanna-be rappers love to toke on their blunts, hollowed-out cigars filled with marijuana. Nothing but uppers and beer in the biker-effect black leather, chain "n" chrome heavy metal universe; Ecstacy, Vitamin K, or the designer drug of the moment is readily available in the "cutting-edge" rave scene where black-garbed industrial noise/techno folks meet to freak.

To the proverbial visitor from another planet, all this behavior seems so clannish, quaint, and tribal, this connection between each music scene and the drugs that go with it. How did these "mores" evolve? What were they to begin with, and in what ways over the past 30 years have they been transformed? How we answer these riddles not only says much about what we are as a nation so totally consumed and obsessed with pop culture but also helps to explain how we got to this point in the first place. There's a common thread running through this naturally: Unless one has chosen to willfully ignore the past 40 years of American social history, it comes as no shock to realize that not only a fair percentage of today's teenagers, unofficially put at more than 40%, but a larger if no longer as well-documented number of former teenagers, i.e., their parents, are now or have been intimately familiar with the meaning of Bob Dylan's song "Rainy Day Women #12 and 39." Granted, some of us no longer follow Mister Zimmerman as closely as we did, we may "not inhale" that much anymore, but just like the song says, "everybody must get stoned."

But we do, we have, four generations of us in one particular fashion. Perhaps "You Can't Always Get What You Want" by the Rolling Stones or "Truckin'" or "Casey Jones" by the Grateful Dead will always raise a knowing crinkle of recognition in future teenage eyes, perhaps not. It's comforting nonetheless in this Post-Elvis Age to realize that many of us cohabit the same musical/experiential universe. Sex and drugs and rock and roll; rock and sex and drugs and roll, these are the familiar rites of initiation into contemporary American adolescence, even if it seems to last into early middle age now. Though the cultural contexts of these songs and newer ones have been substantially modified over time to fit new contexts by their commercial uses, they remain an integral part of our media musical consciousness. Pop music in all its hues, tastes, and varieties, from hip-hop to reggae, from a capella oldies to vintage psychedelia, is the hardest-working component of the material/commercial world of big business; its riffs, catchy hooks, and especially the inherent "attitude" accompany the strutting supermodel parade on the media catwalk before our eyes and ears. There's so much music product to choose from, so much seeming variety, yet paradoxically less and less *music* capable of stirring souls. It may appear that we are not even listening to the same music from the same pew, or as members of the same church for that matter. But though we may hearken to different preachers and sing different doxologies, still each of us is product of and worships at the church of rock and roll. Its images and attitudes inform our world.

Riddle me this: The Beatles, who broke up more than 25 years ago, were in 1996 enjoying their best album sales yet, having sold 6 million out of their own old catalogue and achieved a combined sales figure of almost 20 million for their recently released anthologies. That's astonishing enough given the complexity of the music business, but even more mind-boggling is that an estimated *41%* of those buyers were teenagers who weren't even born when the Beatles were first popular in the early sixties.[1] Listening to *Sgt. Pepper's Lonely Hearts Club Band* through a set of earphones or on a really expensive audio system while investigating and decoding its every musical detail and nuance, checking and noting every overdub, every cross-fade between channels, remains a compelling experience for many more generations now. Hearing for the first time that chair squeak at the end of the orchestra glissando, the conclusion of "A Day in the Life," remains a delicious discovery too. After all this time we're kidding ourselves if we refuse to admit that *Sgt. Pepper's* attention to detail, its textual continuity, is no longer (or never had been) amplified, enhanced, aided, and abetted by judicious applications of marijuana (or LSD or mushrooms, for that matter). That, in short, *Sgt. Pepper's* was created expressly for stoned people and continues to function as a meditational aid in that capacity is, in the words of the veritable Parson Weems, "too true to be doubted."

Likewise the music of Jimi Hendrix and the Doors continues to exert its intergenerational fascination. Perennial backlist mainstays for more than 25 years, the records of these artists annually produce royalties at the six-figure level for heirs and record companies alike.* That observation alone speaks well of the continued popularity and profitability of the "golden oldies" format on "Classic Rock" FM radio stations.

If we look beyond the tale of the commercial tapes for a moment, something less quantifiable but more concrete becomes apparent. These numbers document and underscore the growing hunger of new generations not only for the music of that "old time" space and place but also for the "spiritual" values those works embodied (which flip postmodernists denigrate and dismiss as "all that hippie bullshit"). Still, whether hidden within the subtexts of television commercials or mutated beyond belief by selective motion picture or video recreations, somehow those "old" values continue to induce younger generations to examine them in their pristine forms via CD or cassette and expropriate these essential texts for their own adolescent rites of initiation.

---

* According to a survey conducted by the *Oprah Winfrey Show* in 1996, Jim Morrison of the Doors was the seventh-richest *dead* rock star, with Elvis first and Jimi Hendrix fourth. (There are statistics for everything, Virginia.)

Considering America's present hypocritical ideology concerning drugs, it seems totally out of character that any kind of consciousness and lifestyle could be or ever was ever associated with music. For nineteenth-century American utilitarians, there were two sorts of drugs available: those that cured you (in short supply and virtually nonexistent) and those that doped you up while nature ran its course. The latter, avidly ingested for all sorts of ills, real and imagined, were widely available in large quantities from the patent medicine industry in potions that contained varying doses of opium and cannabis derivatives.

By the nineteenth-century, according to Dean Latimer and Jeff Goldberg's *Flowers in the Blood: The Story of Opium*, the drug trade was starting to be a major staple of American commerce. In 1840 there was so much opium being imported for "medicinal" uses, 24,000 pounds, that the United States Customs Office put a duty on it that raised the wholesale price to $1.40 a pound. Ten years later, 87,000 pounds were imported. By 1860, the price was $4.50 a pound and the United States was importing 105,000 pounds. By 1870, the amount clearing customs had more than quadrupled to 500,000 pounds, while the paid duty cost per pound had been raised to $2.50 per pound. This figure excluded the approximately 25,000 extra pounds that were being smuggled into the country by canny sea captains and traders.[2]

The drug industry grew explosively when opium was further definitively and cheaply refined into its 24 alkaloids. The most powerful and cheapest to produce was morphine,

> much cheaper than alcohol for the euphoric tickle it gave you, and every pharmacy and general store carried preparations of it calculated to appeal to every sort of person alive, whatever the individual emotional quirk or physical ailment. There were lower-proof opiates like laudanum or codeine, in tasty syrups and candies, to inculcate in novices of any age an appreciation of opium's particular extra-therapeutic properties, and to insidiously lead them, through a succession of higher-proof nostrums, to morphine itself.[3]

From corner drugstores or traveling snake oil salesmen, morphine was also readily available to the discerning consumer in tablet, ointment, solution, tincture, suspension, and clyster (enema) form. The mania for self-administered opiate medication in the mid-1880s was given a "boost" by the development,

production, and widescale marketing of high-quality syringes
and needles, while "the appearance of pure, cheap, cocaine
hydrochloride was everywhere enthusiastically greeted, and
sales of more traditional pharmaceutical highs like chloral
hydrate, ether, and cannabis tinctures suddenly took off on
a handsome surge."[4] The industry that serviced the "medicinal" demands for this epidemic of American nervousness grew
by leaps and bounds, and opiate use in the United States grew
at a rate considerably steeper than the general increase in the
population.[5]

It may have been one thing for a nation of white Americans to
self-medicate themselves into a stupor for imagined or real ills,
accounting for the increased consumption by many people who
never wound up being full-fledged addicts and documented as
official statistics. From a peculiarly skewed point of view, however, America's mass underground addiction to codeine-laced
cough syrup (among other concoctions) was a fitting symbol
of nineteenth-century progress and civilization, mirroring and
aping the social problems that England in the Victorian Era
or France in La Belle Epoque had as social consequences of
the trade, a worthy example of capitalism's ability to meet the
demands of the market in the same way. Perhaps, too, this need
for better living through industrial chemistry among the leading
Western powers, this hallmark of a "modern" civilization, was
an essential component of The White Man's Burden. Or even
that addiction was an anthropomorphic indicator of a modern
colonial nation's "masculinity"; that is, if one considers chemical
dependence as an exclusively masculine trait. (This last notion,
currently under revisionist attack, may no longer appear to be as
true in our progressive age of politically correct thinking.)

149

Given all this, it may have been possible to condone such
addictive excess in America among the dominant white population, but never for any nonwhite group, especially the Chinese
and newly enfranchised African Americans. As the century drew
to a close, it became an increasingly acceptable political tactic
to demonize drug use among the Chinese and African Americans and color it with racial stereotypes that neatly deflected
blame away from the ethics of the over-the-counter (or out-of-
the-wagon) patent medicine industry that profited from it. The

Chinese were attacked and ridiculed for their "devious foreign ways," though by their substantial contributions to America during the building of the transcontinental railroads in midcentury they were entitled to American citizenship if they so chose. To their credit, they successfully carved out a separate but coexistent society in large American cities like San Francisco, Chicago, New York, Philadelphia, and Boston, where their culture, crafts, and cuisine were widely available to be enjoyed by those who bothered to investigate them on their own. And yet one of the favored yellow journalist cartoon visions concerned the crafty and sinister opium-smoking Chinese white slaver leading "good" girls to disgrace, a characterization that seemed for a time to appeal to the redneck mother population in the agrarian hinterlands of America.

For native-born, newly enfranchised African Americans, the approach was far more insidious and twisted, because it was targeted against their unique music culture, despite the fact that minstrel and ragtime music was already thoroughly integrated into nineteenth-century American life. To the politicians who encouraged these racist sentiments as well as the newspaper editorialists who promoted them, African-American music was an insidious conveyor of racial impurity and cultural miscegenation, and African Americans were to be feared as "the other"—the designated emotional dark side of the American psyche. It was one thing to listen to this music, to even enjoy it, but not to acknowledge freely or openly the origins or give respect to the culture from which it came. Unless black ragtime and jazz (and, indirectly, the group that created it) were marginalized or limited to function within certain stereotypical parameters, if not suppressed altogether, one risked losing one's cultural identity as an official White Person in Anglo-Saxon America.

And so it was that the associated evils of race mixing that came from the volatile mixture of jazz and opiates circulated in the popular press before World War I along with lurid stories about African American "cocaine-o-mania"—a widely circulated folk myth that African Americans were the only people who had violent reactions to drug overdoses. Authors Latimer and Goldberg cited "Negro Cocaine 'Fiends' are a New South Menace," an article by Dr. Edward Huntington Williams that appeared in the *Sunday New York Times Magazine* in 1914, describing how cocaine turned black men into veritable were-wolves:

> consumed by violent homicidal passions and, worst of all, invulnerable to bullets . . . with the story of a police chief in Asheville, North Carolina, who was called out to arrest a "hitherto inoffensive negro" who was "running amuck" in a cocaine frenzy: "Knowing that he must kill the man or be killed himself, the Chief drew his revolver, placed the muzzle over the Negro's heart, and fired—'intending to kill him right quick,' as the officer tells it. But the shot did not even stagger the man. And a second shot that pierced the arm and entered the chest had just as little effect in crippling the Negro or checking his attack. Meanwhile the chief, out of the corner of his eye, saw infuriated Negroes running toward the cabin from all directions. He had only three cartridges remaining in his gun, and he might need these in a minute to stop the mob. So he saved his ammunition and finished the man with his club.[6]

A variation of these scare tactics was adapted by the Anti-Saloon League and the Temperance Movements at the turn of the century and used to sell the idea of Prohibition to the nation. The Volstead Act of 1919, banning alcohol sale and consumption in the United States from 1919 until its repeal in 1934, proved to be an exercise in misguided altruism with unforeseen consequences. Like the widespread indiscriminate use of opiates, there had always been a problem in America of defining the line between social drinking and alcoholism. The choice to imbibe and how was better left up to individuals or like-minded individuals to decide, not the government, of course. Instead of turning people away from alcohol, the so-called "Noble Experiment" elevated alcohol to the status of an illicit drug whose consumption became an indicator of fashionable modernism. In effect Prohibition *encouraged* people who never thought of drinking or breaking the law to patronize speakeasies where bootleg liquor was served. The generation of law-breakers Prohibition created facilitated the growth of a whole criminal underclass to service the great thirst, much the same way patent medicine manufacturers had leaped into the commercial breach in the preceding decades. (Since the late 1960s, seven presidential "wars" on drugs have apparently ignored or repressed knowledge of Prohibition's moral failure—if not the consequences, its criminal hangover.) But maybe it was easier to get people behind the idea of Prohibition, at least initially, because it was an addictive drug with no cultural overtones attached.

Though they sold papers, inflamed mobs, and sometimes even won elections, these racist campaigns hardly befitted the sentiments of a nation sworn to defend Western civilization against the onslaught of the godless Huns in World War I, if indeed that was the purpose of the politicians and pamphleteers in the first place. In any case, the accomplishments of the Harlem Renaissance, that veritable flowering of black arts in the post-War twenties, definitively should have put paid to the notion of the inferiority of black culture. This especially held true for the "Flaming Youth" of the twenties who discovered this world on their own in the clubs and art galleries that grew up in Harlem and for those who discovered the energy of *le jazz hot* in Paris in the twenties.

From the twenties until the late forties, jazz in its various configurations, like rock and roll in our own time, was at one time deemed "countercultural" too. Whether performed live from radio studios or hotel ballrooms or played on records where black jazz was marketed and segregated as "race" music, it gradually became an integral part of America's musical pulse despite the fact that American society was functionally racially segregated. There were black jazz ensembles who played for predominantly black audiences as well as white "swing bands," like the Tommy Dorsey Band and the Glenn Miller Big Band, who translated the idiom while knocking off the more racy sexual innuendos for white tastes.

However, for the growing number of white jazz buffs who knew the difference, the Big Band Sound was a pale and hollow shuck-and-jive act compared to the authentic item. It wasn't until the midthirties, when Benny Goodman featured black players like Teddy Wilson and Lionel Hampton in his Trio and Quartet arrgegations and used arrangers like Fletcher Henderson and Don Redman in New York's Carnegie Hall Spirituals to Swing in 1938 and 1939, that the cultural barriers between white and black worlds began to crumble. Still, it wasn't until after World War II that integrated jazz bands were the norm and the inevitable mixing of cultures could no longer be ignored or officially marginalized.

This is where those artists, poets, musicians, and writers of the Beat Generation came on the scene and dived right into that rich

musical, very American tradition. Enthusiastically they embraced
be-bop, the counterstatement to the lush overorchestrated big
band sound in the late forties and the "cool" school that grew
out of it. By the early fifties archetypal Beats were mesmerized
by players like Charlie Parker, John Coltrane, Eric Dolphy, Charlie Mingus, Horace Silver, and eternally Miles Davis, whose style
projected their distance from the official "whiteness" of American
culture. Beat poetry, those dense word-notes of cross-hatched
blank verse chanted or scat-sung sometimes with jazz accompaniment, riffed off the hidden social history of black America, a
mirror image of the cool, mournful, meditative, plaintive, intuitive, self-referential worlds the musicians inhabited. Reading
Allen Ginsberg's incantory poem *Howl* or Lawrence Ferlinghetti's
"The Dog" from *Coney Island of the Mind* or virtually any passage in Jack Kerouac's *On the Road*, originally conceived as one
long literary jazz solo written on one continuous roll of paper, is
a literary taste of the jazz universe the Beats inhabited.

By the late fifties and early sixties, the cool of jazz was folded
into a heady cultural stew which was comprised of liberal doses
of nineteenth-century American Transcendentalism (the poet-
ics of Walt Whitman, Ralph Waldo Emerson sentiments) with an
interest in Zen Buddhism brought on by American servicemen's
contact with the Far East. Along with post–World War I French
Surrealism, Dadaism, and post–World War II Existentialism, the
resultant full-field intellectual overview proved to be irresist-
ible for the next generation of college students. When further
refined, the central metaphor came down to one goal: the search
for consciousness, Self and Cosmic, the search for good maps.
Everyone needs them; adolescents in any age need good maps
when first becoming aware of the world at large, when beginning to ask questions not only about their ultimate place in the
scheme of things, but *what it all means*. Knowing where to find
the right kind of maps to get "The Rules" is crucial during that
emotionally painful period of transformation in high school precisely because "the rules" are always changing. Consciousness of
Self centered on the personal knowing and transformation that
would put you in touch with who you were and what you could
become, or so it was thought.

The correlative to Consciousness of Self, Cosmic Consciousness, was supposed to put one in touch and in synch with the larger universe and provide a set of invariant universal maps for behavior; even if they weren't aware of it at the time, the Beats provided for the next generation a set of roadmaps that seemed useful for the taking. In the long run, having the "right maps" in the Cosmic sense was far more useful than being dependent on mutable ones, those that adolescent peer group culture or the consumer society of the fifties were selling. When boiled down further, one's psychic survival revolved around being on The Path, The Way, and how you traveled was more important than the ultimate destination, which would take care of itself. (By the later sixties, the question was further distilled: "Are you on or off the bus?")

For the Beats there were two paths to enlightenment: In occult terms they were characterized as the Path of the Serpent and the Path of the Arrow. The Path of the Serpent was a slow, meandering, but seemingly inexorable journey that required intense contemplative study of many years by the seeker before the inner light was revealed. It was the way of monks. Zen masters, and ascetics like St. Augustine. A far more direct instantaneous approach (as well as a more social path) was the Path of the Arrow, which was entered by the use of drugs, be they caffeine and benzedrex ("benzedrine, the staff of life," was an old beatnik joke), marijuana, psilocybin mushrooms, or opium and its derivatives. Though the visions may have been ecstatic and intense, without the maps, metaphors, and "the knowledge," the Path of the Arrow produced a temporary result, a fleeting glimpse, an imitation of the meditational state.

On the other hand, sometimes a glimpse was all you could get (or all you really wanted or had time for), so the best that one could do under the circumstances was somehow to testify to that reality, to the possibility of attaining that vision, that feeling, and to attempt to translate that ecstacy into art, music, or poetry. Books like Allen Ginsberg's *Yage Letters* or Aldous Huxley's *Doors of Perception* and *Heaven and Hell* or the teachings of Timothy Leary in the latter sixties served as travelogues filled with field notes from these psychoactive excursions, and they conferred on the Path of the Arrow an aura of romance. Without

the proper knowledge to take along on the Path of the Arrow,
there was the temptation to become hooked on the various
ways of "getting there" instead of staying and "being there," the
supposed ultimate purpose of the whole exercise. The perverse
visionary nightmare world of the psychically addicted in William
Burroughs' *Naked Lunch* and *Nova Express* showed the darker
aspects of the Path of the Arrow. For Burroughs, heroin was *the*
working metaphor for the promise of consumer society as well
as the ultimate commodity that consistently provided an ever-
evolving, seductive, all-inclusive "reality"—a terminal addiction
as any shop-a-holic maxed out on credit cards can attest. Burroughs' cautionary tales were also an integral component of the
Beat legacy, and though bleak, were crucial if one was to fully
comprehend the darker consequences of using drugs of transformation that amplified, mediated, and ultimately altered personal reality.

For one who chose to travel the Path of the Arrow, the stakes
were high and the perils had to be addressed responsibly—Not
for Everybody. To undertake this path for the wrong reasons,
haphazardly on a dare without a patient and understanding
guide, was the ultimate foolishness, cheapening and devaluing
the psychic and spiritual initiation process. To experiment with
psychoactive drugs essentially should have been an act built
on faith and, above all, trust. It was the height of psychic folly
to entrust the spiritual development of one's inner being to just
anyone. The guide perforce had to be multifaceted and talented:
a philosopher, therapist, priest, and DJ all rolled into one. The
guide also had to have "been there" consciously enough to be
able to share the experience, to be able to patiently answer whatever questions were raised during the course of the experience
of the neophyte.

Once this knowledge was fully apprehended by the initiate and successfully demonstrated, in time it could be passed
onward to yet another seeker, and so the tradition and the
knowledge could be transmitted from mouth to ear to soul and
back, from individual to individual. Such visions could take
the form of a Mack Sennett movie directed by Federico Fellini
(thanks, Jeff A.) or could be extrapolated by viewing the cycle of
rebirth in a vase of cut wild flowers that withered and bloomed

before one's eyes like a visual tape loop. The visions could and frequently did take the form of laughing the cosmic laugh for hours on end. Visions varied with individuals, as did the form of the lessons with which intuitive and competent guides were familiar. In the main, all such insights were variations built around learning about interrelated global psychic consciousness, eternity, human decency, personal responsibility, and the brotherhood of man—for want of a better word, Love, if only one had the grace to see it. And somehow, without these intuitions and revelations being written down anywhere, but rather orally passed onward and outward in this manner, these maps became part of a brief but living tradition.

From 1962 to 1966, the Paths of the Arrow and the Serpent commingled. Drugs with certain kinds of music made the heavenly spheres dance. It was here that the Beats connected with those who would eventually refer to themselves as Heads, who would themselves briefly integrate the knowledge from both paths and the traditions from which they sprung. To be even an apprentice Beat one had to be attuned to a larger worldwide cultural history. In music, that meant being familiar with the history and development of not only the jazz of Miles Davis, Charlie Mingus, and John Coltrane but also the music of J. S. Bach, the rhythmic dissonances of Bela Bartok and Igor Stravinsky, Middle Eastern music, and American folk songs of Pete Seeger and the Weavers, and the blues of Josh White and Hudie Leadbetter, Ma Rainey and Bessie Smith. The music was to be found in coffeehouses and jazz clubs in the cities where musicians and poets came together, or on late-night jazz shows, or in books "borrowed" from older brothers and sisters who were reading the new poetry in college courses. Following the Beat Way for an apprentice high school Beat required effort, a personal statement, since examining the world from an intercultural as opposed to parochial viewpoint was a conscious act of subversion in the self-absorbed America of midcentury.

Once on this path, good sense and intuition led to other connections the material laid out; it was natural to investigate the poetry and art of William Blake and Walt Whitman, or William James' *Varieties of Religious Experience*, the cosmological theories of Carl Jung, the plays of Samuel Beckett. Why folk, jazz, and pot came together is anybody's guess; maybe it was just a natural organic connection, a potent alchemical mixture that brought the outlaws from mainstream American music and the culture it represented to each other in the end. Before the juggernaut of official commercial culture redirected the purpose of the trip, other forces were at work that also had a hand in defining what "the knowledge" was even as it floated out of the coffeehouse worlds on the McDougall Street–Los Angeles–Boston folk axis.

An equally opposite and far more "official" form of "counter-culture" emanated from the parallel worlds of pop art in New York, Los Angeles, London, and Paris, one over which for a time Andy Warhol presided. Under his influence the timelessness of Cosmic Consciousness was transposed into the morally drained aesthetic universe of the Now, where Art and Celebrity were coequal. Ambition for fame and celebrity defined this world's moral parameters and gave it its edge, where Being There mattered less than Being *Seen* There. The Fame Game universe over which Warhol reigned was totally consumed by social and creative edge-walking and publicity. Hugh Kenner, the critic, described the high-culture variation of the Poetry edge as The Hack's Progress, or How to Make It in London with Poetry:

> By one version, you spend your first two years at Oxford getting known and published in the Oxford little mags. (Getting what published? Well, you know, some *poems*: little sensitive ways to say Lo, Lo or Shrug, Shrug.) In your third year you get your own little mag together, with as many names as you can bag, and launch it with a publisher's cocktail party in London. No second issue ever need appear. You are now ensconced on the carousel where the action is: round and round and round, you-review-me-I-review-you, and together we'll all see just who gets reviewed. This account, an ideal composite, is not alleged to fit anyone in particular; an especially hilarious variant is the story of X, who, alas, did it all and it didn't work. He ended up lecturing in the Farthest East, one version of the doom Waugh invented for Tony Last.[7]

The drugs needed for the pop art world, unlike the poetry world, either helped one maintain that psychic edge or acted as a pillow when one fell off or out of one's edge. In this high-gloss high-powered atmosphere of couture, museum openings, showbiz personalities, and international society, the only "folk" that mattered were the rich folk, and the only cosmic connections that meant anything were those that advanced careers, not the spiritual evolution of the soul. The high-stakes movers and shakers of machine-made culture took barbiturates to sleep, uppers to kick-start the morning, and alcohol to maintain the buzz until it was time to crash and then start the cycle all over again.* This was primarily a culture that thrived on extremes.

The musical equivalent of urban edge in the pop art world, the virtual progeny of William Burroughs, was the Velvet Underground, who came out of Andy Warhol's Factory in the midsixties. The Velvets' shrieking, dissonant, brooding rhythms, when wrapped around lead vocalist Lou Reed's ironic lyric portraits and enveloped by John Cale's dark narcoleptic trance-inducing viola drones, portrayed a seamy seductive universe that romanticized the chrome-plated fashion nightmare in which the denizens of the high pop world existed. Instead of life-affirming and connection-making, the music of the Velvets reeked of sexual ambiguity, death-rush, psychic confusion, paranoia, and betrayal—the mirror image of the heroin edgeworld, which for those looking in from the outside of this kind of city life possessed a morbid fascination.

158

Whether by accident, design, or the fact that Fashion's needs are insatiable, in the eighties when the Velvets reemerged as a pop force, heroin use and addiction had been elevated to mythic status in the developing pop rock world. Over the last 30 years, for a legion of punk bands in Los Angeles and New York as well as any other urban center that aspired to host an artistic avant garde, heroin had come to be the drug of choice for those who craved the pretensions of *high pop* that the Velvets shilled for. Though undeniably dark, after 1967, this heroin lifestyle-aesthetic, the seeking of ever newer and sharper edges, became the operant mechanism that drove the music business through

---

* During and into the late sixties when the pop art world was reigning supreme, there was a "Dr. Feelgood" practicing in New York whom the Beatles memorialized in their song "Dr. Robert." He was known for administering injections containing speed, vitamin B12, and multivitamins to celebrities and socialites alike, providing for a time (until he got busted by the local authorities) that one could speed one's brains out and still be healthy, rich, *and* thin.

successive phases, and continues to this day in the world of rock
and roll celebrity.

Unfortunately, the nature of this slow and gradual organic dissemination of "the knowledge," which had been taking place roughly in the period from 1962 to 1966, was irreparably altered and distorted by its electronic transformation during the so-called Summer of Love in 1967. Consciousness of the kind Heads sought never could be an easily accessible or readily manu-factured mass commodity. Good guides had always been at a premium, in spite of what "straight" journalists, looking for a good catchy hook, advertised as they focused on the external trappings without bothering to burrow underneath. What was "discovered" and publicized was a series of easily comprehen-sible slogans, fashion pictorials, and store-bought goods: posters, faded jeans, tie-dye T-shirts, bongs, cigarette rolling machines, paisley wallpaper, "free" love, communes, the whole catastrophe. Promoted by *Time, Life, Look, Newsweek, Vogue, The New York Times*, and in time, *Rolling Stone*, "Head" consciousness became an irrelevancy; a separate reality was born. Anyone could look like they were "being there" (or had been there) without going through the discipline of the steps. Maybe it was inevitable, given the penchant of the American spirit to think of things in terms of commerce, that the knowledge itself was another failed Romantic effort to turn back the clock (or for that matter, to dis-pense with clocks entirely). What had been Not for Everybody in the early sixties by 1968 was for Anyone; the Nova Express had left the station.

By 1970 and thereafter, it no longer mattered that Heads eschewed alcohol and depressants or had pegged the oblivion express junkies were on for the baleful psychic influence it was bound to become. Heads were scorned as "elitists." Nor would it occur to the next generation for whom "the knowledge" was handily homogenized, commodified, and profitably distributed that Rock Culture, this new composite designer drug, would ultimately prove to be not only an inferior, but also a far more addictive, opiate than anything heads could have imagined.

Whole universes have been traversed since the fifties question "Can you hold your liquor" has become "Are you experienced?"

while "listen(ing) to the color of your dream" seems to have gone out of fashion lately for those who choose the Path of the Arrow today. Fame, designer goods, technology's promise, or the pursuit of pleasure are today's drugs of choice; the culture of addiction that William Burroughs fluidly and eerily explored has been renamed "codependency," reduced to a staple topic for television talk shows. Here's progress for you: While heroin's effects have been superseded by those of crack cocaine, whose ecstatic rush is far more extreme and of shorter duration, inevitably crack has become more cost-effective than heroin for the dealers who traffic in it, individuals and governments alike.

All products change, it's true; fashions in "illicit" drug use fluctuate, wax, and wane—as does the effectiveness of the over-the-counter and prescription varieties that medicate this society's ills. Enough time has passed so that we see the mechanism at work in popular media: *Miami Vice*, the wildly successful television show of the eighties that glamorized the high-stakes, high-edge underworld of the cocaine trade, spawned a thriving fashion subculture that glamorized not only the drug, but also the fashion attitude and music that accompanied it. Ironically, this show was popular during the height of President Ronald Reagan's much-publicized war on the South American cocaine cartels, the ultimate result of which was to bring down the price of cocaine sold on the street to a more affordable level for larger numbers of people, hard-core addicts and the curious alike. The old folk song maxim inherent in the lyrics, "Cocaine's for horses, not for men,/they say it will kill me, but they won't say when" has been definitively transformed into "Champagne don't make me crazy, cocaine don't make me lazy/ain't nobody's business but my own." But again, how can good maps be created when the moral and ethical landscape in which they should guide no longer has any solid foundations or a sense of its own living history? Still, the need for valid and meaningful adolescent initiations remains constant though its forms continue changing over time, as do the lessons they are supposed to uncover and disclose about society.

Music no longer possesses that spiritual/ideological connection; it's all a series of metaphors to mix and match while the Paths of the Serpent and the Arrow have been reduced to a Stairmaster in the living room that goes nowhere in particular but helps pass the time and keeps us in "shape" for the race. Here's what remains of the "knowledge" from that time: David Bowie in all his incarnations continues to inspire the fashionably correct, and if he's just too strange, there's always the midnight screening for *The Rocky Horror Picture Show*, which accomplishes the same ends. We also know that the stoner kids (the apprentice pothead and hippies) are captivated by Phish or the Grateful Dead; the apprentice macho-men or self-styled bad-girls (what used to be considered the "greaser and hood" element in the fifties) check into the regalia-laden feudal world of heavy metal. Rap's and hip-hop's appeal crosses race and class lines to the point where the lyrical and visual conventions have been enthusiastically assimilated by mainstream commercial culture—which meets and matches in the celebrity realms of pro basketball and football. The offspring of the Velvet Underground take to the techno-clubs and grunge parlors equipped with the correct clothing and attitude or flattened-affect. We know we're in the country and western world when we hear on the jukebox "She's acting single. I'm drinking doubles." The nutritionally and psychically correct New Age devotees prize their own trance induction and channeling music. (Is Prozac the psycho-musical equivalent of Muzak in elevators and malls?)

We all know the drill by now, having gone through the changes ourselves. Each generation salvages what artifacts remain from the last, then adds its own little twist to the hippie/punk/new wave/grunge variations. We don't complain, don't ask why, don't even blink, though perhaps we sometimes grit our teeth in frustration. For some reason, we also don't tell the new kids about our own experience, how we've "been there, done that," not as much because they won't listen but because they're convinced that the light only shines for them. Eventually they'll figure that one out, but not soon enough to break the cycle.

What alcohol did for earlier generations of adolescents, music and drugs do now. Whether we choose to avail ourselves of the knowledge their use and abuse provided (and continues to provide now), the ultimate questions revolve around not only how we initially came to our knowledge, but also the quality of our adolescent initiation rites—if not the skill of our guides. The manner in which the Beat/Head initiations of the fifties have been debased in the nineties is a case in point. Twenty-five or 30 years is a long enough span of time in which to examine the consequences of allowing these singular initiations to become, in effect, items of commerce.

In any case, even if the knowledge of those old maps is willfully repressed, discarded, or just neatly stored away in a dusty attic trunk in the Memory Palace, rest assured, the news and electronic fashion media will give us their version of the knowledge music formerly provided and will keep us abreast of the newest fashions in consciousness. We'll always know when heroin has again become chic among the art set or what's the right designer outfit to wear or designer drug to use on the techno/industrial noise club scene, but we'll never know why. That our media provides the wrong answers to the wrong questions seems to be a moot point in our world today. That's the sorrow and the pity of this continuing party, because it *should* deeply matter to us all.

Chapter 9

Don't Touch Me There

Whatever Happened to Foreplay?

Forty years on, rock and roll continues to claim to be about sex. It hasn't been about foreplay for a long while, a concept damn near dead in the nineties, and one wonders not only who killed it but when. Where can one find "make out" music these days? Not on MTV or VH-1, unless condom manufacturers are sponsoring the music buzz clip. On the other hand, there's an awful lot of jingle music to have sex to; pop and rock music accompany almost every form of sexual behavior imaginable, from heavy metal bondage/domination sex to disco sex (pass the poppers, please). The video gangsta-rap variation technically isn't about sex at all, but rather violence, where women are portrayed as willing victims. And when women are the rappers, the men become the beefcake objects of desire attired in their $700 sneakers, club jackets, and gold chains. At the opposite extreme is New Age music sex (or is it sex music?), which is ethereal, nonviolent, and androgenous, without a bottom or backbeat to it. And where's the fun in that?

Admittedly, all this talk seems rather quaint in a decade where children are having sex at younger and younger ages, when the average 8-year-old knows more about it than most 20-somethings a few decades ago, where teenage pregnancies in this most civilized of nations continue to be the meat and potatoes of political rhetoric and a social worker's nightmare. For all the music that's out there to accompany sexual activity, very little of it really seems to concern itself with the needs of foreplay or, for that matter, with the essence of sexual activity itself.

Foreplay was what adolescents of both sexes in the fifties practiced at slow dances to the accompaniment of "Teen Angel" heard over the tinny speakers of cheesy .45 record players or as they dry-humped in the back seats of their parent's cars at drive-in movies or in remote Lover's Lanes while watching the submarine races. Maybe foreplay would (or could) eventually lead to sex, and down the road to making love. Making love happened when two people who'd gotten over the surprise of having sex for the first time had actually discovered how to enjoy each other—but that's Foreplay 305 and we're still trying to deal with the concept of Foreplay 101 and 102. Foreplay (actually petting) was all there was for adolescents, an end unto itself. Within its confines, rules, and rituals, boys were allowed to turn into men and girls into women, and romantic love was always a possibility. It's not that way now; no one is supposed to be tentative, and either one has the mechanics down or one doesn't. He shoots, he Scores!! and there's no room whatsoever for the indeterminacies of the relationships between the sexes in the Post-Elvis Age. That's the problem with this brave new (old) age. "Foreplay? What's that?" I'm not advocating bringing back the fifties. God knows, but there were certain useful rituals back then that were helpful for easing one "into it," that primordial and timeless man/ woman thing.

For boys trying to be men back then, inevitably the whole of male/female relations revolved around "making out," which for guys before MTV dealt with baseball imagery as a working metaphor. Before hitting a "home run" became the norm, adolescent males contented themselves with "running the base paths." Making out was an art, hence the term "make-out artist," and, in many ways, when raised to the level of art, was a more exciting process than "making it"—if only because it lasted longer. That one could only find out after one had been "making out" for a while, but who really knew from that back then? Not men, and only a few women at least until the early seventies. Making out was so delicious precisely *because* each person was under a certain amount of restraint. Which was maddening for an adolescent because one logically didn't know where to go after getting all hot and bothered, all that blood pounding in your ears and you're fumbling about, frantically grinding away to "Teen Angel." There's no real room for stuff like that in the middle of a mosh pit, that kind of tentative, intimate touching; but then again, that's not the function of moshing for the predominance of men who do or the ladies who love them. Gotta have glove, I suppose.

"Making it" and "making out" were worlds removed for men; "making it" was a finite destination, a 3-minute can-you-dance-to-it kind of thing, all very digital, an act with neither mystery or ritual attached. "Making out," on the other hand, was very analog in nature, and that came with the ritual that preceded it: the ritual grope at the movies or in the back seats of cars. And the music of that time was music to fumble to while contemplating and trying to deal with *the rules*. Here in an age when there are virtually no rules, limits, or rituals, having rules took on, in retrospect, an erotic content. In more innocent times, those rituals involved heavy petting and dealing with many layers of clothing, removing the ceremonial panty girdle (which gives away how old the ritual really is). Maybe clothing was the key to the eternal female mystery, the labyrinth of the Great Mother.

Suffice it to say, adolescent foreplay revolved around uninformed gradualism. Guys never went from meeting somebody even to kissing without going through the appropriate rituals. Whatever you "got" was significant: a first date peck on the cheek, even a handshake would do for speculation's sake for "the time being." Which seemed an eternity in high school on Monday, when you wanted to know who you'd be with on Friday or Saturday night. Men/boys extrapolated what women/girls wanted from their "field research"; in retrospect a laughable concept consisting of hurried and/or wildly inaccurate conferences with friends about getting to "second base," what happened when caught stealing third (that situation where a girl would let you french kiss her but you couldn't get her bra off while doing so). Rituals, those little rules!, the mechanics and intricacies of female impedimenta! Those little hooks were difficult for clumsy lust-crazed fingers turning thumbs to dislodge in the heat of the moment. Definitely it was uncool to rip these contraptions off, traumatizing your date and yourself in the process—with the whole of the second balcony looking on.

True, by the early seventies, some women decided no longer to wear bras—as a political statement, mind; something was gained, undeniably and momentarily, but something was also lost in the foreplay area. (These days, though, it appears that undergarments are back in vogue, at least if we can extrapolate from the number of Victoria's Secret, Frederick's of Hollywood, and trashy lingerie stores there seem to be springing up in local malls throughout the country.) So getting the bra off was part of that ritual, but girls had to let you take it off, or at least help when the confident hand slipped to hopeless fumbling. During these strained eternities, when locked into an emotional hyperspace, no one spoke: Thoughts reverberated, check lists were consulted as one's well-programmed but maxed-out emotional computers scanned data banks weighing experience against past research. There was something to be said for research nonetheless.

But back in that early rock and roll time, the largest part of foreplay was spent learning about kissing and slow dancing, the most fun to learn, especially at parties where everyone else was more or less doing the same thing with varying degrees of success. You had to wait until a ladies' choice or a spotlight dance, or any slow dance and then *ask her*, the culmination of yet another set of foreplay rules fraught with a different set of variables. But say one got over that hurdle, in theory with a slow dance, one could be allowed (and maybe even encouraged) to practice and refine those techniques however they were acquired. To be honest and perfectly clear here, guys back then never really knew what girls were thinking. (For that matter, guys today *still* don't, only they project their 'tude better about it all. At the same time, the only reason men might know anything is that women are more vocal, but that doesn't mean that men know what women are *thinking*—they might think they do now, but they don't.) In the land of foreplay, thinking didn't take place on the level of language, but rather in the joint wordless, tactile exploration of a shared netherworld of moist silences, kissing, and slow dancing.

168

I was lucky back then to find a girl who liked me well enough to talk about the whole business to show me how to slow dance because I was such a cluck at it. Especially the technique of how to use my hands to deliberately (if apparently innocently) roam the female back to allow "the energy" build-up. This and more she showed me as we slow-danced in her rec room when her mother was out shopping one afternoon. (Not only was she a good dancer but also a *great* kisser.) The varieties of kissing! The open-mouthed kiss, the clenched-teeth kiss, and the variations in between. You knew you were striking out when you hit

clenched teeth instead of moist lips. Sometimes you kissed off
center then had to sort of work your way around. First kisses on
first dates (assuming you had the opportunity) were problematic,
especially that lead-in, which always seemed to be on the order
of "ah ... goodnight," and you'd steal a quick one before vanishing into the night ... if she let you, for sometimes it took a
few dates before she would. There were all these other steps and
stages to go before "the deed" could have some meaning. Maybe
I'd find out in college.

True, in the evenings from 7:30 to 11:30, the college library
assumed an air of academic eroticism, where footsies under the
table was the fore-foreplay to passing notes, to coffee dates, etc.,
etc., etc. More pitfalls. And if you really were crazy and obsessed
with minute movements, you could very well wind up playing
footsies with a chair leg. Which was embarrassing, but only to
you. Then there were "study dates," which expanded how you
dealt with women in terms of ritual. In college, girls were still
girls, in the sense that the big wet silence still existed.

169

Late sixties psychedelic and early seventies art rock, even if
now considered by some revisionists to be culturally incorrect,
was a boon to foreplay, far more useful for rec room fumbling
than those well-tempered slick Brill Building ditties back in the
fifties. This was especially true for those long instrumental jams
like the Chambers Brothers' anthem "Time (Has Come)." Significant others (though the list can be exhaustive as well as highly
idiosyncratic) included, of course, the Rolling Stones' "Goin'
Home" from their classic midsixties' album *Aftermath*. Mavin
Gaye's "Sexual Healing" and "What's Goin On," and of course Led
Zeppelin's "Stairway to Heaven," a world-class bit of make-out
music if ever there was one. But while foreplay was given a
larger musical context in which to "work" as an environmental
aid for seduction (or whatever was passing for it), the Age of Liberation and Aquarius dawned, bringing with it an ideology intent
on doing away with all forms of inhibiting sexual rituals. Along
with sexism and male chauvinism in all its forms, foreplay, like
God around the same time, was officially declared dead, or if not
dead, then null and void. Damn, I'd just spent all those years per-
fecting my technique!

To be honest, the idea of "loving the one you're with," sappy as it sounds to youth today, when coupled with a wider use of the Pill, almost made foreplay an afterthought. There was lots of *talk* about sex, which everyone claimed to be having however they chose to have it. Everything was allowed: straight, gay, swinging, any kind of sex as long as it didn't cause a murder. It came down to "our bodies, ourselves," however "body" was defined. The neoscientific age was born; the messy age of hormonal humanism was officially in eclipse. Along with the new paradigms for sexual behavior came an inordinate amount of discussion about sexism in rock music among the females who'd formerly been the objects of lust and/or veneration, love or repulsion, but really (as always) approach and avoidance among the men. It was no big secret that the Rolling Stones had made a brilliant career out of their misogyny, as did lots of other groups; good rockin' for some, but where was the line going to be drawn between good old-fashioned rock and roll and new-fashioned ideological correctness? And exactly who was going to draw the line? Manuals abounded to herald the new age, for it was assumed not only that people had forgotten how to make love, but also to whom. (*How to Prolong Climax, How to Make Foreplay. The Joy of Straight Sex, The Joys of Gay Sex, The Consumer's Guide to Self-Abuse, The Harried Guide to Swinging*, or even *The Militant Feminist's Guide to Doctrinally Pure Sex* were never really written, but they might well have been, merely to get around the unscientific and uncomfortable predispositions of foreplay.) If all that doesn't kill foreplay dead, nothing can!

Though foreplay was officially and insistently declared dead by those in the know, vast numbers of people in the hinterlands still hadn't gotten the message. In the Aquarian Age, sex was again or still a commodity, and in terms of consumer satisfaction, no different than a color TV, a new car, a home computer. As with any other consumer product, sex, unlike foreplay, predicated on the expectation that what you put in you should be able to get out (with exception of some women and men who, once you put it in or it was put in to you, you'll never get it out, but this isn't an essay about bondage and domination, a discussion that can be left to the structuralists and deconstructionists in the audience). Maybe we had rock and roll to blame for all of this (and many did blame it), or perhaps that shows how materialism enervates the soul, as de Tocqueville has said elsewhere in this book.[1] That's what happens when there's too much official information. One wonders what he would have written about American adolescents today.

In the late sixties and middle seventies, though, sex, drugs, and rock and roll took the place of foreplay. In retrospect, this may have been the result of a male fantasy that drugs made sex better, presupposing that men and women functioned in the same ways on the same drugs. Back in the Age of Psychedelia, it was assumed that if you dropped acid or mescaline with someone you loved, at least there was a kind of spiritual altruism at play, an emotional/mystical wish that surely it was possible to share an instinctual universe provided both people "peaked" at the same time. Not the case at all, and on further examination, not really such a transcendent psychedelic truth either, since, for the most part, women didn't need psychedelics as they functioned on another level entirely. It is equally true in retrospect that this idea may have been predicated on an essentially male version of the way women's psyches worked, and furthermore, it was *the men* who needed the drugs to break down their own emotional doors of perception. And even if this notion was misguided, it beat the hell out of sex divorced from any sort of emotional involvement at all. Most women were already definitely A-1 out there, thank you very much, Mr. Owsley. Give a woman a hit of Orange Sunshine and you'd never be able to catch up.

171

Did New Age sex come without foreplay? Was it "Love me, love my dogma?" Yes, because the doctrine that supplanted muzzy sixties emotional altruism was disco, a form of music and a social ideology antithetical to the concept of foreplay. Instead of having relationships, one "partied" at the disco, where one had sex in an industrially controlled environment. And not even on the dance floor, but in the toilet (somehow fitting, that). There was no reason to go to the toilet at the disco save to get loaded or have sex, or both. *Everyone* knew that you "went" before you came (depending on your sexual preference, of course). You didn't even have to take your clothes off for disco sex; that was reduced to a kind of impersonal sexual shorthand of fellatio, the blow-job favored by straight and gay men, though this depended on the class of disco one frequented. A snort of

Peruvian marching powder, a quick blow-job, was an act of sexual consumerism that required little emotional commitment and absolutely no foreplay. There was a certain high school aura to doin' it in the bathroom, much like smoking in the boys' or girls' room in high school for earlier ages—times change not much. The disco world was all about the moment. People didn't go to discos to find love but to get laid. Oh, you went to psychedelic dances or peace rallies in the sixties to get laid too, but usually you went somewhere else to do that—your place or mine.

If the late sixties was all about making love and foreplay, the seventies was all about having sex. The sixties may have been about liberation, but the seventies was about license—that you could do whatever you wanted to do with whoever you wanted to do it, and that was all right. One's sexuality was a matter of personal choice, and a fashion statement too. In short, the seventies had brought out the swinging singles mentality, which proposed object love: You made love to someone to prove that you could, not because you enjoyed it. Who knew or cared what women wanted? Who cared what anybody wanted for that matter; a therapy would present itself later on, along with better drugs to dull the pain of concept sex. The age of glam rock and disco sure may have appeared to be a wonderful whirl of fashion, but to adolescents just coming into their own sexual knowledge it merely confused matters more precisely because there were no rules, there was no emotional anteroom, no foreplay.

It did appear, to me at least, that the "New Age" feminism of the late sixties that rose to meet the challenges of liberation and whose effects are still being debated a quarter century later initially robbed women of their singularity. Perhaps this loss of individuality was useful from a doctrinaire point of view, but from the idea of old-fashioned romance, it was totally misleading and nonproductive. Doctrinaire feminism substituted a joyless, humorless, spiritual materialism for sensuality. Wasn't foreplay a humanist rather than a feminist or an economic issue? So now it was okay for women to pleasure themselves but no longer for men to pleasure women—what was happening?

For the conscious men in this heady age of self-knowledge and liberation, foreplay with newly entitled feminists at best

was a chancy proposition, more uncomfortable than any fumbling they'd done at the submarine races a decade or so before.
Whatever a man did or didn't say, do or didn't do, was scrutinized according to the latest ironclad ukases on sexism. And if
one wasn't particularly a male chauvinist at the beginning of
the evening, there was the possibility of becoming a raving one
at the end just for spite. The result was that men became even
more confused, since they were still enamored of the mysticism,
magic, and romance they thought women personified. Men
had been trying to solve the riddle of women for aeons, even if
sometimes the results proved fatal, as Eric Newman remarked
in his seminal study *The Great Mother* when he noted that "the
numerous princesses who present riddles to be solved do indeed
kill their unsuccessful suitors. But they do so only in order to
give themselves willingly to the victor, whose superiority, shown
by his solving of the riddle, redeems the princess herself, who
is the riddle"[2] At last there weren't going to be any more riddles
for men to solve. Who needed women to personify them? To
become them? To pose them? But what was happening to the
vital connection between men and women in the process?

Did feminists want to bore all men to death with no mystery
or ritual? Apparently, but *like*-mindedness was just as constrict-
ing and ultimately frustrating as *no*-mindedness. Apparently
those men who were drawn to the mystery of women were on
to something that women possessed and had presided over for
aeons. Mystery was always the biggest selling point of full womanhood, even with the great Female Acid archetype. Meanwhile,
there were plenty of arguments surfacing that definitively proved
that foreplay was an invidious form of sexually exploitative male
behavior, though exactly who was exploiting whom was never
really satisfactorily spelled out. For a time the message was who
needed men anyway—sisterhood was beautiful provided everyone read from the same press release. Foreplay was either 20
minutes of begging and pleading or a total hype.

When foreplay was declared dead and then reinvented as a
form of socialist sexual egalitarianism, female individuality was
sacrificed. Unfortunately, these new authoritarians overlooked
the fact that instead of rules, women just needed encouragement. Inevitably, feminist rhetoric expanded into the same

dismal and ultimately dumb rhetorical and totalitarian spaces into which leftist male politics had sunk long ago. And how much finger-pointing or guilt-tripping could men endure before a reaction set in? Foreplay, who cares, we don't even have an arena in which to establish a dialogue, said the men who also wanted to evolve. Happily these days, an increasing percentage of women are starting to realize that their "official" stereotypes were just as chauvinist and humanly counterproductive and that men *and* women seek singular satisfactions: hugs, rubs, and companionship. If sex was merely a specific object-oriented consumer good, then sex itself was a barren and soul-enervating exercise.

For all the talk about feminism in the late sixties and early seventies, ironically about the only place where any progress was being made in terms of equality was within the field of rock and roll. Though in some ways hidden under the rubric of "publicity assistant" or "management assistant," women exercised considerable influence. In bands, either women were back-up singers or fronts, rarely musicians on their own. However, it was in the field of rock journalism, formerly a closed shop, where women came into their own. These early pioneers were in a class by themselves, and woe to the man—or for that matter the group—who told them differently! Without benefit of doctrine, unique creations all, these ambitious and fearsomely intelligent women gave as good as they got, to overcome the goddess/groupies stereotype. To be taken seriously by not only their male colleagues but also by the musicians themselves, they had to beat the men at their own sexist game because like it or not, rock and roll had always been a boy's club. These literary ladies could and frequently did out-smoke, out-drink, and sometimes even out-fuck their male counterparts. Some musicians mistakenly thought that if they managed to bed the lady journalist, they'd be assured good reviews. Nothing particularly novel in that thought; some things never change in profile tabloid journalism. Though a lead singer (or lead guitarist or drummer) might or might not be able to perform in the sack, if he failed to deliver on stage, a negative review was the rule, not the exception; so whatever temporary marginal utility performers thought they were gaining over the journalistic process evaporated in a New York minute. Men were men, women were women; but art was art, which most of these rock and roll women journalists never thought of confusing with publicity—something their male counterparts had a habit of doing all the time.

It might appear that the rules have changed in the nineties, but no one has apparently been successful in convincing generations of adolescent males of the fact. They still insist on the same male fantasies that certain forms of rock and roll continue to provide, regardless of what media feminists would like to think. What continues to be offered at least visually and lyrically is the same old product: sex without the courtship ritual attached—which is what foreplay was supposed to provide. Modern entertainers like Madonna play by those old rules, while academic feminists fail to realize that she's not an avatar or creature of their ideology but purely of show business's. And as for the music video sex that bundles her public image, that seems to be just too product- and image-specific to be of much use save as a "self-help" aid. After a while it's all too much of a set piece, the imagery too standardized to allow any room for foreplay, which deals with uncertainties and shades of meaning.

Enough already with chromium motorcycle sluts of various genders in bondage leathers, boots, and garter belts cavorting in pseudo-Gothic dungeons or after-hours clubs or homeboys in their Beamers airing out their bitches in the 'hood. That's not even sex, it's power whose visions have been approved by the OPA (Orgasmic Protection Agency). In music video sex-land there's no room for representations of silences, hugs, and rubs anymore, just more polemics and more manuals for accessing the industrial commodity, not to mention more psychiatrists who specialize in sexual dysfunctions, more naked paper women, more MTV cybersex, more phone sex. No room for rituals here save of the industrial kind.

Though it is said that pop music is about romance while rock and roll is about sex, neither seems to address the issue that women, plain and simple, want to be appreciated for themselves, not held up against a chauvinist checklist of predigested specifications. It appears that women need to be treated with the respect due their position as the other half of the divine equation, so that in sex and in love a third more powerful entity evolves— that state that emerges when, in the middle of love-making, time ceases to exist and a delicious deep wet blackness descends, the kind of experience that reduces partners to a state of astonishment, the "what-was-that?" experience. There's no liberation in the rock and roll music world if sex is reduced to one specific vision or a series of specific visions.

Many years ago *Esquire* magazine published a survey about the perfect woman. No one was surprised that the respondent males wanted someone to take care of the kids, to look presentable, to entertain, do the chores, balance the books, clean up the kiddie poo, pick up the laundry … in short, a wife. Everyone wants one of those, including most women, and why not? That men appear to want a slave, not an ally, shows how frightened they are of themselves, how imprisoned they've become by their own roles that media feminism has foisted upon them. It's also a little sad to think that men want their lives transformed by the *service* not the *love* of a good woman, that men prefer to be maintained in their weakness. And, of course, most men don't understand that male chauvinism is an outmoded industrial concept that is not only psychically damaging but also financially ruinous, especially these days. In truth, women lose their natural transformatory powers by assuming the roles that doctrinaire feminists would like them to play, by ignoring the fact that good sex takes place among equals, not those habituated to roles. Is it any wonder that newsstands are glutted with pictures of buttered buns and air-brushed breasts on MTV vision of women? Whores or goddesses or just regular gals. Still, selling women using men's rules to do it is how music works in the nineties, like it or not.

176

People need more mystery and less science and industry. When a large industrial power is totally involved with sex as an industrial commodity, where is pleasure? If the object of all this technology is to make what is natural into a commodity, people would be better off in politics. It's really the politician's delusion that sex for money is somehow better than freely given sex, but considering what most politicians want a hooker to do to them, is it any wonder they have to pay for it? Everyone knows that working girls never get their due. But if they weren't doing their jobs, we'd all probably have a lot more wars so that politicians could watch. It must be a sign of status to be able to pay for sex, but I guess paying for it somehow makes it seem all right.

Militant feminists have been saying so for a decade or more, what's to disagree?

So while sex has become inextricably tied to politics, romance remains an uncomfortable emotional issue—along with the difficulty of separating love and romance from politics. Rock and roll has always skated on thin ice here; it used to be about foreplay and courtship, but we no longer have any time for those things. If one makes love with the idea of making a political statement, as it seems people have doing lately, then the end result will be unsatisfactory: concept love, gimme some of that concept love. Concept love really doesn't keep you warm at night. If lovers started off as friends first, they'd still have something after the love gave out; any relationship that doesn't have friendship as its basis is doomed to failure anyway. The big lie that pop and rock music continue to promote is that most men are convinced that friendship is impossible with women and that the only way to deal with them is as objects to be manipulated, used (and therefore abused). In truth good friends don't play those kinds of games. If men started off having friendship instead of sexual mastery at the root of their interactions with the opposite sex, they'd be far happier with the results, because friendship can lead to the intelligent man, and evolution takes place.

177

Getting "the woman's point of view" is always helpful when navigating through, getting over, or even starting a love affair. By talking *with*, not *at*, women, one learns about other women and how they perceive men. One learns how to see with the heart instead of the eyes too. And it's amazing just how many women feel limited by the physical body, why they're all so naturally drawn toward the occult. "Gee, I didn't know she had a brain," say men who've evolved to the next level of awareness. Men need to understand that it's just as devastating to be related to by a woman as a hunk with balls. Our bodies, ourselves? Hardly.

It's a shame that Americans have forgotten how useful rituals were for getting to know someone, for breaking the ice, for easing the tensions that allowed nascent feelings to blossom. At the same time, this emphasis on the marginal utility of foreplay has paradoxically lead to increased frigidity and fear; one doesn't tune the string of the violin unless one is prepared to play the tune. How humane and enlightened can a society be if it abolishes foreplay in the name of progress or leaves it to psychiatrists, magazines, sexual politicians, or even rock and roll music, when it makes much more sense to return to simpler pleasures and sensations, to re-create the feeling of that first tentative kiss wherever or whenever it was, no matter how embarrassed one might have been.

Chapter 10

White Punks on Dope

Why Camille Paglia Is Academe's Answer to Betty Page

I too think the intellectual should constantly disturb, should bear witness to the misery of the world, should be provocative by being independent, should rebel against all hidden and open pressure and manipulations, should be the chief doubter of systems, of power, and its incantations, should be witness to their mendacity. For this reason, an intellectual cannot fit into any role that may be assigned to him . . . An intellectual essentially doesn't fit into any pigeonhole completely.

—**Vaclav Havel**[1]

A new generation is coming on the scene. . . . They won't use your knowledge and they will call you "sick" and "way-out" and that will be a sad day, but we must be prepared for it. For on that day they will have abandoned the other world they came here with and will become mundanists, pragmatists and concretists. They will shout loudly about soul because they will have lost it. And their protests will be a shriek, A manic sound. That's just the way it goes, brothers.

—**Ishmael Reed**[2]

When *Mumbo Jumbo*, Ishmael Reed's satiric novel about the twenties' Harlem Renaissance and black and white history appeared in 1972, it was hailed for its fantastical free-wheeling take on American culture. Within the context of those truly psychedelic multicultural times of late sixties and early seventies, the novel was a perfect prism for examining black history, with its sharp-focus sidebars and divagations on his favorite areas of interest: Egyptology and the Osiris myths, voodoo, jazz and the birth of the blues, Masonic conspiracies, ofay hipsters and hepcats, left- and right-hand path magic and mysticism, plus of course (and always underneath as the beat) the struggle of good and evil, themes he still explores today. Though a book of its time, nevertheless, it was timeless in its cultural sweep and in its evocation of the living spirit of American history, segregated as well as integrated, a present with a presence of the past and using the twenties in Harlem to take a snapshot of America *in media res.*

It's not an anachronistic stretch even now to imagine Abdul's diatribe to Papa LaBas (see Ishmal Reed's epigraph above) coming from any of the participants in the debate over multiculturalism or any number of other evanescent intellectual flavor-of-the-month debates raging today. Reed took no prisoners then, figuring no doubt that he'd covered the subject, but almost a quarter-century later he has returned to the debate with *Japanese by Spring*, a picaresque novel of academia about the illuminating journey of a black professor. Charles "Chappy" Puttbutt, in his pursuit of tenure. Existing uneasily in the inter-disciplinary metaspace between the departments of English and African studies, Puttbutt has managed to keep himself as inoffensively aloof as possible while walking the ideological tightrope, much to the annoyance of his erstwhile colleagues who are always in need of allies in their interdepartmental struggles. In the turbulent atmosphere of Oakland University, though the good professor by dint of continually re-creating and reinventing himself has dodged many bullets and is now up for tenure, the forces of contradictory ideologies are conspiring against him.

By happy accident, while studying Japanese to improve his job prospects in case he *is* canned. Puttbutt is taken under the wing of his language instructor, actually the frontman for a Japanese business consortium with designs on his university (cultural conspiracies are nothing new within Reed's cosmology). Because of Chappy's eminent ideological pliability as departmental outsider, when the coup goes down, he becomes his mentor's chief administrative assistant. Instead of the ass kisser, he becomes the kissee in charge of promotion as well as the arbiter of future departmental agendas. Faced with all this power after being the interdepartmental *shlemozel* for so long, Puttbutt has a revelation and opts out of the whole program just as the conspiracy fails. The students finally mobilize after years of passive acceptance of their teachers' constant head games, and things almost return to status quo ante. Puttbutt shuffles off to Buffalo, or maybe it's Hawaii, end of novel, end.

182

After dismissing Puttbutt's self-involved world of academic specialization, which is solely preoccupied with merchandizing and commodifying the theoretical myopia of the moment, Reed added an Afterword, a personal epiphany on multicultural America he experienced on a spring day in Oakland, California, at a large ethnic festival of food and dance. Outside the Ivory Tower lived the authentic unmediated ethnicity of the "real" people, and here he poetically and succinctly provided the perspective the novel lacked. With this premeditated though unexpected act of literary and creative sabotage, Reed implied that the old civilities and literary conventions that formerly governed the academic world have broken down, and the postmodern forms*that are

---

* There is no point getting into an argument about what "postmodernism" really means, because half the fun of the term is writing about it, and writing, and writing. It's like some kind of universal decontextualized widget. It could be alternatively called the "present present," which is modified by variable contemporary media, or even "the corruptible future present," but it's still just another convenient nonspecific packaging metaphor trying to sup-

supposed to replace them are incoherent and divisive, with con- tradictory and criminal consequences for those involved within and without the academy.

Again what makes *Japanese by Spring* so entertaining is that like most of his other novels, Reed's satiric vision informs as well as entertains the reader. Sprinkled throughout this narrative (and essential too!) are barbed and explicit observations on Japanese culture and language and American Far Eastern foreign policy, as well as the linguistic and philosophic quirks of Yoruba language and culture (he is talking about African-American cultural studies after all). Much like *Mumbo Jumbo*, this novel is also an instamatic of contemporary multicultural American experience. However, this richly intriguing tapestry is contrasted and filtered through the tunnel vision of contemporary academia where Puttbutt plies his trade. It is a world of status-obsessed intellectuals engaged in ideological turf wars to promote their ascendence to the pinnacle of the ever-changing Theoretical Top 100 List, a world where the satisfaction of mentoring students is small beer compared to the rush of instant celebrity that comes with being a Theory Expert, a featured and well-remunerated speaker at academic conferences, someone with *serious grown-up power* capable of commanding large study grants or corporate sponsorship for an *institute* as a well as an agent to book celebrity appearances.

It is a world where everyone is fighting everyone else for a piece of the ideological pie and its attendant spoils. In Puttbutt's case, that means in his immediate universe everyone from the high-fiving, jive-talking, dashiki-wearing head of African studies who's afraid he's losing his touch with the younger "bros" in the 'hood to his owlish English department counterpart, who's worried whether his PC quotient is sufficient to deal with the feminists who control the gender and women's studies subdivision

---

plant terms like The Jazz Age, The Aspirin Age, The Silent Generation, The Beat Generation, The Blank Generation, and of course The X-Generation, a generic adjectival phrase that categorizes ideas, trends, and attitudes that haven't come into being yet. Postmodernism is probably one of the more egregious and newest of "weasel words" coined by academe yet. It certainly provides work for a lot of people (I wish it kept them thinking) and encourages them to fistfight at conferences and in the pages of journals, doesn't it?

and who themselves are intent on deconstructing the English department from inside out to promote their unique but equally myopic vision of American cultural life. This is a creepy world of ideological coups and countercoups that makes the Stalinist purge trials of the late thirties a comparative pink tea. Quite obviously, it's not a happy place to work and it's begging for a strong hand to put it out of its misery and start over, exactly what the conspirators have in mind.

It's easy to dismiss *Japanese by Spring* as just another academic novel, since writers have been using higher education as a fictional backdrop for years (those who work within and without it, from Kingsley Amis's *Lucky Jim to* Richard Farina's *Been Down So Long It Looks Like Up To Me* to David Lodge's *Changing Places* and *Small World* to most recently Robert Grudin's *Book*). It's a great format to use to get it all off one's chest, to indulge in some merciless lampooning of one's enemies, to right wrongs, to settle old scores, and, in the process, to endow one's allies (friends and lovers) with godlike qualities. If it's cleverly done, there's no foul, no fault, and nothing changes really.

If the satire is too transparent, you're in trouble and you be gone. At the worst this means being exiled to some kind of academic Siberia after being publicly drummed out of the fellowship, your writing slate broken and your academic gown rent by your departmental chair during an open faculty senate meeting. Barring that you may find a horse head in your bed one evening with a courtesy card from the Faculty Club.

On the other hand, if you're well-known and ornery enough, you'll be the new kick-me icon, target practice for sniping "think" pieces in mainstream literary magazines, Sunday morning TV talk shows, or ivory tower interdisciplinary institutional journals.

Ishmael Reed *has* tenure and *is* ornery by nature; his metaphorical back, like Moby Dick's, is mottled by an intricate network of overgrown scar tissue composed of broken-off harpoons, the detritus from all the hits he's taken for his outspokenness over the years. His is no ordinary academic novel by any stretch of the imagination, since for the Ish, these are not normal times. In attempting to cast the academy wars in a satiric light, he winds up demolishing the whole convention by inserting himself into his own book, though by trashing his work, he succeeds in bringing to the reader a more immediate sense of the desperation he feels at the current situation on American college campuses.

Instead of providing and encouraging an intellectual climate in which debates about meanings are welcomed, where open-ended conclusions are arrived at, in Puttbutt's world, and by extension in the world of higher education in general, debates center around the meaning of meanings, or better, the meaning of the *appearance* of meanings, though both are in reality nothing more than a marketeers' quest for designer packaging (or repackaging, as is so often the case). These days there is only information to be gleaned, insight is transitory and peripheral, an add-on. It's more the stuff of the smoke and mirrors, this business of consumer advertising for market dominance, and less a case of even-handed scholarship than the emphasis on the "cutting-edge" celebrity endorsement that confers a spurious authority.

If we follow Reed's view further, in this "hot" media world it just won't do for a teacher of undergraduates to say that there are no definitive answers to philosophical or ethical problems, only questions and approaches, despite the fact that society at large is predisposed to the belief and expectation that not only does everything have quantifiable answers, but there are invariant "right" ones to which exact formulas can be applied as an alchemical solvent. It's questionable science, if indeed that's the point, and even worse pedagogy. It's also a rude awakening for young minds who have been previously indoctrinated otherwise in primary and secondary school to be told by those from whom they hope to become credentialed that education broadens the periphery of one's ignorance, and accordingly that learning is a lifelong process, where a B.A. opens the door instead of closing it. Anyway, that's not what their parents or they themselves are paying for, is it? Practical useful knowledge for the money—right?

Higher education should be a dangerous and heady drug, a liberating experience though not when reduced to the marketplace where ideas themselves become nothing more than staged events, set pieces that the performer uses for entertainment.[3] If the pursuit of knowledge is nothing more than an exercise in professorial performance art, then it reinforces in students' minds that ideas have no validity outside of their immediate utility as entertainment, and thus in the same way one comparison shops for cars, one can comparison shop for ideas, from which follows the assumption that like any other consumer good, one can "trade up" or "retool" the engine of ideology. Higher education in this light is nothing more than a slightly advanced version of the high school life adjustment curriculum that has been an intellectual tonic in public secondary school education since the fifties, whose basis, as intellectual historian Richard Hofstader observed, is

> the more immediately usable an item of knowledge is, the more readily it can be taught. The value of a school subject can be measured by the number of immediate, actual life situations to which it directly applies. The important thing, then, is not to teach pupils how to generalize, but to supply them directly with the information they need for daily living—for example, to teach them, not physiology, but how to keep physically fit.[4]

If we take Reed's satirical riffs "to the bridge," so to speak, he's pointing out that to carry over this view to higher education for whatever misguided motives is criminal and intellectually dishonest, because it ignores the profound long-term consequences not only for the undergraduates who eventually leave the academy, but also for the teachers (who should know better) who, by giving in, have broken faith with their craft and disregarded what they know in their hearts to be true. By promoting their own fashionable orthodoxies, they have reduced scholarship to an arena of competing products arrayed in the upscale mall of higher education. In doing so, they consciously reinforce the idea that higher learning requires nothing more than the comparison shopper's ability to make the "right" choices from the "right" answers that are already conveniently premixed and predigested for them. If this line of reasoning is carried to its logical conclusion, colleges and universities will be nothing more than purveyors of consumer guides whose diplomas eventually will be imprinted with expiration dates on the backs of the sheepskins—nice and convenient, but no cigar. Why?

This intellectual *fait accompli* encourages students to be lazy, spoiled, and intolerant, while promoting a lifelong cynicism for any kind of intellectual activity save for that which can be digested in a 20-second MTV buzz clip. Though students somehow survive and even thrive in this system, the end result robs them of their powers of discernment as well as their ability to think and reason on their own. They are cut loose, set adrift at sea with a defective compass that knows no true north. In short, academics are being honorable neither to their higher calling nor to their students, and honor is the glue that cements the compact between professors and students. It does not lie in rhetorical posturings, facile ratiocinations, or ideological marriages of convenience that ignore long-term consequences. Maybe it's not the loss of honor after all, but rather a lack of brass balls, since it takes incredible courage to tilt against an official educational ideology as well as a culture in which students are rewarded, encouraged to be, in the words of Benjamin J. Barber, "society smart rather than school smart . . . [where] their teachers in that world, the nation's true pedagogues, are television, advertising, movies, politics, and the celebrity domains they define."[5]

It's a tough audience to please, this postmodern student bunch who are comparison-shopping for cutting-edge informercials, for zappy bon mots to download to their disks. Maybe this is progress after all, and it's a good thing that academics have found a method for enlivening their formerly fusty profession by expropriating the trappings of the hot media world of art. It may appear to be a much sexier universe with more perks, better girls (boys), and money than working as an intellectual, a solitary thinker/teacher; it's the American dream perhaps having it all, but they've only got it half right. Blinded by the klieg lights of momentary media celebrity, they miss the downside that is the killer.

It is a profoundly antiintellectual world in which they ply the trade of thinking within a society predicated on a decontextualized present; it requires courage to go against the grain, to encourage reflection and the importance of living in the present informed by the presence of the past. It takes a foolhardy kind of chutzpa once the rules of the road have been lodged, but anything less is unacceptable if academics really want to assume their duties as serious intellectuals. If academics wish to portray themselves as performance artists, then they must also accept the transient politics of the art world that thrives on com-modification and celebrity as well as its dangers like other savvy pragmatist "artists" whose lifestyles they wish to expropriate. According to Richard Schickel in *Intimate Strangers: The Culture of Celebrity*, he (or she) falls into celebrity trap via the publicizing process

> [which] gives him a status in the society that he might not have found in other eras, a sort of demi-heroism. [which] at the same time denies him that later heroism that a life self-sacrificingly devoted to his calling formerly conferred, especially on creators who were understood to be ahead in their time—a posterity of truly heroic proportions, which proportions can only be shaped out of mystery.[6]

When mainlined into the academic world, this publicity process devalues whatever knowledge teachers have a handle on and is, in effect, a conscious repudiation of the ideals they had before the theory dance started a decade or so ago, when the pickings and perks were leaner, when being an intellectual meant something to people like Vaclev Havel, who, to borrow a cliché from another sexy media world, the music business, had to "suffer to play the blues," and who courageously accepted that suffering as the price one pays for getting out of, in the words of Bob Dylan in yet another context, "going through all these things twice." Maybe it's simply a matter of consumer satisfaction that there's no longer any kick in being a guide and mentor. Possibly it's just an old-fashioned intellectual elitist conceit that has been replaced by something more au courant, newer, and deadlier, a marketplace elitism, as Richard Schickel notes "in which all success is measured quantitatively rather than qualitatively and critically."[7] Ars longa, pecunia longer? Who's to choose and who's to lose?

188

On a more basic level, though, this is a death wish of gigantic and tragic proportions, a bad game where everyone collegially lies to feel better while everyone loses big time: professors, students, and society. There is nothing sadder and more pathetic than being a victim of fashion. It may be the stuff of future talk shows from pop culture pundits or psychologists who service the sartorially and culturally challenged in the upper echelons of California, New York, or Chicago; surely the Internet bulletin board will be abuzz in some backwater road-house on the information superhighway eventually or even now. Be that as it may, it's still criminal to support a system that makes the difficult and frustrating search for knowledge irrelevant. If higher education is to serve higher ends instead of merely being a white collar cre- dentialing mill in the postindustrial age, then college professors need to resubscribe and/or renew their faith in the Havel doctrine or else they wind up taking the heat from Abdul's progeny and become casualties themselves when some new game package or flashier huckster comes along to displace them. It may mean getting lower collective marks on student evaluation sheets for demanding quality work, but it's a risk that must be assumed.

Lest anyone think these kinds of arguments or observations are of our current coinage at the end of this century, one could do no better than to refer to those of educator, social scientist, and founder of Clark University, G. Stanley Hall (see Chapter 5, "Play School"). Gainsayers will protest no doubt that Hall's observations are invalid because he was writing about adolescence at the end of the nineteenth century, before electronic mass media changed everything and everybody, or because he was a friend and colleague of William James, he "shrouded the social problems of adolescence in the pseudoscientific jargons of psychology and biology"[8] (and so much for James too!). They will roll their eyes and point out Hall was also a contemporary of progressive educator and thinker John Dewey, who's an official nonperson now save on ceremonial occasions or, I suspect, and more to the point, that Granville Stanley Hall was just plain elitist and as everyone knows, elitism is not PC in these final decades of the Century of the Common Man. Hall's adolescents may or may not have worn knickers and parted their hair down the middle or been media-challenged, but even back then, good college teachers still knew what they had to do to ignite the spark of adolescent intellectual curiosity—as the good ones do today.

Hall wrote from a kinder, gentler sense of academic time and perspective, less publicity- and celebrity-ridden, true, but nevertheless his thoughts have direct resonance today for those who embrace the idea that with each new generation of undergraduates there is new hope for society, and it is the duty of the college teacher to act as its midwife. It is to speak to this spirit of intellectual renewal and evolution that college teaching aspires and that does not lie in the promulgation of transient fashions or in being intoxicated by the drug of momentary celebrity. When one says aloud to a group of questing minds, "I don't know, but let's see how we can find it out," instead of "It's in the book (or video)," that love of learning and inquiry is passed on. In the present tense atmosphere of huckstering and posturing, it's refreshing to find someone like Hall who laid it on the line even if a century ago:

> If professors made it always a point of honor to confess and never conceal the limitation of their knowledge, would scorn all pretense of it, place credit for originality frankly where it belongs, teach no creeds they do not profoundly believe, or topics in which they are not interested, and withhold nothing from those who want the truth, they could from this vantage with more effect bring students to feel that the laziness [the characteristic student apathy toward "doing the reading before the lecture" many professors meet on a daily basis], that while outwardly conforming does no real inner work, that getting a diploma, as a professor lately said, an average student could do on one hour's study a day, living beyond one's means, and thus imposing a hardship on parents greater than the talent of the sons justifies, accepting stipends not needed, especially to the deprivation of those more needy, using dishonest ways of securing rank in studies or positions, on teams, or social standing, are one and all, not only ungentlemanly but cowardly and mean, and the axe would be laid at the root of the tree.[9]

Hall wasn't the only lumberjack wielding the axe out there in the groves of American academe 100 years ago. He joined William James, a distinguished polymath, psychologist, and humanist, who'd done so earlier in an essay written for the Harvard Monthly in 1903. In "The Ph.D. Octopus," James observed from inside the Harvard academic establishment that the degree itself not only conferred an inappropriate and overblown reputation for erudition and scholarship within the academy but outside it was "in point of fact already looked upon as a mere advertising resource, a manner of throwing dust in the Public's eye."[10] It was, moreover, playing into the disturbing trend Americans already had to revere titles,[11] which sounds familiar enough to us when confronted with the variety of Ph.D. programs in everything from physical therapy to real estate management today.

Of course he was referring to an earlier, more innocent academic age when in American colleges and universities there was a dearth of homegrown scholars, where the prestige doctorates still came from the great old universities in Germany. Back in those dear dead days, the Ph.D. was distinguished by its scarcity, the M.A., less so, and teaching and scholarship proceeded for the most part without anything other than perhaps a B.A. It was innocently thought back then in that characteristic American quantifiable way that the more Ph.D.'s one had on the faculty, the better the school. Then as now there were individuals who did the dance gracefully and easily, who "pass with ease all ordeals with which life confronts them,"[12] and those who succeeded by dint of intestinal fortitude and a thick skin though "not without baleful nervous wear and tear and retardation of their purely inner life, but on the whole successfully, and with advantage."[13]

The octopus's main victims were all the other candidates, in fact the great majority for whom (as can be seen in any number of academic novels over the years, including Reed's persona-damaged one) the doctoral degree dance was (and is) a humiliating intellectual experience. For the journeyman scholar "without marked originality or native force, but fond of truth and especially of books and study, ambitious of reward and recognition, poor often, and needing a degree to get a teaching position, weak in the eyes of their examiners,"[14] it was a poisonous hell that one survived damaged and temporarily enervated of intellectual curiosity in the short term. Ironically, in the longer term, once over the immediate effects, these same recovering damaged scholars tended to perpetuate unconsciously the humiliations they underwent on future candidates—a little bondage, a little humiliation in the exercise of dominance, just like a fraternity hazing.

For James, not only was this state of affairs insupportably dishonest and outrageous, but it also undercut the tenets of scholarship and free inquiry he had always championed throughout his long and productive life:

> To interfere with the free development of talent, to obstruct the natural play of supply and demand in the teaching profession, to foster academic snobbery by the prestige of certain privileged institutions, to transfer accredited value from essential manhood to an outward badge, to blight hopes and promote invidious sentiments, to divert the attention of aspiring youth from direct dealings with truth to the passing of examinations—such consequences, if they exist, ought surely to be regarded as drawbacks to the system, and an enlightened public consciousness ought to be keenly alive to the importance of reducing their amount.[15]

Not! Unfortunately, these are the signature characteristics and perverse "strengths" of the contemporary American academic

experience that *Japanese by Spring* satirically explored before
Reed lost his patience and his cool. Despite his failure or maybe
because of it, Reed put his finger upon the weaknesses that have
been bedeviling higher education for more than 100 years. Can
you blame him if he could find no satiric resolution and bailed
out in disgust?

Though we may have commenced this essay innocently
enough by examining a failed academic novel, we nevertheless
wind up gaping open-mouthed at the spectacle of Camille Paglia
in black leather and holding a whip, renegade feminist, anarchic
Shiva, and academic black sheep bad girl, being profiled in *People* and *Time* magazines for her theories on literature, life, sex,
and death. It's the very image that the Ish may have been pointing
toward, one supposes, the logical end result: the *dominatrix academensis*, the souped-up nineties academic version of Betty Page,
fifties America's bondage pin-up, whose iconography itself echoed
back to earlier Victorian days of Hall and James. In a strange way,
though, that's one hell of a vision of the present informed by a
presence of the past for you: What starts with mumbo jumbo
ends with black leather. And even if the Ish failed to bring it off
completely, he succeeded in piquing our curiosity and exercising our insight, which is, after all, far better than simply striking a
pose and vogueing for the cameras, don't you think?

Da Capo

Back to the head—and that's our *Teenage Nervous Breakdown*. So where do we go from here? The problem's way too big for me to deal with, Walley. Having read this book, you're entitled to ask that question, but unfortunately I can offer no definitive answers, nor did I intend to. For one thing, I wanted these essays to be descriptive rather than prescriptive. You have to know what the problem is and how it manifests itself before definitive action can be taken. Nonetheless, what *is* obvious to anyone who gives a good goddamn is that the powers that be, the ConGlomCos great and small who actually run this world through the electronic media, bank on that fact that *not* only will you *not* give a damn or that you will merely *like*, but ultimately that you will *prefer* how they view the subtotal of your life. That's what I tried to show—damn, I hope I'm not right.

But since you asked, for better or worse, here's what I think: Maybe it starts simply enough with talking back at the TV set when your kids are around and you see something that's just totally bogus and you explain to them why. Things will change when people willfully opt to be informed and question the values of the consumer world, when people prefer not to be anesticized by those values and the goods they seem to represent (and know the difference between the two states), because knowledge is power. I'd say that all of this requires a revolution in our thinking, but "revolution" is too overused a term these days, applying just as readily to dish-washing liquid or 24-hour lipstick as social upheaval. Putting the Evolution back into Revolution is more to my point, because evolution starts with individuals, not consumer affinity groups or target audiences. In its purest form as a cultural statement, that's what I thought the sixties were all about. Evolution had to do with discovering a series of truths that had always been there waiting for me and my generation to rediscover; naively we had hoped future generations would also uncover the same ones as part of their growth, too. That's what happens when one leaves high school behind forever. Boil that down to this: Each generation has a duty to inform the next that the rules of the road have nothing to do with music TV or the consumer world it has birthed.

All of this may indeed be happening, and perhaps I'm not just seeing it yet, though I'm thinking that I should have by now. We can only do the best we can to live up to our potential, but it is crucially important that what is "the best" keeps being further refined and defined: That's what I was reaching for in this book.

Hope you enjoyed the set.

Notes

Preface

1. Vonnegut, Kurt, *Wampeters, Foma & Granfalloons* (New York: Delacorte, 1974).

Chapter 1. "This, Here, Soon"

1. Huizinga, Johan, *America: A Dutch Historian's Vision, From Afar and Near*, translated by Herbert H. Rowen (New York: Harper & Row, 1972), p. 168.
2. Copyright Peggy Garrison 1972 and used with permission.
3. Ostrander, Gilman, *American Civilization in the First Machine Age* (New York: Harper & Row, 1970), p. 224.
4. de Tocqueville, Alexis, *Democracy in America*, edited and abridged by Richard D. Heffner (New York: New American Library, 1964), p. 213.
5. Whitman, Walt, *Prose Works 1892–Volume II. Collected and Other Prose*, edited by Floyd Stoval (New York: NYU Press. 1964), pp. 402–403.
6. "Survey: Too Much Television, Fat in Children's Diet," Associated Press, September 20, 1994.
7. Whitman, p. 474.
8. Pound, Ezra, "Hugh Selwyn Mauberly" (first published in 1920), *Personal: Collected Poems of Ezra Pound* (New York: Horace Liveright, 1926).
9. Huizinga, p. 168.
10. Harountunian, Joseph, *Lust for Power* (New York: Charles Scribner's Sons, 1949), p. 19.
11. Bryson, Bill, *The Lost Continent: Travels in Small-Town America* (New York: Harper & Row. 1989), p. 130.
12. Walley, David G., *The Ernie Kovacs Phile* (New York: Fireside Books, 1987), p. 207.

13. Bloom, Allan, *The Closing of the American Mind: How Higher Education Has Failed Democracy and Impoverished the Souls of Today's Students* (New York: Simon & Schuster, 1987), p. 73.
14. Bloom, p. 75.
15. Walley, David, *No Commercial Potential: The Saga of Frank Zappa* (New York: Da Capo Press, 1996), p. 201.
16. Walley, p. 201.

Chapter 2. Who Stole the Bomp (from the Bomp Sha Bomp)?

1. Frith, Simon, *Music for Pleasure: Essays in the Sociology of Pop* (New York: Routledge, 1988), p. 4.
2. Ward, Ed. "Dedicated to You" in *Stranded: Rock and Roll for a Desert Island*, edited by Greil Marcus (New York: Da Capo Press, 1996), pp. 248–249.
3. Torches, Nick, *Country: The Twisted Roots of Rock "n" Roll* (New York: Da Capo Press, 1996).
4. For a more worked-out account of this mini culture war, see R. Serge Denisoff's *Tarnished Gold: The Record Industry Revisited* (New Brunswick, NJ: Transaction Books, 1986).
5. Willis, Ellen, "Velvet Underground: Golden Archive Series," *Stranded: Rock and Roll for a Desert Island*, edited by Greil Marcus (Da Capo Press: New York, 1996) p. 73.
6. It should be noted here that the amount of press generated is no guarantee of commercial success. CBS in the early seventies even went as far as announcing in the trades that a Blood, Sweat and Tears album had been shipped gold, i.e., had sold 100,000 units; unfortunately, it came *back* gold too—we all laughed.
7. Rockwell, John, "Living in the USA," in *Stranded: Rock and Roll for a Desert Island*, edited by Greil Marcus (New York, Da Capo Press, 1996), p. 188.
8. I should know. I was the boyfriend. For further details, see *Strange Days: My Life With and Without Jim Morrison* by Patricia Kennealy (New York: Dutton, 1992).
9. For a very impressive and exhaustive history of the punk movement in England, see John Savage, *England's Dreaming* (New York: St. Martin's Press, 1992).

10. NcNeil, Legs, and Gillian McCain, *Please Kill Me: The Uncensored Oral History of Punk* (New York: Grove Press, 1996), p. 299

11. McNeil and McCain, p. 334.

12. Ostrander, Gilman, *American Civilization in the First Machine Age* (New York: Harper & Row, 1970), p. 20.

13. Ward, p. 151.

Chapter 3. Blame It on the Sixties

1. Hugh F. Kenner and Don Gifford, correspondence, 1983.

2. Bloom, Allan, *The Closing of the American Mind: How Higher Education Has Failed Democracy and Impoverished the Souls of Today's Students* (New York: Simon & Schuster, 1987), p. 333.

3. Davis, Fred, *Yearning for Yesterday: A Sociology of Nostalgia* (New York: The Press, 1979), p. 31.

4. Davis, p. 111.

5. Davis, p. 122.

6. Geertz, Clifford, *Local Knowledge: Further Essays in Interpretative Anthropology* (New York: Basic Books, 1983), p. 44.

7. See Herbert Gans, *Deciding What's News* (New York: Pantheon Books, 1979), for an accurate assessment of how news is textured and "spun" for public consumption to meet the needs of advertising and ratings by major television news producers and editorial directors. Though his writing style is somewhat stilted, the information is invaluable.

8. Jones, Landon Y., *Great Expectations: America and the Baby Boom Generation* (New York: Coward, McCann and Geoghegen, 1980), p. 68. This well-written basic text lead me to Davis's valuable discussion on nostalgia as a driving force in commercial culture in general and in the sixties in particular. It should be read in conjunction with Abe Peck's *Uncovering the Sixties: The Life and Times of the Underground Press* (New York: Pantheon Books, 1985).

9. James, William, *The Varieties of Religious Experience* (New York: Modern Library Random House, 1902), p. 380n.

10. Clampitt, Amy, *The Kingfisher* (New York: Knopf, 1985), p. 57.

11. Whitman, Walt, *Prose Works 1892–Volume II* (New York: NYU Press, 1964), p. 370.

12. Whitman, p. 396.

13. For an in-the-trenches view of the complexities of cultural revolution sixties-style, one can do no better than read Abe Peck's *Uncovering the Sixties: The Life and Times of the Underground Press* (New York: Pantheon Books, 1985). He manages to give the era a precise, interconnected, and intelligently informed chronology that perfectly captures the spirit, intensity, contradictions, and triumphs. It's the next best thing to having been there. Having been there myself as an underground journalist at New York's *East Village Other* from 1969 to 1973. I happen to agree with him, so there will be some similarities in our approaches if not conclusions in my chapter analysis.

14. For a real example of the mind-set of the media politics and headgames that in some small part contributed to the chaos of the '68 Chicago Convention, see poet, musician, and critic Ed Sanders' *Shards of God: a Novel of the Yippies* (New York: Grove Press, 1970). It could be history, and maybe even is, from one of the era's more articulate and creative "spokesmen."

15. Walley, David, "Abbie in Noshville: The Miami Convention," 1972 (unpublished ms.).

16. Kett, Joseph, *Rites of Passage: Adolescence in America 1790–present* (New York: Basic Books, 1977) p. 272.

17. Kip Cohen, interview by the author, December 20, 1970.

18. Leach, William, *Land of Desire: Merchants, Power and the Rise of a New American Culture* (New York: Pantheon Books, 1993), p. 37.

19. Kennealy, Patricia, "Woodstock '69," in *Jazz and Pop Magazine*, vol. 8, no. 11 (November 1969), p. 22.

20. For a sympathetic account of the Altamont Concert and its aftermath, see *Altamont: Death of Innocence in the Woodstock Nation*, edited and introduction by Jonathon Eisen (New York: Avon, 1970). See specifically "Paradise Loused" by Andy Gordon for a cinematic Mailer-esque account of the concert and the cultural mind-set surrounding it.

21. Cohen, interview by author.

22. Cohen, interview by author.

23. Huizinga, J.H., *In the Shadow of History* (New York: W.W. Norton, 1936), p. 178.

Chapter 4. Boxers or Briefs?

1. Walley, David, *Decadent Memories* (unpublished manuscript, 1980).
2. Pielke, Robert G., *You Say You Want a Revolution: Rock Music in American Culture* (Chicago: Nelson-Hall, 1986), p. 18.
3. Walley, David, *No Commercial Potential: The Saga of Frank Zappa* (New York: Da Capo Press, 1996), p. 203.
4. This paragraph and the one below have been *No Commercial Potential.*
5. "Wal-Mart's CD Standards Are Changing Pop *New York Times* (November 12, 1996), pp. 12.

Chapter 5. Play School

1. Huizinga, Johan, *Homo Ludens*, (London: Routledge & Kegan Paul Ltd., 1949), p. 193.
2. Hall, G. Stanley, *Adolescence: Its Psychology and Its Relation to Physiology, Anthropology, Sociology, Sex, Crime, Religion and Education, Volumes I & II* (New York: D. Appleton and Company, 1907), Volume I, p. xv.
3. Hall, Volume I, pp. xvi–xvii ff.
4. Hall, Volume II, p. 411.
5. Hall, Volume II, p. 488.
6. Hall, II, p. 362.
7. Hall, Volume II, p. 496.
8. Hofstader, Richard, *Anti-Intellectualism in America* (New York: Knopf, 1963), p. 237.
9. Hofstader, p. 342.
10. Hofstader, p. 350.
11. Hofstader, p. 356.
12. See the study by the National Education Commission on and Learning cited in Catherine Manegold's "Only 41% of Schools Day Spent on Academic *New York Times* (May 5, 1994), p. 1.
13. Edward Zwick, a creator of *Thirtysomething,* quoted in Bernard Weintraub's "In Hollywood, a Party Is a Party, and an

Awards Show Is Even Better," *New York Times* (January 23, 1994), p. C11.

14. Ostrander, Gilman, *American Civilization in the First Machine Age* (New York: Harper & Row, 1970), p. 20.
15. Friedenberg, Edgar Z., *The Vanishing Adolescent* (Boston: Beacon Press, 1959, 1964), p. 8.
16. Eckert, Penelope, *Jocks and Burnouts: Social Categories and Identity in the High School* (New York: Teachers College Press, 1989), p. 12.
17. Brake, Michael, *Comparative Youth Culture* (Boston: Routledge & Kegan Paul, 1985), p. 16.
18. Friedenberg, p. 11.

Chapter 6. the Twinkie Defense

1. Schickel, Richard, *Intimate Strangers: The Culture of Celebrity* (New York: Doubleday & Co., 1985), p. 289.
2. Schickel, p. 289.
3. de Tocqueville, Alexis, *Democracy in America* (New York: Washington Square Press, 1965). See especially Chapter "Peculiar Effects of the Love of Physical Gratification in Democratic Times."

Chapter 7. Bad Day at Internet

1. William Gibson, the father of cyberpunk, author of *Neuromancer*, quoted in "On Line with William Gibson: Present at the Creation, Startled at the Reality," article by Peter H. Lewis, *New York Times*, D3, May 22, 1995.
2. Susman, Warren, *Culture as History:The Transformation of American Society in the Twentieth Century* (New York: Pantheon Books, 1984), "Culture and Communications" p. 256.
3. Beard as cited in Susman, p. 258.
4. Susman, p.258.
5. Edward Sapir as quoted by Susman, p. 259.
6. William James, *The Varieties of Religious Experience* (New York: Random House, 1902), p. 142–143
7. Huizinga, J.H. *In the Shadow of Tomorrow* (W.W. Norton: New York, 1936), p. 55
8. Huizinga, J.H., op. cit.

Chapter 8. Asking Alice

1. "Fab Four's Album Sales Soar," *The Transcript*, North Adams, MA, Associated Press, October 22, 1996, p. 16.
2. Latimer, Dean, and Jeff *Flowers in the Blood: The Story of Opium* (New York: Franklin Watts, 1981), p. 180.
3. Latimer and Goldberg, p. 190.
4. Latimer and Goldberg, p. 190.
5. Latimer and Goldberg, p. 190
6. Latimer and Goldberg, footnote, pp.
7. Kenner, Hugh F., *A Sinking Island, "Bards and Bard-Watchers,"* (New York: Knopf, 1988), p. 254.

Chapter 9. Don't Touch Me There

1. de Tocqueville, Alexis; *Democracy in America* (New York: Washington Square Press, 1965). See Chapter 35: Peculiar Effects of "The Love of Physical Gratification in Democratic Times."
2. Newman, Eric, *The Great Mother* (Princeton, NJ: Princeton University Press, 1955), p. 35.

Chapter 10. White Punks on Dope

1. Havel, Vaclav, *Disturbing the Peace* (New York: Knopf, 1990), p. 167.
2. Reed, Ishmael, *Mumbo Jumbo* (New York: Bantam p. 42.
3. Schickel, Richard, *Intimate Strangers: The Culture of Celebrity* (New York: Doubleday & Co., 1985), p. 139.
4. Hofstader, Richard, *Anti-Intellectualism in America* (New York: Knopf, 1963), p. 346.
5. Barber, Benjamin J., "America Skips School," *Harper's Magazine* (December 1993), p. 40. This is an excerpt adapted from Barber's book *An Aristocracy for Everyone: The Politics of Education and the Future of America* (New York: Ballantine Books, 1992). It's a passionate piece of scholarship that centers on the argument that schools ought to provide training in citizenship. His discussion of political correctness. Alan

Bloom's *Closing of the American Mind* controversy, is well-written, witty, concise, and a good primer for those who follow this bubbling tempest—and he's far more polite than Reed when he takes on the canon.

6. Schickel, p. 223.
7. Schickel, p. 242.
8. Nasaw, David, *Schooled to Order: A Social History of Public Schooling in the United States* (New York: Oxford University Press, 1979), p. 88.
9. Hall, G. Stanley, *Adolescence, Vol. II* (New York: D. Appleton and Company, 1907), pp. 400 ff.
10. James, William, *William James: Writings 1902–1910* (New York: The Library of America, 1987), pp. 1112 ff.
11. "It is indeed odd to see this love of titles—and such titles—growing up in a country of which the recognition of individuality and bare manhood have so long been supposed to be the very soul" (James, p. 1118).
12. James, p. 1115.
13. James.
14. James, pp. 1115 ff.
15. James, p. 1114.

Selected Bibliography

Aronowitz, Stanley, *Roll Over Beethoven: The Return of Cultural Strife* (Middletown. CT: Wesleyan University Press, 1993).

Barber, Benjamin J., *An Aristocracy for Everyone: The Politics of Education and the Future of America* (New York: Ballantine Books, 1992).

Bell, Bernard Iddings, *Crisis in Education* (New York: Whittlesey House, 1949).

Bledstein, Burton, *The Culture of Professionalism: The Middle Class and the Development of Higher Education in America* (New York: Norton, 1976).

Bloom, Allan. *The Closing of the American Mind: How Higher Education Has Failed Democracy and Impoverished the Souls of Today's Students* (New York: Simon & Schuster, 1987).

Boorstin, Daniel J., *The Americans: The Democratic Experience* (New York: Random House, 1973).

Boorstin, Daniel J., *The Image: A Guide to Pseudo-Events in America* (New York: Athenaeum, 1980) (originally *The Image: What Happened to the American Dream*, New York: Athenaeum, 1961).

Brake, Michael, *Comparative Youth Culture* (Boston: Routledge & Kegan Paul, 1985).

Braudel, Fernand, *On History*, translated by Sarah Matthews (Chicago: University of Chicago Press, 1980).

Bryson, Bill, *The Lost Continent: Travels in Small-Town America* (New York: Harper & Row, 1989).

Caillois, Roger, *Man, Play, and Games*. translated by Meyer Barash (London, UK: Thames and Hudson, 1962).

Buzzi, Giancarlo, *Advertising: Its Cultural and Political Effects* (Minneapolis: University of Minnesota Press, 1968).

Coleman, James S., *The Adolescent Society: The Social Life of the Teenager and Its Impact on Education* (Glencoe, IL: Free Press, 1962).

Cremer, Lawrence, *The Transformation of the School: Progressivism in American Education 1876–1957* (New York, 1961).

Dallek, Robert, *The American Style of Foreign Policy: Cultural Politics and Foreign Affairs* (New York: Knopf, 1983).

Davis, Fred, *Yearning for Yesterday: A Sociology of Nostalgia* (New York: Free Press, 1979).

Denisoff, R. Serge, *Tarnished Gold: The Record Industry Revisited* (New Brunswick, NJ: Transaction Books, 1986).

Donavel, David F., *High School: The American Walkabout* (Andover, MA: The Regional Laboratory, 1995).

Dragastin, Sigmund, and Glen Elder, editors, *Adolescence and the Life Cycle* (New York: Wiley, 1975).

Eckert, Penelope, *Jocks and Burnouts: Social Categories and Identity in the High School* (New York: Teachers College Press, 1989).

Ehrenfeld, David, *Beginning Again* (New York: Oxford University Press, 1993).

Ehrenreich, Barbara, *The Hearts of Men* (New York: Anchor Books, 1984).

Eliot, Marc, *Rockenomics: The Money Behind the Music* (New York: Franklin Watts, 1989).

Fass, Paula S. *The Damned and the Beautiful: American Youth in the 1920s* (New York: Oxford University Press, 1977).

Feuer, Louis, *The Conflict of Generations* (New York: Basic Books, 1969).

Foley, Douglas, *Learning Capitalist Culture: Deep in the Heart of Texas* (Philadelphia: University of Pennsylvania Press, 1990).

Friedenberg, Edgar Z., *The Vanishing Adolescent* (Boston: Beacon Press, 1959, 1964).

Frith, Simon, *Music for Pleasure: Essays in the Sociology of Pop* (New York: Routledge, 1988).

Fritt, Simon, *Sound Effects: Youth, Leisure and the Politics of Rock 'n' Roll* (New York: Pantheon Books, 1981).

Fukuyama, Francis, *The End of History and the Last Man* (New York: Free Press, 1992).

Fuller, Robert C., *Americans and the Unconscious* (New York: Oxford University Press, 1986).

Gaines, Donna, *Teenage Wasteland* (New York: HarperCollins, 1990, 1991).

Garofolo, Reebee, editor, *Rockin' the Boat: Mass Music and Mass*
Movements (Boston: South End Press, 1992).

Gillis, John, *Youth and History: Tradition and Change in European Age Relations, 1770–Present* (New York: Academic Press, 1981).

Goldman, E. F. *Two-Way Street* (Boston: Bellman Publishing Company, 1948).

Hall, G. Stanley, *Adolescence: Its Psychology and Its Relation to Physiology, Anthropology, Sociology, Sex, Crime, Religion and Education. Volumes I & II* (New York: D. Appleton and Company, 1907).

Harountunian, Joseph, *Lust for Power* (New York: Scribner, 1949).

Henry, Tricia, *Break All Rules! Punk Rock and the Making of a Style* (Ann Arbor, MI: UMI Research Press, 1989).

Hiner, N. Ray, and Joseph M. Hawed, editors, *American Childhood: A Research Guide and Historical Handbook* (Westport, CT: Greenwood Press, 1985).

Hofstader, Richard, *Anti-Intellectualism in America* (New York: Knopf, 1963).

Howe, Neil, and Bill Strauss, *13th Gen (Abort, Retry, Ignore, Fail?)* (New York: Vintage Books, 1993).

Huizinga, Johan, *America: A Dutch Historian's Vision, From Afar and Near*, translated by Herbert H. Rowen (Harper & Row: New York, 1972).

Huizinga, Johan, *Homo Ludens* (London: Routledge & Kegan Paul Ltd., 1949).

Huizinga, Johan, *In the Shadow of History* (New York: Norton, 1936).

James, William, *The Varieties of Religious Experience* (New York: Random House, 1902).

James, William, "The Ph.D. Octopus," in *The Harvard Monthly* (March 1903), from *William James: Writings 1902–1910* (New York: The Library of America, 1987).

Jezer, Marty, *The Dark Ages: Life in the United States, 1945–* (Boston: South End Press, 1982).

Jones, Landon Y., *Great Expectations: America and the Baby Boom Generation* (New York: Coward, McCann and Geoghegan, 1980).

Kett, Joseph F., *The Pursuit of Knowledge under Difficulties: From Self-Improvement to Adult Education in America, 1750–1990* (Stanford, CA: Stanford University Press, 1994).

Kett, Joseph F., *Rites of Passage: Adolescence in America 1790—present* (New York: Basic Books, 1977).

Kline, Stephen, *Out of the Garden: Toys and Children's Culture in the Age of TV Marketing* (New York: Verso, 1993).

Krug, Edward A., *The Shaping of the American High School 1920–1940* (Madison: University of Wisconsin Press, 1972).

Lanza, Joseph, *Elevator Music: A Surreal History of Muzak, Easy-Listening, and Other Moodsong* (New York: St. Martin's Press, 1994).

LaPiere, Richard, *The Freudian Ethic* (New York: Duell, Sloan and Pearce, 1959).

Lasch, Christopher, *The Culture of Narcissism: American Life in An Age of Diminishing Expectations* (New York: Norton, 1979).

Laswell, Harold D., *Democracy through Public Opinion* (New York: 1941).

Leach, William, *Land of Desire: Merchants, Power and the Rise of a New American Culture* (New York: Pantheon Books, 1993).

Lears, T. J. Jackson, *Fables of Abundance: A Cultural History of Advertising in America* (New York: Basic Books, 1994).

Livingston, James, *Pragmatism and the Political Economy of Cultural Revolution* (Chapel Hill, NC: UNC Press, 1994).

Lurie, Alison, *The Language of Clothes* (New York: Randon House, 1981).

Marcus, Greil, editor, *Stranded: Rock and Roll for a Desert Island* (New York: Da Capo Press, 1996).

Mathison, Richard R., *Faiths, Cults and Sects of America: From Atheism to Zen* (New York: Bobbs Merrill, 1960).

Meyer, Donald, *The Positive Thinkers: Popular Religious Psychology from Mary Baker Eddy to Norman Vincent Peale and Ronald Reagan* (Middletown, CT: Wesleyan University Press, 1988).

McNeil, Legs, and Gillian McCain, *Please Kill Me: The Uncensored Oral History of Punk* (New York: Grove Press, 1996).

Modell, John, *Into One's Own: From Youth to Adulthood in the United States 1920–1975* (Berkeley: University of California Press, 1989).

Nasaw, David, *Going Out: The Rise and Fall of Public Amusements* (New York: Basic Books, 1993).

Nasaw, David, *Schooled to Order: A Social History of Public* *Schooling in the United States* (New York: Oxford University Press), 1979.

Nock, Albert J., *The Memories of a Superfluous Man* (Chicago: Henry Regnery Company, 1942, 1964).

Nock, Albert J., *The Theory of Education in The United States* (New York: Harcourt, Brace and Company, 1932).

Orman, John, *The Politics of Rock Music* (Chicago: Nelson-Hall, 1994).

Ostrander, Gilbert, *American Civilization in the First Machine Age* (New York: Harper & Row, 1970).

Pattison, Robert, *The Triumph of Vulgarity: Rock Music in the Mirror of Romanticism* (New York: Oxford University Press, 1987).

Pielke, Robert G., *You Say You Want a Revolution: Rock Music in American Culture* (Chicago: Nelson-Hall, 1986).

Pollock, Bruce, *Hipper Than Our Kids: A Rock and Roll Journal of the Baby Boom Generation* (New York: Schirmer Books, 1993).

Rosenberg, Bernard, and David Manning White, *Mass Culture: The Popular Arts in America* (Glencoe, IL: Free Press, 1957).

Rossitor, Clinton, *Parties and Politics in America* (Ithaca, NY: Cornell University Press, 1960).

Roszak, Theodore, *The Making of a Counter Culture: Reflections on the Technocratic Society and Its Youthful Opposition* (New York: Doubleday, 1969).

Santayana, George, *Character and Opinion in the United States* (New York: Scribner's, 1920).

Scheurer, Timothy E., *Born in the U.S.A.: The Myth of America in Popular Music from Colonial Times to the Present* (Jackson: University of Mississippi Press, 1991).

Schickel, Richard, *Intimate Strangers: The Culture of Celebrity* (New York: Doubleday, 1985).

Scott, John, *Rebel Rock: The Politics of Popular Music* (Oxford, UK: Basil Blackwell, 1986).

Spring, Joel, *The Sorting Machine: National Education Policy since 1945* (New York: David McKay, 1976).

Strauss, Samuel, *American Opportunity* (Boston: Little, Brown, 1935).

Stuessy, Joe, *Rock and Roll: Its History and Stylistic Development* (Englewood Cliffs, NJ: Prentice-Hall, 1990).

Susman, Warren I., *Culture as History: The Transformation of American Society in the 20th Century* (New York: Pantheon Books, 1984).

Taylor, William R. editor, *Inventing Times Square: Commerce and Culture at the Crossroads of the World* (New York: Russell Sage Foundation, 1991).

de Tocqueville, Alexis, *Democracy in America* (New York: Washington Square Press, 1965).

Veblen, Thorstein, *The Theory of the Leisure Class: An Economic Study of Institutions* (New York: Random House, 1934).

Weinstein, Deena, *Heavy Metal: A Cultural Sociology* (New York: Lexington Books, 1991).

Whitman, Walt, *Prose Works 1892–Volume II, Collect and Other Prose*, edited by Floyd Stoval (New York: NYU Press, 1964).

Wicke, Peter, *Rock Music: Culture, Aesthetics and Sociology*, translated by Rachel Fogg, (London: Cambridge University Press, 1990).

Wilson, Edmund, *The Cold War and the Income Tax* (New York: Farrar Strauss, 1963).

Wood, Robert C. *Suburbia: Its People and Their Politics* (Boston: Houghton Mifflin, 1958).

THE ULTIMATE
GIRLS' BODY BOOK

Praise for The Ultimate Girls' Body Book

In my personal research, I have not found a more comprehensive and useful resource for young women looking to understand their bodies. *The Ultimate Girls' Body Book* removes the opportunity for misunderstandings or lack of information that could handicap a girl for life. I'm eager and delighted for both my daughters to have a copy to study with me.

—*Jennie Bishop, author of* The Princess and the Kiss *and* Planned Purity
for Parents, *founder of PurityWorks, Daytona Beach, Florida*

Dr. Walt and Dr. Wohlever have written a thoughtful guide for tween girls and their parents that is scientifically sound, biblically grounded, and entirely practical. They answer the questions that everyone is too embarrassed to talk about.

—*Julian T. Hsu, MD, family physician, assistant clinical professor,
University of Colorado Health Sciences Center, Denver, Colorado*

The Ultimate Girls' Body Book is an amazing resource for parents. We are grateful that a trusted medical professional has taken the time to write this much-needed guide for girls. Dr. Walt Larimore is a unique combination of medical expert, outstanding communicator, and compassionate advisor. He uses those gifts to lead young readers through the often-puzzling journey of adolescence by answering the questions they are often afraid to voice.

—*Mark Merrill, president of Family First and author of* All Pro Dad
—*Susan Merrill, founder and director of iMOM.com and author of*
The Passionate Mom

This book is fun and approachable. It is written with sensitivity, yet it is also realistic and direct. This is something a tween can relate to. I am picky about books, but this is a wonderful resource that can serve as a valuable guidepost for families with tween girls. I plan to recommend it to family and friends.

—*Ann Park, MD, women's development coach and founder of
CoachingwithDrAnn.com, Tampa, Florida*

Other Writings by the Authors

By Walt Larimore, MD

Nonfiction Books

*The Ultimate Guys' Body Book:
Not-So-Stupid Questions About Your Body*

Lintball Leo's Not-So-Stupid Questions About Your Body

*10 Essentials of Happy, Healthy People:
Becoming and Staying Highly Healthy*

Alternative Medicine: The Christian Handbook

*SuperSized Kids: How to Rescue Your Child
from the Obesity Threat*

Why A.D.H.D. Doesn't Mean Disaster

*His Brain, Her Brain: How Divinely Designed
Differences Can Strengthen Your Marriage*

*The Honeymoon of Your Dreams:
A Practical Guide to Planning a Romantic Honeymoon*

Workplace Grace: Becoming a Spiritual Influence at Work

*Workplace Grace: Becoming a Spiritual Influence at Work —
Groupware™ Curriculum*
(Includes video, DVD, leader's guide, and participant's workbook)

*Grace Prescriptions: Becoming a Spiritual Influence
in Healthcare*
(Small-group curriculum with leader's guide and participant's workbook;
coauthored with William Carr Peel)

The Saline Solution: Becoming a Spiritual Influence in Your Medical Practice
(Small-group curriculum with DVD, leader's guide, and participant's workbook; coauthored with William Carr Peel)

Autobiographical Books

Bryson City Tales: Stories of a Doctor's First Year of Practice in the Smoky Mountains

Bryson City Seasons: More Tales of a Doctor's Practice in the Smoky Mountains

Bryson City Secrets: Even More Tales of a Small-Town Doctor in the Smoky Mountains

Novels

Time Series Investigators: The Gabon Virus

Time Series Investigators: The Influenza Bomb
(coauthored with Paul McCusker)

Hazel Creek: A Novel

Sugar Fork: A Novel

Websites

Dr. Walt's website is www.DrWalt.com.

Dr. Walt's health blog is www.DrWalt.com/blog.

Purchase autographed books at
www.Dr-Walts-store.hostedbyamazon.com.

Morning Glory, Evening Grace Daily Devotional,
available at www.Devotional.DrWalt.com

By Amaryllis Sánchez Wohlever, MD

Nonfiction Books

Walking with Jesus in Healthcare: A 120-day devotional to refresh your soul as you care for others

Bible commentary published in The Journey

Faith in Action: Living a Life of Blessing
(a study of James and the Beatitudes)

Marks of the Kingdom (based on the Gospel According to Matthew)

Prayer in the Early Church (based on Acts of the Apostles)

The Radiance of God's Glory (a study of the book of Hebrews)

Turning Points of the Faith

Study of the Gospel According to Mark

Studies of Paul's Letters (Philippians, 1 Corinthians, 1 and 2 Thessalonians)

Study of Letters of Peter, John, and Jude

Websites

Dr. Mari's blog is www.DrMarisFaithStop.com.

Dr. Mari's author website is www.faithfulmd.wordpress.com.

Dr. Mari writes devotions for Good News Daily *and* Bible *commentary for* The Journey
(published by Bible Reading Fellowship — www.biblereading.org)

Learn about Dr. Mari's writing, editing, and Spanish translations at www.DrMarisFaithStop.com.

Not-So-Silly Questions
About Your Body

THE ULTIMATE
GIRLS' BODY BOOK

Walt Larimore, MD
Amaryllis Sánchez Wohlever, MD

ZONDERkidz

Zonderkidz

The Ultimate Girls' Body Book
Copyright © 2013 by Dr. Walt Larimore and Dr. Amaryllis Sánchez Wohlever

This title is also available as a Zondervan ebook.
Visit www.zondervan.com/ebooks.

Requests for information should be addressed to:

Zondervan, 3900 *Sparks Dr. SE, Grand Rapids, Michigan* 49546

ISBN 978-0-310-62130-0

Agent line goes here if needed.

Cover design: Cindy Davis
Interior illustration: Guy Francis
Editor: Kim Childress
Interior composition: Greg Johnson/Textbook Perfect

Printed in the United States of America

14 15 16 17 18 19 20 /RRD/ 20 19 18 17 16 15 14 13 12 11 10 9 8 7 6 5 4 3 2 1

For Anna Katherine and Sarah Elisabeth
May you always be as beautiful on the inside as you are
on the outside.

Pop

For Hannah, whose pure heart and love of God will
forever make her beautiful.
And for Mami, whose legacy of love lives on.

A.S.W.

Disclaimer

This book contains advice and information relating to health and medicine. It is designed for your personal knowledge and to help you be a more informed consumer of medical and health services. It is not intended to be exhaustive or to replace medical advice from your physician and should be used to supplement rather than replace regular care by your physician. Readers should consult their physicians with specific questions and concerns. All efforts have been made to ensure the accuracy of the information contained within this book.

CONTENTS

This book is enhanced with QR codes that link to valuable articles and websites. Look for these codes throughout the book.

NOTE TO PARENTS

The Ultimate Girls' Body Book was written to help equip girls and the adults who love them during the change-packed years of puberty. We know it can be tough to approach subjects like their changing bodies, moods, and the world of boy-girl relationships. So we've provided conversation starters to help you embrace this time of change, learn together, and enjoy the journey.

Puberty means body changes, acne, and menstrual periods. It means talks about hormones, boys, and sex. It also means texts, phone calls, slumber parties and, yes, more texts. No worries. This book will help you talk about all this and raise a healthy daughter. You can reassure her that puberty is a normal, God-designed process that helps her transition from girl to woman. Your loving guidance will make all the difference.

As Christian family doctors, we want you to have accurate medical information that is biblically sound. So we reviewed the latest research and national guidelines through the lens of a biblical worldview. We also had every chapter reviewed by the Christian Medical Association and researchers, physicians, dietitians, psychologists, coaches, educators, and mom-daughter teams (they're listed under Acknowledgments).

Let us share a word of caution. We care deeply about preserving your daughter's innocence and know she may not be ready for certain topics. Yet, we can't ignore the dangers that lurk in a broken world. The latter part of the book contains more mature subjects. Help guide her reading and stay engaged. Decide which topics should wait. You know her best.

We recommend that you read the book together. Be available for discussions while cooking dinner or driving to school, at the mall or during nightly walks. A simple question like, *What did you think about the chapter on friendship?* may open a door to new ways of relating. Reading together will make it easier to establish healthy boundaries for your family.

Another option is to read the book on your own first. If it seems appropriate for her maturity level, let her read it. But be intentional. Keep track of her progress and give her opportunities to ask questions. You won't have all the answers, but you can show her you care by sharing the journey.

Consider journaling about your feelings and questions. Share your awkward puberty stories and laugh. Pray together and have fun. The seeds you plant now will bear fruit for a lifetime.

> Start children off on the way they should go, and even when they are old they will not turn from it.
>
> *Proverbs 22:6*

NOTE TO GIRLS

Welcome to puberty! *To what?* Yes! You're near or smack in the middle of the exciting (and puzzling!) time called *puberty*. Do you like roller coasters? Awesome! Buckle your seatbelt as you learn all about God's plan to grow you from girl to young woman.

You may wonder, *When will I start wearing a bra and shaving my legs? And what on earth are periods?* We'll answer your questions and make you laugh too. You'll learn about dealing with pimples and what true beauty is all about. We'll talk about your changing body, liking boys, texting, bullies, and more.

Read this book with your mom or another trusted woman. Choose fun spots to chat with her about all you're learning. Talk while painting your toenails. Go hiking or shopping together, then share a smoothie and ask questions.

You may feel awkward or shy about some of these topics. No problem. This book will make it easier to talk and laugh about all this.

Puberty is part of God's plan for you. It's true! God wants you to grow and learn to trust him. Yes, young girls can learn to trust God.

Did you know Mary was a teen when the angel Gabriel visited her? When she learned God chose her to be Jesus' mother, Mary could have said, "No way!" or "I'm too young." But Mary trusted God, and that helped her believe God could do amazing things through her.

Mary said yes. God chose a teenager with a heart of faith. Wow!

So for nine months, Jesus—the Author of life—grew inside this young girl. God honored Mary's body by living there. Wow, again!

God gave *your* body such respect and dignity too. This book is about your body and much more. It's about God's purpose for your life, including puberty.

So get ready for a fun adventure! Puberty comes only once, and with the changes and moods come many joys and treasures too.

> Trust in the LORD with all your heart and lean not on your own understanding; in all your ways submit to him, and he will make your paths straight.
>
> *Proverbs 3:5–6*

QUESTION 1

What does it mean to be healthy?

Have you ever been in an automobile when a tire blew? The loud KABOOM scares everyone in the car. Then the whole vehicle starts to wobble. The driver tightens her grip, slows down, and pulls over to the side of the road. As the car slows, the shaking lessens, and you hear the *plop, plop, plop* of the flattening tire. When you finally stop and get out of the car, the tire is as flat as a pancake. So much for your plans for the day.

Believe it or not, your body is designed in a similar way. Here's how.

Two of my (Dr. Walt's) very first books were *God's Design for the Highly Healthy Teen* and *10 Essentials of Happy, Healthy People*.

In the books, I discuss how authentic health is about a lot more than simply not being sick or trying to have the best body. I explain that health is made up of four separate parts that work together:

- Your physical health
- Your emotional/mental health
- Your relational/social health
- Your spiritual health

For example, when you have a cold (physical health), it affects your mood (your emotional health) and how you react to others (your relational health). When a girl is emotionally ill—with depression, for example—it can affect her immune system (physical health) and her relationships with her family and others (her social health).

In other words, your overall health is kind of like a car with four tires. Each tire represents an aspect of your health: your physical, emotional, relational, and spiritual health. If any one of the tires is not fully inflated, or if even one of your health wheels is not aligned correctly, it affects how the whole car rides—how well you are.

If one of your health wheels is off balance, your entire "health ride" will be bumpy. You will have to slow down to prevent a crash! And if one of your tires blows—BOOM!—your failing health stops you cold.

So even though our book is titled *The Ultimate Girls' Body Book*, it's about much more than your physical body. We'll also explain how emotional, relational, and spiritual health contributes not only to a healthier body but also to an overall healthier you.

Kate is one of the healthiest girls I (Dr. Walt) have ever known. If you met her when she was growing up and just looked at her physical body, you'd think she was not very healthy. She was born with a brain problem that keeps the muscles on her left side from working normally. As a result, they are stiff and contracted. She has a bit of a speech problem and, as a child, could only walk with braces and great difficulty. Her crossed eyes and contracted legs often caused her to stumble and fall. She was bullied frequently by kids who would mock and laugh at her.

Kate doesn't sound like the picture of health, right? Yet despite her physical disabilities, Kate's charming, genuine personality drew people to her. Most of her classmates and teachers loved her. Despite her physical challenges, Kate carried herself with class and self-respect and became highly healthy emotionally, relationally, and spiritually.

Growing up, her attitude was usually upbeat, and her infectious laugh made others smile. If she dropped something, she wouldn't get mad or frustrated; she'd just giggle. If her left hand didn't do what her brain was telling it to do, she'd say cheerfully, "That left hand has a mind all its own."

Kate loved to read and laugh out loud. She was lighthearted, even though many with similar disabilities can be heavyhearted. Not Kate. Her smile could light up the darkest room. She was also wise in choosing her friends and, as a result, was surrounded by a group of great friends who loved and helped care for her. When she needed to be in the hospital, they were always there to support her.

But most of all, Kate's deep faith in God impressed everyone around her. No one ever heard her question why God had allowed her to have such a devastating disorder. Instead, Kate would share what God was teaching her through her disabilities.

As a young woman full of kindness, gratitude, and hope, Kate was healthier than most tweens and teens I've known. Although her physical wheel was a bit out of balance, her extremely healthy emotional, social, and spiritual wheels gave her a smooth ride in life.

I had the immense pleasure of watching her grow up, and now she's a highly healthy young adult. I'm very grateful for all she's taught me. I'm even more grateful to be her dad.

So think about your health car and your four health wheels. Is there anything you can do to prevent a flat tire in your health? Or to prevent a wreck caused by a blown tire?

The answer is yes. That's the whole point of this book. There is so much *you* can do.

The first step involves prevention, which keeps things from going wrong in the first place. Like cars, people need to take good care of themselves, and they need regular checkups. During these "tune-ups," the mechanic will check the "tires" to see that they are aligned and fully inflated. If they're not, the mechanic will make the adjustments so you'll have a safe ride on the road.

I (Dr. Walt) designed a test you can take to determine if your four health wheels are healthy, or if one or more of them is flat, out of alignment, or ready to blow. You can find a link to these free evaluations for parents and tweens/teens using this QR code or the URLs included in our list of resources.

Assess Your
Health-Teens

The second step involves choosing to drive on safe roads that will help keep you healthy. Throughout the book, we help you learn how to drive safely when it comes to your health, and we show you what the safe roads to great health look like. As you read each question, consider how healthy you feel and what steps you need to take to get healthier if needed. We pray that this book will be a road map to becoming a healthy and godly tween and teen girl who will grow up into a healthy, godly woman.

And now, let's learn more about this exciting time of life called *puberty*.

QUESTION 2

I'm changing. What's happening to my body?

How often do you or your friends use the word *puberty*? Probably not at all. But *all* of the physical and emotional changes that you're going through are part of an ongoing conversation for most girls during the tween and teen years.

Since we are doctors — so we like medically reliable terms — we'll go with *puberty*. Here's our definition: puberty is the process that develops and changes your body physically from a girl to a woman. Here's your definition: "Wow, what's up with my body? A lot of stuff is going on!"

During puberty, your body will grow faster than at any other time in your life — well, except for when you were in your mother's womb and when you were a tiny baby. You will grow taller, you will develop hair in new places, your private parts will change, and your breasts will grow. Surely you've heard about girls getting their periods. Maybe you're wondering about *your* first period. What in the world is going on with that?

You'll also experience a roller coaster of new feelings and emotions. You can feel super confident one moment and ultrasensitive the next. In the morning, you may have it all together, only to fall apart in a single second by the first bite of your lunch. You'll have to deal with mean girls, bullying, and attraction to boys. Not to mention TV shows, movies, the Internet, videos, and video games bombarding virtually every thought you have.

We'll talk about all those things, but first let's discuss puberty, which involves three main events: the growth of your breasts, the growth of pubic hair, and your first menstrual period. Typically, the changes unfold in exactly that order and can take anywhere from two to five years. Although these changes may seem weird or even scary, they are normal, healthy, and God-designed.

Girls go through puberty at different ages and at different rates. It usually starts between the ages of eight and twelve. Over the last few decades, more girls have begun puberty before the age of eight—even down to age six or seven. And your ethnicity can make a huge difference.

If puberty starts before you're eight years old (or has not started by the time you turn twelve), you should see your doctor just to be sure everything's all right.

So what kicks off the process? Hormones do. A *gland* is a part of your body that makes the chemicals called *hormones*. The bloodstream then carries the hormones to another part of the body (like from your brain to your breasts). Puberty begins when your brain releases a bunch of these chemicals.

The hormones called *estrogen* (made primarily in your ovaries) and *human growth hormone* (HGH, made in your brain) cause most of the changes in your body during puberty. Get ready for some drama!

When these hormones reach the muscles and bones, your body's growth speeds up. If someone tells you, "You're all hands and feet," in a way they're right. During puberty, your extremities grow first, then your trunk (back, chest, and abdomen). Most girls grow fastest about six months before their first period (which is called *menarche*, but more on that later).

You'll grow taller during puberty. You'll gain weight in different places. You'll develop awe-inspiring superpowers—okay, just kidding about that last one.

Most girls will notice more body fat along the upper arms, thighs, and upper back. Your hips may grow rounder and wider, while your waist can narrow. This is all totally normal and divinely designed (that's always nice to know).

For most girls, breast growth is the first sign of puberty; estrogen causes it. Some girls will first notice hair growing in their pubic area, while a few others first notice hair growing on their arms, legs, and armpits (*axillae*). Menstrual periods usually don't come until later, typically when you're twelve or thirteen.

We know these changes can seem scary and strange to you and to other girls who go through them. But don't worry! As you learn more about what's happening, it will make sense, and you'll feel better. Trust us.

So let's begin to address the many questions that are swirling around in your mind about these amazing, God-designed changes.

> "Before I formed you in the womb I knew you, before you were born I set you apart."
>
> *Jeremiah 1:5*

> "Your Redeemer ... formed you in the womb."
>
> *Isaiah 44:24*

QUESTION 3

Why are there things about my body I just don't like?

I (Dr. Walt) was speaking to a group of fifth-grade girls at their school about their changing bodies. I looked at one of the girls, who seemed quieter than the others, and asked, "Sara, do you have any questions?" She thought for a moment and said, "How come there are some things about my body I just don't like?"

I looked around and noticed many other heads nodding. "How many of you are thinking the same thing?" Slowly, nearly every girl raised her hand. I was not surprised at all. You see, this is one of the questions we get asked most when we talk with girls about all the changes they are experiencing before and during puberty.

No matter how old you are, your body has grown, developed,

and changed over the last year. And if there is one thing we can guarantee you, even more changes are coming!

Most girls become self-conscious about their physical development during puberty. They can worry about everything—their height, weight, even the shape of their little toe. But these changes can cause even more embarrassment if your friends or parents—or even worse, boys or bullies—tease you or talk about them.

We want you to learn about and become more comfortable talking about all these changes. First, you need to consider this fact: God created you just the way you are. The Bible says God fashioned you; he formed you.

> My frame was not hidden from you when I was made in the secret place, when I was woven together in the depths of the earth. Your eyes saw my unformed body; all the days ordained for me were written in your book before one of them came to be.

> *Psalm 139:15–16*

God literally knit you together while you were still in your mother's womb, which the writer of the Psalm figuratively calls "the depths of the earth." In fact, the phrase "woven together" is a single word in the Hebrew that can also be translated "embroidered."

Some of you know what embroidery is: fancy and delicate stitches hand-sewn onto cloth that add beauty and value to the material. That is the word used to describe how God made *you*.

One Bible teacher wrote, "It describes the delicate embroidery of the body, the things that tie us together so that one organ supports another. The lungs need the heart, and the heart needs the lungs; the liver needs the kidneys, and the stomach needs both; all the parts are amazingly embroidered together."

In other words, God designed you. He caused your body to form and grow, like a weaver creates an art piece with yarn or string.

The Rooster Crowed

When I (Dr. Mari) got my first period, I was home with my older brother. We were watching a movie while we waited for Mom to come home. I must have taken twenty trips to the bathroom, since I didn't have a pad or any supplies to use except for toilet paper. It was a long afternoon!

When Mami (that's what we called our mom) finally came home, she was thrilled to hear the news. She hugged and kissed me and looked at me proudly, smiling, with a tender look on her face. She gave me everything I needed, like pads and some supercute undies she'd bought ahead of time to celebrate this special event. We had a great time chatting about growing up.

This beautiful mother-daughter moment was interrupted when a neighbor stopped by to borrow some sugar. Seeing all my supplies on the couch, mom's friend realized what had just happened. So at the top of her lungs, she exclaimed, "The rooster crowed!" Then, hugging me, she began to crow, "¡Qui-qui-ri-quí! ¡Qui-qui-ri-quí!"

Can you imagine?

The rooster crowed? What on earth was she talking about? The lady seemed to have lost her mind. Turns out that expression is about how a rooster crows to announce the dawn of a new day — and a new day had dawned for me. With the arrival of my first period, I was one day closer to becoming a woman.

Truth is, I still laugh every time I think about her excitement at watching me grow up. Thanks to my mom and our exuberant neighbor, I'll never forget that special day.

You are wonderfully made, which means you are special—a wonder. Your Creator has designed you to be completely unique—*one of a kind*. And he is *still* growing you—using all of these changes to shape you into the woman he has designed you to be.

> For we are God's handiwork, created in Christ Jesus to do good works, which God prepared in advance for us to do.
>
> *Ephesians 2:10*

The Greek word for "handiwork" (sometimes translated "workmanship") is *poiema* (POY-ay-mah), which means "that which is made personally." *Poiema* is also the origin of the English word *poem*, which tells us something amazing: God the Creator not only personally made you, but you are his poetry. You are his artwork. You are his masterpiece.

You are absolutely one-of-a-kind. No one else in the past or in the future has your fingerprints, your DNA pattern, your exact personality, or even the exact pattern of the veins you have on the back of your hand.

Not only does God have a blueprint just for you and your body, but he also designed a special life plan just for you. Here are two verses describing this:

> Many are the plans in a person's heart, but it is the LORD's purpose that prevails.
>
> *Proverbs 19:21*

> For it is God who works in you to will and to act in order to fulfill his good purpose.
>
> *Philippians 2:13*

God's plan for you includes using what you or others may see as imperfections. Perhaps you feel parts of your body or personality are "design flaws"—mistakes, even—but they're not. God can use all that for your benefit. He made you the way he made you for a purpose.

Do you remember Kate's story in question 1? She could have complained about her physical imperfections. Instead, she chose to see how God would use them in her life. Her disabilities allowed God to use Kate to serve in the speechwriters' office of the President of the United States. She shared the story of God's work in her life not only around the country, but also in Washington, D.C., the very center of our government.

God's plan is perfect. And God knows you. He loves you. He created you. He designed you. If you trust him, over time you will understand his design and plan for you better. This will make you more willing to follow him and even thank him for the way he made you—and even the fact that he made your little brother, who wakes you up every morning by burping your name.

You may say, "Well, it's not fair that _____." (Fill in the blank with the words "I have zits," or "I'm too short," or "My nose is too long," or any other things you simply don't like about yourself.) But if you dwell on that, aren't you really saying, "God, I don't trust your design for me. I think I know what I need better than you do."

Really?

Imagine you are God. You created the universe. You designed all of the solar systems, plants, and animals. Then you make a little girl who begins to grow into a young woman. You know why you put her together just the way she is. Everything the girl sees as a flaw, you made for a specific purpose. You know what is best for her, and you already know the end of her story. You know where she will go to school, what profession she'll choose, whom she'll marry, and what she'll accomplish.

You love that girl more than she will ever love herself. In fact, you are building an eternal home for her—so you can be together forever. And, most important, you know that at the end of her

The Hidden Masterpiece

A story is told of a young girl who was riding home from school on the subway. She'd been bullied at school that day about her looks — her acne, her tangled hair, and her hand-me-down clothes. Tears welled up in her eyes.

An older woman sat next to her and pulled out a jumble of thread that spread out several inches in each direction. There were knots everywhere, and all kinds of colors. The whole thing looked like a confused muddle of filaments going every which way.

With needle and thread, the woman began working on the mess of string. The harder she worked, the more messed up the whole thing looked. The girl laughed out loud and then covered her mouth to silence a chuckle.

"What?" the woman said, smiling. "What's so humorous about this?"

"Your sewing," the girl replied. "It just looks funny."

The woman laughed and said:

My life is but a weaving, between my Lord and me;
I cannot choose the pattern, but He works steadily.
His weaving looks confusing, as I, in foolish pride,
Forget He sees the upper, and I the underside.

The wise old woman turned the fabric over to show the girl the other side. The teen's mouth fell open as she gazed at the perfect embroidery.

The woman turned her work back over to the jumble of thread and said, "When I was your age, I would often be sad about my looks or my lot in life. I think it's true of most girls."

Years passed, and the now-grown girl reflected back on the magnificent piece of art and thought, "Only later did I learn to see myself as my Creator did. His weaving is always perfect."

life, when she meets you in heaven, she'll look back and see that your design and plan for her were perfect.

Then imagine that little girl looking in the mirror, frowning in disgust, turning red-faced in anger and pointing a finger at you, "I can't believe you made me this way. This is not fair."

If you were God, how would you feel? We know you'd still love that little girl with all your heart. But you'd want to pull her into your lap—to hug her and say, "Hang in there. Just trust in me. I don't make no junk." (Though God's grammar would be perfect.)

Part of becoming a faithful young woman who follows Jesus involves trusting that his ways are better than your ways. It might help to know that what you're going through does not surprise God.

It's perfectly okay to wonder, *God, what are you doing? What's your plan here? What are you trying to teach me?* It's honest and healthy to admit to him that you aren't comfortable with certain things. But it's wise to understand that God is God and you are not. We hope that, as you read on, this will become more and more real for you.

> "For my thoughts are not your thoughts, neither are your ways my ways," declares the LORD. "As the heavens are higher than the earth, so are my ways higher than your ways and my thoughts than your thoughts."
>
> *Isaiah 55:8–9*

> Oh yes, you shaped me first inside, then out; you formed me in my mother's womb. I thank you, High God—you're breathtaking! Body and soul, I am marvelously made! I worship in adoration—what a creation!
>
> *Psalm 139:13–15 MSG*

Hot-Cross Bonds

When pastor and author Louie Giglio looks at creation — from distant galaxies to the intricate human cell — he can't help but see the work of Jesus.

Jesus even holds our bodies together with a symbol of his never-failing love.

Pastor Giglio talks about a substance called *laminin*, which is part of a family of proteins that holds our cells together. Think of it as body glue.

Scientists who study the human cell under incredibly powerful electron microscopes have found that all laminins discovered so far are in a cross-like shape.

"How crazy is that?" Pastor Giglio says. "The stuff that holds our bodies together, that's holding the linings of your organs together, that's holding your skin on, is in the perfect shape of the cross of our Lord Jesus Christ."

God's design, love, and power are truly on display in all of creation — even in places that the human eye cannot see.

For in him all things were created: things in heaven and on earth, visible and invisible, whether thrones or powers or rulers or authorities; all things have been created through him and for him. He is before all things, and in him all things hold together.

Colossians 1:16–17

QUESTION 4

Why isn't my body changing like I expected?

I (Dr. Walt) remember having this question when I was a boy. It seemed like I was developing more slowly than all of my friends. In the ninth grade, I was a short, ninety-eight-pound weakling, with no body hair or big muscles. It seemed all of my friends were growing up faster than I was. And I *so* wanted to grow up more quickly.

We've noticed that our young patients (and their parents) sometimes worry that their growth is either too slow or progressing too quickly. If your development is ahead or behind that of your friends, you may wonder if you are normal. Chances are everything is just fine and you're right on target for your divine design.

But those girls who are on the slower end of things when it comes to their physical development tend to worry the most about this. They wonder when their breasts will grow, when they'll begin shaving hair on their legs and under their arms, or when their first period will come.

And if you're developing more quickly than other girls in your class, this can become even more painfully obvious when older boys start staring at you instead of talking to you.

It is completely normal for physical development to start at different times and move along at different rates for each girl. Once the first changes of puberty begin, it usually takes several years before all of them are complete—and on top of this, changes vary from girl to girl.

So during the teenage years, two girls who are the same age and developing normally can appear quite different from one another. You likely know some girls who look much older and more physically mature, while other friends look younger and less mature, right? But the one who starts slower will usually catch up in time.

Although your changes will be different from those of your friends, they won't be very different from your mom's (believe it or not). So if you can talk to your mom about when and how she developed, this may give you an idea of what's ahead for you.

Still, it's important to know that these days, most young girls start to grow and develop at a younger age than their moms did (about nine months earlier on average). Also, they are growing taller (about one inch taller on average) and weigh more (about ten pounds on average) than their mothers.

So how will your body change during puberty? Here are some averages:

Eight to thirteen years: Your breasts begin to grow.
Eight to fourteen years: Pubic hair begins to grow (usually after your breasts begin to grow).
Nine and a half to fourteen and a half: Your body growth speeds up and you head toward your growth spurt. *My what?* Don't worry; we'll cover that in question 5.

Nine to sixteen: You may notice hair under your arms starting about two years after your first pubic hairs show up.
You may begin to have acne. Your sweat glands begin to
produce more sweat, and it begins to smell (a.k.a. body
odor or BO—more about that in question 20).

Twelve to thirteen: Your first menstrual period occurs (usually after breast and pubic hair growth begins). More
about that in questions 12 and 13.

Sixteen to eighteen: You are nearing your full adult height
and your body shape is mature.

Remember, these are examples of *average* development. At any
milestone of puberty, there is a wide range of ages.

Also, the order of events can vary from one girl to another.
For example, some girls will have hair growing under their arms
at the same time their leg hair is beginning to grow. Other girls
could grow hair much later or much earlier.

So use these timelines as a general guide. Each of these steps
will happen in the timing that God has designed for your unique
system.

> Many, LORD my God, are the wonders you have done, the
> things you planned for us. None can compare with you;
> were I to speak and tell of your deeds, they would be too
> many to declare.
>
> *Psalm 40:5*

Your Breasts

Breast development happens in stages. The first stage, *breast budding*, starts during the earliest part of puberty. Yes, like flowers, your breasts start off as small buds.

A breast bud is simply a small raised bump behind the nipple. After breast budding, the nipple and the circle of skin around the nipple (called the *areola*) get bigger and a little darker. Then the area around the nipple and areola starts to grow into a breast.

As breasts keep growing, they may be pointy for a while before becoming rounder and fuller. A girl's breasts continue to grow throughout her teen years and even into the early twenties. Breast size is determined mostly by your heredity and your weight. So if your mom's breasts are small, it's likely that you'll have breasts of similar size. And a girl with more body fat will often have larger breasts.

Let us give you a warning: There are many companies that want you to spend money on products they claim will make your body develop faster (if you are delayed) or slower (if you are early), but the only things guaranteed to get bigger are *their* bank accounts as they take your money for products that *will not* help.

You can't do anything to make your body develop faster than God designed. Of course, you should eat a nutritious diet, stay active, and get enough sleep — we'll talk about these things later in the book. But special diets, food supplements, herbs, vitamins, or creams won't do anything to make normal puberty start sooner or happen more quickly.

Breasts are just one of many signs that you are on your way to becoming a woman. If you have questions or concerns about breasts or bras, ask your mom or a trusted adult. She knows exactly what you're going through. Also, we'll answer many of your questions about breasts in question 15.

QUESTION 5

Am I growing — or is the ceiling dropping?

Have you ever heard someone say to one of your friends, "You shot up like a weed"? Well, weeds grow much faster than regular plants and flowers, and so will you when you have your growth spurt.

Spurt is a word used to describe a short burst of activity, or something that happens in a hurry. So a *growth spurt* means your body is growing really fast.

You'll experience two kinds of growth spurts during the teen years. First, there is your *height spurt*, when you grow taller. Second, there is your *weight spurt*, when you'll gain more body fat, especially in your hips and thighs. This is God's design to make your body curvier and more feminine.

You may be surprised to learn that your height spurt is actually a series of growth spurts. You may grow a couple of inches over a few months, then grow at a normal rate for a few months, and then grow extra fast in another spurt. At some point, you will level off and stop growing once you reach your adult height.

To see if your height (also called *stature*) is normal for your age, you can use a standard stature-for-age chart like the one located at tinyurl.com/n92u7sh. In this chart, you'll notice that what's considered normal (between the 5th and 95th percentile) varies greatly. For example, on average, a twelve-year-old girl can be anywhere from fifty-four inches (about four and a half feet tall) to sixty-four inches tall (about five and a third feet tall). That's nearly a foot difference!

If you're super tall or extremely short, then your doctor should evaluate you. But if your height is in the normal range, then you may wonder how tall you will be after puberty.

A good way to predict this is to look at your parents, who gave you the *genetic code* (the unique way your individual cells are designed and arranged) that determines your height. Here is a simple formula you can use to predict how tall you *may* be when you reach your adult height (at least within three to four inches):

Note your biologic dad's height (in inches).
Subtract five inches.
To this number add your mom's height in inches.
Then divide this number by two.

BMIP Calculator

Voilà! That's a guesstimate of your height when you're fully grown. However, several more accurate Internet tools can help you predict where you might end up. One tool helps you estimate your adult height based on your biological parents' adult heights. Click on this QR code or see the URLs in our resources list at the back of the book. But remember that these are simply estimates. In most cases you'll just have to wait to see how tall you become.

During puberty, a girl can grow two to ten inches in just a few years. Your feet and hands grow first, then your facial bones, and the rest of the body follows. When your facial bones start growing before the rest of your body, your face may appear to be "long." You may feel like your nose is starting to take over your face. Your forehead will widen and your hairline will move back. But don't worry. This is all normal, and you're not going bald (even if your dad is).

Once your height spurt ends, you will not grow much taller. Toward the end of this growth spurt, the *growth plates* of your bones will fuse so that they won't grow longer. This is when you've reached your final adult height.

Although the typical girl is usually about one inch taller than most boys before puberty, women are, on average, more than five inches shorter than men. Why? Although guys generally start growing tall later than girls, their growth spurts last a lot longer. So boys catch up and eventually pass most girls.

Occasionally we'll see kids whose growth is lagging way behind. This is called *constitutional growth delay* and can cause a girl to be a slow grower or a late bloomer.

When we doctors see this, we order X-rays of the girl's bones and compare them with X-rays of what's considered average for that age. The bones of teens with constitutional growth delay look younger than what is expected for their age.

The good news is that most of these girls will have a height spurt, although a bit delayed, and continue growing and developing into womanhood. They usually catch up with their peers by the time they're young adults.

Although you may go through a stage when you feel like an ugly duckling because everything seems out of proportion, this stage will pass. You will emerge as a beautiful swan with a more mature look about your face.

In fact, you can relax, for three very good reasons:

1. You are much more aware of these changes than those around you.
2. Your trunk, or torso, will begin its growth and then your body will even out.
3. This is all part of God's perfect design for you — to transition you from a girl into a woman.

Another common worry during this stage of puberty is clumsiness, which can be embarrassing. Here's why this happens: When you grow slowly, your brain has time to adjust and learn. But when you're growing quickly, your brain has no time to catch up.

God created your brain to know where your hands and legs are at all times — even if your eyes can't see them. Don't believe it? Just close your eyes and move your fingers, hands, or feet. Your mind's eye knows exactly where they are because of a brain process with a big fancy name: *proprioception.*

Your brain works this way so it can very skillfully help guide your fingers and toes, your hands and feet, your arms and legs.

But your body can develop more quickly than your brain. So it can take your brain a little time to adapt. And while your brain is learning and catching up, you may be a bit clumsier than usual. Perhaps that's why you keep running into your dog.

But don't worry. Although this phase can be awkward and embarrassing, it will be over before you know it.

In the meantime, you can speed up your brain's learning by staying active. Exercise and active games are great ways to speed up your brain's learning and reduce clumsiness. We recommend outdoor activities and games, but for those who for safety reasons need to stay inside, games at a local gym or exercise-based video games may help.

Instead of looking down at your feet, staring at your face in the mirror, or worrying about your clumsiness, we recommend you look up to God during this time. Ask him what he's up to with you. Use this critical time in your life to take your focus off of yourself and focus on him more and more.

> The LORD makes firm the steps of the one who delights in him; though he may stumble, he will not fall, for the LORD upholds him with his hand.
>
> *Psalm 37:23–24*

Your Amazing Brain

Your brain is one of the most powerful supercomputers on the planet. The average brain weighs in at only three pounds but uses 20 percent of the oxygen you breathe and 25 percent of the calories you eat. In addition, about 20 percent of the blood flowing from the heart is pumped to the brain. Your brain is busy!

The brain needs all this constant blood flow, oxygen, and food to keep up with the heavy demands of its 100 trillion connections (*synapses*) that operate at the speed of light. The average brain has 100 billion brain cells (*neurons*) — which is amazing when you consider that the entire Milky Way galaxy is said to contain roughly 100 billion planets and stars. There's a whole universe inside your head (but don't let that give you a headache).

Your brain can handle 10 quadrillion instructions per second, which is ten times the theoretical maximum speed of the top supercomputer.

And your brain is standing by to be trained and to make you less clumsy. In fact, by practicing an action over and over, your brain can have your body do it perfectly.

If you're feeling clumsy and want to get more coordinated, try these exercises:

- Balance on one leg while moving your other leg out to the side, in front, then behind you.
- Jump in place and try to spin a perfect 180 or 360 degrees.
- Jump rope by yourself or with friends — or play hopscotch.
- Play a team sport with friends like basketball, volleyball, soccer, or field hockey.
- Stand with your feet shoulder-width apart. Lift your right knee up as you cross over your left hand and touch the outside of your right knee. Repeat by lifting your left knee and crossing over your right hand to touch it. Continue "marching" in place and touching your knee with the opposite hand.
- Run in a figure eight. Then do it backward.

QUESTION 6

Sleeping Beauty sounds boring. Who needs sleep?

If you're the average tween or teen girl, it's probably safe to say you are *not* getting as much sleep as you need. These days, more and more young people are staying up late and falling asleep at school. And children arrive late at school more often now because they oversleep.

If you're seven to twelve years old, you need ten to eleven hours of sleep each day. Yet studies show the average kid this age only gets eight to nine hours of sleep. That's not enough. When you get into your teen years, you need at least nine to ten hours of sleep each night. But most girls this age only get six or seven hours of sleep.

This is not healthy. Your mind and body need sleep to be in tip-top shape. If you don't get enough Zs, you may air ball every shot at the basketball tryouts or mess up your pirouettes at your next recital—bummer. You'll have trouble getting up in the morning, concentrating, and learning at school. You may start acting like Grumpy, Dopey, or Sleepy, and you may fall asleep in class.

Also, your grades may start slipping. Kids who get the least amount of sleep are more likely to get Cs and Ds. Although study habits also play a huge role, children who sleep the most are more likely to get better grades. So getting your Zs may help you get A's and Bs.

So sleep helps your grades and it helps you stay healthy. Restful sleep reenergizes you. It allows your body and mind to recover from all of your day's activities and prepare for the next day. Restful sleep also:

- Promotes healthy bone growth
- Helps form red blood cells that deliver oxygen to your body and brain
- Stimulates the release of human growth hormone, which helps tissues grow properly
- Strengthens your immune and nervous systems

Here's a little-known fact: The more sleep you get, the less likely you are to be overweight or obese. And if you're already overweight or obese, increasing your sleep can help you lose weight.

People who sleep fewer than seven hours a night tend to weigh more. Scientists think extra rest shuts down a gene that is tied to obesity. Less sleep also means less *leptin* (a hormone that makes you less hungry) and more *ghrelin* (a hormone that makes you hungry). People who get less sleep tend to eat a lot more, especially high-fat foods like ice cream. Hmm... perhaps Sleeping Beauty was on to something.

Yes, there may be something to the old idea of "beauty sleep." Research shows that people who don't sleep enough appear grumpier, more tired, less attractive, and unhealthier than those who are well rested. So, you see, you don't need makeup. You can just snooze your way to an ever cuter you.

Getting a good night's sleep will help you. You'll be healthier in your body and in the way you feel (your emotions). It will help

Do's and Don'ts for Healthy Zs

- Do avoid caffeine after 4:00 p.m., such as sodas, energy drinks, coffee, or chocolate. (Yes, chocolate has caffeine.)
- Do avoid exciting, violent, or scary shows, movies, or stories before bedtime. They can keep you up.
- Do stop watching TV at least thirty minutes before bed — sixty is even better. And don't use a computer or play video games for the last hour or so before bedtime. The light from the screen sends signals to your brain that it's time to wake up.
- Do keep naps short, or you might have trouble falling asleep later. You'll get the most energy from a ten- to twenty-minute "power nap."
- Don't wait until the night before to study for a big test (we sound like your parents, don't we?). Staying up all night can mess up your sleep cycle and affect how you do on the test. Plan to study ahead of time.
- Don't sleep with a pet — especially dogs — as they move around all night and can keep you from deep sleep. And if they like chewing socks and licking feet, the tickles will wake you up. This is why I (Dr. Mari) had to kick our puppy off the bed.
- Do exercise regularly, but not right before bed, which can make it harder to fall asleep. People who exercise for at least thirty minutes most days have more restful sleep than those who don't.

your relationships with your family, friends, teachers, and God. You may even become a better student and athlete.

So what are you waiting for? Go take a nap so you won't be grumpy or mean.

- Do try to go to bed and wake up around the same time each day. A *circadian clock* in your brain regulates your sleep-wake cycle. If one part of the cycle is off, it messes up the rest. Consistent bedtimes and wake-up times will help your body's clock work better. Try not to sleep in too much on the weekends, except to catch up during the occasional poor sleep week.
- Do get into bright light in the morning. It will wake you up and get you going.
- Do unwind from the day by praying, reading your Bible or a peaceful book, or journaling. Establish a regular, relaxing bedtime routine such as soaking in a warm bath and then reading or listening to soft music. This helps separate your sleep time from activities that can wake you up or stress you out.
- Do keep all computers and cell phones outside your bedroom. And turn them off at night. Keeping them on in your bedroom may keep you from having a good night's sleep, and a midnight text sent by a night-owl friend could keep you up for hours.
- Do make sure your room is cool, quiet, dark, comfortable, and free of *any* interruptions. Consider using blackout curtains, eye shades, ear plugs, "white noise," humidifiers, fans, and other devices to help you get the great night's sleep that is part of God's divine design for you.

When you lie down, your sleep will be sweet.

Proverbs 3:24

Even youths grow tired and weary, and young men stumble and fall; but those who hope in the Lord will renew their strength. They will soar on wings like eagles; they will run and not grow weary, they will walk and not be faint.

Isaiah 40:30–31

Do I really need calcium
for my bones?

Each year about two million broken bones (*fractures*) occur in older women because of weak bones. And many of these fractures can be prevented—especially if you take good care of your bones now, during your tween and teen years.

Calcium is a building block for strong bones. When there's not enough of it in your bloodstream, your body tries to pull calcium from your bones, which thins and weakens them—not cool. Over time, this can cause a disease called *osteoporosis*, which leads to breaks and fractures. Older people usually get this, but what you do now can keep you from getting it later.

By the time you are in your early twenties (which will be here before you know it), you'll have acquired almost 90 percent of the bone strength that you will have for the rest of your life. We doctors call this your *bone mineral density* (BMD). And from your thirties onward, no matter what you do, your BMD drops.

To have the strongest bones possible, you have to begin to take good care of them during your tween and teen years (when girls are less likely than boys to get enough calcium). Less than 10 percent of girls ages nine to seventeen get the 1,300 mg of calcium experts say you need each day. Yipes! So what can you do to get what you need?

Almost all North American girls get 300 to 400 mg of calcium each day in the foods they eat. If you add a serving of fat-free milk, soymilk, yogurt, or calcium-fortified orange juice to your breakfast, you'll get another 300 mg or so. Now you're over halfway to what you need.

Then if you add another serving of dairy (skim milk or yogurt) with a calcium-fortified whole grain cereal, you can get another 600 to 900 mg of calcium. This healthy formula will give you all the calcium you need in a day—just with a good breakfast.

We join most experts in recommending you get as much calcium as you can (if not all) from food—not pills.

If you can't get enough calcium from what you eat, your doctor or pharmacist can recommend a supplement.

Also, we can't talk about calcium without mentioning vitamin D. Your body won't absorb calcium without its BFF—vitamin D. Since it's hard to get enough vitamin D from food and potentially risky to get it from the sun, most experts currently recommend that teens take a supplement of 1,500 to 2,000 IU of vitamin D_3 daily with a meal.

Your pharmacist can help you find tasty chewable calcium and vitamin D supplements. However, when it comes to vitamin D, most multivitamins do not have what you need. Since these recommendations may change over time, be sure to discuss these suggestions with your doctor.

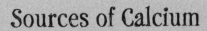

Sources of Calcium

This great list of calcium-rich foods comes from the CDC's Best Bones Forever website.

FOOD	PORTION	MILLIGRAMS OF CALCIUM
MILK		
Fat free	1 cup	306
Lactose reduced, fat free	1 cup	300
YOGURT		
Plain, fat free	8 ounces	452
Fruit, low fat	8 ounces	343
CHEESE		
Pasteurized Swiss	2 ounces	438
Ricotta, part skim	1/2 cup	335
Pasteurized American	2 ounces	323
Mozzarella, part skim	1.5 ounces	311
FORTIFIED FOODS		
Soy drink with added calcium	1 cup	368
Orange juice with added calcium	1 cup	300
Tofu with added calcium	1/2 cup	253
Cereal with added calcium	1 ounce	236–1043
Cereal bar with added calcium	1 bar	200
Bread with added calcium	1 slice	100

Did You Know? Fun Facts About Your Bones

Here are some fun facts about human bones from the blog *Healthy Times*:

- You have over 230 moveable and semi-moveable joints.
- Your smallest bone, the *stapes* or stirrup bone, lives in your middle ear. It transmits sound vibrations into your hearing system in the brain and measures about a third of a centimeter — that's one tiny speaker!
- Your thigh bone (called the *femur*) is stronger than concrete. It's the biggest and strongest bone in your body.
- Babies don't have kneecaps. Their kneecaps are still soft cartilage that gradually hardens into bone. This process is called *ossification*.
- At birth, you have up to 350 bones. As you grow, the number drops to 206. No, they didn't go join a percussion band. But between ages twelve and fourteen, some of your smaller bones fuse together into larger, bigger, and stronger bones.
- More than half of a grown-up's bones are located in the hands and feet.
- Your ribs move about 5 million times a year — every time you breathe.
- Did you know that humans and giraffes have the same number of bones in their necks? Seven. Giraffe neck vertebrae are just much, much longer.

Besides getting the right amount of calcium and vitamin D each day, what else can you do to have the strongest bones possible?

Stay active. Step away from the computer. Girls who spend most of their time sitting have a higher risk of osteoporosis later in life than active girls. Walking, running, jumping, dancing, and light weightlifting (for older girls only) can help strengthen and maintain healthy bones.

Avoid alcohol. Beyond all the other problems caused by alcohol, which we'll talk about in question 29, drinking also increases your risk of weak bones and fractures later in life.

Avoid tobacco. Smoking causes bad breath, stains teeth, and kills people from lung and heart disease and cancer. Smoking also weakens bones. It's just another reason to never even think about smoking.

Always remember that a nutritious diet, regular exercise, and some supplements (if needed) will go a long way toward giving you the healthiest bones possible.

> Did you not ... clothe me with skin and flesh and knit me together with bones and sinews? You gave me life and showed me kindness, and in your providence watched over my spirit.
>
> *Job 10:10–12*

QUESTION 8

Makeup, hairstyles, clothes — what makes me beautiful?

Beauty. Our culture is obsessed with it. Only, most people are obsessed with the wrong kind of beauty.

In our culture, it's all about how you look on the outside. Yet, to God, your beauty begins on the inside — in your heart — and comes from that place where you were "fearfully and wonderfully made." Did you ever hear that phrase? It comes from Psalm 139.

> I praise you because I am fearfully and wonderfully made; your works are wonderful, I know that full well.
>
> *Psalm 139:14*

> The Lord does not look at the things people look at. People look at the outward appearance, but the Lord looks at the heart.

1 Samuel 16:7

So whether you realize it or not, you *are* a wonderful creation. That's a fact. But do you believe it? Do you feel like God's wonderful handiwork, or do you compare yourself with the supermodels on TV?

We have great news for you. Your days of rating yourself against the external beauty of photoshopped models can come to a screeching halt today. And here's why: You are, in fact, a God-designed, God-shaped, beautiful, and wonderful creation.

Regardless of how you feel or how you think you look, you are beautiful in the eyes of your Creator. God's Word says that he made you *wonderfully*. He took extreme care to craft every detail. You don't need to put on a drop of makeup or fix your hair for God to look at you and smile. He made you just the way you are, and he considers his creation—you—beautiful.

And here's more: Not only are you beautiful in God's eyes, but also your imperfections have a purpose. Did you ever think of that? Even though you are not perfect, every part of you was planned perfectly. Nothing about you is an accident. Nothing!

Your worth, value, and beauty do not come from anything outside of you. Your worth comes from having been created in the image of a good and loving God. Your beauty and value come from the love and dignity that God placed within you. It's a done deal; God made you that way.

So here you are, a young lady—beautiful in God's eyes—in the midst of a world obsessed with the wrong things. Our culture yells out lies about true beauty at every turn, from commercials to advertisements to the latest TV shows and movies. You don't have to watch for too long to see what they're selling—if you're not big-chested, tall and skinny, all made up, and willing to show some skin, you're not beautiful—at least in *their* opinion.

This message is a lie—a hurtful and destructive lie. But when the message is repeated continually, it begins to stick without you even noticing it. If you're not careful, it can become your yardstick, even your goal.

The truth is that inner beauty affects your outward appearance. Beauty that comes from the inside out reveals itself in love, joy, peace, gentleness, and kindness. It attracts others because it is true beauty.

Perhaps your grandmother or an older woman in your life can help you understand beauty in a new way. When I (Dr. Mari) was growing up, a lady in her eighties named Mary lived across the street. After her husband died, the neighborhood kids became her new family. She taught us to play card games and dominoes, and she shared with us an unlimited supply of soda and treats. Games and sweets—her house was a hit.

Mary's face was full of wrinkles, and her spine was curved. As she got older, she got shorter, and her head shook when she spoke. Although Mary's face would never end up on the cover of a beauty magazine, she radiated true beauty.

Mary loved us, and we knew it. It was her love that made her beautiful in our eyes. I loved to look at Mary, listen to her talk, and watch her play with us. She was beautiful!

Another great example was Mother Teresa. Though she was full of wrinkles in her old age, her acts of love and kindness made her absolutely beautiful. Her compassion, her deep love of God, and her servant heart inspired me (Dr. Mari) to become a doctor.

For over forty-five years, Mother Teresa ministered to the poor, sick, orphaned, and dying. She founded the Missionaries of Charity, which has grown to 610 missions in 123 countries. She even ranked first in the list of Most Widely Admired People of the 20th Century. Mother Teresa's life shows what happens when

God's love fills you and overflows onto others. Find out more about Mother Teresa in our resources list at the end of the book.

We find another wonderful example of true beauty in the Old Testament story of Esther. An orphaned girl raised by her uncle, young Esther was as beautiful on the inside as she was on the outside. She was physically pretty. But because of her genuineness and inner beauty, not simply her outer looks, "Esther won the favor of everyone who saw her" (Esther 2:15).

When an ungodly man threatened to destroy her people, Esther chose to trust God and risk everything to help them. A whole generation of Jewish men and women was saved because of her compassion, character, and courage. The beauty of what she did for others out of love surpassed her physical beauty.

Here's a different way to think about beauty:

> Your beauty should not come from outward adornment, such as elaborate hairstyles and the wearing of gold jewelry or fine clothes. Rather, it should be that of your inner self, the unfading beauty of a gentle and quiet spirit, which is of great worth in God's sight.
>
> *1 Peter 3:3–4*

This Scripture doesn't mean that you shouldn't wear jewelry or accessorize; that can be a lot of fun, and attractive. It simply emphasizes that true beauty goes much deeper and begins in your heart—where your thoughts and feelings originate.

Your thoughts and feelings lead to your actions—things you do that spread either good or bad in your surroundings. Acts of kindness, love, and respect will add to your beauty. Violence and angry outbursts will not.

Too much focus on outer beauty can lead to a poor body image, insecurity, and low self-esteem. Our culture's obsession with outer beauty contributes to all these problems and many more for today's young woman.

Beauty Around the World

It has been said that beauty is in the eye of the beholder. In various parts of the world, beauty is defined in very different ways.

- In some countries where many people have dark skin, they use whitening products to lighten it, whereas fair-skinned people in other nations, including the U.S., often flock to tanning salons to darken their skin. Go figure.
- Some Asian cultures consider a long neck beautiful. Girls as young as five years of age wear metal rings around their necks, adding more as they grow older, to give the perception of a longer and more attractive neck.
- Others believe that beauty lies in soft, unmarked skin, so they enrich their food with collagen, a protein, hoping for "flawless" skin.
- In some countries, people turn bird poop into a powder that's used as a facial mask to improve their complexion. Any takers?
- In other parts of the world, tattoos on different parts of the body indicate a person's social status.
- In yet other cultures, being heavy with bigger curves is considered most beautiful, and being skinny is frowned upon.

As you can see, outer beauty is, to a large extent, a matter of opinion — except when it comes to your Creator. To him, you are beautiful no matter where you live or what you look like. To him, you are absolutely precious — you are his pride and joy.

Yes, makeup and fashion are fun if done right at the right age. Your parents or a trusted adult can let you know what clothes are appropriate and what's the right age for you to start using makeup. But it's not good to focus primarily on pretty looks, because such beauty doesn't last, and it's not what true beauty is all about.

No matter what you do, outer looks will fade over time. Yet the beauty that comes from your heart will make you beautiful on the outside too. This kind of true beauty will last.

So your inner beauty comes from *who* you are and *whose* you are, *not* what you look like or what others say about you. Such beauty is pure, it is genuine, and it adds worth to everyone it touches. This type of loveliness—this true inner beauty—is a worthy goal for every young woman. And as you love and care for others throughout your life, you will reflect God's beauty and goodness even more.

> Charm is deceptive, and beauty is fleeting; but a woman who fears the LORD is to be praised.
>
> *Proverbs 31:30*

We talk more about beauty and the media in the next question. Meanwhile, you have a choice to make: you can let your culture define what's beautiful for you, or you can believe God's definition. Choose well—for the decision you make now will affect the rest of your life!

> Let the king be enthralled by your beauty; honor him, for he is your lord.
>
> *Psalm 45:11*

QUESTION 9

Why do I look so different from the girls I see on TV?

I (Dr. Mari) love going on media walks with my kids at the mall. We point out ads or displays in store windows and rate them as family-friendly, neutral, or an absolute disgrace. The mall gives us plenty of material for discussion, like half-naked women in displays and ads that are just plain disrespectful of girls and women. My kids now spot what's inappropriate in no time.

Take a look around the mall and study the billboards along the road. Consider the commercials on TV and online. How are girls and women portrayed in movies and reality shows?

These are the images from our culture's classroom. A bright young woman will ask herself, *What do they teach me about beauty, femininity, and sexuality?*

As you flip through the TV channels, you may wonder, *What does a skinny woman in a tiny bikini have to do with football? Why is a woman with cleavage and tight shorts selling hamburgers or cars?*

The reality is that ads often try to sell a product by misusing or exploiting something else, like a woman's body. One study suggests most people "are exposed to over 2,000 ads a day." Many of these ads *use* a woman's body to try to sell a product while stripping the models of what makes them human. Women (and even girls) are depicted as "things" and part of the merchandise rather than as people. As one article pointed out, "It's like they are 'bodies' rather than 'somebodies.'"

Sadly, in our sex-obsessed culture, "sexy" is what sells, and advertisers know it. They use a woman's sexuality to catch people's attention to try to sell more of their product. "Sexy" sells, and they make money. Jackpot! Trust us—if they discovered that squirrels riding bicycles would sell their products, they'd show that.

So how does this trend impact the models they use and the people who watch these ads? Every year, models and actresses get skinnier. Many admit they're obsessed with working out and dieting to attain a body that may look "sexy" to some but is actually quite unhealthy (more on that in question 10). Everything they do revolves around maintaining a "sexy" image. They neglect everything else to focus on their outer looks, while often feeling ugly, empty, and sad inside.

These models go to great lengths to maintain the image needed to survive in the fashion world. Some have collagen (a protein) injected to thicken their lips. Others get injections to soften wrinkles. Many others have surgeries like tummy tucks or breast enlargements. Believe it or not, some will even have ribs removed to eliminate *normal* skin lines so they will look even thinner. They go through risky operations, removing *normal* body parts, simply to look "beautiful." They starve themselves and work out for hours, becoming more and more unhealthy not only physically, but also in mind, heart, and soul.

A Fashion Faux Pas

Did you know that nobody actually looks like the models in fashion magazines? The models themselves don't even look like that in real life. Nobody does.

After photo shoots, digital retouching (known as *photoshopping*) takes place to remove natural blemishes and reshape models' bodies to make them look "sexy" and "beautiful" according to the magazine's definition of beauty.

Several models were interviewed following a photo shoot. After they'd posed for hours in front of the camera, every one of their photographs was photoshopped. Expecting to find the usual computerized touches that *create* a thinner waist and smaller hips and *remove* beauty marks, one model was shocked to find something else missing — a whole leg. An overzealous photoshopper kept thinning out her thigh until the leg vanished from sight altogether. Oops.

Don't let such lies become your standard for beauty. Such "beauty" is unattainable, unhealthy, and *not* God's plan for you. Choose to believe what God says about beauty instead — it doesn't need any touching up.

He has made everything beautiful in its time. He has also set eternity in the human heart; yet no one can fathom what God has done from beginning to end.

Ecclesiastes 3:11

Although most girls don't enter the fashion world planning to change their bodies, this becomes their reality. And the rest of the girl population grows up bombarded with these images that can become the standard for what you think *you* should look like. But those images aren't even real.

Pictures and video images of models are airbrushed, and their so-called "imperfections" (which are part of God's design for them) are removed with software programs. What they look like is completely unreal, a *visual lie.*

While the media and advertising experts try to define beauty for you, you can choose to think differently—to think wisely. You can sharpen your eyes and your mind, strengthening your heart with truth, to replace the lie that says you're not good enough or beautiful enough unless you look a certain way.

You may be asking, *How can I do this? How do I protect myself from this pressure to look like a supermodel? How do I invest in true and lasting beauty?*

The Bible sets a foundation to answer these important questions:

> Above all else, guard your heart, for everything you do flows from it.
>
> *Proverbs 4:23*

Your identity is not determined by your looks or who you are on the outside. You are the daughter of the Creator of the universe—a King who loves and accepts you as you are. After all, he made you that way, and he doesn't airbrush or photoshop anyone! As a young lady in a sex-crazed world, you must know who you are and whose you are.

As you get to know God better and experience his goodness and love, you'll begin to embrace yourself just as he made you. As you understand his plans for your life, you'll learn that his commands are there to keep you safe.

When you pursue *God's* best for your life, you will like yourself more—exactly as you are—while trusting him to transform you in those areas where *he* wants you to change. Not your culture. Not your friends. Not that boy in history class who snorts when he laughs. But your God.

It is possible—even in this culture—for God's standard to become your own. It takes time and courage, and the choice to walk closely with him. It's the harder path. But it's the best and safest path. Like Jesus said:

> "Small is the gate and narrow the road that leads to life,
> and only a few find it."
>
> *Matthew 7:14*

To stay on this path, you need to fill your mind with God's truth to oppose the culture's lies. Part of guarding your heart and mind involves protecting your ears and your eyes. So watch what you watch.

TV shows, movies, and music affect your mind and heart, so choose well. Refuse to look at or dwell on things that are not edifying or good, such as sexual images or books that demean or exploit girls. Why waste your precious brain cells adding more unrealistic images to your brain? Read a good book instead, or choose a movie that will make you feel good about yourself, not worse.

Avoid magazines that make girls look sexy or older than they are. Think about those girl models. They need to be treated with respect, not used and abused. Check out our list of resources at the end of the book to find some magazines that are fun and informative and that treat girls with dignity and respect. They will help you see yourself through God's eyes and live to honor him.

Invest your money, time, and energy in things that build you up and reinforce God's definition of beauty. Pursue things and people who help you fulfill your purpose in life rather than move you away from it.

It is difficult to go against the tide of our culture's emphasis on physical beauty and sexiness. But it is totally possible with God's guidance, with your parents' coaching, and with some good friends who will help you keep making wise choices.

If you've been obsessed with your looks in unhealthy ways—thinking too much about or spending too much time or money on your outer appearance—you are not alone. But today, you can choose a new way to look at yourself and others—with a deep appreciation for the gift of your body and your femininity.

The life the media is selling young people is empty and can lead to depression and eating disorders. Become a voice among your peers that upholds the dignity of all people—boys and girls, men and women. You and your friends can empower one another to become more aware of the impact of the media on your soul and heart.

Embrace your femininity as a beautiful gift to be nurtured, not exposed. Guard your heart, treat your body as the gift that it is, and move away from people (and things) who mistreat, demean, or try to exploit you.

> Do you not know that your bodies are temples of the Holy Spirit, who is in you, whom you have received from God? You are not your own; you were bought at a price. Therefore honor God with your bodies.
>
> *1 Corinthians 6:19–20*

QUESTION 10

Should I go on a diet?

A young woman wrote to me (Dr. Walt): "I think I may be over-weight. I'm thinking of trying one of the latest diet plans. Which one do you recommend?" Good question—listen in.

Incredible pressure is placed on girls to be thin. You'll hear about all sorts of ways to lose weight—a few that are healthy, but many that are unhealthy. We want you to be healthy in mind, body, soul, and spirit, and dieting is usually a very unhealthy behavior for tweens and teens. Here's why.

Going on a diet can mean making great choices about nutrition, like eating more fruit, vegetables, whole grains, fiber, and heart-healthy proteins and oils, while cutting back on fatty, fried foods, high-sugar foods, and highly processed food (so much for your new deep-fried brownie recipe).

But to many girls, going on a diet means making harmful choices, like skipping meals, eating too little, making themselves throw up, or not eating enough healthy, nutritious food. Not one of these is good.

Unfortunately, some girls turn to harmful (even dangerous) dieting to try to change their bodies and feel better about themselves. But they become less healthy and end up feeling worse.

Here are some disturbing facts about teen girls and dieting:

- About one in every two teen girls has tried dieting to change the shape of her body.
- Of teen girls at a *healthy* weight, more than one in every three try to diet anyway.
- Teens who don't feel good about themselves are more likely to diet.
- Compared with teens who don't diet, teens who do diet:
  - are more unhappy with their weight.
  - often *feel* fat even if they're at a healthy weight.
  - have lower self-esteem.
  - feel less connected to their families and schools.
  - feel less in control of their lives.

The bottom line is that if you want to achieve and maintain a healthy weight, going on a diet is usually *not* a good solution. In fact, it is often unhealthy.

First, diets rarely work. Second, over time, you are more likely to *gain* weight if you try to diet. In other words, unhealthy dieting actually causes many girls to gain weight in the long run. Why? Going without food makes your body feel deprived, and you feel sad, both of which can make you overeat later.

Dieting can make you feel hungry and preoccupied with food (thinking about it all the time). It can make you feel distracted and tired, sad and unmotivated, cold and dizzy, and deprived of foods you enjoy.

Some forms of dieting can be dangerous, such as skipping meals, using weight loss pills or laxatives, going on "crash" diets, or vomiting after eating.

As a teen, you are growing rapidly and need the right amount of nutrients to be healthy. Eliminating entire food groups or taking in too few calories when you are still developing can make you sick.

Healthy Minds and Healthy Bodies

Have you ever heard of eating disorders? This is when someone becomes so obsessed with being thin that she starts doing extreme and unhealthy things. She is afraid to gain any weight at all.

Girls with the eating disorder called *anorexia* don't eat enough. They often work out way too much, becoming way too thin. Girls with *bulimia* overeat (binge) and then they make themselves throw up (purge). Both extremes are very, very bad for their bodies and minds.

If untreated, eating disorders can harm the heart, stomach, and kidneys and can alter menstrual periods, which can also weaken a girl's bones. Girls with eating disorders can get dehydrated and have trouble sleeping. Frequent vomiting can stain their teeth permanently and lead to very bad breath.

Many of these girls have a very poor body image. They often feel fat when they're actually at a healthy weight or even too thin already. They end up not getting enough nutrition and becoming more unhealthy — even if they *look* thin or fit.

It's common for tween and teen girls to feel self-conscious, since you're changing so much. But it's not normal or healthy to feel guilty when you eat or to worry about your weight and feel bad about your body all the time. This is called having a *negative body image*. Girls (and boys) who have a negative body image often lack confidence in other areas of their lives as well.

If you worry too much about your weight or a negative body image is interfering with your life, tell an adult you trust, like a parent, teacher, coach, school counselor, youth pastor, or doctor.

Doctors don't know the exact cause of eating disorders. But we do know that society's obsession with "perfect" looks and thinness contributes to the problem. People with eating disorders are not simply obsessed with food and their weight. They are using food to deal with feelings they have about their bodies and who they are. Some of them are depressed, or they worry a lot about things they can't control. They may have family problems or very poor self-esteem, feeling like they're not good enough.

For this reason, girls (and boys) with eating disorders need professional counseling, including a doctor, a psychologist, and a dietitian. This team of experts can help a lot. But it takes time to identify and deal with the emotions that are at play behind eating disorders. It also takes time to develop a healthier relationship with food and weight, both of which are essential parts of God's design for healthy, growing girls.

You can find more information and advice at the website for the National Eating Disorders Association by using this QR code or the URL included in our list of resources.

National Eating Disorders Association

They can help you. And if the first one you ask doesn't help, ask another.

Now let's take an objective look at your weight and see if yours is healthy. It's not okay to simply guess whether your weight is normal. To objectively determine (not guess) if you're at a healthy weight, follow these steps:

Step 1: Measure your height and weight accurately. Go to **http://tinyurl.com/n2x8o8j** for tips on how to do this.

For the next step, you'll need to know your height to the nearest ⅛ inch and your weight to the nearest ¼ pound. If you have trouble doing this at home, your school nurse or your doctor's medical assistant can help.

Step 2: Find your Body Mass Index Percentile (BMIP). Now, follow these directions carefully. First you'll need to write down your birth date, your height (to the nearest ⅛ inch), your weight (to the nearest ¼ pound), and the date you measured your height and weight. Then, go to **http://tinyurl.com/q853fr** and enter this data. When you click on "calculate," it will come up with your individual BMIP.

BMIP Calculator

Once you know your BMIP, here's how to interpret the number:

- Below the 5th percentile: You are UNDERWEIGHT.
- Between the 5th and 74th percentile: You are at a HEALTHY WEIGHT. Hooray!
- Between the 75th and 84th percentile: You are at a NORMAL WEIGHT but AT RISK to become overweight. If this is your BMIP, you'll learn how to lower your risk in the next question.

- Between the 85th and 94th percentile: You are OVER-WEIGHT and AT RISK for becoming obese. If this is your BMIP, be sure to read the next question to learn how to avoid this.
- In the 95th percentile or greater: Your weight falls in the OBESE category. If this is the case, be sure to study the next question, "What can I do if I'm overweight?" There's a lot you can do to get healthier starting today.

Again, if you're between the 5th and 84th BMI percentiles, your weight is considered normal. But notice the tremendous variation in what's considered normal. For example, at age twelve, a girl is at a normal weight anywhere from 68 to 138 pounds—that means the normal weight for a twelve-year-old can vary by seventy pounds.

If you're in the 75th to 84th percentile, your weight is considered normal, but you are at risk to become overweight. I (Dr. Walt) recommend an Eight-Week Family Fitness Plan I developed for my patients in this category. You can find out more about this plan in the next question by using this QR code or the URL in our list of resources.

Eight-Week Family Fitness Plan

If you fall in the underweight, overweight, or obese category, see your doctor for a checkup. Don't put this off. Girls in each of these categories are at risk for significant health problems. Now is the time for your doctor to evaluate you and recommend some ways you can improve your health.

For girls who are at risk to become overweight or who fall in the overweight or obese categories, we've devoted the next question to you and your family. We share examples and simple tips that will help you get healthier and stay healthier—check it out.

Get Active

How many TV commercials do you watch every year? Take a guess.

The American Academy of Pediatrics (AAP) estimates that the average North American kid sees 40,000 commercials each year. That averages out to nearly 110 commercials every day. That means a lot of kids are spending a ton of time in front of the TV.

Studies show kids between eight and eighteen years old spend nearly four hours a day in front of a TV screen and another two hours on the computer. That's almost as much time as a full-time job.

Since you're only in school for around nine months a year, it's very possible that you spend more time in front of a screen than you do in a classroom.

If you want to live a healthy life and build a strong body and a strong mind, one of the best things you can do is get away from the TV and computer (yes, it can be done.). You don't have to join a sports team. Just walking the dog, helping with yard work, riding your bike, or playing outside with friends can help make you fit and strong.

If you really want to be radical, suggest to your parents that your family go without TV for a few weeks, a month, or even several months. Consider it a family fast. Believe it or not, many families who try this end up getting rid of their televisions.

When kids stop watching so much TV, they discover things they love to do. They also realize how much they were missing out on by not being physically active. They start to feel healthier and learn how to spend more quality time together as a family. Check out more great ideas on the "TV-free" websites using this QR code or the URLs included in our list of resources.

Get active, and get outside. Your body will thank you for it, and you will feel better too.

Become TV-Free

QUESTION 11

What can I do if I'm overweight?

We've talked about body image and society's obsession with outer looks and thinness. We've also discussed the importance of defining beauty through God's eyes rather than the hottest TV show or magazine cover. Although an obsession with weight, shape, and appearance is unhealthy, maintaining a healthy weight and BMIP *is* critical to your health. Thankfully, this is not something you need to achieve overnight.

The decisions you make now—about nutrition, activity, exercise, sleep, and the use of tobacco, alcohol, and drugs—will make a difference for the rest of your life. Are you willing to decide right now to live a healthy lifestyle so you'll live longer and better?

Medical studies confirm that the nutrition, exercise, and sleep habits you begin in middle school and high school are the habits you'll likely continue for life. So choosing now to eat well, exercise, and get a great night's sleep is a wise investment in your future. These are great ways to become healthy and feel better physically and mentally. Even if you're overweight now, you can regain control of your health with some simple, consistent new choices.

Do not, for a minute, believe that excess weight will disappear without you making some real changes. Most overweight and obese girls who do not make healthy changes will *not* outgrow it. If you don't start making some changes, and start soon, chances are you will be overweight or obese as an adult. You're developing habits now that may be harder to break later on. But there's a lot you and your family can do starting now.

You may be asking, *Why does this matter?* Well, if you're obese as a young girl, you have a much higher chance of developing heart disease or diabetes as early as your twenties. Worse yet, you're also more likely to die younger than your friends who have a healthy BMIP. Overall, obesity can shorten your life by somewhere between five and twenty years. Who wants that?

We're not telling you this to scare you, but to inform you of the risks of staying at an unhealthy BMIP. In every question of this book, we want to give you information that is medically reliable and biblically sound—even if the news is bad.

Why? Because in most cases, any bad news we give you can be balanced by some very good news.

Even if your weight is normal, this information can help you develop and maintain a permanent healthy lifestyle. The most common choices leading to overweight and obesity include:

1. Eating too many foods high in bad sugars (sweets or sugary drinks) and bad fats (including processed, junk, and fast foods)

2. Too much screen time (TV, computer, video games, texting, social media, etc.) and not enough active play and exercise

3. Staying up too late and getting less than nine or ten hours of sleep every night (covered in question 6)

These poor choices can lead to physical diseases (such as heart problems, high blood pressure, diabetes, arthritis, stroke, and some types of cancer), emotional problems (such as depression, anxiety, and a poor self-image), and relationship problems—all at surprisingly young ages. In fact, being overweight or obese is associated with more lasting medical and emotional problems than smoking or drinking alcohol. Yikes!

If you're an overweight or obese tween or teen, believe it or not, your body could already be building up to diseases that can harm you, even if you feel well right now. To help prevent these problems, here are some strategies to help you and your family start making better choices today.

Strategy 1: Choose healthier foods.

- Eat a wide variety of foods every day from all the food groups.
- Eat a healthy breakfast every day.
- Serve your own food, and serve it on a smaller plate. Kids who serve their own food on smaller plates eat less and feel as full as kids who eat off larger plates.
- Eat when you are hungry, and stop when you are satisfied (no, you don't have to finish all of the food on your plate—be sure to tell your mom we said this).
- Choose water or fat-free (skim) milk instead of soft drinks or juice.
- Choose foods that are high in whole grains like bran, wheat, and rye.

- When you eat out, watch your food portions. In many restaurants (especially fast food) portions are much bigger than most people need. Why not split a meal with a friend or two?
- Don't rush. Be sure to enjoy conversation with your friends or family during a meal. You'll eat more slowly, you'll eat less, and you'll fill up more quickly.
- Don't use food to make yourself feel better when you are bored, sad, or upset.
- Don't eat in front of the TV or computer.

Not all calories are healthy calories. Be aware of the amount and quality of food you eat—without obsessing over it. Learn to read food labels. Look for nutritional content. If you don't know how, you can learn by using our list of resources, or from your parents, school nurse, or a registered dietitian.

Eating foods high in protein and healthy fats helps your body and overall health. Dried fruit and nuts, bananas, avocados, string cheese, and peanut butter give you energy and are healthy choices. But foods that give you calories with little to no vitamins or minerals are known as *empty calories*. Sodas are a great example of empty calories. Sodas make you gain weight while providing no nutrition at all. So leave the soda for Yoda.

Follow this formula: 5–2–1–0.

Five: Eat five servings of fruits and vegetables every day.
Two: Two-hour screen time limit (Internet, TV, video games, phone) or less.
One: Exercise (do something active) one-half to one hour most days.
Zero: Consume zero sweetened beverages (like soda) daily.

Strategy 2: Reduce screen time and increase active time.

Physical activity is an important part of maintaining a healthy weight. It's also a great way to feel good about yourself. Spend some time every day doing physical activities you like with people you like. Start slowly, building up to the recommended 150 to 180 minutes per week—which can be, for example, thirty minutes a day, five or six days a week. The minutes you exercise each day do not have to be all at once. Ten minutes here and ten minutes there can really add up.

It's also a good idea to build up a little muscle with strength training. But don't confuse strength training with weight lifting, bodybuilding, or power lifting, which can put too much strain on young muscles, tendons, and areas of cartilage that haven't yet turned to bone (called *growth plates*). Strength training (done right) can be very helpful, and not just for athletes. Here are some benefits:

- Stronger muscles and greater fitness
- Stronger bones and joints, which means fewer injuries
- Healthier blood pressure and cholesterol levels
- A more active metabolism
- Helps you stay at a healthy weight

You can do many strength-training exercises with your own body weight (like push-ups) or by using inexpensive resistance tubing. Free weights and machine weights, used carefully and with adult supervision, are other options, but they're for older teens and adults.

Children under eight years old should not begin strength training. But as early as eight years old, strength training can become a valuable part of an overall fitness plan—as long as you use proper technique.

Strategy 3: Get a good night's sleep—every night.

Most teens need nine to ten hours of sleep a day—and most get only six to seven hours. Not getting enough sleep can make it hard to pay attention at school. That means lower grades. And it can make you cranky and emotional, affecting your relationships with your family, friends, and teachers. Ever see cartoons of Donald Duck? He's got a pretty short fuse, right? Not getting enough sleep makes you a bit like that—nap so you won't quack.

And get this: not getting enough sleep can make you gain weight because of two hormones called *ghrelin* and *leptin*. Ghrelin causes you to gain weight, while leptin helps you lose weight. The less sleep you get, the more weight-gaining ghrelin and the less weight-losing leptin you produce. Who wants that?

If you get enough sleep each night, exercise most days, and eat nutritious foods, you're much more likely to reach and maintain a healthy weight. (See the answer to question 6.)

So, do you think you're making wise decisions in these areas? Do you want to know for sure? I (Dr. Walt) developed a simple quiz you can take to test your nutrition and exercise habits. You can find the SuperSized Kids Test at www.supersizedkids.com /resources/quiz/index.

After you finish the quiz, you'll receive three grades in three areas: activity, nutrition, and family BMI. Completing this questionnaire will give you an instant snapshot of your risk status. If you don't make straight A's, don't be alarmed. Very, very few teens do.

To help you improve your health grade, I (Dr. Walt) joined with nutrition expert Cheryl Flynt, RD, MPH, and the experts at Florida Hospital in Orlando to develop and test an eight-week family fitness program that you and your family can use to get healthier. The program is easy and fun and designed for everyone in your family (except babies). In many families, the tween or teen can become the organizer and encourager for her mom, dad, and siblings. You can get the Eight-Week Family Fitness Plan for free using this QR code or the URL included in our list of resources.

Eight-Week Family Fitness Plan

Show your ideas to your parents. Schedule a family meeting to discuss any challenges you identified when you took the quiz on exercise and nutrition. Talk about possible actions you could take as a family. See if your siblings and parents have any other ideas and find out what you'd all be willing to try.

Once you have a plan, it's time to get started. Remember, small changes can result in big benefits. The simple steps in the eight-week plan will work. In fact, you can meet other families with kids your age (on the SuperSized Kids website) who have used the plan with success. Go to tinyurl.com/bklelw4 to check it out.

Don't give up. At the end of the eight weeks, retake the Super-Sized test to see how much you've improved. If your family enjoys the first eight weeks, a second eight-week plan that's a bit more advanced is available at http://tinyurl.com/bxabe94.

By the way, the eight-week plan can be done once a week for eight weeks, or twice a month for four months, or once a month over eight to ten months. How quickly or slowly you do it doesn't matter. The main thing is to get started and to finish together.

One last word of encouragement. Adults who are overweight or obese have only one way to get their BMIP into a healthy range. They must lose weight. But as a tween or teen, you're getting ready to enter into a growth spurt. Growing in height means that, for many overweight girls, there may be no need for weight loss at all. As your height increases, your BMIP may just slowly drop into the normal range.

That's why we encourage girls to begin developing healthy habits—to become fitter and healthier—as opposed to dieting or trying to lose weight. Some girls may have some weight to lose—but this should only be done under the direction of your doctor.

Becoming fitter and healthier takes discipline, work, and time. But think of it like this: If you put a little money in a savings account each week, the interest builds slowly, barely noticeable at first. But as time goes on, the interest grows faster and faster.

It's the same way with your health. Good habits now build interest for a long and healthy life. Even if you don't recognize it

The Lopez Family — Daughter Age 11, Son Age 13

Angel Lopez is a single father with two children, Aimee, age eleven, and Angel III, age thirteen. He wanted to rescue his children from the obesity threat and motivate them to take better care of their health.

With a family weight of 549 pounds, Angel looked for something that would help them make lasting changes in their eating and activity habits. Angel III realized this would not be so easy for him. He loved to watch TV and play video games — both of which are linked to weight gain.

Aimee and her dad decided they could start by going for walks together before preparing dinner. They decided to watch less TV and never eat in front of the TV. When they went out to eat, they tried to choose healthier food. And Aimee and her dad began working out together at a local fitness center.

Other changes that helped them succeed included:

- Spinning classes at the gym
- Adding "screen-free" nights
- Eating more whole grains and protein
- Spending more time playing outside than looking at a screen

The results after eight weeks were remarkable. The Lopez family lost forty-two pounds.

now, as you get older, you'll be thankful for the choices you made. To a large extent, you control how healthy you will be. God gave you an amazing body. It's your job to feed it right and make sure it gets enough exercise and sleep.

> Long life to you! Good health to you and your household!
> And good health to all that is yours!

1 Samuel 25:6

QUESTION 12

Some of my friends are having periods; others aren't. What's up with that?

So you've arrived at the question that part of you has wanted to read—and part of you has wanted to avoid. But there's no way around it. Menstrual periods (or *menses*, what most girls call periods) are a normal part of every girl's development.

Perhaps you've already had periods. If not, your first one may be just around the corner, or you may still have a few more years to wait. The first period comes at different ages for different girls. This is normal. But here are some guidelines to help you estimate when your first period will arrive, though not to the day.

Most girls begin to develop *secondary sexual characteristics* when they're eight or nine. These include growing breasts and body hair, among others. In general, your first period will come about two years after your breasts begin to grow. This is usually between the ages of ten and sixteen.

About six months or so before your first period, you might notice more clear discharge on your panties. This is very common. In general, there's no need to worry about this *vaginal discharge* unless it has a strong odor or causes irritation, itchiness, or other symptoms. See your doctor if you're not sure.

When your first period arrives, you've reached the stage of puberty called *menarche*, and your body's clock has begun a cycle that will repeat itself about every twenty to forty days. A *menstrual cycle* is the length of time (in days) between one period and the next. So if you got your period on January 1 and the next one started February 1, that cycle lasted thirty-one days.

Although you may have heard that the typical menstrual cycle lasts twenty-eight days, that figure is just an average. This means that, for most girls, the time between one period and the next *averages* twenty-eight days, but a completely normal menstrual cycle can be as short as twenty days or as long as forty days. And the cycle length can be different from cycle to cycle, especially in puberty. All this is very normal.

You may wonder how long the typical period lasts. Here again, this varies a lot, but most girls will have about three to five days of bleeding, although it can last up to ten to twelve days.

In the two years after your very first period, your cycles will vary a lot (how long they last, how many days you bleed, and how much you bleed). Your cycles can be quite irregular. You may have a period with light bleeding or spotting that lasts a week, then no period for two or three months. Then you get a longer one, say, for about ten days, with heavy bleeding, then you skip another month and have a shorter one, and so on. You may feel cramps with some periods. Other times, you may feel nothing at all. Every part of your cycle can vary like crazy.

Then, after that first year or two of somewhat erratic periods, your menstrual cycle becomes more consistent and your periods become more predictable. Yes, this day will come. Just be patient.

Let us caution you about something that has become popular. Because of the availability of birth control pills (called *the pill*), girls and their moms will sometimes ask doctors for this medication to "regulate" a girl's cycle. Have you heard of this?

In general, this is not a good idea and rarely needed. The pill is a combination of powerful hormones (estrogen and progestin) that can cause many serious side effects. Your periods will improve over time on their own without the pill. So why risk the side effects (like nausea, headaches, depression, and blood clots) that can arise from taking extra hormones that you don't really need? Learning about your cycles and the normal monthly changes in your body will help a lot.

Since your initial periods will likely be unpredictable, you need to be prepared. So always carry one or two sanitary pads with you. There are a few different types from which to choose.

One type is an external pad that attaches to your panties just outside of your vagina. A second option is a "plug-in" pad, known as a *tampon*. Either type can keep the fluids that come with each period from getting on your clothing.

You can keep sanitary pads and extra panties in your purse, backpack, and/or locker. That way when a period comes unexpectedly, you'll be ready.

Even so, your period may still catch you by surprise at times. If it does, don't worry. You can fold toilet paper into a rectangle and use that as a sanitary napkin until you can get a pad. Usually other girls or women—a friend, teacher, school nurse, coach, or office staff—will have some extra pads. It's perfectly okay to ask for one. If someone helps you, you can bet that this has likely happened to her too.

When it comes to choosing between a pad and a tampon, talk to your mom or a trusted adult. She will help you get the right products for you. Most girls use a sanitary liner (a pad) rather

Premenstrual Blues

Periods are a part of life for growing girls. Period. You're either on your period, getting over your period, or about to start your period, and each one of these stages of your monthly cycle is caused by changes in hormone levels. You had no idea that being a girl had so much to do with science, did you?

As hormone levels go up and down, so does your mood. Did you ever hear about *premenstrual syndrome*, or *PMS*? This simply describes how you may feel right before a period. You may feel super moody, more tired, or just plain blah. You may feel down and unmotivated, irritable or cranky. PMS is common and happens to all women to some extent, and you can do a lot to keep it under control.

To prevent or decrease PMS symptoms, be sure to

- eat well,
- exercise, and
- get enough rest.

If you do this consistently, studies show that your whole monthly cycle will be much better. You will feel less crampy and less achy, and your moods will be more stable. Why not give it a try?

Stay active right before and during your period. This is extremely helpful. Also, healthy eating makes a huge difference. Girls with high-fat, high-carb diets, especially right before their period, will have lower "lows" than those who eat more fruits, vegetables, and fiber-rich foods.

If you have extreme PMS symptoms every month, you may have moved from PMS to what is called *premenstrual dysphoric disorder* (PMDD), where the symptoms of PMS begin to really affect with your life. If you consistently have what seems to be severe PMS month after month, see your doctor to get help.

than tampons. Most doctors recommend external pads because they are safer, especially for nighttime use.

Some external pads come with wings, which means they extend to the sides, not just front and back. They protect your underwear better, especially on heavy flow days. You can find brands that are thicker and more absorbent—they're for heavier periods. You can use thinner pads on light flow days. You may want to have both types around, since your flow can be heavier the first few days of each period and then lighten up.

Rachel's Timely Period

Menstrual cramps have been around since Adam and Eve. We know this because the Bible talks about periods in Genesis, where we read a story about Rachel trying to hide some items she had stolen from her father. She placed the items under her camel's saddle and sat on them. And then:

> Rachel said to her father, "Don't be angry, my lord, that I cannot stand up in your presence; I'm having my period." So he searched but could not find the household gods.

> Genesis 31:35

She got away with using her period as an excuse and a distraction—sneaky Rachel.

It could be tempting to use your period as an excuse to sit around and do nothing for days, but there's no need for that. Nowadays, there's a lot you can do to reduce your cramps and continue to enjoy life during this time of the month.

Still, you may feel moody or irritable, and your breasts may feel swollen. You may feel bloated and get cramps or soreness

A tampon is an absorbent cotton "plug" that's inserted into the vagina with a plastic or cardboard applicator. Your mom, an older sister, a trusted woman, or even your doctor's nurse can show you how to safely insert a tampon into your vagina. Tampons are particularly useful during athletic activities. They can even be worn while swimming. But we want to stress that tampons are for *daytime* use only.

If you choose to use a tampon, you've got to remember to change it every few hours. Why? You want to avoid the risk of

over the uterus and pubic area. Sometimes your lower back or upper thighs may feel uncomfortable. This is common, typically mild, and it doesn't have to interfere much with your life.

Warm baths can help your tummy feel better. A warm towel or heating pad (on a low setting) placed over the lower abdomen will also help. You can also take an over-the-counter medication like acetaminophen, ibuprofen, or naproxen. This can be extremely helpful, and when taken as directed, it is usually safe. Ask your doctor or pharmacist which medication is right for you. To help reduce bloating, stay away from salty foods and caffeine and drink more water.

If these simple measures don't control the cramping and mild discomfort that come with normal periods, or if you have moderate or severe symptoms, make an appointment with your doctor.

But don't be like Rachel — you'll feel a lot better if you get off your camel and move.

a serious infection known as *toxic shock syndrome* (TSS). TSS can be horrible. It can make you seriously ill, or rarely, it can even be fatal. Because of this, tampons are *not* a good option for someone who is forgetful. It could be very dangerous if you forget that you're wearing a tampon and leave it inside for too long. That's another reason we never recommend tampons for nighttime use.

Vitamins and Minerals for PMS

Although most girls don't need to take anything at all for PMS, some vitamins or minerals may help those girls who have more symptoms right before their periods. The doctors of pharmacy at the Natural Medicines Comprehensive Database recommend:

- Calcium: Taking 1,000 to 1,200 mg daily seems to lessen water retention, pain, and "the blues" that can come with PMS. You can read more about calcium in question 7.
- Pyridoxine (vitamin B$_6$): Taking 50 to 100 mg daily can improve PMS-related breast soreness and gloom.

Before you try any natural medicine (herb, vitamin, or supplement), be sure to discuss it with your physician or pharmacist. Even though these medicines are natural, they can still cause unexpected symptoms. So don't take them on your own and never take more than your doctor recommends.

The good news is that you can continue to play sports and be as active as you want even while on your period. You can go running or biking or practice almost any sport you like. You may want to use tampons for activities such as swimming or gymnastics.

Staying active during your period will minimize cramping and help you feel better, so keep moving and eat healthy foods. Remember to change your pad often (every three to four hours) and you'll be just fine.

Occasionally, a problem may present itself through a change in your normal periods. See your doctor if:

1. You have persistent bleeding between periods.
2. There is a sudden change in the normal pattern of your periods.
3. You soak more than seven or eight pads per day for longer than a week to ten days.
4. You develop severe tummy pain at any time.

Thankfully, these problems are not very common and most periods are mild and easy to manage.

Well, you did it! You got through this awkward section. We know periods are a little weird to talk about at first, but they are a *normal* part of becoming and being a woman. It's okay to feel a bit embarrassed.

God made your body this way—periods and all—for a reason. We'll talk more about that in the next question because we know you're wondering: *Why do I have to have periods in the first place? And why do periods have to come every month?*

Keep reading. Everything is about to make sense.

QUESTION 13

How do periods work, anyway?

One of my (Dr. Mari's) friends got her very first period on the day of her fourteenth birthday. She was the last of her friends to get her period. She had invited her friends over that night for a pajama party to celebrate her birthday. Here's what she says happened next:

> That day, I came home from school to get ready for the slumber party, went up to the bathroom, and discovered that I had "become a woman." My mom had already supplied me with the "necessities," so I quickly took care of it.
>
> That evening when my friends and I were all in the bathroom getting ready for bed, the discussion turned to our periods.
>
> When my friends discovered that I had mine, one asked, "How long have you had it?"

I said, "Awhile" (technically not a lie), and the look on her face was priceless.

Thereafter, I always felt like my period was God's birthday present to me. That made all of the unpleasantness that goes along with it so much easier to bear.

Although your first period may not come on your birthday, it is still a wonderful gift. Why?

You have hormones (with names like *FSH, LH, estrogen,* and *progesterone*) that rise and fall in predictable ways throughout your monthly cycle for a specific purpose. Their ups and downs are preparing your body for something special. Your periods have a lot to do with another gift you may receive someday. It is the gift of motherhood, one of the most amazing experiences a woman can have.

Here's how it's all related: From birth, girls have *ovaries, fallopian tubes,* and a *uterus.* Your two ovaries are oval-shaped, about the size of small pecans, and sit on either side of your *uterus* (womb). They are located in the very lowest part of your tummy, called the *pelvis.* When you are born, your ovaries each contain thousands of eggs, also called *ova.* Each egg (or *ovum*) is microscopic—smaller than the period at the end of this sentence.

Your two fallopian tubes are long and as thin as a piece of spaghetti. Each fallopian tube stretches from an ovary to the uterus, which is a pear-shaped organ that sits right in the middle of and at the very bottom of the pelvis.

The muscles in a woman's uterus are incredible—they can slowly stretch to the size of a basketball and hold a fully grown baby. Ever hear of Elastigirl? Your womb muscles are a bit like that— stretchy and strong. So you do have some superpowers after all.

According to *Guinness World Records,* the largest baby ever born (and, thus, held inside the mother's uterus) was twenty-three pounds and twelve ounces. That's the average size of an eighteen-month-old child! After all that stretching for nine months, the strong muscles of the uterus are able to begin to contract (we call that *labor*) and then push the child out when it's time for the baby to be born. Amazing!

As you enter puberty, your pituitary gland releases strong hormones (FSH and LH). These two hormones get your ovaries to make estrogen and progesterone, which cause many of the physical and emotional changes we've been talking about, including your menstrual cycles.

About once a month, a tiny egg (ovum) will be launched from one of your ovaries—a process called *ovulation*—right into the abdominal cavity. The fallopian tube is way cool. Its mouth, which is near the ovary, has amazing finger-like pods that are designed to draw the egg inside. They stretch out and then tighten—just as your fingers do when you open your hand and then make a fist. Once a finger touches the egg, all of the fingers contract and push the egg into the fallopian tube.

Once the egg is inside, the fallopian tube contracts rhythmically to push the egg toward the inside of the uterus. You can find absolutely amazing video of this on the Internet using the URL in our list of resources.

Anyway, in the days before you ovulate, estrogen will stimulate your uterus to build up its lining with extra blood and tissue, making the walls of your uterus (the *endometrium*) thick and lush. This prepares your uterus for a possible pregnancy each month. Why?

If you've already begun to have periods (or if you're just about to have your first period) and you have sexual intercourse with a male, you can get pregnant. Did you know that? Yes, as long as you're having periods, you can get pregnant if you have sex.

Let's say that again. Even while in middle school, you can get pregnant if you have sex, even if your period doesn't show up every month. (If you don't know much about sex, this would be a good time to ask your mom or trusted adult about it.)

So how does this happen? If a woman's egg joins up with a man's sperm cell, at that instant, the egg and sperm cells miraculously combine to create another human being—a new life. Once *fertilization* takes place, a brand-new, unique human being exists.

Then the newly formed human will travel down the fallopian tube to your uterus and attach, or implant, to the cushiony wall of your uterus. There, it will continue to develop as your unborn baby. Wow! By attaching to the lining of your uterus, he or she begins to grow in the safety of his or her new home. A woman's womb is the safest place on earth for God's miracle of new life.

So how is all this related to your periods? Here's how:

If your egg is released and not fertilized by a hopeful sperm—which is the case during most monthly cycles—then your body recognizes that you are *not* pregnant. Since there's no baby growing in your womb that month, those tissues that thickened within the uterus are not needed. So guess what happens? The uterus begins to contract and the excess lining (tissue and blood) leaves through the opening of the uterus (the *cervix*), into your vagina, and out of your body.

That's when your period comes. All of this blood and tissue is known as *menses*. After your period, the lining of the womb gets thin again. Then the whole cycle begins all over again, reminding girls and women that God made our bodies with a unique purpose.

This cycle happens almost every month for several decades (except, of course, when you're pregnant) until you reach the stage in life called *menopause*, when your periods stop. On average, you can wave periods goodbye around age fifty. Your periods won't last forever.

This is the science behind your menstrual period. But there are also spiritual realities involving your period that are just as important to recognize. As you begin to understand the awesome privilege of having a female body, we believe you will begin to see your periods as the gifts that they are.

Every period can remind you that God entrusted you with a gift and a responsibility. Everything that is unique about the female body, even having breasts that can nurture an infant with

Blot the Spot

Have you ever heard of "spotting"? This is when you see menstrual-like fluid during a time of the month when you're not having a period. It can look like your period is starting, but it never does. You simply "spot" for a day or two.

These are good days to wear panty liners to keep your underwear from getting stained. Such spotting is especially likely during those first two years of irregular periods. However, after that time, recurrent or painful spotting can signal a problem, such as an infection or a lesion on the cervix. If this type of spotting is an issue, see your doctor to figure out why.

milk, revolves around the possibility of the divinely designed gift of motherhood within marriage.

We've covered a lot of ground, and it all started by talking about your periods. Your monthly cycles are a great reminder of God's plan for you as a girl and as a woman who may one day be someone's mom—in God's perfect time.

So, with each period, when you are tempted to complain about the messiness or cramps, let your period remind you of the gift and responsibility that God has entrusted to you. You can even use any discomfort or messiness as an opportunity to pray.

Pray that God will help you honor him with your soul, your body, and your purity. Pray that he will help you see yourself through his eyes—every part of you. Even your periods, cramps, and moods.

What an amazing gift your body is—it's God's masterpiece. This whole process is an awesome part of God's creation.

QUESTION 14

What's that on my underwear?

I (Dr. Mari) have an embarrassing story to share with you. Years ago, I had a sleepover at my neighbor's house. The next morning we went to the beach. I was eleven years old, smack in the middle of puberty. My friend's sister was eight and hadn't started developing quite yet.

I went to the bathroom to change into my bathing suit and left my underwear on the floor. When we returned after hours of snorkeling, my friend's sister found my underwear. With a curious look on her face, she dangled my undies in front of me and asked, "What's *that* on your underwear?"

I was so terribly embarrassed. I wanted the earth to swallow me up and take me to the Land of Oz or somewhere far, far away. Thankfully, no one else was around for this awkward moment.

If I could go back in time, my answer about the normal discharge stain on my underwear would have been matter-of-fact and blush-free. The fact is that all girls see normal mucus appear on their underwear beginning around age nine or ten. About six months to a year before your first period, you may begin to see and feel mucus coming from your vagina. This is perfectly normal—God made you this way.

As all the hormone changes affect your breasts, hair, skin, brain, and moods, they also lead to fluids that end up on your underwear. What's on your undies is completely normal and God-designed.

So what exactly is this vaginal discharge? It is part of how your female reproductive organs stay clean and healthy. Your vagina and cervix (the lowest part of your womb) form fluids and mucus that carry away dead skin cells and bacteria. This can help prevent infections in the womb. Your discharge is a little bit like earwax, which keeps your ears clean. We know—double *yikes*.

You may wonder if normal discharge is stinky or what it's supposed to look like. Normal discharge can be sticky, stretchy, slippery, gooey, or tacky, and it can be clear, transparent, or a milky white shade. Although it has a natural scent, it's not a bad smell, and you'll get used to what's normal for you.

You may notice a strong odor if you're sweaty, as during sports, but washing with soap and water will remove that smell. If an unpleasant odor persists despite washing, get that checked by your doctor.

Normal discharge shouldn't itch, burn, sting, or hurt, but infections can be quite bothersome. If you become infected with a type of germ called *yeast*, it can be very itchy. These germs can overgrow in moist areas that don't "breathe" well, like under your breasts or inside your vagina. Vaginal yeast infections cause a cottage cheese–like discharge.

If you become infected with a type of germ called *bacteria*, your discharge may be frothy and yellow or green. The discharge may also burn, itch, or just feel uncomfortable. In either case, it's worth going to your doctor to check it out.

You may wonder what's the "right" way to wash the vaginal area. Soap and water is all you need. Your normal vaginal mucus takes care of cleaning the vagina itself—there's no need to help it along.

Have you heard of *douching*? This is *not* the right way to wash your vagina. Douche is a French word that means to wash or soak. Douches are mixtures of water and baking soda, vinegar, iodine, and other products that are squirted into the vagina to "clean" it. Yet most doctors and medical organizations recommend *not* doing this. It is unnecessary and can lead to infections being jetted right up inside you. So don't douche!

Observe the normal changes in your mucus throughout the month to get to know your body better. You can even identify when you're ovulating (when an egg is released from your ovary) by observing the day-to-day changes in your mucus closely. When it gets clear, stretchy, and slippery, it's egg time. This is the fertile time of the month. If a girl has sex with a boy when she's ovulating, she can get pregnant.

The next menstrual period will usually occur about two weeks after the egg is released—no matter how irregular your cycle. As you get to know your cycles, you can learn what to expect in terms of moods, breast tenderness, and other physical and emotional symptoms that may come each month.

Itch, Itch, Go Away

PREVENTING SKIN YEAST INFECTIONS

To help keep the skin around your vagina from getting sweaty, itchy, or infected with yeast:

- Wear cotton underwear, and avoid tight-fitting undies and pants. The goal is to keep those parts dry. Moisture will make yeast germs overgrow.
- If you're an athlete or dancer, bring extra underwear to practice and games.
- After a workout, wash and dry yourself and change into dry undies. You can sprinkle athletic powder in this area to help keep it dry.
- Avoid staying in a wet bathing suit too long.
- Avoid *scented* feminine pads or tampons, sprays, soaps, powder, and lotions. They can irritate your skin and contribute to infections.
- Bottom line: let your private parts breathe and keep them dry.

PREVENTING VAGINAL YEAST INFECTIONS

To prevent yeast infections inside the vagina (especially if you get them often):

- Eat a balanced diet rich in fruits, vegetables, whole grains, and nonfat dairy products.
- Some women think that eating foods with *Lactobacillus* organisms, such as yogurt or acidophilus milk, will prevent yeast infections. There's no medical evidence for this, but these foods can be part of a healthy diet.
- Ask your doctor or pharmacist about taking probiotics. These friendly bacteria can keep the harmful yeast germs under control.

- If you're getting yeast infections that are frequent or tough to treat, your doctor may need to check your sugar levels to rule out diabetes.

PREVENTING URINARY TRACT INFECTIONS

- In girls and women, the *urethra* (the tiny tube that carries urine from your bladder to the outside) is very short.
- Bacteria from your skin can travel up the short urethra and cause an infection in your bladder, a urinary tract infection (UTI). UTIs can hurt and cause burning when you pee. Ouch.
- To help prevent UTIs, wipe carefully after having a bowel movement. Always wipe front-to-back. After pooping, wiping from *back to front* can spread a troop of poop germs to the skin near the urethra — not a good move! Front-to-back wiping ensures that stinky troop of germs will stay far from your urethra and vagina. Hooray!

TREATING VAGINAL YEAST INFECTIONS

- If you develop the itchy, cottage-cheesy vaginal discharge that is so typical of vaginal yeast infections, you can buy an over-the-counter vaginal yeast treatment like *miconazole* to treat it.
- Just follow the instructions on the container.
- See your doctor if the infection gets worse or lasts more than a few days.

QUESTION 15

My breasts aren't growing. What's wrong with me?

By now you probably know exactly what we're going to say: Each girl develops at a different rate. And if your breasts aren't growing yet, they will begin to grow exactly at the time God intended— at the right time for *you*.

Sometime between the ages of eight and ten, you will notice two small, firm bumps under your nipples. You learned in question 4 that these bumps are known as *breast buds*. Initially, they may be a little sore, but that won't last very long.

One bud may emerge before the other, so don't be alarmed if things look a bit unequal at first. For most girls, one breast is a little bigger than the other. But you can always ask your doctor if you're not sure what's normal for you.

The beginning of breast development is called *thelarche*. It can begin slightly earlier for some girls or a bit later for others. Some girls seem to grow breasts overnight while their friends wonder, *Will my breasts ever grow?* It's different for each girl because God creates each of you uniquely.

During this part of puberty, some girls wonder if they can do anything to make their breasts grow faster or bigger. Despite what advertisements and magazines say, there is no magic cream, pill, or exercise that can speed up the process or make your breasts larger than they are designed to be.

Whether your breasts are already growing or just starting to "bud," you may wonder when to start wearing a bra. I (Dr. Mari) recently overheard some seven-year-olds talking about bras. They were surprised that a girl in fourth grade was already wearing a training bra. Then one turned and asked, "When will I need to start wearing one?"

I was amazed that, in second grade, girls talk about training bras. I explained that girls' bodies develop at different rates and that she likely still has a few more years to go. Some girls begin wearing a bra in late elementary school, whereas others start in middle school. Both are perfectly normal.

Rather than wearing a bra early on, some girls prefer a light undershirt. Talk to your mom or a trusted adult about what you prefer and do what's most comfortable for you. One thing we've noticed is that some girls are thrilled to be old enough to start wearing a bra, whereas others are not at all excited. These are both common reactions, and you'll soon get used to the whole thing. Do what makes you feel most at ease during this time of change.

Bras can be very helpful. They help support your growing breasts, especially during exercise, and they also help you dress more modestly as your breasts grow larger.

When your breasts begin to grow, you can wear a training bra, which is a lightweight, pullover type of bra for growing girls.

A lot of girls prefer to start off with a camisole, which is a comfy and lightweight tank top.

Breasts come in all sizes, and they change over time. But whether your breasts are like buds, fried eggs, growing apples, or full-grown watermelons, all girls eventually need a few good bras. Songs have been written (and sung brilliantly) about the importance of a comfy "over-the-shoulder-boulder-holder." So be sure to have some fun with this.

Shopping for Your First Bra

Once your breasts begin to grow, it's time to shop. You get to handpick your first few bras. Plan a fun day out with your mom, aunt, or older sister and go shop for bras together. Let her help you find the right style and, more important, the right size. You want a bra that's comfortable and doesn't slide all over the place or feel tight.

It can take a little while to get used to wearing that first bra — they can be tricky. They can be difficult to fasten and adjust. They may dig in, ride up, slide off your shoulders, or peek out of your clothing, especially if you don't have just the right bra for your body shape and activity.

A bra can even snap open right as you spike a volleyball with all your might — WHAM! POP! Uh-oh! Yes, that happened to me (Dr. Mari) in high school.

Several department stores offer free bra fittings. We know what you're probably thinking: *Fitted? I need to get fitted? What is this — the prom?* Don't worry. No need to fret over that first fitting. (You can do measurements at home first. While at home, have your mom or sister or trusted adult measure your chest size all the way around the fullest part. Then measure around your chest under your breasts. Write down these two numbers and

Have you noticed the numbers and letters on bras, like 28A, 28AA, 32B, or 36C? In bra language, the *number* refers to your chest size (the total inches at the widest point around your chest) when measured with a measuring tape. The *letter* refers to cup size (the measurement of the breast itself), as in the triangular section that covers your breast like a bikini top.

As your breasts grow larger, your cup size increases. You may start out with an A or AA cup. Lots of girls may start with a

bring them with you.) Then choose a department store to go try on some bras.

Most stores have a clerk who is trained to help fit girls for their first bra. She can help you figure out your cup size (the letter) and can teach you how to adjust the straps. Although you may feel awkward going there and asking for help, the ladies in the bra section do this all the time. It will really help to have a woman trained to fit bras measure you and suggest the best bra size for you. Fittings at these stores are done discreetly in a fitting room, so it will be private and not embarrassing.

One of our reviewers, who works at one of these stores, wrote:

> I see young girls coming in for their first bra fitting all the time. They are usually really nervous and shy and maybe feel a little awkward about getting a fitting, but it is very important that they do come in to some professional place for that fitting ... [and] start off with the right bra from the beginning.

It's perfectly normal to feel a bit embarrassed when bra shopping for the first time, but don't worry. All girls and women go through this. We're all in this together.

sports bra, which provides support for running, jumping, and more active days. Not all bras are alike, so you'll have to try some on or get fitted.

Once you know your size, walk around and pick out your favorite designs. If you're looking to smooth out your growing breasts and nipples, a training bra will do the trick. If you want more support for your active lifestyle, a sports bra is the way to go. For all other needs, a regular bra will suffice.

Your new bra should feel comfortable. If it feels tight, choose a different style or a larger size. Adjust the straps if needed; that can really help when a bra wants to ride up and dig in. Along the way, ask questions about bra styles and don't forget to laugh. You'll likely remember this day for a very long time.

Before we finish this question, let us give you a warning. There's one thing you may experience that can feel awkward: While in school or playing sports, you may be sent to the locker room to change into your physical education (PE) or sports clothes. You will notice that some girls change in front of each other, whereas others prefer the privacy of a bathroom stall. Many girls feel uncomfortable when thrown into the chaos and rowdiness of a locker room, and both sides can get teased.

Some girls will tease each other's looks when they change in public. Occasionally, they may also tease the one who chooses more privacy. Try to relax without worrying about what the other girls think, say, or do. We know this can be easier said than done, but remember that girls often tease to deal with their own discomfort. And anytime you're getting naked, privacy is not a bad idea.

Speaking of locker rooms, when you change clothes with other girls, you may notice the tendency to compare yourself with how other girls look. You may wonder, *Are my breasts too big, or are they too small?* And because of our culture's influence, here's what often happens: If they're small, you want them bigger, and if they're large, you wish they were smaller. Sound familiar?

Breasts: An Architectural Feat

Did you know that the human breast is a work of art? It's true. Just like a rose begins with a small bud, the human breast starts with a tiny bud and grows into a mature breast that's fully equipped to nurture a growing baby. The breast continues to change throughout a woman's reproductive years, forming a complex system of lobes and ducts that house and transport milk through the nipple. Isn't that neat?

During your menstrual cycle, your breasts are changing too. Just like the uterus is getting ready for a possible pregnancy, the breasts get ready too.

During the first part of your menstrual cycle, the milk ducts in your breasts grow as estrogen is released. In the second part of your cycle, after ovulation, progesterone rises and milk glands form. As these glands enlarge in the second half of your monthly cycle, your breasts may feel "lumpy." This is normal.

These hormonal effects likely explain the soreness or swollen feeling of your breasts, especially right as your period begins each month.

As your period starts, your breasts return to their normal size, and the whole cycle begins again next month.

Are you starting to recognize that your body is magnificent, beautifully and wonderfully made for God's purposes? Your breasts are another reminder of the gift of your body — God's masterpiece.

Breasts don't simply add curves to a girl's body. If you become a mom one day, you'll have the wonderful opportunity to breastfeed your baby. Breastfeeding provides the best and healthiest milk a baby can have, and that's pretty amazing.

What do you think about all this? God gave you *your* body for a reason, and you're still growing and changing. Embrace yourself just how God made you; appreciate his design for you. Thank him for who you are, whose you are, and who you will become.

Even the Scriptures use a bit of humor and poetry to describe your changing body. Take a look:

> Your breasts are like two fawns, like twin fawns of a gazelle.
>
> *Song of Solomon 7:3*

> Your stature is like that of the palm, and your breasts like clusters of fruit.
>
> *Song of Solomon 7:7*

One last thing: when it comes to your breasts, dressing modestly will help keep the stares off, which will make this transition go more smoothly for you. Pretty soon, you'll get used to your new twin gazelles, and they'll remind you of the precious gift of your femininity.

QUESTION 16

When do I get to shave my legs and underarms?

My (Dr. Mari's) daughter is a girly girl. Although lately she's grown to love the whole spectrum of the rainbow, for years she's been all about pink and purple, and now she favors blue. Her bedroom is a definite girl zone, featuring the likes of Rapunzel and a host of Pixie Hollow fairies. It's another world in there—magical and mystical.

We love doing things together—from crafts to chats to cuddles. Recently my daughter and I started our own foot soaking tradition. If she needs some cheering up, I invite her to soak her feet with me. She lights up right away. Somehow, as the soapy, warm water hits her feet, her lips get going. We laugh, joke around, and chitchat about everything. I love the opportunity to hear her questions and help her as much as I can—with big and small things.

As you walk through puberty, you too have many questions. You may wonder things like when you can start shaving or when it is appropriate to start wearing makeup. Talk to your mom or another trusted adult about all this. Your friends have their own families, and their viewpoint and rules might be different from yours.

In general, most girls begin shaving between the ages of nine and sixteen. There is quite a bit of variation here, and you can choose not to shave too. This is not a medical necessity by any means; it is more of a cultural and family decision. In some cultures, women shave their underarms and lower legs, but not their thighs. In others, women don't shave at all.

One thing to keep in mind is that, once you start shaving, your hair will grow back differently in that area. It will be less smooth and more prickly. The most important thing is not so much when to shave, but to get permission from your parents before picking up that razor.

Your mom might mention different choices you have, like a handheld razor, an electric razor, or hair-removing cream. She will teach you never to shave your legs while they're dry; that can cause a lot of itching, discomfort, and even a rash. Also, if you're going to swim in the ocean, shave the day before, or your legs will likely start burning as soon as they touch the water. Ouch!

Waxing is not as convenient as shaving, but you can be hair-free for weeks, or longer. Your mom or trusted adult can help you pick out the right wax at any convenience store and help you use it correctly. Read the directions carefully, test it on a small part of your body (to make sure you're not allergic to it), and wait at least six hours before you proceed.

Around the time when your breasts begin to grow, you'll likely notice some hair in the pubic area as well. This usually happens after your breasts bud, but a few girls get pubic hair before their

Will My Hair Grow Thicker After I Shave?

In a word, no! As it grows, each hair tapers, getting thinner at the ends. This is why longer hair bends more easily than shorter hair. This can sometimes lead to those *split ends* you're so glad to get rid of after a haircut.

This is also why shorter hair feels more stubbly than longer hair. The blunt end of shaved hair may feel temporarily coarser, but it's not because it was shaved, but because it's shorter. It's all part of how God made hair.

breasts grow. At first, this hair will be smooth and fine, but as it fills in, it will become coarser and curlier. A year or two after your pubic hair appears, expect to see some hair show up under your arms as well. Woo-hoo.

Through all these changes, make sure you get your mom's or a trusted adult's permission *and* help before shaving anything, especially near your groin (along the inner thighs). Girls don't really need to shave there at all, but some choose to so hair won't show when wearing a bathing suit. Be super careful!

Shaving this sensitive area with a razor can lead to tough-to-treat skin infections that can grow into painful bumps called *boils*—we don't recommend it. And if you do it incorrectly, it can be quite uncomfortable. Using a safe, hair-removing product might be a better alternative at your age, though it's probably best to leave that hair alone.

Remember that, although it's great to talk to your girlfriends, they're learning too, so their answers aren't always correct. If in doubt, ask your mom, an older sister, or a trusted woman. They went through everything you're going through—and more.

Get me off this roller coaster.
Why am I so moody?

See if this sounds familiar. You wake up full of energy. You put on your favorite shirt, cute shorts, and matching socks, and head to the kitchen for breakfast. As you sit down to eat, your little sister spills her milk and your mom asks you to clean it up.

Without warning and for no good reason, you blow up. Your sister starts crying. Your mom sighs. And your brother walks in, still half asleep, to quite a scene. He burps loudly, and you greet him by yelling at him for sleeping when he could have been helping.

Not a great way to start a morning, is it? But this is exactly the kind of chaos that moodiness can create. Nobody likes it, including you.

Moodiness can mean that one moment you're skipping along, feeling happy, and the next instant you're a grump. Ever feel such contrasting emotions in the same day, even within the same five-minute period? Welcome to puberty.

As a young woman on your journey through puberty, your mood can change in a matter of seconds. You can go from gentle swan to ferocious tigress without so much as a blink. These ever-changing moods can be explained, in part, by a word you're starting to love — *hormones*.

Yes, the same hormones that God designed to guide puberty can also make you moody. But here's the thing. You can't blame everything you feel on these chemicals, and you can't let moods run your life.

Although hormones can make you feel like you're riding an out-of-control emotional roller coaster, we have good news for you. Regardless of how you *feel*, you can control how you respond. God equipped your body with hormones and your spiritual life with fruit:

> The fruit of the Spirit is love, joy, peace, patience, kindness, goodness, faithfulness, gentleness, self-control; against such things there is no law.
>
> *Galatians 5:22–23,* NASB

When life feels out of control, you can choose to exercise *self-control*. And God-given self-control is more powerful than *any* hormone.

I (Dr. Mari) wonder if God gave women hormone shifts partly to help us learn to *exercise* our self-control. You see, regardless of your circumstances or feelings, you *always* have a choice. You can hop off the roller coaster, or at least slow it down, and gain some control over your life.

Here's what can happen when you stay on that loopy roller coaster — it happened to me (Dr. Mari) when I was about twelve.

Before Christmas, my brother and I checked the mail every day, eager to get our favorite toy catalog. One year, it finally came, and he got to it first. Bummer. I waited and waited, and he wouldn't give it up.

I asked nicely again and again, but he refused to share. So what did I do? I stomped out of the room and slammed my bedroom door—WHAM! Everyone heard me, probably even the neighbors. And then someone came to my door.

Still fuming, and certain it was my brother, I let him have it, yelling out words that I can't repeat here. It wasn't pretty. When I finally stopped yelling, I saw my father standing there shocked—and not at all amused. He had kindly brought the catalog and planned to serve it with a smile. Big oops!

When you feed your moods and emotions rather than try to manage them, you end up feeling worse. Sometimes you hurt others too. Has that ever happened to you?

The good news is that, although some moodiness is a normal part of going through puberty, you don't have to live by how you *feel*. You can live by what you *know*. And you know that kindness is better than rudeness and respect is better than rebellion.

So when you wake up feeling down, when you're upset or angry, you have a choice to make. You can exercise self-control in any situation. You can stop yourself before saying something hurtful. You can think *before* you say or do something you might regret. You can regroup, gather your thoughts, and decide if that's the wise and godly choice or not.

It also helps to remember that most bad moods don't last long, so be patient with yourself. Count to ten; maybe take some deep breaths. Walk away—quietly, without stomping—and talk to God about how you feel.

If you need to, have a good, cleansing cry. Go hang out with a cheerful friend, or laugh with your goofy little brother. Read a good book, turn up some good music, and pray. Perhaps you can call a friend or talk to your mom or sister or a funny neighbor.

You can go for a run or a walk or pet your dog. Doing something nice for someone else may help take your mind off yourself. Next thing you know, you're feeling better.

It's important to recognize that, whereas some moodiness is normal, being irritable all the time or very often can signal a problem. If moods get to be too much, and if you also feel extremely tired, sad, or hopeless, you may be getting depressed. If you feel down often or stop enjoying life, talk to your mom or dad or a trusted teacher or adult who can help you. You may need to see a counselor, psychologist, or doctor if these feelings don't go away. We talk much more about depression in the next question.

All the healthy habits we've discussed can help keep your stress level down and balance your moods. And speaking of stress, puberty can be a time of significant stress from school, family, and relationships—and even from your body changes. You may feel like more is expected of you now, and you're right. But you can make this transition smoother and minimize stress.

Did you know that a certain level of stress is good? It energizes you and helps prepare you for what you need to do. But stress that isn't managed well can drain your energy and make you procrastinate and worry. As you learn to use stress to your advantage, you will benefit from the stress hormones that motivate you while minimizing the stress effects that drain you.

So what can you do to cope with stress? As with managing moodiness, eating a healthy diet, staying active, and getting enough rest are critical. Thankfully, there are many fun ways to manage stress. Usually they involve doing the stuff you love to do.

Do you like to sing or dance? Do you love to run? Do you feel better when you're outside surrounded by nature? Make sure you do some of these things you love every day; you will feel happier and less stressed.

When I (Dr. Mari) was twelve, my best friend gave me a journal I've kept all these years. If I felt confused or sad, I would write about it. I felt better and I learned more about myself. Writing

Stressed, Moody, Tired — or All of the Above?

The word *hormone* comes from the Greek word *hormo*, meaning "to set in motion." Hormones set many things into motion, including your metabolism, your growth and development, and, yes, your mood. Hormones like estrogen, serotonin, and beta-endorphins can contribute to a "good mood." Sometimes it's all about hormones, but not always.

Many young people visit their doctor because they feel tired. They lack energy and wonder if something's wrong with their bodies. For most of the girls with these types of complaints, the solution is clear. They need to make better choices. Most of them need:

- *More sleep.* Most tweens and teens need at least nine to ten hours every night (read more about how to get a better night's sleep in question 6).

- *More physical activity.* Exercise gives you energy and speeds up your metabolism (that means your body's wide awake). It also helps you burn fat for energy instead of muscle. And staying physically active helps you feel better during the day and sleep better at night.

- *Better nutrition* (you can read more about this in questions 7 and 10).

- *More fiber.* A high-fiber diet helps you have more energy throughout the day. High-fiber foods include nuts, whole grains, fruits, vegetables, oatmeal, corn, beans, avocados, and others.

- *Less soda and caffeine.* Sugary drinks and caffeine (found in many "energy drinks") can dehydrate you. They remove too much fluid from your body, making you tired. They provide no nutrition at all, only empty calories. Choose water instead.

- *Less bad fats.* A diet high in bad, or *saturated*, fats can slow down your metabolism (your body takes a nap) and make you sluggish. Bad fats can also increase your risk for obesity, heart problems, and diabetes. Instead, consider good fats such as *monounsaturated* fats (found in olive oil, canola oil, sunflower oil, avocados, and nuts) or *polyunsaturated* fats (found in soybean oil, walnuts, sunflower/sesame/pumpkin seeds, flaxseed, fatty fish [salmon, tuna, mackerel, herring, trout, sardines], and soy milk).

- *Stress management.* If stress is not handled properly, it can affect how you feel, how well you do in school, and your relationships. It can make you tired, anxious, or depressed. If you feel stressed out, get help from your parents, teachers, school counselor, and/or a psychologist.

- *No smoking, alcohol, or drugs* (you can read more about these in question 29). All these substances contribute to moodiness, depression, fatigue, anxiety, poor sleep, and countless other problems. Be wise and stay away from all that.

Controlling Your Moodiness

Here are some tips for moody teens from WebMD:

- Think about something or someone you are thankful for.
- Do something nice. It's hard to be in a bad mood when you're helping someone.
- Listen to some upbeat and uplifting music.
- Realize that you're not alone. Talk to a friend about your moods. It might surprise you to discover that others are going through the same mood swings as you.
- Don't keep your feelings to yourself. This can make problems seem much worse than they actually are. If a friend or parent is not available, talk to a teacher or counselor.
- Do something active. Get outside if you can. Go for a walk, ride your bike, play tennis or another favorite sport. Or just take a deep breath and enjoy the fresh air.
- Get enough sleep every night. Being tired can make you feel gloomy and irritable, and it makes it harder to cope with your moods.

can help you deal with stress and moods. It's also a great way to communicate with your parents about tough or embarrassing topics. Give it a try.

Do you enjoy reading? A good book at the right time can bring peace and comfort, or it can simply be fun. Reading the Bible every day will help you know God and his plans for your life. It will also keep you growing all the fruit of the Spirit.

Your friends can also help you deal with the stresses of life. While in middle school, I (Dr. Mari) grew close to three girl-friends, and we're still like sisters. We've cried together, laughed together, and figured out life's messes together.

Some of the friendships you're making now may last a lifetime. So nurture good friendships starting now. Choose your friends well and treat them with love, kindness, and respect. They will often be the ones who give you the most grace on those moody days that we all face.

> The words of the reckless pierce like swords, but the tongue of the wise brings healing.
>
> *Proverbs 12:18*

> Be completely humble and gentle; be patient, bearing with one another in love.
>
> *Ephesians 4:2*

Emotions and the Bible

Did you ever read the story of Job? It's about a good man who lost everything overnight, including his home, riches, and family. Job was depressed for a long time as he tried to make sense of his new life, his suffering, and God. Three friends tried to help him and failed. But God never failed him.

In his grief, Job said:

> "If only my anguish could be weighed and all my misery be placed on the scales! It would surely outweigh the sand of the seas — no wonder my words have been impetuous."
>
> Job 6:2–3

Impetuous means reckless, hotheaded, saying words one might regret. Job's sadness was so deep that even his friends didn't know how to help him. So Job talked to God, sharing his true feelings rather than denying the awful way he felt.

When God answered, Job gained a whole new perspective. Job felt God's love for him once more and said:

> "My ears had heard of you but now my eyes have seen you."
>
> Job 42:5

Job then forgave his friends, and God blessed him.

When we are moody, we can talk to God (by prayer) and listen to God (by reading his Word). I (Dr. Walt) have found that when I'm moody, the books of Psalms and Proverbs are particularly helpful. Here's what I do:

- I look at the date. For example, when I was writing this, it was the third day of the month.
- Then I read one chapter in the book of Proverbs (there are thirty-one chapters in Proverbs) that matches the date: Proverbs 3.
- Then I read several psalms. I take the day of the month and add thirty, again and again, up to 150 (the total number of psalms). So I would read Psalms 3, 33, 63, 93, and 123.
- With the exception of Psalm 119, the psalms and proverbs are short. So I can read one chapter of Proverbs and five chapters of Psalms in just a few minutes.

Our emotions are not a surprise to God; he made us this way. So trust God with the uncertainties of your life, including the changes that come with puberty. He will never fail you.

QUESTION 18

Can my moods be dangerous?

I (Dr. Walt) saw a young woman in my office about six months ago. I'll call her Sophia. She told me she had not been feeling like herself. She kept feeling worse and worse, and her family and friends began to notice.

Sophia felt unmotivated, like her get-up-and-go had got up and gone. She had trouble with her sleep, both trouble going to sleep (we call that *insomnia*) and trouble staying asleep; she would wake up at all hours during the night. So she felt sleepy all day. Even worse, she didn't enjoy her good friends anymore, or the activities she used to love, like biking and shopping.

This wasn't all. Sophia had always been a good student. But over the last three months her grades dropped like a rock. She couldn't concentrate or think as clearly as before. For the first time in her life, she even forgot to turn in an assignment. She denied using any drugs, and a physical exam and lab work at her student health center were all normal.

She was overeating and gaining weight. But worst of all, she just felt like sitting around all day and crying. "I feel sad all the time, Dr. Walt."

Sophia and her mom hadn't thought of it, but I was pretty sure she had depression.

I asked questions and did some additional tests to rule out other possible causes (like a difficult relationship or a hormone problem), but all the tests came back normal. A depression questionnaire confirmed that she was very depressed.

"I can't be depressed," Sophia insisted. "I thought only old people got depressed. Or people who have a friend die." Sophia was wrong on both counts.

Many people don't understand depression. You see, depression can be both a *symptom* that comes and goes and a *disease* that lingers. Although we all feel depressed (sad, down, or just kinda blah) at times, that does not mean we have the *disease* called *depression*. Moods come and go; full-blown depression stays.

Since depression is so common, let's talk about it. The more you know about it, the more likely that you will be able to help others—and maybe even save someone's life. Here's why.

Depression is a deep sadness and despair (think of Job) as well as discouragement that can last weeks, months, years, or a lifetime. People who are depressed often feel hopeless and inadequate. They can feel such gloom and desperation, they even think about hurting themselves or actually do try to hurt themselves or others. So, yes, depression can be very dangerous.

At any one time, about one in five teens (20 percent) has depressive *symptoms*, like persistent sadness, sleeping problems, and irritability. But when it comes to the *disease*, about 6 to 8 percent of teens have some form of depression at any time.

Signs of Depression

People who are depressed show it in different ways. A person may have three or four of these symptoms or just about the whole list. And, with depression, you can't seem to shake them off — they continue to weigh you down day after day. Here are some of the most common symptoms of depression:

- Sadness that won't go away
- Hopelessness
- Persistent boredom
- Unexplained irritability or crying
- Loss of interest in usual activities
- Eating and/or sleeping more or less than normal
- Difficulty falling asleep, or waking up too early
- Missed school or poor school performance
- Threats or attempts to run away from home
- Outbursts of anger, shouting, complaining
- Reckless behavior
- Self-injury, such as cutting or beating oneself
- Aches and pains that don't get better with treatment
- Social isolation, poor communication
- Extreme sensitivity to rejection or failure
- Thoughts about death or suicide
- Alcohol or drug use

In other words, if you're in the average school, and there are 1,000 kids in your school, over 200 will have depressive *symptoms*, like those listed above, while about sixty to eighty will actually be suffering from the *disease* of depression. Yipes! Think about that the next time your school is gathered in a gym or auditorium.

Before the teen years, equal numbers of boys and girls are depressed. But by age thirteen, a dramatic shift occurs. More than twice as many girls as boys are depressed as teens—and this proportion persists into adulthood. Does anyone know why? Well, it turns out that medical detectives have some clues.

A girl's fluctuating hormones lead to real mood shifts during puberty. Sadness, discouragement, and feeling down are natural human emotions that affect all of us at times, but even more so for girls during puberty. Boys also have these emotions, as expressed in many of King David's psalms, which seem to have been written in times of torment, discouragement, sadness, or downright depression.

> Why, my soul, are you downcast? Why so disturbed within me? Put your hope in God, for I will yet praise him, my Savior and my God.
>
> *Psalm 42:5*

You likely have felt sad after a disagreement, argument, or fight with a family member or friend. You naturally would be down after someone close to you moves away. No doubt you've been discouraged if you've done poorly on an assignment, test, or competition. And something like the death of someone we are extremely close to can lead to the saddest of sadness—grief.

However, and this is key, most of the time we deal with these emotions and, over time, we get over them. They pass. Things get better. This is *not* true about the illness of depression when it's not treated.

As Sophia learned, depression affected more than her emotional health. It affected her energy, motivation, concentration, appetite, sleep, and weight. Worst of all, it kept her from enjoying the good things in life she normally enjoyed so much—such as her hobbies, good meals, and her relationships with God, her family, and her best friends.

Why Do People Get Depressed?

There is rarely a single cause for depression in any one person. Many factors can play a role, including:

- Genetics. You can inherit the tendency to develop depression from family members who had it (even as far back as your great-grandparents).
- Past or ongoing emotional abuse, bullying, or trauma.
- Living in a difficult family or social environment.
- Lack of exercise or light (such as during winter) and not getting enough sleep can make depression more likely.
- Inadequate nutrition from an un-healthy diet and/or eating disorders like bulimia and anorexia (you can read more about eating disorders using this QR code or the URL in our resources list).

National Eating Disorders Association

- Alcohol and/or drug use.
- Many medical disorders can cause or coexist with depression.
- People who are pessimistic (negative — think Eeyore) or melancholic (naturally sad or pensive) can be more prone to depression.
- Sometimes a person can become depressed for no obvious reason at all.

Regardless of the contributing factors, an imbalance of chemicals in the brain results in depression — chemicals like *serotonin*, *norepinephrine*, and *dopamine*. If these *neurotransmitters* get all out of whack, you may start sounding and acting like Eeyore. Like Charlie Brown on bad days, you may begin to sound like you've lost hope.

She was the perfect example of what we talked about in question 1: If one health wheel is out of alignment, it can affect the other three. Sophia's flat emotional health wheel impacted her physical, relational, and spiritual health wheels.

Sophia was like many of our depressed patients in that she did not even realize she was depressed. Like others we see with depression, she mistakenly began to think of herself as a failure, a bad person, a poor student, a quitter, and a loser. And Sophia's mother thought her daughter just had "a bad attitude" or, even worse, was abusing drugs and not admitting it.

I reassured them that it's very common for depression to go unrecognized. "But now that we know what's wrong," I told them, "we can do something about it." We then talked about all the different ways we could begin to help Sophia get better.

When a girl with depression gets the right care, she can get better. But if depression is not diagnosed and treated, it can get worse—sometimes a lot worse. Left untreated, teen depression dramatically increases the risk of attempting suicide or having thoughts about harming oneself. This is especially true for girls, who are more than twice as likely to attempt suicide as boys. Tragically, suicide is the third leading cause of death in people ages ten to twenty-four.

If you have a friend you think is depressed, encouraging them to get the help they need may literally save their life. The good news is that depression is one of the most treatable diseases. The National Association of School Psychologists says, "Virtually everyone who receives proper, timely intervention can be helped." That means getting the right help at the right time.

This is why we tell people who think they are depressed not to wait to get help while hoping it will go away on its own. And if you or a friend might be depressed, getting help should include both of these:

1. *Get a medical checkup.* Your doctor can check for any
   health problems that might be causing symptoms of

Help for Depression

Beyond the medicines that are sometimes needed to treat depression, so many things can help the disorder. Here are some of them:

- Counseling and/or therapy, preferably from a Christian mental health expert (counselor, psychologist, or therapist). This can be extremely helpful.

- Daily physical activity such as a brisk walk, a bike ride, jogging, or dancing, especially if done with a friend or exercise buddy.

- Getting outside in daylight and enjoying nature and fresh air can lift your mood.

- Good nutrition. One person with depression might overeat while another has no appetite. It's important to eat plenty of fruits and vegetables, drink plenty of water, and not skip meals.

- Healthy food choices, avoiding bad sugars and bad fats, which can make you sluggish.

- Setting aside time to relax and/or learning stress-reduction skills.

- Playing, petting a dog, or doing fun things with good friends.

- Finding something to laugh about—a funny movie or book perhaps.

- Exercising one's imagination (reading, journaling, painting, drawing, doodling, sewing, writing, dancing, composing music, etc.) to get creative juices flowing and loosen up some positive emotions.

- Sleeping well. Good sleep helps people recover from depression more quickly (you can read more about this in question 6).

- Looking on the bright side. Depression affects normal thinking, making everything seem gloomy, negative, and hopeless. I (Dr. Walt) encourage my patients to make an effort to notice the good things in life. I also encourage them to consider their strengths, gifts, and blessings.

- I (Dr. Walt) tell patients to journal each night about five blessings from that day. Then I have them think about these blessings and pray, thanking God for all of them.

- Setting aside quiet time with God each day — talking to him (through prayer) and listening to him (by reading the Bible).

- Studying what God's Word says about sadness, depression, and grief.

- Memorizing Scripture verses that are meaningful and encouraging.

- Joining (or starting) a small group of trusted Christian friends for fellowship, accountability, and prayer.

- Most of all, it's important to be patient. Depression takes time to heal.

depression. For example, having diabetes or a lazy thyroid gland (*hypothyroidism*) can cause a depressed mood, low energy, and tiredness. *Mononucleosis* (mono) is a viral infection that can also make a person feel very tired and even depressed.

These medical problems mimic depression. They make a person look and feel depressed, but when you treat the medical problem, they feel better. Seeing your doctor and getting help for these conditions can make a huge difference.

2. *Talk to a professional counselor.* When someone has depression, "talk therapy" with a therapist or counselor is usually very helpful (even if your doctor also recommends a medication). Here are just a few of the ways talk therapy helps:

- A counselor will help people with depression understand the disorder and how it affects their emotions. The counselor may teach them how to journal or put their feelings into words. This can help people feel understood and supported.

- A Christian counselor will point people to helpful Bible verses and help them understand how God can use depression in their lives (like God used the physical challenges in Kate's life from question 1).

- A therapist will help people develop a plan to work out problems and overcome the negative or self-critical thinking that feeds depression.

- A Christian counselor can help people develop more positive and biblical ways of looking at things. This helps them learn to accept themselves, which improves their self-esteem.

- Therapists help people build the confidence they need to deal with depression.

A Simple Screening Test

A simple, two-question *screening* test helps doctors and counselors identify people who might be depressed. They ask: Over the past two weeks, have you been bothered by either of the following problems?

1. Little interest or pleasure in doing things
2. Feeling down, depressed, or hopeless

If you answer, "Not at all," you likely don't have the disease of depression. If you can't answer, "Not at all" to *both* questions, the next step is to talk to a trusted adult about your feelings. They can help you contact a counselor who can help.

The same week that I (Dr. Walt) wrote the first draft of this question, I saw Sophia and her mother back in my office. They'd done much of what I recommended. In her follow-up visits over six months, she continued to get better.

Thankfully, she went back to feeling and acting like a bubbly teenager. At the end of the visit, I asked, "Sophia, what was the most important thing God taught you during your depression?"

She thought a moment, then smiled. "I learned how to trust and obey him even in my darkest moments. And," she said, smiling gratefully at her mom, "he taught me the importance of my family."

She looked back at me. "And now he's given me a ministry with other girls who are sad and depressed. I've found the Bible is true when it says, 'God is our merciful Father and the source of all comfort. He comforts us in all our troubles so that we can comfort others. When they are troubled, we will be able to give them the same comfort God has given us.'"

"Second Corinthians?" I asked.

She smiled and nodded. "Chapter 1, verses 3 and 4. It's from the New Living Translation. It really speaks to me."

"Me too," I replied. Before they left, we prayed and thanked God for being so faithful and so good.

> Even though I walk through the darkest valley, I will fear no evil, for you are with me; your rod and your staff, they comfort me.
>
> *Psalm 23:4*

> "But I will restore you to health and heal your wounds," declares the LORD.
>
> *Jeremiah 30:17*

QUESTION 19

Acne and tanning — how do I win with my skin?

TANNING

An old expression says, "Beauty is only skin deep." By now, you know that this is not true from God's perspective. He considers you his beautiful creation because he created you in his image.

Still, most girls have two areas of concern when it comes to their skin: (1) the annoying reality of acne and (2) the *perceived* benefits of tanning. So what do you need to know to have the healthiest skin possible?

Let's start with acne, which is a normal and natural (and, yes, annoying) part of growing up. The primary cause of acne is overactive oil glands in your skin, especially on your face, neck, chest, and back. The same hormones that lead to puberty rev up these oil glands.

Since different girls have different reactions to their hormones, some will get more acne than others. Stress can also worsen acne. But the good news is that there's a lot you can do to reduce the number and severity of breakouts.

You'll be delighted to learn that foods like pizza and chocolate do *not* cause acne. However, it is possible that these foods, dairy products, or diets high in sugars may cause or worsen acne in *some* kids. The American Academy of Dermatology (AAD) says:

- If you think a food might be worsening your acne, consider avoiding that product for a time.
- Be patient. After you start avoiding that food item, it may take up to twelve weeks for your acne to improve.
- If you're convinced that dairy products worsen your acne and decide to limit or avoid them, talk to your doctor or pharmacist about taking a calcium and vitamin D supplement.

An over-the-counter acne medication can often clear up mild breakouts of acne. Look for a product with benzoyl peroxide (BP), a peeling agent that helps clear pores. Here are some of our BP tips:

- Sometimes BP can bleach clothing, so it's better to use it at night.
- Start with a product with 5 percent BP. Apply it at night after washing your face.
- Since BP causes dryness and flaking, use a moisturizing lotion after the BP.
- We recommend lotions instead of creams, as they are less likely to clog your pores. Make sure the lotion is fragrance-free, oil-free, and non-comedogenic.
- After about five days of daily use, if your acne hasn't improved much and your skin isn't irritated, use the 5 percent lotion twice a day. Or you may switch to a lotion with 10 percent BP and use it once a day (at bedtime).

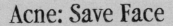

Acne: Save Face

Here are some effective ways to help prevent acne — or at least reduce the number of attacks:

- Keep your skin clean. This helps remove excess oils and dead skin cells that can clog your pores. But washing too much can dry out your skin or irritate existing acne.
- Keep it simple. Wash your face with a moisturizing soap twice a day. Some physicians recommend an antibacterial soap. Ideally, it should be a *noncomedogenic* soap, which means it won't cause or worsen acne.
- Wash your face and body with your hands rather than a washcloth, and never scrub.
- Avoid harsh alcohol-based or oil-based cleansers.
- Wash after exercising; sweat and dirt can clog your pores and worsen acne.
- Gently pat dry with a clean towel.
- Keep hair gel and other hair products away from your face as much as possible. Many hair products contain chemicals that can worsen acne.
- Try not to pick at your face or lean your chin on your hands, which can worsen your breakout.

- After another four to five days of consistent use, if your acne still hasn't improved and your skin isn't irritated, use the 10 percent BP twice a day.

If these tips don't work and your acne does not get better (or if it worsens), see your family's doctor. Your doctor is trained to help get your skin to look its best and probably also dealt with acne as a teen.

Acne will usually improve with simple prescription gels or creams, oral medications, or a combination of both. But you'll need to be very patient. It may take weeks or a few months to find the exact combination of medicines to help clear up your acne. There are many, many options, and one will help, eventually. So don't give up too soon.

While you wait, you may be tempted to squeeze and pop a big pimple. This may actually worsen your acne by pushing the infected material deeper into the skin and causing even more swelling and redness. Popping pimples may even leave a purplish mark that stays on the skin for weeks. Squeezing pimples can also lead to scarring. Don't do it!

The best news of all is that, in general, acne gets better and is often greatly improved or gone by the time you complete puberty. Prescription treatments usually work if you follow your doctor's advice.

Acne isn't the only thing affecting your skin that can show up during puberty. You need to make some very important decisions about tanning—whether in the sun or in a tanning salon.

As I (Dr. Walt) was writing this chapter, I saw a sad news report about a young woman who was told her chance of survival was only 20 percent. As you can imagine, she was devastated. What disease threatened her life? It was a type of skin cancer. But what caused her cancer was the real surprise—the twelve indoor tanning sessions she had just before her wedding day.

Only six years after getting married, this young woman was diagnosed with one of the most dangerous and potentially fatal forms of skin cancer—*melanoma*—and it had spread throughout her body.

More and more women with skin cancer are teaming up to warn young girls like you about the dangers of tanning.

Many of our young patients (and their parents) are shocked to learn that sunburns and tanning are major risk factors for getting skin cancer. In fact, having one or more blistering sunburns as a child or teenager increases your risk of developing skin cancer as an adult. Would you believe that one in two young people reports having had at least one sunburn in the past year?

But not all skin cancers come from outdoor tanning. Many come from indoor tanning.

Most girls believe that sun exposure is good for their health and that tanning salons are perfectly safe. Unfortunately, although many, if not most, tanning salons claim to be healthy and safe, they're not.

Did you know that teens who use indoor tanning beds have a 75 percent increased chance of getting melanoma? And if you tan indoors, your chance of another type of skin cancer—*basal cell carcinoma*—is 69 percent higher than those who never do. No wonder many states and countries have banned the use of indoor tanning devices for those under eighteen.

No wonder the AAP points out that "indoor tanning is a potent source of ultraviolet radiation, especially UVA," which "can be as much as 10 to 15 times more powerful than midday sunlight."

And there's more. Using a tanning bed may become addictive. According to one small study of people who do this often, their brain can look (during a tanning session) like the brain of people on drugs.

Also, indoor or outdoor tanning can cause wrinkles and premature aging. It's true. Tanning can cause both skin cancer *and* wrinkles. Yikes! You can see why we tell people that "no tan is a safe tan."

The bottom line? *No* indoor tanning is safe—especially for kids and teens, whose skin is far more susceptible to these harmful, cancer-causing sources of UV rays.

So what can you do to have healthier skin that's less likely to wrinkle or get skin cancer? Avoid too much sun and all tanning and sunburns. Wear sunscreen when outdoors. This will decrease your risk a lot.

On any given day, if you'll be in the sun for more than fifteen minutes between 9:00 a.m. and 4:00 p.m., wear sunscreen or a moisturizing lotion with ultraviolet (UV sunlight) protection. Remember that it takes at least twenty minutes for the sunscreen to be absorbed into the skin and begin to work.

Look for products with a sun protection factor (SPF) of at least 15 that protects against both damaging types of sun rays— ultraviolet A (UVA) *and* ultraviolet B (UVB) rays. You'll notice that many sunscreen products have an SPF of 45, 50, or even 60. But an SPF greater than 30 offers very little advantage. The difference in skin protection above SPF 15 is minimal. And the higher the SPF, the greater the cost and the greater the risk of adverse effects like a rash or an allergic reaction.

We recommend products with an SPF of 15 or 20 for most girls. But for those who are more sensitive to the sun, an SPF of 30 should be plenty.

Also, the SPF ratings only apply to UVB protection. UVA rays are less likely to burn, but they penetrate deeper into the skin and can lead to wrinkles, sagging, discoloration, and redness or rashes. UVA also contributes to your risk for dangerous forms of skin cancer. That's why we tell our patients to buy a *full* or *broad-spectrum* sunscreen that protects against UVA *and* UVB rays.

How much sunscreen should you apply? According to the American Academy of Dermatology, a heaping handful of sunscreen (at least one to two ounces) should be applied to exposed skin every day—including your face, ears, neck, and arms (as well as your legs or feet if exposed).

And speaking of the sun ... have you noticed you sweat a little more these days? We'll talk about this normal change in the next question.

QUESTION 20

Why do I sweat? It makes me feel like a boy.

Like body hair, sweat-ing is not just for boys. Too bad, right?

The good news is that there are many ways to deal with sweat and its partner, body odor (BO). We're sorry to say it, but girls have BO too. You know, smells that are not terribly pleasant or "feminine," or, to put it bluntly, smells that just stink. There—we've said it. Even girls— cute girls, adorable girls—can be stinky at times.

Of course, it's good and normal to sweat when you're working out or playing. It's part of God's divine design to help cool you down when your body heats up. But normal sweat can get quite stinky. My (Dr. Mari's) son loves telling jokes. He recently asked, "Mom, what do you call a fairy that doesn't take a bath?" You'll love the answer: "Stinker-bell."

137

Anyway, you can keep the Stinker-bell and sweaty days to a minimum. With just a little help, stink can turn pretty pink in no time. And girls can have more fun with this than boys, since we have so many fragrances and fun products to choose from.

Did you ever shop for body lotions with your mom or girl-friends? You can find balms, lotions, sprays, creams, powders, bubble bath, gels, soaps, and oils. By using only products that are safe for young skin, you can have a lot of fun with these.

You could spend hours exploring all the fragrances and products out there that help make being a girl so fun. There's ginger, lavender, pomegranate, vanilla, and every kind of berry. You can enjoy jasmine and honeysuckle.

Yet, along with beautiful scents, God allows us to have stinky smells and BO, doesn't he? Let's talk about why this happens and how you can prevent it and deal with it.

Sweating is one way the body cools itself down — it's part of the miracle of your perfectly integrated body. And did you know that sweat is actually odorless? Sweat is stink-free until it combines with bacteria that normally live on your skin. So you can blame those pesky germs for stinking up sweat.

The first thing you can do is to dry up. Less sweat means there's less fluid for the bacteria to mix with, which means less odor. Washing your underarms with water and a mild soap every day and after sporting events will always help.

Early in the puberty years you can start using an antiperspirant (which helps you sweat less), a deodorant (which removes and covers up smells), or a product that combines the two. But remember to wash before using deodorant, or you'll just be covering up BO without getting rid of it. You can end up with some very interesting smells that way.

If a traditional deodorant doesn't work well for you, a few products are available without a doctor's prescription that are much stronger. Your pharmacist or doctor's office can recommend one. These products work differently and are usually applied at bedtime. After a few nights of use, daytime sweating usually improves a lot or goes away. You can then continue to use this every other night or as needed to keep sweating under control.

Some people sweat so much that it starts to affect their lives. They may choose white shirts more often to hide sweat marks, or they may not raise their hands in class to hide their embarrassing wetness. Don't let this be you.

If you cannot control sweating from your underarms, palms, or soles, see your doctor to figure out why. Some people sweat more than others. Excessive and unpredictable sweating, called *hyperhidrosis*, is usually hereditary, but occasionally it's related to medical conditions. In most cases, your doctor can prescribe a safe but stronger product that will usually work.

What about stinky feet? In some places, people are expected to leave their shoes at the door when they enter someone's home. This could be embarrassing if your feet smell, but this too can be prevented. Here are some tips:

- Don't wear the same shoes all the time. Let them breathe between wears.
- Wash your feet every day, and avoid wearing wet shoes or sneakers. They can get very stinky when wet, so let them dry out, or ask a parent if the shoes can be thrown in the dryer. Ask first, though; you don't want to ruin the dryer or the shoes.
- It also really helps to wear socks every time you wear closed-toe shoes. If you don't, get ready for a big "phew" moment.
- Sprinkle your shoes and feet with foot powder, which absorbs the wetness that contributes to smelly feet. You can even use antifungal powder. This will help prevent athlete's foot, an itchy fungal infection similar to yeast infections. (You learned about yeast infections in question 14.)

"Tanning" Your Smelly Feet

My (Dr. Walt's) friends Joe and Teresa Graedon, who write for the website *The People's Pharmacy*, have a tip on preventing sweaty feet that I've used with teens for years:

> Sweaty feet can lead to foot odor and increase the risk of athlete's foot. One dermatologist we consulted offered the following home remedy: Boil five tea bags in a quart of water for five minutes. When the solution cools, soak your hands or feet for twenty to thirty minutes nightly.

One day on Oprah's TV show, Dr. Mehmet Oz said, "There are a quarter-million sweat glands on your feet. You can generate about a half a liter of sweat from your foot in a day. It really does make a lot of juice." Like the Graedons, he recommended, "Brew up some mild iced tea and put your feet in it for about thirty minutes a day for a week. The tannic acid in the tea will actually tan your foot a little bit, which will dry it out."

The only catch is that using this treatment can stain the feet a bit — leaving a slight yellow tint on the skin.

You may have heard about *athlete's foot*. It's a common infection of the skin on the feet caused by a germ called *fungus*. People who spend a lot of time wearing sports shoes like cleats, dance shoes, or sneakers get these itchy infections more often. Shoes that don't "breathe" well get moist and sticky on the inside, which helps the fungus overgrow. It also makes your feet get softer and more susceptible to this unwelcome guest. When the fungus overgrows, the web area between your toes gets irritated and uncomfortable and can even crack open.

These infections are one reason I (Dr. Mari) loved growing up in the tropics. When you walk around barefoot, you don't need to worry about athlete's foot. Yes, you're right—you may have to worry about stepping on a rusty nail, sharp rocks, or an open stapler—yep, I did that when I was ten, ouch!

The good news is that athlete's foot is usually easy to treat with over-the-counter creams like *terbinafine* or *clotrimazole*. But it's critical to keep your feet dry so the infection doesn't keep coming back. If it does, see your doctor.

We think that God allows some unpleasant things in our bodies to remind us that we all share some of the same difficulties. Perhaps this helps us all be more compassionate. In 2 Corinthians 12:7 the apostle Paul described a "thorn" in his flesh that he prayed about repeatedly. Still, God chose to let him keep it for a purpose. This thorn reminded Paul that in every circumstance God's grace was enough to get him through it.

So whether you're challenged by sweat, acne, or stinky feet, ask God to help you deal with it. As with Paul, there might be a thing or two you'd rather change but can't. Sweating might be one of those things you'd like to get rid of, or perhaps you'd rather never deal with acne. We understand.

The good news is that with most of these annoying body changes, there is a lot you can do, even on those stinky-and-not-so-girly-pink days.

> Perfume and incense bring joy to the heart, and the pleasantness of a friend springs from their heartfelt advice.
>
> *Proverbs 27:9*

My (Dr. Mari's) family was leaving Disney World when my seven-year-old daughter, Hannah, began to sing and twirl. I asked what she was singing. She replied softly, "Mami, faith dresses me and makes me beautiful in God's eyes. That's what my song is about."

Yes, I thought. *You're right.*

Hannah's song hints at something wonderful—she knows that God's love is the source of true beauty. As she loves him back, she begins to see herself through his eyes. That is beautiful.

Here's what amazes me about the song of my daughter's heart. She sang about true beauty while surrounded by princesses dressed the part. I mean, who doesn't love to look at Cinderella and Belle? Their dresses are gorgeous, and their feminine grace makes them look even better.

Yet, while admiring them, my daughter thought, "Faith dresses me and makes me beautiful in God's eyes." Her song reminds me of these words from the Bible:

> So in Christ Jesus you are all children of God through faith, for all of you who were baptized into Christ have clothed yourselves with Christ.
>
> *Galatians 3:26–27*

> I delight greatly in the LORD; my soul rejoices in my God. For he has clothed me with garments of salvation and arrayed me in a robe of his righteousness, as a bridegroom adorns his head like a priest, and as a bride adorns herself with her jewels.
>
> *Isaiah 61:10*

Rather than focus on your outward clothes, it's critical to first think about what you're wearing on the inside—what clothes your heart.

God loves you just as you are. But do you feel like you're dressed with Christ's love and acceptance? This inner clothing is essential to why modesty matters. Talking about outer looks apart from this understanding makes modesty seem like one more annoying rule to follow. It is far from that.

The desire and willingness to dress modestly comes from the heart that knows its most important clothing is on the inside—God's love and acceptance.

Our deepest desire is that, while reading this book, you will recognize that you've been called to be a princess who is loved, accepted, and embraced by an awesome King.

Did you know that you already have your own Prince Charming? His name is Jesus. Your Prince loves you so much that he

Naked and Spiritually Dead, Dressed and Inwardly Alive

In the Garden of Eden, Eve chose to listen to the serpent, and Adam chose to listen to Eve. Neither one listened to God. After Adam and Eve sinned, they suddenly realized they were naked. Until then, it had not even fazed them. Yet after choosing their way over God's way, they felt ashamed of their nakedness. So they made some clothes from fig leaves and hid. And do you know what God did?

Even though they had sinned and rebelled against him, God still clothed them. He made even better clothes for them than they had made for themselves. His were leather garments — made to last (at least compared to leaves).

God did not want his creation dressed in guilt and shame. Even though they'd just slapped God in the face, he was merciful and made new clothes just for them.

In the same way, Jesus died on the cross to take our sin upon himself and dress us in his righteousness — his goodness and grace. The Sinless One took up our sin and gave those who follow him a new heart — a clean heart. That awesome gift is available to you as well.

Do you want this inner clothing, this new heart? Then ask Jesus, now, if you'd like, to clothe you in his righteousness. He will. In his goodness and love he will send his Holy Spirit to live in you and to change you from the inside out. And there is no better wardrobe than this.

> "I will give them an undivided heart and put a new spirit in them; I will remove from them their heart of stone and give them a heart of flesh."

> Ezekiel 11:19

rushed into this world to battle for you. He came to rescue you. He fought a mighty enemy and gave his life for you. For *you*.

This Prince considers you worthy of his love and his tender care. To him, you are worth more than diamonds and rubies — you are priceless. His life wasn't too high a price to pay. To this Prince, you are beautiful, precious, and one in a billion, since it's estimated that just over one billion humans have lived on the earth since the dawn of time.

God's love, the source of your inner beauty, can become the driving force of your life. It can wake you up every morning and guide every choice you make. Here's what can happen:

You recognize that the one who created you loves you like no one else. He knows your thoughts, including what you like about yourself and what you don't. He knows your every secret. He knows every good and bad thought you have. He knows you intimately. And, knowing you, he loves every bit of you — from the top of your head to the tips of your toes.

The more you recognize how much he loves you, the more you want to live according to his best plans for you. Little by little, the choice to delight God above all else affects everything you do — the music you choose to hear, the movies you watch, what you say and do — even what you think.

One of these choices involves the way you look on the outside — in particular, the clothes you wear, the makeup and jewelry you wear, even the words you use. The way you present yourself to others says something about who you are, what you want, what you care about — and, most important, whose you are. It also impacts how others perceive and treat you. So modesty is not simply about rules that say do this and don't do that.

> Charm is deceptive, and beauty is fleeting; but a woman who fears the LORD is to be praised.
>
> *Proverbs 31:30*

Pure Fashion

Pure Fashion encourages teen girls to live, act, and dress according to their dignity as children of God. They focus on guiding girls ages fourteen to eighteen "to become confident, competent leaders who live the virtues of modesty and purity in their schools and communities." Their goal is "to show the public that it is possible to be stylish, cute, and MODEST."

Pure Fashion writes:

> We understand that many young women today are losing their sense of innocence at a very young age, and Pure Fashion aims to reverse this trend by offering a fun, exciting and effective program.
>
> Pure Fashion is a character formation program that enhances not only a young woman's external appearance, but more important, her interior beauty and balanced self-confidence.

You can learn more about Pure Fashion using the URL in our resources list at the back of the book.

She is clothed with strength and dignity; she can laugh at the days to come. She speaks with wisdom, and faithful instruction is on her tongue.

Proverbs 31:25–26

We love the verses from Proverbs 31. They describe a woman of virtue. She is "clothed with strength and dignity," and "she speaks with wisdom." She reminds me (Dr. Mari) of the most influential woman in my life: my mother, Mami. She was beautiful—inside and out—like Esther. She was generous, loving, and kind, and she had a servant heart. She loved to laugh and she loved helping others. Her quiet strength and dignity came through in the way she spoke, walked, and dressed. Everything about her radiated confidence, beauty, and strength.

Mami exemplified modesty and made it fun. She loved jewelry, accessories, and nice clothes. Her wardrobe was full of cute blouses, sparkly pins and belts, and, of course, awesome shoes.

We already pointed out how the feminine grace with which you carry yourself enhances the way you look. This is how Mami was. Her inner beauty and dignity made everything she wore more beautiful. Her clothes didn't have to be expensive, sexy, or glamorous to look great. She knew you don't need to show a bunch of skin to look beautiful.

When it comes to feminine grace, Mami was my Cinderella. No, she did not wear evening gowns to the mall. But everything about her taught me about modesty and true beauty.

So what is this dress called *modesty* that true beauty wears?

Modesty is about showing good judgment and restraint. Modesty makes you avoid what's indecent and favor what's appropriate. Granted, what's acceptable, trendy, and cool is often defined by the culture we live in. But God's principles define what's right and proper for girls.

Clothing, thoughts, and good choices — what's the connection?

In the last question, we laid a foundation for why modesty matters. If you haven't read question 21, please read it now before you go on; that background is too important. Here are three important reasons why modesty matters:

1. It affects you.
2. It affects others.
3. It affects your relationship with God.

Why? Let's look at how the Bible views modesty:

> I also want the women to dress modestly, with decency and propriety, adorning themselves, not with elaborate hairstyles or gold or pearls or expensive clothes, but with good deeds, appropriate for women who profess to worship God.
>
> *1 Timothy 2:9–10*

Again, that doesn't mean that all jewelry, accessories, and attractive clothing are out. Not at all. It means that your inner beauty is *most* important. It also emphasizes that, when excessive or inappropriate, clothing and jewelry can be a distraction. They can cause you and others to focus on the wrong things.

God calls us to honor him in our hearts, in our minds, and with our bodies. If your body is for God, and God for your body, then what dress is appropriate for you? That which is proper and decent. Clothing that is dignified and not revealing, that shows you respect yourself and others, and that guards the gift of your sexuality.

Modesty is about recognizing the gift of being a girl and becoming a woman. As you keep reading, ask your mom or a trusted adult questions. The need for modesty exists partly because you are not only a spiritual being, but a relational, sexual person. What does that mean?

Here's a bit of background. The Bible teaches that when we ask Jesus to live and reign in our hearts, when we become followers of Jesus, we become a temple of God's Holy Spirit.

> Do you not know that your bodies are temples of the Holy Spirit, who is in you, whom you have received from God? You are not your own.
>
> *1 Corinthians 6:19*

Why is that word *temple* used? A temple is a place that is sacred, holy, *set apart* for a special purpose. God is telling you that he has set your body apart as the home of his Spirit — to live there — within you. That is a very big deal. So you want to treat your body in a *very* special way.

Your body is an important part of God's divine design for you. As you grow older and if God ordains it, his plan for you may include the opportunity to get married. You may then be blessed to bring a child into the world. Through your body, you can participate in the miracle of a new life. Wow!

Your body, amazing as it sounds, has been reserved for one man — if God calls you to marry. If not, then your body is set apart for God, and God alone. Thinking about your body in this way will impact the way you treat your body, which includes how you dress.

Just as you might like someone's wit, sense of humor, or loving personality, you might also like how someone looks, right? While in high school, I (Dr. Mari) saw a boy who was so gorgeous he took my breath away. As he walked by our lunch table, I had a brilliant idea. "Hey, girls, a moment of silence ... here comes Pete." Our chatter paused as the five of us admired him. Then one sighed, another giggled — and we all burst into laughter.

Finding boys attractive is, of course, completely normal. In fact, it is part of God's design for relationships and marriage that girls find boys handsome and boys find girls cute. Because of this natural attraction between boys and girls, modesty is not just about you. It is also about caring for others, because the way you dress will impact the boys who see you.

Boys and men are very visual. That's just how their brains are wired. Dressing sexy can make a boy focus on your looks so much that it's distracting. It can make him start thinking about wanting to kiss or hug when you're just trying to talk. Dressing immodestly can lead him to focus on your body rather than *all* that you are — inside and out.

Here's an example. Suppose a girl chooses to wear a really tight shirt that shows lots of cleavage. She then starts talking to a boy at school. She shares about her trip to the beach while the young man, trying to be respectful, fights the urge to stare at her chest and down her shirt.

If he cares about guarding his eyes, his mind, and his heart for his future wife, he'll try hard to look into the girl's eyes, but her choice of clothing can make this much more difficult. He'll have to work to listen to her story. Her clothing actually makes it harder for him to see and appreciate who she is.

"Who Says It Has to be Itsy-bitsy?"

I (Dr. Mari) recently watched a video where actress Jessica Rey shares the story of the bikini and why she decided to design her own line of swimwear. Her goal is to "disprove the age-old notion that, when it comes to swimsuits, less is more … You can dress modestly without sacrificing fashion." Her inspiration was Audrey Hepburn, who is "timeless and classy" and dressed very modestly. "I don't think people think of Audrey Hepburn and think frumpy, dumpy, and out of fashion."

Rey goes on to explain that "modesty isn't about covering up our bodies because they're bad. Modesty isn't about hiding ourselves. It's about revealing our dignity."

Reminding girls and women that we were made beautiful — in God's image and likeness — she ends with this challenge, *"How will you use your beauty?"* Check out the video and her swimsuit designs using this QR code.

Jessica Rey
Swimwear

Imagine a painting with a fancy frame that is so overdone, the frame takes your attention away from the painting. You end up admiring the frame rather than the work of art. It's the same idea. Your outer appearance is like a frame that either distracts from or enhances your inner beauty. Which will it be?

Of course, you are *not* responsible for others' thoughts, but how you dress can contribute to those thoughts. And the Bible gives you this instruction:

> Make up your mind not to put any stumbling block or obstacle in the way of a brother or sister.

Romans 14:13

Again, you are *not* responsible for the way others choose to act in response to how you look. But your outer appearance is like a traffic light. The way you dress can be like a red light that says, "I respect myself and you, and I know there's much more to me than my looks."

Also, the Bible teaches, "In humility value others above yourselves, not looking to your own interests but each of you to the interests of others" (Philippians 2:3–4). I (Dr. Walt) can tell you that many guys would greatly appreciate your help by not presenting them with unnecessary temptation.

In one survey, 97 percent of Christian teen boys said they believe that girls and women can dress attractively while being modest. They agreed with the statement that guys definitely notice and appreciate when a woman dresses modestly.

So you can help boys out and respect yourself by wearing appropriate clothing. Of course, you are free, in most schools, to wear what you want. But what's allowed and what's best are totally different choices.

Modesty also means that you dress your age. Experts warn that girls whose clothing, accessories, and makeup make them look older are at greatest risk for sexual sin. And a study by psychologists found that girls who dress older than their age or who dress sexy are more likely to have eating disorders, low self-esteem, and depression.

So modesty matters, but it's not simply one more rule to follow. It's also not about being ashamed of your body. Not at all. The body God gave you is a beautiful gift. Modesty is about loving God and wanting to honor him with your choices. It's about valuing and treating your body—and others—with respect.

I (Dr. Walt) was so happy to hear about the courage of high-school freshman Saige Hatch. In 2012 she organized what is said to be the first modesty club in America at South Pasadena High School in California.

Saige told one reporter that she was sick of seeing her peers

Modesty Is Humility Expressed in Dress

Jenni Smith writes in the GirlTalk blog, "Modesty is humility expressed in dress, a desire to serve others, neither promoting nor provoking sensuality or lust." The Women of Spirit blog says, "The essence of modesty is not setting rules about skirt length, but living a life that brings glory to God rather than ourselves. Dressing to show off is a huge temptation for many women."

Did you ever wonder what boys think about how girls dress? In a study that surveyed 1,600 Christian boys, most of them said that skimpy skirts and bikinis are not modest. Most boys (70 percent) felt that showing any cleavage is immodest. What about pants with words across the rear end? A big no-no. What about low-cut tops layered with more modest shirts? Most of the boys felt these were all right. Formfitting skirts? About evenly split.

You can find more of the results of The Modesty Survey with the URL in our resources list at the back of the book.

revealing too much skin when she came to school each day. She was surprised at her fifteen-year-old friends wearing midriff-grazing tops and short shorts, while exposing their cleavage.

A statement on her club's website says, "A shift is coming, sneaking through the literal fabric of our culture. Our bright heroic women are being made the fool. A fool to think that to be loved they must be naked. To be noticed they must be sexualized," or dress sexy.

Saige writes, "I noticed from elementary school to middle school, and now in high school, a lot of girls were dressing

Secret Keeper Girls

Author Dannah Gresh encourages girls to keep the secrets of their God-given beauty for their future husband. Check out these cool Truth or Bare Fashion Tests from her website, which you can find with the URL in our list of resources:

1. How short is too short? Sit in front of a mirror — crisscross your legs if in shorts, or sit in a chair with your legs crossed if wearing a skirt. If your underwear or a lot of thigh flashes you in the mirror, those shorts or skirt are too short. Give them to your little sister and go shopping for new ones with Mom.

2. What about your shirt? If a lot of chest skin shows up in the mirror when leaning forward, that shirt fails the modesty test. You want to keep all that beauty to share with your future husband, not everyone at school. Consider layering shirts (with a tank top underneath) or wearing a different one.

For more tips, including how to shop for fun, attractive, modest swimwear, visit Dannah's website, secretkeepergirl. com. You can also learn about their cool pajama parties for girls and moms. Secret Keeper Girls surround themselves with wise friends who, like them, believe God's definition of beauty and choose to live a godly life for him. They help each other keep making right choices, they value modesty, and they love to have fun.

Also, ask your mom to get a copy of Dannah's book, *8 Great Dates for Moms and Daughters*. I (Dr. Walt) especially liked taking my daughter on the "tea date." For me (Dr. Mari), tea parties at home are weekly opportunities to have fun, laugh, and talk about beauty, modesty, and lots more with my daughter. Check out Dannah's book using our resources list at the back of this book.

immodestly. I wanted to bring awareness and remembrance to the value of modesty."

Her Modesty Club website, which you can find with this QR code or with the URL in our list of resources, now has members from all fifty states and fourteen countries. They agree with these modesty club standards:

Modesty Club

- If it's too tight, it's not quite right.
- Shoulders and busts are graciously covered.
- Revealing lines are warning signs.
- When I pass this test, I'll be dressed for success.

Have fun with the way you dress, but remember that a pure heart is more beautiful than any clothing you'll *ever* wear.

And don't judge others simply by how they look. It is possible for a girl who wants to be pure but hasn't learned about modesty to dress in a way that looks sexy. It is also possible for a girl to dress modestly and harbor impure thoughts. Most people learn how to dress from their families and culture, and there's quite a bit of peer pressure to look trendy, sexy, and cool.

This might be the first time you've heard this topic presented in this way. So from now on, consider your choices in light of God's call to modesty. Talk to your parents after reading this together if you have questions about what's considered appropriate for you. Before choosing your wardrobe, ask yourself, *What will the way I dress say about me—who I am, whose I am, what I care about, and how I see others and myself?*

Attention, All Girls

Consider this poignant appeal we've seen on several social media websites:

Dear Girls,

Dressing immodestly is like rolling around in manure. Yes, you'll get attention, but mostly from pigs.

Sincerely,
Real Men

Before you dress, we pray that your heart will sing, "God's love dresses me and makes me beautiful in his eyes!"

Like a gold ring in a pig's snout is a beautiful woman who shows no discretion.

Proverbs 11:22

QUESTION 23

Nails, makeup, and hair — how much should I care?

So we all have body hair—some of it we shave off, while some of it we keep, enjoy, and style.

I (Dr. Mari) will never forget my neighbor growing up. She was a cute girl with long, straight hair. One day she returned home after a haircut and perm, and Mami and I heard screams coming from her bedroom. We listened in and heard her cry out, "This is the worst day of my life, Mom. I hate my hair."

This was her first attempt at a perm, and I'm pretty sure she never tried it again.

Her story may sound silly, but you know what I'm talking about. There's just something about girls and hair. And here's what I've noticed: Girls with naturally curly hair (like me) sometimes long for straight hair, and girls with straight hair want curls and waves.

When Mami and I saw my neighbor's hair, we thought it looked really cute. Still, she went back and had it cut even shorter, and complained about her new hairstyle that whole month. Perhaps it helps to remember that we all have bad hair days, and, thankfully, hair always grows back. At least it did for my daughter when, at age three, she cut off a clump of her hair while pretending to be Mulan.

Whether you have naturally wavy or straight hair, enjoy different hairstyles and have fun with your hair. From braids to bows to hairbands, styling your hair can be a wonderful way to enjoy your femininity and spend fun time together with your mom and girlfriends.

Different hairstyles can be so much fun. If you have natural curls, we recommend a book called *Curly Girl: The Handbook*, by Michelle Massey and Lorraine Bender. It's full of great tips to nurture your curls and help you manage frizz. Read it when you wake up with a lion's mane. A good book for all hair types is American Girl's *Hair-Styling Tips and Tricks for Girls*. Check out Tips and Tricks using this QR code or the URLs in our resources list at the back of the book.

Hair-Styling Tips and Tricks for Girls

One thing we see often, especially in girls with lots of hair, is a flaky scalp. This is very common and often related to not scrubbing your scalp well enough when you shampoo. Just like the skin on your body, your scalp cells are constantly being turned over. Since your hair is in the way, your scalp skin needs extra scrubbing to remove those dead skin cells. Lovely thought, isn't it?

If scrubbing doesn't remove all the flakiness, try some over-the-counter dry skin or dandruff shampoo. If the problem persists, talk to your doctor.

So what about makeup? The first thing is this. Although makeup can be fun to wear, remember where your true beauty comes from. Girls look best with a natural look without excessive makeup.

Wearing too much makeup can make you look older, which is not such a good idea. Don't let the culture's obsession with outer beauty steal your innocence and push you to grow up too fast. Enjoy being your age—it will only come once.

Speaking of your face, did you know that young girls and teens have sensitive skin? It's important to treat your face gently, as you learned in question 19. One way to be gentle with your face is by not overdoing it with makeup and products that may irritate your skin. Be careful how you treat your face, and it will smile back at you.

As far as painting your nails, here's what I (Dr. Mari) have noticed: Many moms let their girls paint their toenails earlier than their fingernails. In our home, experimenting with fun, multi-color shades is for little toes. For fingernails, we keep it simple, using lighter shades and less striking colors. This has worked well for us but, again, different families have their own guidelines. Make sure you know what's acceptable in your family. But remember to always present yourself in a way that honors God and reveals your self-respect and dignity.

> You are altogether beautiful, my darling; there is no flaw in you.
>
> *Song of Solomon 4:7*

> "And why do you worry about clothes? See how the flowers of the field grow. They do not labor or spin."
>
> *Matthew 6:28*

QUESTION 24

Diamonds or sterling — are body piercings bad?

Body piercing and tattooing are all the rage. It's hard to find a celebrity or sports star without one or both, or a lot of both. We bet you know more than one girl who has expressed her independence and personal style with a piercing.

What you won't find are very many girls who know the risks of body piercing. In fact, when I (Dr. Walt) talk to girls your age, less than one in twenty is aware of the risks. We want you to be smart. You may even help your friends make some wise decisions.

Did you know that body piercing is illegal for minors in almost every state? There are many good reasons for this.

Unlike hair and nail shops, which are strictly regulated by each state, body-piercing shops are pretty much unregulated in

America. With little or no regulation, shop owners don't have to answer to anyone about the safety of their procedures and equipment. They have little incentive to protect you and your friends against infections and other health risks. This is why experts who care about your health and safety, like the American Academy of Dermatology, stand against *all* forms of body piercing with one exception: the earlobe.

Also, the American Dental Association (ADA) opposes all oral piercing, which includes the tongue, lips, and cheeks. The ADA even calls it a public health hazard. Why? Tongue jewelry can frequently cause chipped or damaged teeth, and it can also cause nasty and dangerous infections.

The U.S. and Canadian Red Cross organizations will not accept a blood donation from someone who's had a body piercing within the last year. Why? Because piercing can spread infections to you (like hepatitis B or C) that can then spread through your blood to others. These infections can harm your liver and even kill you. There is no cure for hepatitis B or C, and the costly treatment of these infections can make you very sick. Who wants that?

The mouth is the area with the most complications from piercings. Besides the general risks, the mouth carries extra dangers:

- Swallowing the jewelry
- Altered eating habits
- Loss of taste
- Injury to your salivary glands

Other problems that are frequently reported include:

- Worn tooth surface
- Damage to your gums and jawline from wear
- Aspiration (inhaling) of a loose piece of jewelry into the lung
- Beaded jewelry becoming trapped between teeth
- Infection and swelling of the tongue

Also, when tongue rings are placed incorrectly, they can cause a nerve problem (*neuropathy*) that really hurts. Some kids who get this say they have shooting pains up to forty times a day. The only thing that helps them is to remove the tongue ring and allow the hole to close up.

So why is it okay to pierce the earlobe? The ear lobe is made of fatty tissue and has a great blood supply. If it gets infected, high levels of infection-fighting cells from the bloodstream protect the earlobe. Still, the equipment used must be sterile and brand new. Although earrings can be sterilized before use, most *reusable* piercing guns are not sterilized between procedures. Ear piercing systems that use disposable sterile cassettes are the safest, and that's what we recommend.

Many types of ear piercings have become popular, especially piercing through the cartilage of the middle to upper ear. Unfortunately, these *high ear piercings* have many more complications than lower earlobe piercings, including poor healing and more serious infections. This is because ear cartilage contains very few of the blood vessels that bring infection-fighting cells to the area pierced.

Cartilage infections in the ear typically occur in the first month after piercing. The significant scarring that can result from these infections may last a lifetime or require plastic surgery to repair.

Body piercings can also have social and emotional consequences. Think about this. How many politicians, business leaders, pastors, physicians, attorneys, judges, and newscasters do you see with exposed piercings? Not very many, right? Why do you think this is?

We think it's because, right or not, people with body piercings are judged. That's just the way it is. Many people make negative value judgments about people with piercings—especially girls and women. We're not saying these judgments are correct. They

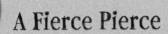

A Fierce Pierce

Other risks of having a body part pierced include:

- Infections (especially staph infections) and boils (painful infections under the skin that can lead to ugly scars)
- Nerve damage causing local paralysis, numbness, or lasting pain
- Skin allergies to the jewelry that's used
- Scarring (especially around the lips or eyes)
- Sepsis (a blood infection sometimes called *blood poisoning*)
- Raised, noticeable scars called *keloids*
- Excessive bleeding requiring an expensive emergency room visit
- Permanent holes or deforming scars in your nose or eyebrow
- Chipped or broken teeth (with tongue piercings)
- A speech impediment (while the tongue jewelry is in place)
- Rarely, hepatitis B, hepatitis C, tetanus, or HIV

More than 35 percent of people who get body piercings experience one or more of these problems. So if you're thinking about piercing, ask yourself, is the pierce worth the fears and all the future tears? There's a lot of regret associated with such a small piece of jewelry.

likely are not. But the truth is that such judgmental attitudes could prevent you from getting a job you want down the road. Even if you remove the jewelry, the hole it leaves can be that telltale mark that can be used against you.

So here's the bottom line. Don't think that we're telling you all this stuff to frighten you. We're not. We simply want you to be wise in the decisions you make about your body.

If you are considering a body piercing, we just want you to understand ahead of time that it can lead to lasting problems even if you don't have complications from the piercing. Before you get one, make sure you're prepared for any of the dangers and social consequences that may come with body piercings.

Think long and hard before you get anything other than your ears pierced. You'll usually need a parent's permission and signature anyway, so talk it over with them and pray about it.

If your parents say to wait until you're older, trust that they have good reasons. And if your best friends or that *still, quiet voice* deep inside your soul says wait, trust that advice too.

> Do you not know that your bodies are temples of the Holy Spirit, who is in you, whom you have received from God? You are not your own; you were bought at a price. Therefore honor God with your bodies.
>
> *1 Corinthians 6:19–20*

QUESTION 25

Thinking about inking — are temporary tattoos safe?

Have you been tempted to get a heart, butterfly, or tiny flower tattoo somewhere on your body where most people won't see it? Or do you have friends who already have a tattoo?

If you'd never get a permanent tattoo (which we'll talk about in the next question), have you considered getting a temporary one at a tourist shop or attraction while on vacation?

When we say temporary tattoos, we're not talking about the kind you put on with a wet washcloth. We mean the so-called "temporary" tattoos that are usually made with black henna and are meant to fade over days or weeks.

You're probably wondering what on earth black henna is. No, this has nothing to do with hens or any type of poultry. Henna

165

is a plant that's been used for thousands of years to dye anything from leather to hair, skin, and fingernails.

Since henna can be applied without piercing your skin, it is technically not a tattoo. Tattooing is placing a permanent mark on the skin by inserting pigment or dye *into* or *under* the skin. Though black henna marks are technically not tattoos, they are *not* necessarily safe.

Although henna markings on the skin pose almost no risk of hepatitis, AIDS, or the other serious health risks associated with traditional tattoos, henna markings can cause other problems such as severe allergic reactions, bad skinburns, and even permanent, ugly scarring.

The U.S. Food and Drug Administration (FDA) does *not* approve henna for direct application to the skin. Henna is approved only for use as a hair dye. Its use on a person's skin is illegal, yet henna "tattoos" sure are easy to obtain.

Many parents have filed lawsuits against distributors of black henna after their children were scarred by black henna markings—but the damage has already happened. In each case, neither the girls involved nor their parents knew of the potential danger. But now you do. So you'll be able to warn any of your friends who are considering this type of tattoo.

Although most girls won't experience a problem with henna tattoos, some could be permanently scarred with a forever reminder of their "temporary" poor decision.

> So whether you eat or drink or whatever you do, do it all
> for the glory of God.
>
> *1 Corinthians 10:31*

QUESTION 26

What about permanent tattoos?

With so many athletes, TV celebrities, and movie stars sporting tattoos these days, you may think it's a cool idea to get one someday. Although tattoos used to be a guy thing, tons of people get tattoos nowadays, including women.

In 1936, *LIFE* magazine estimated that only about 6 percent of people in America had at least one tattoo—and they were mostly men. But by 2012 the American Medical Association (AMA) reported 36 percent of eighteen- to twenty-five-year-olds had a tattoo, and nearly one in five of them were women.

Sadly, most people who get tattooed don't know the health risks. I (Dr. Walt) think that all tattooing should require a signed consent form outlining all the risks—the most obvious one being a major case of remorse. One-half of people who get a tattoo later wish they hadn't. Also, did you know it's illegal for minors to be tattooed in most states? And even within states, the laws can be different from town to town.

So what are some of the risks of getting a tattoo? Tattooing can be very painful. And once done, if you change your mind, tattoos are even more painful (and very expensive) to remove. A tattoo that costs several hundred dollars could require several thousand dollars and many laser sessions to remove. And removing tattoos can leave ugly scars.

And get this! There's no regulation that requires tattoo inks to be sterile (clean and free of infections). Can you believe that? It's true. Worse yet, tattooing can infect you with diseases that make you very sick.

In most states, tattoo parlors are not regulated. Unclean equipment, ink, or technique can infect you with a lifelong, incurable infection—such as HIV (the virus that causes AIDS) or hepatitis B or C (which can harm your liver and cause liver cancer or death). Tattooing can also spread syphilis, tuberculosis, and other diseases from one person to another.

One study reported that the commercial tattoo industry may be the number one distributor of hepatitis C. They found that you are twice as likely to be infected with hepatitis C from getting a tattoo than by shooting up dope (injecting drugs into your veins). That's pretty scary.

Because of the risk of these infections, the American Association of Blood Banks and the Red Cross won't accept blood donations until one year after a person gets a tattoo. They wait a year to see if an infection shows up. They know that if you get a tattoo, you can end up with a two-for-one deal: a forever tattoo with a side order of hepatitis. Not such a happy meal, is it? And if you get a tattoo, there's likely another needle in your future. Your doctor will want blood work to check for this cancer-causing and potentially deadly virus.

More Risks of Having a Tattoo

- Tattooing can cause skin infections, including MRSA, which is tough to treat and can lead to scarring.

- Even tattoo artists who use clean tools and technique have clients who have been infected with a germ similar to the one that causes tuberculosis.

- Some unlicensed tattoo artists use printer ink rather than tattoo ink and guitar strings instead of needles (no, that doesn't mean your tattoo will sing). Do you think that's all clean and infection-free? *No way!*

- Bumps called *granulomas* can form around tattoo ink — especially red ink.

- Tattooing can lead to a keloid, a scar that gets very thick and raised.

- Since some of the dyes used are not approved for use in people, your skin can stay irritated for years.

- Although rare, some people have allergic reactions to the pigments. These reactions can be severe and cause terrible ulcers or scarring. We've seen patients with severe scarring from both tattooing and tattoo removal.

While we were writing this book, a mysterious outbreak of nasty skin rashes in upstate New York was traced to contaminated water in tattoo ink.

An Unusual Tattoo

Years ago, I (Dr. Mari) saw such an interesting tattoo, I had to ask about it. While doing a physical exam on a college student, I noticed a black vertical line above her nipple. When I asked her why she had a line on her breast, she sighed.

"It used to be a small butterfly," she recalled, "but after I gained weight, my breasts grew, and the tattoo stretched out too. So now I have a line above my breast. Who wants that?"

Then she added, "Please tell other girls to think twice before they do something like this. You never know how things will change."

Many tattoo inks contain an unknown mixture of chemicals. Many of these chemicals were intended for use in writing and printer inks as well as car paint—but never for use in or under the skin. It is impossible to know for sure what's in tattoo ink. There's also concern that some ingredients in tattoo ink may contribute to or cause cancer.

By far the most common "side effect" of a tattoo is regret. We can't count the number of people we've cared for who wish they had thought twice before getting a tattoo. We've even seen people who wanted their tattoos removed within a week of getting them.

Researchers at Texas Tech University report some reasons why people change their minds about tattoos. These include problems wearing clothes, embarrassment, and concerns that tattoos could adversely affect their job or career.

Most people who want to get rid of a tattoo are women. Studies show they feel more judged, like they've been marked with

Are Tattoos Okay for Christians?

Dr. Linda Mintle, a licensed marriage and family therapist and expert on family issues, writes:

> Christians need to consider their motivation for wanting a tattoo.
>
> If the motivation to get a tattoo is to conform to this world and fit in better, bring attention to self versus glorify God, disobey parents and cause the people around them to stumble, then it is not a good idea.
>
> For those who are radically saved and new in Christ, the motivation may be to witness to those who are lost. The bottom line is you have to judge your heart against the Word. God knows your heart and your motives, so an appraisal of motivation is needed.

more than the heart or pony or whatever design they chose. They sense that having a tattoo affects how others see them, which affects how they feel about themselves.

To remove a tattoo, a person often needs ten or more laser treatments several weeks apart. Experts say the average tattoo costs $2,000 to $3,000 to remove. Sadly, after spending all that money, one in four people cannot have their tattoo successfully removed.

So what's the bottom line? Never get a tattoo without giving yourself time (weeks, months, or even years) to think and pray about it. Listen to your parents and never get an illegal tattoo. Double-check your motives for getting a tattoo with someone you admire and trust. And remember that permanent probably means forever, and temporary might too.

Perhaps the most important question is the one that one of our teen reviewers recommends we each ask: "Am I considering doing this for God's glory, or my glory?" Great question.

> And you also were included in Christ when you heard the message of truth, the gospel of your salvation. When you believed, you were marked in him with a seal, the promised Holy Spirit.

Ephesians 1:13

Before Getting a Tattoo, Ask Yourself ...

- Why do I want a tattoo?
- Does my motivation to get a tattoo line up with what the Bible teaches?
- What are my heart and conscience saying to me?
- Is the Holy Spirit telling me to do this or encouraging me not to?
- Am I 100 percent sure I'll still want this tattoo or piercing years from now?
- What might my future husband think about this?
- Am I willing to give up potential educational or job opportunities for this tattoo?
- Will I cause a weaker sister or brother to stumble if I get a tattoo?

QUESTION 27

Why are some girls so mean?

Imagine you're at lunch when your friends start making fun of a shy girl who's new to the school. She's sitting all alone, with a near-empty tray of food and a blank stare.

Will you laugh at your friends' comments about her clothes and hair, or will you go sit next to her and help her feel more comfortable?

It's your choice. It's *always* your choice.

If you want to do what's right but worry about what your friends will say or think, you're experiencing peer pressure. A peer is someone your age who is affected by similar stresses and challenges as you. Everyone has peers, regardless of their age. And everyone experiences *peer pressure*—the pressure to fit in or to go along with the crowd. Peer pressure can make you compromise your values and beliefs simply to get a laugh from your "group" or so they will continue to "like" and "accept" you.

The Bible is clear that the wrong kind of peer pressure can keep you from God's best:

> Do not follow the crowd in doing wrong.
>
> *Exodus 23:2*

> And so I insist—and God backs me up on this—that there be no going along with the crowd, the empty-headed, mindless crowd. They've refused for so long to deal with God that they've lost touch not only with God but with reality itself. They can't think straight anymore.
>
> *Ephesians 4:17–18 MSG*

Part of maturing means learning to make wise choices consistently. That means you make good, healthy, and smart choices based on God's plans for your life. But even though girls' brains mature at a young age, they don't always behave like it. You may have experienced this at school or in your neighborhood. Sometimes girls are just plain mean. These girls don't always choose to be nice or *act* maturely even if their brain is capable of it.

Still, *you* can choose to be kind to the new girl in school even if it feels uncomfortable. You can choose to be different. You can decide to be yourself, even if it means that your "friends" won't accept you.

And here's the truth about that. If you need to change who you are so that others like and accept you, they are not true friends.

You can choose to do what's right—which may often be the hardest of the choices you'll have. And, yes, some people might make fun of you, but your heart will be at peace knowing you did the right thing. And who knows? Maybe you'll make a new friend for life.

How to Keep Your Cool

You may experience the same emotions as a mean bully, but you can choose not to behave in angry ways that hurt others. So what can you do when you're angry?

- *You can* take a deep breath and count to ten.
- *You can* walk away from the situation.
- *You can* find someone to talk to, like a parent, your sister, or a good friend.
- *You can* do something active like jogging or biking — great ways to burn off steam.
- *You can* pray and recall scriptures that help you remember who you are and God's best for you.
- *You can* choose not to be mean or hurtful to others or to yourself.
- *You can* choose to be kind when it would be easier to offend or insult others.
- *You can* think of something you love to do and add it to this list!

So, you see, there is much *you can* do when you're angry. Just don't stay angry. That's not good for anyone, especially you.

Even if you make good choices, the reality is that some people choose to be mean and even enjoy bullying others. But bullying is not God's plan for anyone. God never wants us to be mean to others.

Boys tend to be mean by hitting, pushing, or being physical, while girls are often mean in more verbal and relational ways, such as through insults or ignoring. Boys tend to intimidate through their strength or physical attributes. Girls often hurt others emotionally by excluding, teasing, and mocking. Ouch.

None of this is good for anyone, but it happens a lot. You may see it more during the tween and teen years. It helps to know what's happening, and understanding will help you know how to respond.

So what's the difference between meanness and just being moody, which we all experience at times? In question 17 we addressed moodiness as a normal part of growing up that can be managed in various ways. Moods are one thing; meanness is quite another. Moods are usually short-lived, whereas meanness can become a habit, even a way of life. Moods come upon us unexpectedly, but meanness is a choice.

We all go through tough times, and we all have bad moods or sad days. We all feel angry at times, but we don't have to act out in sadness or anger toward others. As with moodiness, we can learn to manage how we *feel* and choose to act upon what we *know* instead.

> "In your anger do not sin": Do not let the sun go down while you are still angry, and do not give the devil a foothold.
>
> *Ephesians 4:26–27*

God gave us our emotions, but he also gave us the ability to make good and wise choices. Although at times we will be angry, confused, and frustrated, we must avoid sinning because of how we *feel*. If we stay angry, this Scripture passage says we give the devil a foothold. What happens if someone grabs your foot? You trip, right? And land flat on your face.

Staying angry is like opening a faucet so that water keeps gushing out. Until we shut off the faucet of anger, it can lead to more angry actions. It gets easier to sin when tempted because our emotions are out of control. Letting bad feelings control what we do can turn meanness into bullying or violence if we're not careful. So we need to shut off that faucet for good.

Still, not every girl makes these wise choices. Perhaps no one taught her how to be nice to others. Maybe someone yells at her at home and she takes it out on others at school when no adult

Dealing with a Bully

- Do not give in to a bully's demands. Remember: they want to control you by shocking you, upsetting you, and putting you down. Stand up tall, and tell them to stop.

- If they don't stop, keep cool and walk away. When bullies come upon that kind of boldness, they will usually find someone else to pick on.

- If you get an email, text, or instant message that's mean or hurtful (cyber bullying), or if someone posts inappropriate pictures of you or lies about you, tell your parents and/ or teacher immediately. This is not acceptable, ever, and must stop.

- Choose friends who are not rude, abusive, or offensive. Don't spend your time with people who enjoy gossiping, being mean to others, or criticizing. Pray for them, but invest your precious time with someone else — someone who really cares about you. Someone who builds you up and encourages you rather than insults you.

- Although a bully's mean behavior may be a cry for help, what he or she is doing is wrong and needs to be handled by an adult. Many bullies need help from a counselor or therapist with special training.

is watching. Sadly, this is the situation for many bullies. They may mistreat others because they're hurting inside, and that's how they've learned to behave.

Some girls use technology to be mean to other girls. It's called *cyber bullying*. Although we know you've heard of this and may have been exposed to it already, let's define some terms so we're all on the same page.

A bully is someone who continually picks on someone else, usually another kid who is smaller, shy, or insecure. Bullies love to get a response; they feel powerful if they can control someone else by demeaning, insulting, or just being mean.

Although bullying in person is more common for boys, girls are more likely to cyber bully. They send emails, instant messages, or texts loaded with hurtful words they wouldn't dare say in person—but will say behind the "safe" cover of technology.

A new form of bullying is called *burning*—what we call *bullying on steroids*. This is a cruel game where everything someone says is turned upside down and distorted into a joke. Girl bullies write "burn books" packed with hurtful lies about a girl, spreading rumors or making fun of the way she looks or who she is.

Typically, a cyber bully singles out someone, opens an Internet page in that person's name, and posts gross and hurtful lies about her. This is wrong and illegal. Social media sites and schools have worked together with police officers to take down these burn pages. Those responsible face possible criminal charges and can even be thrown in jail.

Beyond these types of bullying, some girls seem to enjoy putting other girls down by gossiping about them. Gossip, while not the same as bullying, is another dangerous and hurtful practice that, for some girls, becomes a way of life. Through gossip, these girls criticize or make fun of the way other girls look, talk, dress, or behave—pretty much anything. We like this saying: *Gossip* is saying behind someone's back what you wouldn't say to their face, while *flattery* is saying to someone's face what you wouldn't say behind their back. Both are wrong.

Did you know that the Bible speaks about the destructive power of gossip?

> Avoid godless chatter, because those who indulge in it will become more and more ungodly.
>
> *2 Timothy 2:16*

Though some tongues just love the taste of gossip, those who follow Jesus have better uses for language than that. Don't talk dirty or silly. That kind of talk doesn't fit our style. Thanksgiving is our dialect.

Ephesians 5:3–4 MSG

Mean people spread mean gossip; their words smart and burn.

Proverbs 16:27 MSG

Listening to gossip is like eating cheap candy; do you want junk like that in your belly?

Proverbs 26:22 MSG

So what can you do when girls are mean through gossip?

Start by avoiding these types of conversations. If someone gossips, don't throw more wood in that fire. Instead, get in the habit of saying something like, "I prefer not to talk about that because I don't know if it's true," and change the subject. That's a great way to extinguish the spreading flames of gossip.

If they don't stop after a minute, you can say, "Okay, okay. Can we talk about something else now?" Or you can be more direct and say, "I don't like gossip. Please stop talking like this."

Or you could ask, "Would you say that to the face of the person you're talking about?" Usually, they wouldn't.

As you do this more and more, your friends will recognize that you don't like gossip. You may even help them rethink what they are talking about.

An important way to deal with meanness is by choosing your friends well. Is a girl nice to you one day and mean the next? Does she talk about others all the time? Does she criticize you or make you feel bad about yourself? If so, ask yourself, *Is this a girl I really want to hang out with?*

If you're involved in a conflict with a friend, try talking about your feelings. Take your friend aside, and just between the two of you, say:

- "It hurts my feelings when you say these things about me."
- "It made me feel bad when you made fun of my [clothes, hair, etc.]."
- "I had asked you not to say anything about that, and I'm really mad that you did."

A true friend won't be angry with you for saying something. Or she may be upset at first but then apologize later. It takes courage to be honest, but every time you speak the truth, you'll feel better inside. You may also help others when you take a stand for what is right and speak up.

If you and a friend get into a fight, or the rumor mill spreads something untrue, don't let your anger linger. Go to your friend right away and set the record straight.

- "Did you really say that about me?"
- "I'm sorry. I didn't mean to hurt your feelings."
- "Your friendship means so much to me. Can we talk about what happened?"

If you wait, your mind may make the problem into something bigger. You can start to imagine things that are untrue, and pretty soon you feel worse and worse. Don't hesitate. Make things right as soon as possible. Pray for the words. Pray for wisdom. Though conflict is hard, every time you take a brave step, you will grow stronger in your faith. And it will be easier the next time something happens.

> "Therefore, if you are offering your gift at the altar and there remember that your brother or sister has something against you, leave your gift there in front of the altar. First go and be reconciled to them; then come and offer your gift."
>
> *Matthew 5:23–24*

The Making of a Good Friend

What makes a good friend? Here's how my (Dr. Mari's) son recently described his best friend. "He makes it easy, Mom. I never have to worry about what I say or do. I can just be myself. He accepts me just the way I am."

He's right. Being with a good friend makes you feel good, not stressed. A good friend doesn't try to change you in order to love and accept you, but he or she challenges you to be your very best every day.

I've had three "best friends" since middle school. We are true BFFs. We're all different. Two are teachers, one's a musician, and I'm a doctor and writer. We also have many things in common. These are some of the things that have made us great lifelong friends:

- We love, encourage, and help each other.
- We tell the truth, especially when it's hard.
- We stand by one another in good times and bad.
- We've shared important life experiences, like going to school and serving others.
- Our families know and trust each other; we are close to our parents and to one another.
- When going through tough times, like when my parents split up, we always help each other.
- While in school, we always looked out for one another at parties.
- Now, as adults, we stay close even while living miles apart.

Some girls are mean, but thankfully, most girls are not. Good friends are one of the best things in life.

A friend loves at all times.

Proverbs 17:17

If you or a friend continues to be bullied despite your best efforts, tell a teacher or school counselor and discuss it with your parents. Don't keep it to yourself. Tell your parents or guardians what's going on so they can help you. If you'd prefer, your mom or dad can talk to your teacher. And if your parents can't or won't help, consider asking another trusted adult (like a teacher, school principal, or coach).

Remember, if it's happening to you, it is probably happening to others in your school. Stopping abusive behavior will help many people, including you, your friends, and even bullies.

So why are some girls so mean? Because they choose to be. But *you* don't have to. Surround yourself with people who love and respect you, and remember to pray for those who don't.

> Make sure that nobody pays back wrong for wrong, but always strive to do what is good for each other and for everyone else.
>
> *1 Thessalonians 5:15*

> Whoever of you loves life and desires to see many good days, keep your tongue from evil and your lips from telling lies. Turn from evil and do good; seek peace and pursue it.
>
> *Psalm 34:12–14*

> Be kind and compassionate to one another, forgiving each other, just as in Christ God forgave you.
>
> *Ephesians 4:32*

> Likewise, the tongue is a small part of the body, but it makes great boasts. Consider what a great forest is set on fire by a small spark.
>
> *James 3:5*

QUESTION 28

Social media is fun, but how much is too much?

Can you imagine life with no Internet? No mp3 players, no texting? No iPods or TV? None of this was around when we (and your parents) were kids, but now they're in every home and pocket— including yours, right?

Today's technology is mind-boggling. The Internet connects us with the world like never before. Families and friends keep in touch through social media: Skype, Facebook, Twitter, Pinterest, Face Time, Google Plus, online gaming, Instagram.

All this technology can be great, but when can it become harmful?

It's critical to understand that the Internet is potentially dangerous. It brings good and bad into your life, including things you may not otherwise look at. Sexy images and even people with bad intentions are as real and up close as your next email, IM, or pop-up.

So how can you make the most of the Internet and social media while avoiding the bad?

Here's a great starting point. Never post anything online, in an IM, email, or social media site, that you wouldn't say or do in person—or that you wouldn't want printed in the school newspaper or yearbook!

Before you post anything at all, ask yourself, *Would I say this to someone face-to-face? Will I be proud if the word gets out that I posted this?*

Ask yourself these questions when using social media:

1. What does this text or photo say about what I value and about me?
2. How might this text or photo impact those who see it?
3. Does this post, text, or photo bring glory to God?

These questions will serve as a wise filter to help you do the right thing while using technology. Even pictures of people in bathing suits posted on social media can cross a line pretty quickly. Remember, if what you post doesn't show that you respect yourself, and if you don't protect your dignity as God's child, will others?

We like the saying, "Everything speaks." Everything you see, hear, and read conveys a message. And *everything* that goes online, whether in an email or a text, stays there *forever*—and can become public at any time in your life. So think twice before you post, text, or write anything at all.

The average teen sends 3,339 texts per month. That's about 110 per day and climbing. Texting can take over your life if you're not careful.

Since girls value communication and connection so much, texting and social media can get out of hand very quickly. Sadly,

WWJTXT?

There is now a *What Would Jesus Text?* movement among tweens, teens, and young adults. A thumb ring reminds you to think before you text. The ministry, which you can find with this QR code or the URL in our list of resources, is based on this verse:

What Would
Jesus Text?

> May these words of my mouth and this meditation of my heart be pleasing in your sight, LORD, my Rock and my Redeemer.
>
> Psalm 19:14

Here's the message that comes with each thumb band:

> When texting, we are sometimes faced with temptations that can be hard to overcome. Because we're human and not perfect, we sometimes make mistakes. Let this thumb band be a gentle reminder to do what's right. Ask yourself, "What would Jesus text?" So, when you look back at the end of the day, you'll have no regrets.

You can also write a scripture like Psalm 19:14 or a note on your computer, tablet, iPod, and phone to remind you to be wise in all things, including social media.

research has found that girls who spend a lot of time on social media (like Facebook or Twitter) tend to dislike their bodies and themselves more. They are also more likely to have depression and lower self-esteem. This is not surprising, since the media in general—including social media—is obsessed with the wrong kind of beauty (as you learned in question 9).

Girls who overuse social media get extra doses of the lie that skinnier and sexier is better. Then when they look in the mirror and don't see a skinny-sexy-photoshopped model, they may begin to feel discouraged, even depressed. This makes perfect sense. Research shows that the more screen time for girls, the less happy they are with their weight and body image, and the more obsessed they are with thinness and outer appearance.

So don't overdo it with social media and the Internet. These are great tools to use for learning and connecting with friends and family, but they can harm you as well. Be careful and use limits, like spending no more than thirty minutes to an hour a day online (or less).

So what else can you do to protect yourself from the dangers of social media and the Internet?

- Keep all electronics outside your bedroom. Have one room in the main part of the house for all electronics: smartphones, mp3 players, tablets, and computers. This will keep the whole family more accountable.
- When you get home, don't keep your phone and iPod in your pocket. Park them in the computer room. This way, when Patty and Susie text you three times in a row to plan the next movie night, you're not tempted to answer immediately while ignoring your family or your studies. You'll enjoy people more if you stay focused on them.
- Discuss with your parents when to turn everything off. Consider these guidelines:

  Tweens: No video games, social media, or Internet (apart from homework) after 6:00 p.m., and none unless you've been physically active and/or played outside for a while—which is fun and so good for you.

  Teens: Phones, computers, and all electronics go off no later than 9:00 p.m. on weeknights. No texting after 9:00 p.m. on school nights, possibly a bit later on weekends. All electronics sleep in the "off" position in the designated family computer room—not in your bedroom.

Text, Sext — What's Next?

Sexting is sending sexually explicit messages or photos, usually between cell phones. One study found that nearly 40 percent of tweens and teens have received an "offensive or distressing" sexual image by text or email.

Not only is it illegal to send or store a sext of a minor, it's also wrong, unwise, and potentially dangerous. Some teens who have sexted photographs of themselves, or of their friends, have been charged with spreading child pornography. And others, who have received the images, have been charged with possession of child pornography. These are both crimes.

Many states have laws requiring mandatory sentencing of *anyone* who has photos like that of someone under sixteen, even if they didn't ask for it to be sent to them. The bottom line is that if it's found on your phone or computer, you are breaking the law and could end up in trouble with the cops. Do yourself a favor and avoid that at all costs.

All ages: No access to video games, TV, social media, texts, or email until all homework is complete unless a parent makes an exception.

You can ask your parents if these guidelines can be relaxed as rewards for good behavior, on special occasions, and on weekends. And remember these tips:

- Don't overdo it with technology. It's not good for you or your relationships.
- Be considerate. Sitting in front of someone at the dinner table while texting away is rude. It sends the message that

the person you're texting is more important than the person in front of you. Stay present with the people around you.

- Respect your siblings, parents, teachers, and friends. If they're in front of you, give them your full attention.

Remember, once a text, email, or sext is on the Internet, it's *always* on the Internet. It cannot be erased. And *any* sext, no matter who sends it, can end up on a porn site. The Internet Watch Foundation estimates that nearly 90 percent of sexts were stolen from their original upload location (typically social networks) and posted on other websites — especially porn sites that collect inappropriate images of children and young people.

Imagine anything you write or any picture you send being seen by your parents, your friends, your pastor, or your priest. What would it be like if your future husband or your future children saw a sext of you? You'd *never* want them to see something embarrassing or inappropriate you posted, would you? Then don't do it.

Believe it or not, we've even heard of kids who didn't get into college or didn't get a job they really wanted because of this. Why? Because colleges and employers routinely Google those who apply to their schools and jobs. Anything inappropriate they find can be used against you, even a picture posted as a joke. They also search social media sites like Facebook to try to find out more about you. So be smart, and do the right thing.

If someone asks you to sext, tell your parents or a trusted adult immediately and unfriend or block posts or texts from this person. Avoid sexting at all costs — sending *and* receiving. If you get a sext or inappropriate message, tell your parent or teacher, a counselor, or a trusted adult. Don't let it go on.

Another great idea is to have electronics-free weekends and screen-free breaks to rest your mind and focus on other things. This may sound awful, but you'll thank us.

How Many Ways Can You Say No?

Recently I (Dr. Walt) heard an ad from the Ad Council on the radio where a preteen tested different ways to say no if someone asks her for a sext. We added some of our own one-liners to her clever list. Can you think of any others?

- No way, José!
- I'm camera shy.
- I already said no.
- It's against my religion.
- I'm giving my dog a bath, you can have pictures of that.
- Pressure gives me hives.
- Under my clothes I'm a robot.
- Hold on; let me ask my mom.
- Sorry, a horse ate my webcam.
- I'm worried they'll get passed around school.
- Unfortunately I just had my clothes surgically attached to my body.
- If they got out I might never be president.
- Not even if you were all three Jonas Brothers.
- I have a rash.
- I have lizard skin.
- The more you ask, the uglier you get.
- Is there a bug in your ear?
- You're not the boss of me.
- Did you forget I said no?

The ad ends by saying, "When someone is pressuring you to do something you don't want to do, how many ways can you say no before they get the message?" Can you and your friends come up with more ways to just say no?

Sexting Invaded My Home

One of our reviewers shared this personal story:

My parents gave me a cell phone for safety reasons when I went to middle school. We all were very naive and didn't think about having some guidelines to go along with it.

My parents never read the texts that were coming in or going out. They also didn't realize that I should have time restraints with phone use. This caused me to have less sleep as well, staying up late to answer the texts of my night-owl friends.

Without my parents knowing it, a boy in my school began sexting me. It was both gross and embarrassing — especially since I only wanted a good relationship with him. But because my parents and I didn't have any ground rules, clear expectations, clear communications, or an open-phone policy, I was scared to tell my parents about it.

The sexts kept coming and caused me a great deal of confusion and heartache. I didn't know what to do, until the communication with him was suddenly blocked. How? Thank goodness my parents finally figured out what was going on and put a stop to it.

It would have been so much easier to stop things before they started if my parents and I had only been on the same page. By sharing my experience with other girls my age, I hope to spare others some of the pain our family encountered.

So when your parents read your texts, know that they're trying to protect you.

Go outside. Take walks without being tied to a cell phone or iPod. Breathe in some fresh air. Ride your bike. Write a letter to a friend or to a grandparent, aunt, or cousin. Send a card to someone serving in the military. Read a good book, or visit your local library. Do a puzzle, or paint something. Visit someone at a nursing home. Volunteer to serve food at a homeless shelter or soup kitchen. Work at a food pantry. Find a new hobby. Just stand on your head—anything. You may discover a new talent if you turn off the TV, shut down your computer, and put away your phone. Give it a try.

And speaking of good books to read and movies to watch, be selective. What you read and watch feeds your mind, your heart, and your soul. Be wise, and choose well. Some books and movies that are promoted to young girls shouldn't even be read or watched by adults.

Ask your parents or other trusted Christian adults before deciding on a book or movie that someone recommends. Before you read something, ask yourself if it will be informative or entertaining in a way that helps or harms you. If you're not sure, find something better to do.

> Do not conform to the pattern of this world, but be transformed by the renewing of your mind. Then you will be able to test and approve what God's will is—his good, pleasing and perfect will.
>
> *Romans 12:2*

> May God himself, the God of peace, sanctify you through and through. May your whole spirit, soul and body be kept blameless at the coming of our Lord Jesus Christ.
>
> *1 Thessalonians 5:23*

Plugged In

Have you ever seen a movie preview and thought, *That looks like a really cool movie?* Then you go see it and it's not at all what you expected. It's boring, scary, or totally inappropriate. If you use resources like Plugged In, you won't ever have that happen again.

Both of our families like Plugged In, a website that analyzes and rates movies, videos, music, TV, and games. You can trust the reviewers to give a thumbs-up or a thumbs-down to media you're thinking of listening to, watching, or reading. They also have a really cool blog and weekly podcast that will keep you and your friends in the know about media.

A typical Plugged In review will assess a movie's:

- Positive elements
- Spiritual, sexual, and violent content
- Drug and alcohol content
- Crude language
- Other negative elements

Next time a friend invites you over for a movie, remember to "plug in" before you buy in. You can find Plugged In with the URL in our resources list at the back of the book.

QUESTION 29

What if my friends want to try alcohol, drugs, or dangerous games?

In question 26 we mentioned that many people regret getting a tattoo within a week of getting it. Some regret it the next day. You know why? Because they were drunk, stoned, or high on drugs when they got it.

Imagine waking up one morning, looking down your arm, and doing a double take. Shocked, you realize the lizard you just spotted there will now walk with you everywhere—'cause it's tattooed on your arm. That's the kind of stuff people sometimes do when they drink or use drugs. Not such a great idea, is it?

You may not feel tempted to drink alcohol, but some kids you know are likely already drinking or talking about it. Sadly, nearly one in four girls starts drinking alcohol before age thirteen.

A lot of girls we talk to don't know that alcohol in all forms

193

(wine, beer, and liquor) is a drug—an illegal drug if you're under twenty-one years of age. So for followers of Jesus, underage drinking is a sin because it breaks the law. For a lot of girls, this is enough to help them decide alcohol isn't worth the trouble.

Did you know it's easier to get hooked on alcohol or other drugs when you're younger? This means you want more and more of it each day; you're *addicted*. People who get hooked on alcohol or drugs make very poor choices, like stealing or hurting others to get money to pay for more booze or drugs. So one sin leads to another and another. It's a terrible cycle that's best to avoid completely.

Girls who drink before age fifteen are five times more likely to have problems with alcohol later in life. So if you or your friends start drinking at your age, you are much more likely to get hooked on alcohol even as a teen.

Addiction to alcohol is known as *alcoholism*, and people with this addiction are called *alcoholics*. Being hooked on alcohol (or drugs) traps you in a prison of sorts—physically, emotionally, relationally, and spiritually. Using drugs affects *everything* about you. The good news is that this is totally preventable, especially when you realize that most alcoholics begin drinking when they are very young. So don't.

Drinking even small amounts of alcohol affects girls differently than boys. Girls are much more sensitive to the effects of alcohol than boys, so it is much more dangerous for women than it is for men. Did you know that? More female alcoholics die from suicide, alcohol-related injuries, circulatory disorders, and a bad liver disease called *cirrhosis* than male alcoholics.

Having even one drink per day increases the risk of at least eight types of cancer (mouth, pharynx, larynx, esophagus, liver, breast, colon, and rectum) and many other serious conditions (such as seizure disorders, inflammation of the pancreas [a digestive gland], stroke, heartbeat irregularities, cirrhosis, and high blood pressure).

Did You Know?

The National Center on Addiction and Substance Abuse at Columbia University published some interesting facts about girls and substance abuse:

SMOKING

- Nearly one in every four high school senior girls smokes.
- Girls get hooked on cigarettes quicker than boys.
- Many teens who take birth control pills also smoke. Taken together, cigarettes and the pill can cause heart problems and dangerous blood clots.

ALCOHOL

- Nearly half of high school girls drink alcohol.
- Nearly one in four girls starts drinking before age thirteen.
- Drinking before age fifteen quadruples the chances of getting hooked on alcohol.
- Teen girls who drink a lot are way more likely to have sex (particularly unwanted sex) than girls who don't drink.
- Compared to boys, girls get drunk faster, get hooked on alcohol more quickly, and develop heart, liver, and brain problems sooner.
- For girls, one drink usually has the same effect as two to three drinks for a boy.
- Teen girls who drink often are almost six times more likely to attempt suicide than girls who never drink.

OTHER DRUGS

- Girls who smoke marijuana have more suicidal thoughts and suicide attempts than girls who don't.
- Painkillers are the most abused prescription drugs among teen girls.
- Teen girls are more likely than boys to use over-the-counter drugs to get high. And these medicines can be just as dangerous as prescription drugs.

For females, including teens, even one drink a day increases the risk for breast cancer. Women who have three or more drinks a week have a 15 percent higher risk of breast cancer. And the chances go up even more for each additional drink women regularly have each day. So for girls and women, when it comes to cancer prevention, there's no amount of alcohol that can be said to be safe.

The bottom line is that drinking alcohol can harm your health. So be smart and choose to say no to alcohol and all illegal drugs.

Pot's the Pits

Teens in Colorado, where recreational marijuana (pot) use is now legal for adults, believe these lies about it:

- They think pot actually helps brain cells grow and develop.
- They know smoking pot is bad for your lungs, but they think it's safer than smoking cigarettes.
- They think pot helps you focus in class.

But *none* of these beliefs is true. Here are the facts and just a few of the reasons we tell teens (and everyone) to avoid marijuana:

- Marijuana, also known as *pot*, *weed*, or *joints*, is a drug.
- Marijuana is bad for you, your brain, and your life.
- Teens make bad decisions when they smoke pot, including:
  —Driving and wrecking a car—potentially killing themselves or someone else.
  —Making sexual choices that are unsafe or out of character.
  —Saying or doing dumb or hurtful things they later regret.

The Bible teaches that, as Christians, we are to be wise and cautious in the way we live. We are not to be foolish, and we are not to get drunk:

> Be very careful, then, how you live—not as unwise but as wise.... Therefore do not be foolish, but understand what the Lord's will is. Do not get drunk on wine, which leads to debauchery. Instead, be filled with the Spirit.
>
> *Ephesians 5:15, 17–18*

- Marijuana can also affect your judgment about other drugs. While high on pot, you may drink too much or use drugs you never even planned to try.
- Pot affects your memory and your ability to solve problems. It can also contribute to depression and anxiety, and it can mess up your periods.
- Teens who use marijuana are almost twice as likely to exhibit psychotic behaviors (like seeing or hearing things that aren't real) compared to those who don't.
- Marijuana cigarettes have no filters and contain more tar than nicotine cigarettes. They are even *worse* for your lungs than regular cigarettes (which are bad enough).
- Long-term marijuana use can lead to lung problems like infections, trouble breathing, and cancer.
- Teens are much more likely than adults to get hooked on pot.
- Teens who use pot more than once a week can lower their IQ (a measure of intelligence) for life. In other words, smoking pot can make you dumber. Like one of our teen reviewers said, "No wonder they call it dope."

To be *filled with the Spirit* means to be controlled by, guided by, and empowered by God's Spirit—led by God, not by selfishness. It means to be in control, not out of control.

> You are all children of the light and children of the day. We do not belong to the night or to the darkness. So then, let us not be like others, who are asleep, but let us be awake and sober. For those who sleep, sleep at night, and those who get drunk, get drunk at night. But since we belong to the day, let us be sober, putting on faith and love as a breastplate, and the hope of salvation as a helmet.
>
> *1 Thessalonians 5:5–8*

Here are some of the lies about drugs that you may hear from other kids (and the lies apply to alcohol, marijuana, other inhaled or puffed drugs, and any other drug not prescribed for you):

Lie No. 1: "Drugs will help you deal with your problems."

The truth is, many people use a drug to "numb" their pain. They use it to escape from problems or to forget their troubles. But guess what! When the drug effect wears off, their problems are still there. And now they have even more problems caused by the drug use itself, like wrecking their car or fighting with their best friend. Drugs will never, ever help you solve what is wrong with your life. Drugs will only make things worse.

Lie No. 2: "Drugs will make you look cool."

The truth is, people who drink or use drugs do incredibly uncool things—like stumbling or falling, slurring their speech, having accidents, saying things that hurt others, vomiting their guts out, losing control of their behavior, and many other stupid things.

Worse yet, girls who drink or use drugs and drive end up killing or hurting themselves or others almost every day. Each year, thousands of fifteen- to twenty-year-old drivers are killed in drug-related car accidents, while nearly 300,000 are injured. That's not cool at all.

Lie No. 3: "Drugs will make you happy and help you have a good time."

No doubt about it, drinking alcohol or taking drugs can give you a "buzz" — especially when the drug first begins to affect your brain. And it's not just your brain that's drunk or drugged, but also your entire nervous system. But alcohol and other drugs *never* make a person happy. Alcohol is a depressant. It eventually makes most people feel down and drowsy. It makes them move and react much more slowly than normal.

At first, someone who's drinking alcohol or doing drugs might seem to lose their inhibitions. They "loosen up" and do or say things they normally wouldn't. This is why some people seem wild or out of control when they drink or do drugs. But even if someone seems "pumped up" when they drink, the drug ends up making them sluggish, slow, and unable to make wise decisions.

Experts who work with adolescent sex offenders who were drinking or on drugs often hear the perpetrator say, "It was the alcohol," or "It was the drugs." But these experts say the drug does not make a person do something they don't want to do. The drug makes it easier for a person to cross the boundaries of what they know is right and wrong. You are less likely to think of the consequences of doing something when you are drinking or high on other illegal drugs.

Lie No. 4: "If you just use a little of these drugs, you won't become addicted."

Totally false.

Some kids believe drinking wine or beer is safer than hard alcohol (like whiskey or vodka). The fact is, beer, wine, and hard liquor all contain the exact same drug: alcohol! Also, some kids think trying someone else's prescription drug or smoking a little marijuana won't hurt. But it does.

Many girls we've cared for say they tried alcohol or drugs because their friends were doing it. Peer pressure can be overwhelming—and not just to drink alcohol, but to use or take any drug that is not prescribed for you by your doctor.

In school and in the neighborhood, in clubs and on teams—even in church youth group—you will feel peer pressure to do wrong things. But it's never right to do what's wrong, is it?

There are always consequences for doing wrong things—there's always a price to pay. And sometimes that price can be very, very high.

Think about it. If you are tempted to drink or take another drug because your friends are pushing you to, then it's time to ask a very important question: What would happen if you told them you're not interested in alcohol or drugs?

Would your friends not want to hang out with you anymore because of your decision? If so, were they true friends in the first place?

Of course not. A real friend, a true friend, will respect your decisions, and she won't try to force you into things that are bad for you. Think twice about hanging out with that "friend" anymore. If she's pushing you to try drugs, she hasn't learned how to be a good friend.

Here are some more tips for handling the pressure to try dangerous games, alcohol, or illegal drugs:

- You don't have to do *anything* that you don't want to do.
- You should not do *anything* that is not right to do.
- Giving in to peer pressure never solves problems, but it often *creates* problems.
- Giving in to peer pressure will *not* make people like and respect you more—even if they act like it. Most people actually respect those who stand up for what they believe.

The Choking "Game" — Breathe or Die

As I (Dr. Walt) was writing this chapter, I read a sad headline in our local paper: "A Colorado Springs ninth grader died as a result of playing the 'choking game,' making him the second student to die after playing the game in the last three years."

I remember playing this "game" with friends when I was in elementary school. But this is no game, and no one warned us of its dangers. No one told us that we could die! Sadly, most of the kids who have died playing the "choking game" were eleven to sixteen years old.

So how is this deadly "game" played, and why? Kids do it to get a brief "high." They either choke each other or use a noose or rope to choke themselves. It's crazy! A kid can pass out from this in seconds, get seriously hurt, and even die.

Anything that blocks the arteries in the neck that bring oxygen to the brain will make you pass out. Within three minutes, memory, balance, and other brain functions start to fail. Death occurs shortly after. The choking game has also been called the *pass-out game*, the *strangling game*, *space monkey* or *space cowboy*, *suffocation roulette*, the *fainting game*, *blackout*, *flatliner*, *California choke*, *purple dragon*, or *cloud nine*.

Don't ever play any of these so-called "games." Be smart, and stay safe! You can learn more about the dangers of this game from this QR code or the URL in our resources list at the back of the book.

The Dangers of the Choking Game

With each temptation that comes our way, God provides a way of escape:

> No temptation has overtaken you except what is common to mankind. And God is faithful; he will not let you be tempted beyond what you can bear. But when you are tempted, he will also provide a way out so that you can endure it.
>
> *1 Corinthians 10:13*

You may wonder, *How can I escape the temptation—the pressure?* Remember, it's always okay to just say no. You don't have to give a reason. You don't have to explain yourself.

If you're offered alcohol or another drug, you can suggest an alternative: "I think I'd rather have a soda" or "I'd rather not" or something like that. Or you can simply say, "No, thanks."

Choosing to do something that is wrong may be fun for a brief period of time—but it will always catch up with you. There's *always* a price to pay.

If you've already fallen to temptation with alcohol or other drugs, know that Jesus (who faced many temptations too) understands completely and wants you to talk to him and tap into his power.

> For we do not have a high priest who is unable to empathize with our weaknesses, but we have one who has been tempted in every way, just as we are—yet he did not sin. Let us then approach God's throne of grace with confidence, so that we may receive mercy and find grace to help us in our time of need.
>
> *Hebrews 4:15–16*

As an example of the power of faith to help you make the right choice, think about Moses. As a young man, Moses was tempted to do many wrong things, but he chose not to.

Everybody's *Not* Doing It

At a point in your life (maybe it's already happened), someone will challenge you to do something with the words, "Everybody's doing it."

The temptation might come in the form of shoplifting, going too far sexually, or trying drugs or alcohol. But no matter what the temptation is, know this fact: everybody is *not* doing it.

When it comes to alcohol, studies show that nearly 60 percent of twelve- to seventeen-year-olds have never had a drink. Although some girls have said yes, most girls are saying no.

Experimenting with alcohol is dangerous, and trying other illegal drugs can be even more dangerous. It can even kill you! Taking somebody else's prescription pills, huffing, or trying harder drugs, such as cocaine, can kill a person the very first time they try them.

A very dangerous practice these days is mixing different drugs together — even prescription drugs. At what are called *bowling parties* or *pharm parties*, different pills are thrown in a bowl and people grab handfuls and take them. This is extremely dangerous — people can die after one such party. One expert writes:

> There are dozens of chemicals that can render you friendless, jobless, and despondent — if not outright kill you — all by themselves. That makes taking them together a bit like throwing a mixture of gasoline and fire at your own body. Too much of drug A may cause liver failure, say. Add a little of drug B and it might happen two hours sooner. Toss in drug C, and maybe you'll stop breathing before your liver even gets involved.

So even if someone says "everybody's doing it," when it comes to alcohol and drugs, weigh the consequences, turn to Jesus, and walk away from the crowd.

By faith Moses, when he had grown up, refused to be known as the son of Pharaoh's daughter. He chose to be mistreated along with the people of God rather than to enjoy the fleeting pleasures of sin. He regarded disgrace for the sake of Christ as of greater value than the treasures of Egypt, because he was looking ahead to his reward. By faith he left Egypt, not fearing the king's anger; he persevered because he saw him who is invisible.

Hebrews 11:24–27

Notice, Moses was able to make the right decision by *faith*. His faith became a resource—it strengthened his will to choose right over wrong.

Today, God gives the gift of the Holy Spirit and his Word to guide us to make right decisions. We'll talk more about how to stay strong when tempted in question 34.

We know saying no isn't always easy. But by standing strong, you may find that many of your friends secretly agree with you. They'll likely respect you even more because they know deep down that you are doing the right thing. It may even give them the courage to also say no. You can be an important positive influence in your friends' lives. It takes courage to do what is right even if it seems "uncool." So be brave.

If you continue to get pressured, talk about it with your mom or dad, a teacher, or another trusted adult.

Wine is a mocker and beer a brawler; whoever is led astray by them is not wise.

Proverbs 20:1

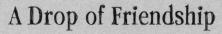

A Drop of Friendship

One of our young reviewers, now in college, has the following advice for you:

Though I believe it is a person's choice whether they want to drink alcohol, I've never been sorely tempted to myself.... It's not the smartest of ideas.

When you drink ... your judgment is altered, and it makes people do really stupid things. You don't need to drink to have a good time. I've gone out with friends and had a good time without a single drop of alcohol in my system.

We agree. I (Dr. Mari) have awesome childhood memories. I hung out with my three BFFs almost every weekend. We had sleepovers at each other's houses and spent tons of time talking, laughing, and having fun. We didn't need to have a drop of alcohol to have fun. All we needed was to be together.

Don't drink too much wine. That cheapens your life. Drink the Spirit of God, huge draughts of him. Sing hymns instead of drinking songs! Sing songs from your heart to Christ. Sing praises over everything, any excuse for a song to God the Father in the name of our Master, Jesus Christ.

Ephesians 5:18–20 MSG

QUESTION 30

Sex — part of God's plan? Are you serious?

God created the universe in a series of steps. And after each step of creation, God said it was all good. But after creating the entire universe, God was not done — the highlight of creation was still missing.

> So God created mankind in his own image, in the image of God he created them; male and female he created them.

Genesis 1:27

After creating a man and a woman,

> God saw all that he had made, and it was very good.

Genesis 1:31

Once he created humans, only then did his entire creation become "very good." Why? Because women and men, girls and boys were the only creatures in the entire universe made in the image of God. God first created the man, Adam. And then he said something surprising: "It is not good ..." (Genesis 2:18).

Why was it *not good*? Everything else in creation was either good or very good. Did God goof up when he made man?

My (Dr. Walt's) daughter, Kate, and I were talking about this once. She smiled and said, "I know why."

"Please go on," I replied.

Kate laughed and said, "Well, it's in the Bible. It says that after God made a man, he said, 'It is not good. I can do better than that.' Then he made a woman."

"What version of the Bible did you get that from?" I asked, laughing.

"The Modern Woman Version," Kate said, joking.

Well, the real reason is *not* that God goofed or that he thought he could do better. Not at all! Men and women are God's beloved creation. Yet God created the man with a very specific need:

> The LORD God said, "It is not good for the man to be alone. I will make a helper suitable for him."
>
> *Genesis 2:18*

God's design is that a man will leave his parents and be united to his wife and become *one flesh* with her (Genesis 2:24). Biblical marriage is a very big deal to God. Jesus emphasized this by saying:

> "Haven't you read ... that at the beginning the Creator 'made them male and female,' and said, 'For this reason a man will leave his father and mother and be united to his wife, and the two will become one flesh'? So they are no longer two, but one flesh."
>
> *Matthew 19:4–6*

God's design for men and women is to have a sexual relationship (to be united and become one flesh) only in the union of marriage where they can then embrace his gift of children. It's all tied together—a man, a woman, sex, and children go together by divine design.

In creating you, God gave your body the ability to carry a child—God's future gift to you and your husband. He designed your womb to carry and nurture a child and to give birth.

Think about it. God created the world in such a way that the creation of people won't happen without the participation of a

Virgin by Grace

A virgin is someone who waits until marriage to have any sexual activity. Unfortunately, some boys and girls are robbed of this choice through sexual abuse. Some young people have been forced into sexual activity by people who are sick, evil, or have bad intentions. Sexual abuse is a crime and a terrible sin. Beyond hurting the child, such abuse hurts God's heart deeply, and God offers those children healing, mercy, and grace.

If this has happened to you, a trained Christian counselor or therapist can help you heal from abuse. Most life-affirming pregnancy centers (also called *crisis pregnancy centers* or *pregnancy resource centers*) have counselors who will talk to you for free. You can find one near you using the URL in our resources list at the back of the book.

Talking to your parent is also extremely important so they can help keep you safe.

If there's been abuse, getting help is very, very important, as is praying and asking God to bring healing to your heart, body, and soul. God can do it.

man *and* a woman. God has trusted us with the best part of his creation—another human being.

This awesome responsibility is a great reason to focus on godly friendships with boys rather than dating while you're still young. In our culture, unless a boy and a girl are very intentional and committed to waiting until marriage to have sex, dating can progress into a physical relationship that neither of them is ready for and both of them may one day regret.

Because physical attraction is so strong, waiting until marriage to have sex can be difficult. It's not impossible, but it takes

Have you ever heard of *secondary virginity*? This is the decision to wait until marriage before having any sexual activity even if you've had sexual activity in the past (whether by choice or through abuse).

The idea is that you can start over *today* regardless of what happened *yesterday*. You can have a fresh start *now* if your choices or experiences robbed you of God's original plan for sexuality.

Although temptation and sin are alive and well in our world, so are God's mercy, forgiveness, and healing. Take him up on his offer of a new life starting right now. Get help from a professional if you haven't already, and believe that God can do great things in you as you trust him with your life, including your sexuality. God promises you hope and a good future.

> "For I know the plans I have for you," declares the LORD, "plans to prosper you and not to harm you, plans to give you hope and a future."
>
> Jeremiah 29:11

a strong commitment. If you decide *now* that you will *not* have sex until marriage, it's much easier. Especially since God will help you. He will answer your prayers and help you stay on his best path for your life.

> How can a young person stay on the path of purity? By living according to your word.
>
> *Psalm 119:9*

How cool is that? God gives you the tools you need to use his gift of sex according to his purpose for your life:

1. He gives you the Bible to guide you.
2. He gives you his Spirit to live in you, to teach, and to lead you.
3. He'll give you good Christian friends to walk the path with you.
4. When you are tempted, he'll even give you a way to escape.

So decide *now* and commit not to open the gift of sex until God intends — in marriage — and with the person, the only person, he wants you to have sex with — your husband.

> Marriage should be honored by all, and the marriage bed kept pure.
>
> *Hebrews 13:4*

At your age, rather than focusing on boyfriends and dating, learn instead what makes a good *friend*. Then you will know what qualities to look for in a husband. How else will you know who a boy really is in his heart and soul unless you spend time becoming close friends long before you marry and have sex? You cannot become a soul mate with a guy until you know his soul (mind, emotions, and will/decision making) and his heart (his character — who he really is) deep down. That takes a long time.

This shift in focus away from boyfriends and dating to making great friends will allow you to pray, make good choices, and wait on God's leading for a good husband—a true best friend forever who will love you as Jesus loves you. A man who is a trustworthy companion, your best friend, *and* your soul mate—forever.

Your mom and dad (if you're blessed to have both) can be the key people in your life to help you live this beautiful story. They can help you understand how to make healthy choices in friendships and dating. There are also a lot of great books about dating, courting, and a godly marriage. We've only skimmed over an important topic—one we recommend you learn much more about.

If it is God's will for you to marry and become a mother someday, pray that he will help prepare you for all that's ahead. You can even pray for your future husband to remain pure in heart and body, as you commit to do the same.

> Flee from sexual immorality. All other sins a person commits are outside the body, but whoever sins sexually, sins against their own body.
>
> *1 Corinthians 6:18*

> Flee the evil desires of youth and pursue righteousness, faith, love and peace, along with those who call on the Lord out of a pure heart.
>
> *2 Timothy 2:22*

Have you heard about PAP tests (or *PAP smears*)? These special tests sample cells from your cervix to ensure they're healthy. With this and other tests, doctors can diagnose HPV (human papillomavirus), other sexually transmitted infections (STIs), and cervical cancer—a form of cancer caused by an STI.

Although STIs are quite common, there's only one way to get them—through sexual activity. So you can dramatically reduce your risk of catching *any* STI by avoiding any and all sexual activity until marriage.

Although we hope and pray that you will wait until marriage to become sexually active, we want you to be informed. So let's talk about STIs.

STIs are infections that can be transmitted through *any* sexual activity. This includes any activity in which genital or oral fluids that have the STI germs are spread from a person who is infected to one who is not. You can only get these infections by having sexual activity with someone who's already infected.

Most young girls who begin to have sex *will likely* develop an STI. If you have sex as a young person, you can just about count on becoming infected with something. Why? STIs are very common and can spread easily. And the younger you are, the more likely you are to catch an STI.

Girls often come to our offices with concerns about an abnormal vaginal discharge that started after having sex for the very first time. Even more common, they see us within a year or two of their first sexual encounter and we discover an infection they didn't even suspect. Tears follow, as well as broken hearts.

Even if you only have sexual activity with one person, you can still get one or more STIs from him if he had sexual activity with an infected person. Sadly, we've both had to break the bad news to young girls who caught one of the STIs that can't be cured. When they find out, they're shocked and often say, "But he's been my only boyfriend." They usually have no idea how many other people he'd had sex with already.

Some STIs can cause cancer. Others can keep you from having a baby by causing infertility. Although many STIs can be treated, some of them (like herpes, hepatitis B and C, and HIV [which causes AIDS]) cannot be cured. The best way to "treat" these infections is by *preventing* them.

When STIs lead to symptoms, they can cause burning with urination and/or a vaginal discharge that's thick and gray, brown, yellow, or green. They can cause pain in the lower abdomen and pelvis. If STIs become more severe, they can cause fevers, nausea,

Learn the N.I.C.E. Way to Say No

If you're ever in a situation that goes against your values to remain pure, it helps to plan and even rehearse some ways to say no. The following tips are adapted from the website It's Great to Wait, which you can find with this QR code or the URL in our list of resources:

It's Great to Wait

N Say *no*. Not "maybe" or "later." Set limits and be decisive. If you decide now that you're not having sex until marriage, it will be easier to say no if someone pressures you or tempts you to say yes.

I Follow your "no" with an *"I"* statement: "I'm not going to have sex until I marry." Or "Sex isn't part of my game plan right now." And move on.

C If the pressure continues, *change*. Change the *subject*: "Did you see the game on TV last night?" Or change *who* you're talking to: "I need to go ask Julie something." Or change the *location*: "I'm going back into the kitchen."

E If these strategies don't help, you need an *exit* plan. Leave a bad or unsafe situation *immediately*—no need to be sweet or gracious. Call your parent to get picked up right away. Have a prearranged code phrase that means "Come pick me up. And hurry."

vomiting, a sore throat, rashes, joint pains, and more. They can make you very, very sick.

The most common STIs among young people include HPV (which can cause warts in your private parts and cervical cancer), chlamydia, and gonorrhea. Syphilis, an infection that can even affect the brain, is also on the rise.

Probably the most significant possible consequence of having sex before marriage is pregnancy, since it also impacts another human being—a new life—along with the baby's mother and father and their families. Once a girl starts having periods, even if she doesn't have one every month, she can get pregnant if she has sex!

Although your health teachers at school may tell you that a condom will protect you from some STIs (*not all!*) some of the time, as author Pam Stenzel so wisely said, "There is not a condom in the world that can protect your heart, your reputation, your character, and your values."

Shut That Door

When an STI causes symptoms or damage to your body, we call it a *sexually transmitted disease* (STD). The problem with STIs is that, very often, girls (and boys) don't even know they have them. Here's what happens.

Let's say boy A has the STI called *chlamydia* and doesn't know it, since he has no symptoms. He meets girl B and they have sexual activity, and she gets infected with chlamydia. They don't even have to have sexual intercourse—they may just be touching or kissing each other's genital areas and can spread some STIs like that.

In any case, girl B now has chlamydia and doesn't even know it. She could get symptoms from it, like a yellowish or green discharge or burning with urination. But many times, there are no symptoms.

A month goes by and boy A and girl B break up. They haven't had treatment for their STIs because they don't even know they're infected. Three months later, girl B meets boy C, and they engage

You have some powerful weapons in the battle against STIs: (1) You have the spiritual tools God gave you, and (2) you have your brain and the ability to make good choices.

You can avoid all STIs by choosing to wait on a sexual relationship until marriage *and* by marrying a man who committed to wait for you long before he even met you.

More and more teens and young adults are choosing to live with sexual integrity. This means (1) making choices that keep you pure *now* and (2) waiting for sexual activity until marriage.

in sexual activity. Now boy C, though he never even met boy A, has the same STI, because girl B passed it from one to the other.

Boy C meets girl D. They start making out and end up having sex. She too gets chlamydia, though she has no idea she's carrying the infection. So now four people who don't even all know each other have the STI.

You get the picture. It's not pretty, but this is exactly what happens. We see it in our offices every single day. When it comes to STIs, having sexual activity with one person means you're having sex with everyone he's ever had sex with. Yech!

The revolving door of sex and STIs can be avoided with a simple choice: Shut that door. Have *no* sexual activity of *any* type with *anyone* until marriage. All the public health authorities agree this is the best plan. It's also the plan designed by your Creator. But it's up to you to shut the door to STIs and the heartache and physical consequences they bring.

Dressed to Win

Remember the story about Adam and Eve — how God dressed them after they sinned? Well, God dresses you, too, during your spiritual battles to help you do the right thing and not mess up. He's given you a special uniform that you can put on:

Therefore put on the full armor of God, so that when the day of evil comes, you may be able to stand your ground, and after you have done everything, to stand. Stand firm then, with the belt of truth buckled around your waist, with the breastplate of righteousness in place, and with your feet fitted with the readiness that comes from the gospel of peace. In addition to all this, take up the shield of faith, with which you can extinguish all the flaming arrows of the evil one. Take the helmet of salvation and the sword of the Spirit, which is the word of God.

Ephesians 6:13–17

Our advice? Don't take off God's special clothing — ever. Check out the following sites with your mom or a trusted adult to learn more about living a pure life *every* day. You can find links to each with the URLs in our resources list at the back of the book:

- True Pink
- TeenSTAR Program
- Abstinence Clearinghouse
- Best Friends Foundation
- Legacy Institute
- True Love Waits

Jesus said:

"Blessed are the pure in heart, for they will see God."

Matthew 5:8

Nurturing a pure heart and mind will help you keep your body pure. It will also grow your relationship with God, who is the key to all purity. If you make a mistake, by the way, he is the one who forgives you and can help you get back on track.

The good news is that the majority of girls and boys graduating from high school these days have *not* had sexual intercourse. And that majority is growing year by year, as young people learn the truth about and the wisdom of saving *all* sexual activity for marriage. When friends say, "Everyone's doing it," you can say, "No, they're not. *Most* boys and girls are not."

Of those who have sex as teens, three out of four regret that decision and wish they had waited. You can choose to keep yourself pure and preserve all sexual activity until marriage. Not only will you be following God's plan for sexuality, but you'll also avoid the many emotional, spiritual, relational, and physical consequences of these dangerous and costly infections.

Remember the huge responsibility you've been given as a young lady, and protect your gift, your body, and your soul by choosing to live with sexual integrity. You'll be glad you did.

QUESTION 31

Talk to my parents about sex? Are you crazy?

Most parents know that at some point they need to talk to their daughter about love, sex, and her relationships with boys. But most parents say this is not always an easy topic to bring up. For some parents, it's downright stressful!

If one of your parents has not approached you to talk about these things, it could be that he or she is just as nervous about discussing it as you are. Your parent may even be more nervous. So if you feel embarrassed, know you're not alone. It's normal to be a bit apprehensive, shy, and nervous.

We want to make these conversations easier and more meaningful for all of you. We have some ideas to help you start talking about this with one or both of your parents. And if your parent(s) cannot or will not do this, then we'd like to recommend ways for you to pick a trusted Christian woman to talk to.

Now, we're not talking about a onetime "birds-and-bees" talk. We recommend ongoing discussions about sex and sexuality starting now that will continue for years (yeah, it's that important). These conversations should include topics like these:

- What it means to live according to God's Word
- God's gift and plan for sex and sexuality
- How and when to date a young man
- How to apply this information and these principles to your life
- How to choose good friends to help you keep your commitments

As we talked about earlier, the Bible teaches that God designed sex and gave it to married couples as a gift to enjoy. It's a good and wonderful gift. After all, it's from the Creator himself. It's *his* divine design.

As he does with every gift he gives us, he provides some clear rules or boundaries for using the gift of sex. This is an amazing and good thing. Some people think God's rules are meant to keep them from having fun, but that's not true. They're meant to keep you safe—and healthy. God sees sexuality as a beautiful gift, and he loves you enough to tell you how to use it.

Think of it this way. If you're a musician and someone you love gives you a beautiful, fragile, and expensive violin, you'd be a fool to use it as a hammer or baseball bat, right? It would completely ruin it.

Well, your sexuality is an incredibly beautiful, fragile, and precious gift from your Creator. Use it very carefully and wisely. Value and protect it as the treasure it is.

Now, a special note for you girls being raised by a single dad— especially those of you whose mother is no longer with you.

First, three cheers for your dad. Being a single parent is one of the most difficult jobs in the world. He needs your full support, obedience, love, trust, and prayers.

Second, your father can teach you what it means to be treated properly and respectfully by a boy. After all, he once was a boy, he went through puberty, and he can give you some wise advice and warnings about how to dress, how to act around boys, and how to stay safe.

Fun Learning About Sex — Really!

Many ministries offer day or weekend retreats that help moms and daughters start talking in fun and creative ways. Here are the ones we like the best. You can find some links using the URLs in our resources list at the back of the book.

Secret Keeper Girl (for tweens) and Pure Freedom Live (for teens) have live events around the country. You can even go with your mom and your best friends and their moms.

Ideas for mother-daughter weekends away can be found in Family Life's Passport2Purity. These could be some of the most memorable weekends of your life. One of our reviewers noted:

> Although Passport2Purity was originally designed to be done by a mother and daughter, my husband and I took our daughter, age thirteen, away for a special weekend to do this program together. Despite our initial concern that it might be awkward for her to discuss some of these issues with her dad present, it turned out to be such a wonderful addition to have my husband there to communicate the male perspective on the importance of his daughter's purity.

Still, girls are typically most comfortable talking to a woman about sex and sexuality. So if your mom's not around, talk to your dad about choosing a special trusted Christian woman with whom to talk about all this. It may be an aunt, a female youth pastor, an Awana leader, a coach, or some other godly woman you admire and respect.

Another important thing about sex: don't believe everything you see on TV and in the movies. And watch out for books that target tweens and teens but teach you lies about love and sexuality.

Biblical Blueprint for Sexual Integrity is a DVD series designed by the Legacy Institute for parents and their child. The series provides the biblical framework for healthy relationships and an understanding of the divine design of men and women. It will help your parents understand how to explain what it means to be a godly woman.

The Legacy Institute also has a resource called Relationships With Integrity, which has materials for every grade and is ideal for youth groups or small group settings. You might really enjoy going through this series with some of your close Christian friends.

Other great resources to help you understand God's design for your body and sexuality include *Theology of the Body for Teens* and *Theology of the Body for Teens: Middle School Edition.*

Last but not least, we like a Bible study for thirteen- to nineteen-year-old girls called *True Beauty.* This study is designed to teach you what it means to be truly female and truly beautiful. Each chapter teaches you about God's plans in a refreshing and fun way, allowing you and your friends to learn together. Some of the topics you'll talk about include identity, beauty as a gift from God, clothing that reflects true beauty, living whole and balanced lives, nobility, kindness, and much more.

The Talk

For decades, when a parent sat down with a daughter to discuss sex for the first time, it was simply known as "the talk." The problem is that not a lot of parents and daughters are *talking* about sex these days.

Studies show that teens most want to hear about sex and sexuality — believe it or not — from their parents. But that's not what usually happens. Most girls learn about sex through their friends and the media (TV, movies, magazines, social media, videos or DVDs, songs and music channels, the Internet, and porn sites or magazines). Not a great classroom!

The trouble is that what you learn about sex through those sources is usually *not* the best information. Much of it is misleading, a fair amount is just plain wrong, and some of it is meant to harm you or to lead you to make decisions you will regret.

To truly understand and appreciate sex, you have to consider what God says about it in his Word. Since he invented sex and gave it to you as a gift for the future, don't you think he might have a thing or two to say about how to best receive and enjoy this gift?

Research shows that girls who know and live out what the Bible teaches about sex have a more satisfying, fun, and healthy sexual relationship with their future husbands. So we recommend that any talk or talks you have on this topic take place with your mom or dad, or a mature Christian woman, and always include God's Word.

When it comes to your sexuality, make sure to get your information from the best sources you can find—which will usually be your parents (or another trusted Christian female), books like this one and others we recommend, and God's Word.

> Keep your father's command and do not forsake your mother's teaching. Bind them always on your heart; fasten them around your neck. When you walk, they will guide you; when you sleep, they will watch over you; when you awake, they will speak to you. For this command is a lamp, this teaching is a light, and correction and instruction are the way to life.
>
> *Proverbs 6:20–23*

QUESTION 32

Is there a monster in my computer?

Like many girls your age, you probably leaf through teen magazines sometimes. You may look at pictures of pop stars and keep track of their concerts and shows. You may even follow some of them on Twitter or other websites.

Unfortunately, many of these magazines or websites go over the top, and some of them are downright crude. They show pictures of young artists and teen celebrities half naked, wearing just underwear or very provocative clothes. Though this is inappropriate, it's become a normal part of our culture.

Such sexual images are now a part of every girl's life. You literally cannot avoid them. They are in almost every magazine, TV show, and movie, and they're plastered on billboards along many roads. They are everywhere.

Ninety percent of girls your age, those eight to sixteen years old, say they've seen sexual pictures or videos online. In other words, if you're a tween or young teen who spends time on the Internet or texting friends, you're at a high risk of being exposed to sexual images.

When images are sexually explicit (showing private parts or sexual activity), we call them *pornography*, or *porn*. Although looking at these images might seem like harmless fun, it can actually be very dangerous. This is especially true of the super-graphic images on some Internet sites and pop-ups.

The people who make money by hooking others on these images use the Internet as a weapon. You may end up on a site with inappropriate content you weren't even looking for. As you try to get out of it, you realize you're stuck on that awful page. The site has traps built in to keep you there called *mousetrapping*. When you try to click off to leave, a new pop-up appears with even worse images, and the cycle goes on.

If this ever happens to you, stop looking at the images and either power off your computer or use keyboard shortcuts rather than your mouse to click off. Then go find a parent and tell them what happened. Together, you can keep this from happening again.

Mark Kastleman wrote a book about pornography titled *The Drug of the New Millenium*. He says that the chemicals the brain releases when people view sexual images are so intense that experts say they're the most powerful drugs ever known.

You may wonder why this is so dangerous. Here's why. Looking at sexual images, especially if it continues, begins to *change* your brain chemistry, creating a powerful addiction that is tough to break. That's why Kastleman calls porn a powerful drug.

Besides harming your mind, watching sexual images misses the mark of God's best intentions for you. God knows how dangerous this is for your mind *and* heart.

There *Is* a Monster in Your Computer

Looking at sexual images may seem different than staring into the eyes of a dangerous, grotesque, massive monster. But at its core, pornography is a monster that can be hard to control.

If you think porn isn't a worldwide problem, think again. Pornography is a monster with only one goal in mind — to control you and change your view of God's amazing gift of sex. And this monster is aimed right at you.

A U.S. government commission found that the porn industry actually targets twelve- to seventeen-year-olds. Makers of porn know that if they can hook you when you're young, they may have a customer for life.

One expert said showing pornography to teens is like giving crack cocaine (a super-addictive drug) to a drug addict. Their addiction can be extremely hard to break. Sadly, nearly one-third of teens watch pornography often, and nearly every teen has seen at least one pornographic image.

If you have never looked at sexual images on your computer, don't think you're weird or that you're missing something. In fact, we applaud you. You're keeping your mind clean and clear of destructive and disturbing images.

When it comes to pornography, think about it as a monster. Stay away from it. Run from it. Don't think you can chain it up in the basement of your mind. It can still break free and hurt you. Instead of digging around in places on the Internet where you shouldn't go, strive to walk a clean path and honor God with what you put into your mind.

And if you do have a problem with pornography, don't wait to tell a parent or trusted adult. By being open and honest about your secret now, you can start the healing process and kick this monster out.

The number of girls affected by pornography is soaring. One in three kids under ten has been exposed to porn online, and three out of four teens will see a porn image before age eighteen. For most girls, porn is not something they go looking for online, but it's easy to come across these images if you're not careful.

Girls who get hooked on porn say they feel worthless and degraded by their habit. They also say it affects their relationships with others. So remember, the decisions you make now will make a difference for years to come. If your friends are into this and try to get you to join in, choose to guard your heart and mind, and say no.

Don't believe the lie that this is just a problem for guys. That is simply not true. And remember, it helps to look at things through God's eyes—especially when choosing what to look at or listen to.

Sexual immorality (sexual sin) covers many activities that the Bible says are wrong—and you should work hard to avoid them all. Some girls may think, *It's just a picture, or it's just a chat room on the Internet. I didn't actually do anything physically. Therefore, it's not wrong or sinful.*

Except for one thing. Jesus said:

> "You have heard that it was said, 'You shall not commit adultery.' But I tell you that anyone who looks at a woman lustfully has already committed adultery with her in his heart."
>
> *Matthew 5:27–28*

Some girls say, "Guys are gorgeous; they're hot—private parts and all. I'm just admiring God's creation. It's like looking at Michelangelo's naked statue of David. It's art, right?" Sounds innocent enough. Except for the fact that God created that man for his wife to admire and stare at and enjoy—not you.

Also, viewing sexual images can become addicting. Sounds crazy, right? Like all addictions, it starts small but can grow into an ugly monster. And once a girl starts viewing sexual images, she is much more likely to begin acting out sexually. In other words, what goes into your eyes and your mind will affect what you do—your actions.

One of our young female reviewers struggled with this problem for years. She wrote:

> I think the most important thing a girl can do if she is already ... drawn to porn is to reach out. It is so hard, because you feel alone and ashamed and weird, but the more it stays in your mind, the more dangerous it is. So if you can talk to your parents, great. If that is too hard, finding someone older or someone you know will be patient with you is crucial. Also, I think emphasizing to do something now rather than later is important. The longer you wait to stop, the more difficult it is.

We think it is critical that you tell a parent or trusted adult if you're struggling to stop looking at sexual images, since it can affect every area of your life, including your friendships and your schoolwork. Your parents can help find a professional counselor for you to talk to who can help you learn what to do.

Many women who are addicted to sexual images began viewing porn *before* high school. So remember, the decisions you make now will impact the rest of your life.

Now you know why parents set up rules about the kind of TV shows and movies you can watch and which Internet sites you may visit. Certain shows and movies are rated as inappropriate for your age for good reasons—watching them can steal your innocence and harm your mind and heart.

Protect yourself by being choosy about what you allow yourself to watch—whether on TV, DVDs, video games, magazines, or the Internet. Even some commercials are just too much sexually. And guard what you allow yourself to listen to, especially music that plays alongside sexual images like you may have seen on MTV or YouTube.

Bad Apples

We hope your parent has taught you that your private parts are private. No one has a right to touch or see your private parts without your and your parent's permission. No one.

However, people with bad intentions may want to try. Sometimes these people are coaches, teachers, church leaders, Scout leaders, or other youth leaders. We don't want to scare you — most church and youth leaders and teachers are moral and devoted to God, to you, and to their work. But there are a few bad apples in each of these categories. Those bad apples first earn your trust and your parent's trust. And then, when no one's around, they may try to take advantage of you or a friend.

One report found that one in fourteen girls in fifth to eighth grades had been sexually abused by a teacher or coach. For high school girls, the number was one in nine. And these bad people know that most of the girls they abuse will not tell anyone. They use threats and scare the girls to keep them silent. Again, we don't want you to be afraid of all adults in your life — we just want you to know about a real and serious problem that you or your friends may encounter.

No one has found a surefire way to keep these bad apples away from young girls. So you and your friends need to be watchful. You need to know how to protect yourselves and stay safe.

If someone tries to see, photograph, or touch your private parts — or wants you to touch their private parts — forcefully say no and leave. Scream it as loud as you can if you have to! Get away from them. Run to a safe place, and immediately tell your mom or dad or someone in authority, like your principal or a cop or security guard.

Not only will you save yourself from a potential bad guy, but you'll likely save many other girls too.

If TV or Internet programs are causing you problems, turn them off. Choose what you allow to influence your mind, your heart, and your daily thoughts. Ask yourself these questions:

- Would I watch this particular TV show, movie, or website if Christ was in the room?
- Is what I'm doing drawing me closer to God and strengthening my relationship with him or harming it?

Your answers to these questions will help you make wise decisions about what you listen to and watch.

There's one more danger to keep in mind. Looking at porn and visiting chat rooms on the Internet can expose you to *real* bad guys—sexual predators—people who are there to try to take advantage of you or hurt you. So do not ever communicate in chat rooms through IMs, email, or in any way. This is just one more reason to stay away from all that!

As we mentioned in question 28, we suggest that families keep *all* electronic devices, especially those with Internet access, in the living room, family room, or another common room in the house. That way the screen can be seen by anyone in the area. This helps keep the whole family safer and more accountable.

Ask your parents about Internet filters and accountability software to keep your computers safe—we suggest some of our favorites in our resources list at the back of the book.

Also, if porn or a chat room tempts you, consider getting rid of Internet access for a while, and tell your parents and your older siblings so they can help you too.

Throw away any sexually explicit music, magazines, books, or videos you might have and stay away from friends who are into that. Look for a mature Christian woman and some good friends who can hold you accountable and whom you can call if you're tempted.

Remember, don't chat online or exchange messages with *any-one* you haven't met in person, regardless of who they *claim* to be. And if a boy or girl you know tries to message you with sexual images or topics, click "ignore" or "hide" and tell a parent. The best approach is to "unfriend" or block anyone who sends sexual images, since it will probably happen again if you don't.

Your thoughts and actions are important to the Lord — and critical to your future. They will shape the woman you will become. That's why the Bible teaches:

> Whatever is right, whatever is pure, whatever is lovely, whatever is admirable — if anything is excellent or praise-worthy — think about such things.
>
> *Philippians 4:8*

Choose to fill your mind with thoughts of the Lord and what he is doing in your life. As a follower of Jesus, you are not simply to avoid these images; you are to run from them.

> Don't let anyone look down on you because you are young, but set an example for the believers in speech, in conduct, in love, in faith and in purity.
>
> *1 Timothy 4:12*

Take captive every thought to make it obedient to Christ.

> *2 Corinthians 10:5*

QUESTION 33

If sex is so great, why should I wait?

The time will come to fall in love and explore the wonderful world of romance—when you're older. Until then, of course you'll be curious, and you may find yourself scoping out boys at times and giggling about it with your girlfriends.

If you start to get very interested in boys and get tempted to act on it physically before God's timing for you is right, it will help to have a plan. It helps so much to make up your mind *now* about how you want to live your life.

So decide now to enjoy being a girl—having good friends and being a good friend. Decide now to spend your time and focus your energy on planning for a good future. Decide now not to have to worry about sexually transmitted infections, teen pregnancy, and the many complications that come from getting involved in sexual relationships outside of God's will.

And remember this important truth. You don't need to have a boyfriend to be someone's special girl. You're *already* someone's special girl. You are God's special girl. You are your parents' special girl. And you are your future husband's special girl.

God has such great plans for your life. He wants you to have a good life, and one of the ways he wants to protect you is by helping you live a pure life in every area—including your sexuality.

Sex *binds* a couple together in physical, emotional, *and* spiritual ways. Having sexual activity with someone other than your husband can cause feelings of guilt and shame. Why? Because God designed sex as a wonderful gift that is meant to be enjoyed within marriage. And deep down, most boys and girls know this is true.

Besides the physical act, sex is an *intimate, spiritual* act where two people "become one," and it's not to be taken lightly. When you have sex, you give a huge part of yourself—your body, heart, and soul—to another person. Doing this outside of marriage can have lasting, painful consequences affecting (1) your physical body, (2) your mind and emotions, and (3) your relationship with the person with whom you had sex, your parents, your friends, your future husband, and God.

Think of it like this. When you have *any* form of sexual activity, it's like giving a piece of your heart away to the other person. Do this too much and pretty soon you'll have little of yourself left and less to offer your future husband.

Do you want a husband who will commit his entire life and his entire heart to you? Of course. That's the only kind of man to whom you should consider giving your whole self. You want a man who will wait for you, just as you commit to wait for him to share the precious, God-given gift of yourself.

Without a doubt, waiting to have sex until marriage can be difficult! Every girl will have her sexual nature awakened, often around puberty. One day you're happy enough walking around the mall chatting with your girlfriends. The next day, you suddenly notice every cute boy who walks by. You wonder if he noticed you. You think about going over to meet and talk to him. You tell your girlfriends, and you all check him out and giggle.

This is all normal and can be fun for sure. Yes, do have fun getting to know your girlfriends and boys too—we're all so different. Having good boy and girl friends will help you understand people and your world better. It will also enrich your life.

Risky Business

Here are some of the risks of getting involved in a sexual relationship outside of God's plan:

SEXUALLY TRANSMITTED INFECTIONS (STIs)

- Of the 18.9 million new cases of STIs each year, nearly half are among fifteen- to twenty-four-year-olds.
- Human papillomavirus (HPV) is very common among fifteen- to twenty-four-year-olds who have sex. This virus can cause cancer of the cervix and mouth and painful warts in the private parts.
- Teens, especially girls, are much more susceptible to STIs than adults. That means it's easier for teens and girls to get infected with an STI when exposed to it.
- Some STIs can cause infertility, making it difficult to get pregnant later on when a woman wants to start a family.

TEEN PREGNANCY

- Each year, almost 750,000 young women ages fifteen to nineteen become pregnant.

So enjoy being young following God's plan for your life, and save yourself from the hassles and pain that can come from the wrong relationship at the wrong time. Sex is for later. It's for marriage. It's a gift for you and your future husband. It's also God's plan for bringing new lives into the world.

Choosing to wait until marriage to have any sexual activity helps build a much closer relationship with your future husband — a marriage that's built on trust and love. And that's one important reason why it pays to wait.

- Ten of every 100 babies born in the U.S. have teen parents.
- Teen mothers and fathers are more likely to experience depression, anxiety, single parenthood (splitting up), less education, poverty, and homelessness.
- Children born to teen mothers are more likely to experience health problems, abuse, neglect, poverty, and incarceration (being sent to jail).

TEEN ABORTION

- There are usually more than 200,000 abortions every year among fifteen- to nineteen-year-olds.
- More than one in four pregnancies among fifteen- to nineteen-year-olds ends in abortion each year.
- Most girls and women who have an abortion later experience guilt, shame, and regret similar to *post-traumatic stress disorder* (PTSD), the stress reaction that follows traumatic events. They can also develop severe infections and many other physical, spiritual, and emotional consequences, like depression, poor self-esteem, and guilt.

Accountability Partners

Good friends with similar values and beliefs can help you stay on target, follow God's ways, and make good choices throughout your life. For example, if your close friends are all committed to waiting for a sexual relationship until marriage, it will be easier for all of you to follow through if you have each other. If one of you is tempted, the others can step in to remind her why it's important to stick with God's plan.

Your parents, trusted teachers, and good friends — as well as knowing God's Word — will help you with every choice, like staying away from alcohol and drugs and keeping your mind, heart, and body safe and pure.

A young woman on our review panel wrote:

I can't overemphasize the importance of pursuing relationships with Christian friends. Mine were great. My best friend and I paired up as accountability partners in high school. We then knew we were there as a support for each other but also knew that we could call each other out in love if we were struggling with something. It was so great because someone who was dealing with similar things as me was there to help me through rough times.

Another wrote:

A group of my Christian friends and I made a covenant to be accountability partners when we were in middle school. We agreed to talk to and check on each other often. We agreed to pray for each other. We agreed to ask each other the hard questions about relationships, sex, and sexuality. But most of all, we agreed to be there for each other at all times — 24/7/365. Remaining sexually pure in our culture is never easy. But walking this path with good friends made it so much easier.

It's been just over twenty years since we all became best friends and accountability partners. The last one of us is getting married this summer. We were all able to walk the aisle, sexually pure, because of the help of our Lord and our friends.

> For the LORD will be at your side and will keep your foot from being snared.
>
> Proverbs 3:26

Our Purity Ring

One of our book reviewers shared this story with us:

Once I made a commitment to God and to my future husband to be sexually pure until marriage, I began to wear a purity ring on the ring finger of my left hand. When I got engaged, I began to think about the ring I wanted to buy for my husband — his wedding ring.

After thinking and praying about it, I came up with an idea. I talked to a jeweler who helped me design this really cool ring. What the jeweler did was take my purity ring and build my future husband's ring around it.

From the outside it looks like a normal man's wedding band. But when he takes it off, he sees my purity ring on the inside. So it's my ring, stretched out, that is against his finger.

So my wedding ring was a double gift to him — not only my commitment to him on that day, but also a commitment I had made to him long before.

There is a time for everything, and a season for every activity under the heavens.

Ecclesiastes 3:1

QUESTION 34

I want to make wise choices, but how do I stay strong when tempted?

As you grow older, you will face more and more peer pressure. At times, you may consider doing something that could harm you, like smoking, drinking, experimenting with drugs, looking at sexual images, or having sex before marriage. So how do you stand firm when tempted? And how do your choices affect your faith and your relationship with Jesus?

Curiosity is natural and normal. It's normal to wonder about trying a cigarette when you see other kids smoking. It's normal to think about sex when you're bombarded by images every day on TV, in magazines, on the Internet, and even in school. Temptations exist all around you, and they will be there every day of your life.

Being tempted simply means we're human. But the more you learn, the better prepared you will be to make wise choices. Being

239

aware of what's out there can give you discernment, or the ability to use good judgment. Discernment gives you a gut-feeling kind of reaction that helps you determine if something you want to do is right or wrong, or if a situation should be completely avoided. The conscience God gave you also helps you, as does knowing God's Word.

Think about what is important to you right now. How do you want to live? How do you want others to think of you? Do you want to be thought of as a hardworking athlete? A good student? A caring and considerate person? Do you want to stay away from drugs and alcohol? Do you want to be sexually pure until marriage? Deciding ahead of time how you want to live will help you stand strong, even when your friends disagree with you.

As a Christian, your body is a temple, a way to worship God, and God wants you to remain pure. Does this mean that if you mess up God won't forgive you? Absolutely not. But several Truths may help you when temptation strikes.

Truth 1

God may test you. He may allow trials to purify and strengthen you, but he will never lead you into sin. In our culture, people commonly blame their mistakes on peer pressure, leaders, parents, upbringing, genetics, the mailman, their dog, their little toe—whatever. As long as you look for someone or something else to blame, you will have a tough time fighting temptations.

> When tempted, no one should say, "God is tempting me."
> For God cannot be tempted by evil, nor does he tempt anyone.
>
> *James 1:13*

Jesus was tempted in every way, just as we are, and he suffered when tempted. So he knows what it's like, and it's good to have him as our defender.

> For this reason [Jesus] had to be made like [us], fully
> human in every way, in order that he might become a mer-
> ciful and faithful high priest in service to God, and that he
> might make atonement for the sins of the people. Because
> he himself suffered when he was tempted, he is able to help
> those who are being tempted.
>
> *Hebrews 2:17–18*

Truth 2

Everyone faces temptation. None of us is tempted in some new or
unique way. While we are each completely unique, the temptations we face are basically the same ones that have confronted all
people throughout history.

> No temptation has overtaken you except what is common
> to mankind.
>
> *1 Corinthians 10:13a*

Truth 3

The Bible tells us that when we are tempted, God won't let us
be tempted more than we can stand. He will always provide an
escape route.

> And God is faithful; he will not let you be tempted beyond
> what you can bear. But when you are tempted, he will also
> provide a way out so that you can endure it.
>
> *1 Corinthians 10:13b*

The tricky part is choosing to follow that escape route, which
could mean turning off the computer or avoiding certain books,
movies, or friends. Sometimes escaping can mean literally running away.

Yes, this can be easier said than done. But there are steps you
can take to escape temptation—besides running away.

1. Pray. When tempted, quickly pray to God about what you're experiencing. These on-the-spot, lightning-quick prayers allow you to ask your Father in heaven for grace, wisdom, and strength to avoid the temptation—and to take the way of escape he has provided.

> "Watch and pray so that you will not fall into temptation. The spirit is willing, but the flesh is weak."
>
> *Matthew 26:41*

2. Read Scripture. No matter what happens in your life, the Bible gives you a guide to live by. God's Word gives us rules and advice to help in every situation. Even though the events described in the Bible happened thousands of years ago, its words of wisdom still apply today.

> Your word is a lamp for my feet, a light on my path.
>
> *Psalm 119:105*

> You guide me with your counsel.
>
> *Psalm 73:24*

Plus, memorizing and reciting Scripture can help during times of temptation. Think about your favorite Scripture when your thoughts turn negative.

> How can a young person stay on the path of purity? By living according to your word.... I have hidden your word in my heart that I might not sin against you. Praise be to you, Lord; teach me your decrees.... I meditate on your precepts and consider your ways. I delight in your decrees; I will not neglect your word.
>
> *Psalm 119:9, 11–12, 15–16*

The Word of God is powerful. Jesus used Scripture to defeat Satan when he tempted Jesus in the desert.

3. Avoid temptation in the first place. Don't put yourself in situations where you know you will be tempted. That greatly increases your chances of messing up. Since you're too young to date, even if you're just hanging out with guys, be careful who you spend time with and where you go. And make sure your parents know who you are with and where you are. Always go out with a group. Also, avoid friends who encourage you to watch movies or go places you know your parents wouldn't allow—or tell those friends in advance you won't participate.

On several occasions, Christ told his disciples to pray that they might not fall into temptation. He knew that prayer makes a huge difference.

> "This, then, is how you should pray: 'Our Father ... lead us not into temptation, but deliver us from the evil one.'"
>
> *Matthew 6:9, 13*

4. Encourage one another. Since we are all tempted in similar ways, we can help, support, and learn from each other. As Christians, God wants us to help each other and build each other up in our faith (Ephesians 4:15–16). Having a group of girls who can talk and pray together can really help you avoid specific sins that so many young women fall into.

Here's what one of our teen reviewers said about friends:

> During your teen years, your friends are a huge part of your life, so choose them wisely. You go to school with them for seven hours a day and they make a huge impact on your life whether you realize it. Choose friends who will uplift you in the good and bad times and challenge you in your walk with the Lord.

5. Confess. When you fall, pray and ask for God's forgiveness and for strength to avoid the temptation the next time. Tell a parent or trusted friend about your mistake. Ask her to pray for you. Confession clears your heart and mind.

> Make this your common practice: Confess your sins to each other and pray for each other so that you can live together whole and healed. The prayer of a person living right with God is something powerful to be reckoned with.
>
> *James 5:16 MSG*

Finding good friends and mentors will help you stand strong when facing the temptations common to the teen years. Think about what makes friends good. Do they encourage you or put you down? What do you talk about together, and what do you watch and read? Where do you hang out? Is your friend a Christian?

Think about friendships like strong trees. So what does a tree have to do with encouraging others and finding people who will help you avoid temptation? A lot actually. Coastal redwoods grow to huge heights—the tallest one grew higher than a football field is long—but these trees have shallow root systems. Their roots only go four to six feet deep and spread out more than one hundred feet. These redwoods are able to survive terrible winds and rains by growing close to each other and interlocking their roots to strengthen one another.

By supporting each other, redwoods live thousands of years and become mighty trees.

Good friends help each other grow stronger in their faith. They also make life a lot more fun. So put down roots with some Christian girlfriends who share your goals and values and grow some lives that stand out for Christ.

> "A new command I give you: Love one another. As I have loved you, so you must love one another."
>
> *John 13:34*

> It's better to have a partner than go it alone. Share the work, share the wealth. And if one falls down, the other helps, but if there's no one to help, tough!
>
> *Ecclesiastes 4:9–10 MSG*

Congratulations. You got through thirty-four key questions about your body and puberty. Can you believe how much you've learned? Imagine trying to navigate the difficult path of adolescence without all this information. We've been so happy and blessed to walk this path with you.

You probably have other questions we haven't answered. But by now we hope your relationship with your parents or another trusted adult has given you a safe person to whom you can bring any question or concern.

Now we want to cover one last question every young girl has: When will I be a woman?

Becoming a woman is not about a specific date. It doesn't magically happen when you get your first period or when your breasts begin to grow. It certainly doesn't happen when you get that first pimple. It is a process. You are, right now, becoming a woman. The goal is to grow each day into the young woman whom God created you to be.

Our culture defines your purpose in strange ways. We hope by now you understand and believe that you are much, much more than how you look. We've talked about our culture's obsession with a not-so-beautiful outer "beauty" that's shallow on the inside and leaves girls feeling empty, thinking they don't measure up. Our prayer is that you will not fall for those lies.

Instead, we pray that you will see yourself through the eyes of your Creator, the one who knows and loves you like no one else. This is, in fact, every girl's dream — to know that she is loved just the way she is. And you are! You are precious and loved just as you are.

Once you choose to become a follower of Jesus, once God is the God of your heart, you become a temple of God's Holy Spirit. You are what the Bible calls a jar of clay. Yes, that's right. This is a metaphor for a remarkable truth about the source of your inner beauty and spiritual strength — God's life within you!

> But we have this treasure in jars of clay to show that this all-surpassing power is from God and not from us.
>
> *2 Corinthians 4:7*

Like clay, you are fragile on the outside but house a treasure on the inside. Nowhere in the Bible are you called to focus excessively on the jar. Instead, you are told to guard your *heart* — above all else.

> Above all else, guard your heart, for everything you do flows from it.
>
> *Proverbs 4:23*

Jesus' emphasis always moves you from focusing on the outside to the inner life. He wants you to focus on your heart.

> "The LORD does not look at the things people look at.
> People look at the outward appearance, but the LORD looks
> at the heart."
>
> *1 Samuel 16:7*

I (Dr. Mari) recently bought a devotional book for tweens to read with my daughter. I looked forward to reading a chapter a night with her and learning together. When I gave it to her, she leafed through it briefly and went right back to playing. I could almost hear her thoughts: *I'm playing now, Mami. Maybe later.*

That night, when I entered Hannah's wonderland to tuck her in, I found her reading. She said she couldn't put down her new book. "You didn't wait for me," I said, and she smiled.

Hannah didn't wait for me the next day either, or the next day. She read the whole book that week. Like you, she was thirsty for the truth. She wanted to learn more about life and what's important for girls to know about themselves and about God.

For weeks, we talked about the stories in the book. We soaked our feet, had tea parties, and laughed a lot. Months later, she still brings up the stories she read, which gives us another chance to chat about life. I cherish those moments with her — your loved ones do too.

Just this week we had another special moment, this time at the mall. After getting some cool nail polish, I noticed Hannah looking away when we walked by store mannequins in their underwear. She did what she'd learned in one of the stories she read. She was guarding her eyes and her heart.

I'm not sure exactly what she was thinking, but as we walked on, she suddenly said, "Mami, I am a faith girl that's dressed in God." Even at a very young age, girls can learn to think with God's mind, focusing not on their bodies but on their hearts.

Her beautiful (and true) statement reminded me of what she'd said months earlier while surrounded by Disney princesses: "Faith dresses me and makes me beautiful in God's eyes." She is so right.

As a young woman, you are beautiful in God's eyes. He loves his special and unique creation—you. And when you let his goodness and love shine through you, you look even more beautiful.

We hope and pray you'll think about true beauty for the rest of your life. A beautiful, godly woman brings glory to God and displays his character to everyone she meets. And this is precisely what you are called to be and what we pray you are becoming—one day at a time.

When you choose to live according to God's ways, he helps you live a life that's pure, holy, and true. When you offer yourself back to your Creator, you begin the greatest adventure of all. A life of knowing, following, and loving God is better than any fairy tale—it is the adventure of a lifetime.

We invite you to stop reading for a moment to think and pray about these questions:

- Who am I?
- Whose am I?
- Why does it matter?

Consider jotting some thoughts in your journal. Your answers are important because the way you see yourself comes through in the things you say and do—in the way you live.

For the rest of your days, choose to nurture your inner life with God's love and truth, focusing on your heart, and the rest will take care of itself. Focus on being a courageous, committed, and faithful woman of God—like Esther. Choose to be obedient and surrender to God's plans—like Mary. Choose to serve others—like Mother Teresa. All three of them became women of God when they were very young. So can you.

Find God's path for you in your gifts and godly passions—those things you love to do. And focus on growing the garden of your spirit, bearing its fruit of love, joy, peace, patience, kindness, goodness, faithfulness, gentleness, and self-control.

Such a harvest spreads Jesus in the world and makes your heart glad. Self-respect is beautiful. Kindness and goodness are beautiful. Thoughtfulness and gentleness are beautiful. Your inner beauty will shine through in the way you treat yourself and others.

You may be thinking, *This sounds great, but it's hard to do all the time.* We agree. Living like Esther, Mary, or Mother Teresa is not easy, but it *is* possible with God's help and the help of those who love you.

Continue to use your journal to work through your emotions, thoughts, and feelings, and share with your mom and trusted adults as you continue to grow up. Stay close to godly role models and friends. No one has all the right answers, and neither will you, but God does. His wisdom will keep you safe.

Respect and treat yourself with the same kindness and gentleness that you'd want to offer to the friends you love. Identify and use your God-given gifts—this will bring you joy and enrich your life and those around you. And make going to church a priority. Although it may not always be fun, staying in church means you continue to hear God's Word and learn to apply it to your daily life. This will help deepen your faith and keep you close to God.

Ask for help when you need it. God blessed you with parents, teachers, role models, friends, and family. Many people love you and want God's best for your life. Talk to your parents and siblings when you need help or have questions—that's what they're there for.

Embrace the gifts of your femininity and sexuality, and keep yourself pure as you await the blessing of marriage. Be smart. Don't go with the crowd. Don't blend in with those who don't follow Jesus. Be different. If you want to find a crowd to follow and imitate, choose a group that honors God and demonstrates godliness.

Although this way of life may *feel* lonely at times, you are *not* alone as you choose the path of righteousness—of thinking and doing right things.

Throughout the world, young men and women are speaking out for godliness, truth, and a pure life. Join them. Become a voice for purity and godliness. Become a voice of hope to your generation. Like Mary and Esther, you can choose to be courageous and live dressed in the beauty of God's love.

> Therefore, if anyone is in Christ, the new creation has come: The old has gone, the new is here!
>
> *2 Corinthians 5:17*

> So then, just as you received Christ Jesus as Lord, continue to live your lives in him, rooted and built up in him, strengthened in the faith as you were taught, and overflowing with thankfulness.
>
> *Colossians 2:6–7*

FINAL WORD FOR DAUGHTERS AND PARENTS

When my (Dr. Walt's) daughter, Kate, turned six years old, my father called her to wish her a happy birthday. I beamed like any proud dad, and then Kate turned to me. "Pops would like to speak with you," she said as she handed me the phone.

"Congratulations." my father declared.

"For what, Dad? What did I do?"

"It's Kate's one-third birthday."

That made no sense, so I pointed out, "She's six years old, Dad."

"Yes, but one-third of your life with her is over."

One-third? You mean I was one-third of the way through raising this little pipsqueak of a girl who favored coloring books and story time? It didn't seem possible. She was so tiny. But I instantly understood what my father was saying: at eighteen, she would leave home—my child-rearing days would be over, and Kate's childhood days would be past.

You may be wondering what this has to do with you. Well, if you're twelve, two-thirds of your time with your parents as a child is gone.

And for you, parents, your child-rearing days are two-thirds complete.

You're both more than halfway through. You're rounding the clubhouse turn, and the finish line is in sight. Just like any race, though, the homestretch can be the toughest ground to cover.

For you tweens and teens, if you haven't figured it out by now, what matters most is not the *things* you get from your parents.

You need *your parents*—their love, their cheerleading, their advice and guidance, their steering and teaching, and, most of all, their time and prayers.

Every tween and teen needs her parents to spend quality time with her. It's critical to learn that quality time can only occur within quantity time—a concept I learned when I read a book written by my friend, family physician Richard Swenson. In *Margin: Restoring Emotional, Physical, Financial, and Time Reserves to Overloaded Lives*, Dr. Swenson explains how the health of families is being destroyed by parents (especially dads) who leave little room in their schedule for their kids.

I was blessed to read this book just as God used my dad to urge me to spend more time with Kate and her brother, Scott. Back then, my day started with early hospital rounds, followed by eight or more hours of patient care in the office and then evening hospital rounds. This schedule left little margin for me to spend time with my wife or children.

My father's encouragement and Dr. Swenson's book inspired me to do something about that. I met with my medical partner, and we agreed to a new work schedule: On Tuesdays and Thursdays, I'd stop seeing patients at 2:00 p.m. so I could meet one of our children at the bus stop by 3:00 p.m.

Tuesday afternoons and evenings were for Kate, and Thursdays were for Scott. My time with Kate involved helping her with homework, and then we'd take walks, read together, or go get a milk shake. Sometimes we'd just sit for a while and have long talks about anything and everything.

I had a blast with this time set aside for my children. And so did they. I came to know and love my kids in a new way, which never could have happened any other way. I learned that quality time occurs only in the midst of quantity time. In other words, to have many special moments together, you need to spend time together regularly.

When Kate was nineteen, I was invited to introduce Dr.

Swenson at a medical conference. Kate was with me, and when she heard that Dr. Swenson was there, she asked to introduce him. Here's what she said that afternoon:

> Ladies and gentlemen, when I was a little girl, my daddy read a book that Dr. Swenson had written. The book was called *Margin*. In that book, my daddy learned that if he wanted me to be as healthy as I could be physically, emotionally, relationally, and spiritually, he would have to spend some time with me—a lot of time.... So my daddy took time away from work and spent every Tuesday afternoon and evening with me.... I'm embarrassed to tell you that I don't remember a lot of the gifts my parents have given me during my childhood, but I will never forget the memories I have from those days with my daddy.

Then Kate turned to Dr. Swenson and said, "Dr. Swenson, I want to thank you for teaching my daddy. Because of what he did, I will never be the same."

So our final word to you is this: Create some margin—open up space for each other in your life—and spend precious time *together*.

Highly healthy girls will spend time with their moms and their dads. Parents who give their kids both love *and* time help them become healthy and whole. Moms and dads, if your parents didn't give you this gift, you have a chance to break the cycle with your children.

And, girls, if you feel like you don't get enough time with your parents, pray about it and pray for them. When the time is right, have a heart-to-heart chat and let them know how you feel. Let your mom or dad know how much you want to and need to spend more time with them.

Believe us, it will be worth it.

> Let us not love with words or speech but with actions and in truth.

1 John 3:18

Last, thanks for allowing us to be a small part of your journey from girlhood to womanhood. Our prayer for you is that you mature into a wonderful woman of God—that you choose to develop and practice the character traits of a woman of integrity—traits that must be learned and practiced. God's life in you—his wisdom and grace—will help you grow into the woman he created you to be.

As you grow into all God has planned for you, choose to follow his ways. Remember that God's rules and limits are designed to protect you—because he loves you. So choose to do what's right even when parents and teachers and police officers aren't around.

God's love calls you to honor and obey your parents and teachers. As a young woman of character, do all you can to get along with your parents. And thank them for working hard so you can have a home, clothes, food, and everything you need.

A great way to thank your parents is by understanding that food, clothes, furniture, water, and electricity cost money. So don't waste them. Take care of your clothes and your room. Be sweet to your siblings and help care for your pets and home. Be a good steward of all things entrusted to your care.

As a growing, young woman of God, be honest, loyal, and trustworthy. Be a good friend and serve others without expecting thanks or a reward.

Nurture a pure heart that will help you wait until marriage to have sexual activity. Commit to a pure life now and do everything you can to wait for and then remain married to one person for life.

Commit to read the Bible to hear God speak to your heart, and speak to him through prayer and quiet time every day. Attending church will also bring you closer to your family, your church family, and to God.

Finally, get to know yourself—your heart, feelings, and dreams—and be genuine, sharing your feelings and thoughts with trusted friends. Learn to respect others' feelings and beliefs. And be authentic. God didn't make you to be someone else. He made you to be you!

How does a young girl do and become all of this? Simply by walking with Jesus through *each* day, letting him be the God of your heart and choices, listening to him, and learning from him.

Still, every woman of God will make mistakes, and it's great to know that God's heart is full of grace for you. He loves you so much just the way you are. And he gives you his Spirit to guide and lead you. As Paul writes:

> Be on your guard; stand firm in the faith; be courageous; be strong. Do everything in love.
>
> *1 Corinthians 16:13–14*

A life spent following God is full of "love, joy, peace, patience, kindness, goodness, faithfulness, gentleness, self-control; against such things there is no law" (Galatians 5:22–23, NASB). As you devote yourself to being a woman after God's own heart, your Creator—the God of the universe—is on your side. You will be blessed, and you will be a blessing to many.

> Trust in the LORD with all your heart
> and lean not on your own understanding;
> In all your ways submit to him,
> and he will make your paths straight.
> Do not be wise in your own eyes;
> fear the LORD and shun evil.
> This will bring health to your body
> and nourishment to your bones.
>
> *Proverbs 3:5–8*

ACKNOWLEDGMENTS

W'ere thankful to a volunteer panel of expert advisers who spent considerable time reviewing this book and have, with their corrections, advice, and wisdom, made it much more accurate and reliable:

Psychologist

Arlyn Brunet, PhD (psychologist, San Juan, Puerto Rico).

Authors/educators/youth specialists/pastoral professionals

Carrie Abbott (family/youth educator, Kenmore, WA); Carrie Archual (youth specialist, Indianapolis, IN); Jennie Bishop (author, Daytona Beach, FL); Mary Margaret Collingsworth (youth specialist, Franklin, TN); Robert Fleischmann (pastor/theologian, Hartford, WI); Leah Kilcoin (pastoral professional, Matthews, NC); Jessica Lubbers (youth specialist, Mechanicsville, VA); Yvette Maher (pastoral professional, Colorado Springs, CO); Mark Merrill (attorney and family/youth specialist, Tampa, FL); Susan Merrill (family/youth specialist, Tampa, FL); Diane Passno (family specialist, Colorado Springs, CO); Kate Ritz (youth specialist, Colorado Springs, CO); Jessica Sanders (youth specialist, Denton, TX); Angie Schlossberg (educator, Wynantskill, NY); Lynnette Simm, EdD (educator, Prosper, TX); Becky Wood (pastoral professional, Baton Rouge, LA).

Medical professionals

Ruth Bolton, MD (family physician, Madison Lake, MN); Freda Bush, MD (obstetrician/gynecologist, Jackson, MS); Vicki Clark, CMA (Certified Medical Assistant, Colorado Springs, CO); Patti

Francis, MD (pediatrician, Moraga, CA); Lauren Franklin, MD (family physician, Niceville, FL); Darla R. Grossman, MD (family physician, Evansville, IN); Ed Guttery, MD (pediatrician, Fort Myers, FL); Susan A. Henriksen, MD (family physician, Glen Rock, PA); Leanna Hollis, MD (internal medicine, Blue Springs, MS); Paula Homberger, PAC (physician assistant, Colorado Springs, CO); Julian Hsu, MD (family physician, Centennial, CO); Pearl Huang-Ramírez, MD (family physician, Kissimmee, FL); Kim Jones, MD (pediatrician, Los Altos, CA); Gaylen M. Kelton, MD (family physician, Cicero, IN); Mark Lytle, MD (pediatrician, Birmingham, AL); Nicole McVay, RN (nurse, Tulsa, OK); Mary Anne Nelson, MD (family physician, Cedar Rapids, IA); Ann Park, MD (women's development coach, Tampa, FL); Kent Petrie, MD (family physician, Avon, CO); Amarillys Sojo, MD, (Swansea, IL); Patty Stitcher, RN (nurse, Littleton, CO); Alice Ko Tsai, MD (obstetrician/gynecologist, New York City, NY); Paul R. Williams, MD (pediatrician/neonatologist, Pisgah Forest, NC); Laurel Williston, MD (family physician, Tulsa, OK); Joanne Woida, PT (physical therapist, Orlando, FL); Jean Wright, MD, MBA (pediatrician/health system executive), Mint Hill, NC; Gentry Yeatman, MD (adolescent medicine, Tacoma, WA).

Mothers

Valerie Alexander (Birmingham, AL); Carey Clawson (Larkspur, CO); Zanese Duncan (Norcross, GA); Idaliz Good (Kissimmee, FL); Shannon McLaughlin (Celebration, FL); Kathy Norquist (Eagle Creek, OR); Lois Osborn (Larkspur, CO); Jenny Rapp (Falmouth, MA); Sally Zaengle (Greene, NY).

Young women

Harper Alexander (Birmingham, AL); Julia Campbell (Troutdale, OR); Brianna Clark (Colorado Springs, CO); Grace Clawson (Larkspur, CO); Christianna Bishop (South Daytona, FL);

Meredith Clawson (Larkspur, CO); Kelly Gutrich (Tinley Park, IL); Lindsay Henriksen (Glen Rock, PA); Jessica Jones (Los Altos, CA); Annie McVay (Tulsa, OK); Arlyn Moret-Brunet (San Juan, Puerto Rico); Hannah Osborn (Larkspur, CO); Gracie Roberts (Moraga, CA); Courtney Runn (Austin, TX); Casey Lee Sheffey (Lake Mary, FL); Jennifer Sojo (Tallahassee, FL); Hannah Woida (Orlando, FL); Bethany Wright (Mint Hill, NC).

In particular, Carrie Abbott; Carrie Archual; Freda Bush, MD; Robert Fleischmann; Darla R. Grossman, MD; Diane Passno; and Pearl Huang-Ramírez, MD, spent significant time helping us with their extensive review of early manuscripts of the book. Thanks to Andrea Vinley Jewell, Patrick Dunn, and Barb Larimore for over-the-top editorial assistance. Appreciation is due to Ned McLeod and D. J. Snell for legal and contract assistance. We're also grateful to Kim Childress and the team (including Cindy Davis, Guy Francis, and Greg Johnson) at ZonderKidz for the trust they extended in asking us to write this book.

But we're most thankful to God for calling us into the unmatched privilege of being his children. We pray that this book will bring honor and glory to him, his name, his kingdom, his word, his Son, his Spirit, and his church.

Walt Larimore, MD, Monument, CO
Amaryllis Sánchez Wohlever, MD, Orlando, FL

December 2013

RESOURCES

Question 1: What does it mean to be healthy?

God's Design for the Highly Healthy Teen. http://tinyurl.com/arfzmdz
10 Essentials of Happy, Healthy People: Becoming and Staying Highly Healthy. http://tinyurl.com/amcbhzy
God's Design for the Highly Healthy Teen Assessment. http://tinyurl.com/ao4wnxu

Question 3: Why are there things about my body I just don't like?

My life is but a weaving ... adapted from Grant Colfax Tullar's poem "The Weaver" http://tinyurl.com/l2zkdhl

Question 5: Am I growing—or is the ceiling dropping?

Stature-for-Age Chart:
  • http://tinyurl.com/n92u7sh
Predicting your adult height:
  • http://tinyurl.com/ygfe2o
  • http://tinyurl.com/264hutv

Question 7: Do I really need calcium for my bones?

Best Bones Forever. www.facebook.com/bestbonesforever

Question 8: Makeup, hairstyles, clothes—what makes me beautiful?

Mother Teresa. http://tinyurl.com/s6k5p

Question 9: Why do I look so different from the girls I see on TV?

Photoshopping examples:
  • http://tinyurl.com/yfbeeka
  • http://tinyurl.com/bb25wuw
Magazines we recommend:
  • *Sisterhood* (for teens). http://tinyurl.com/azz82nc
  • *Discovery Girls* (for tweens). http://tinyurl.com/yzqmj2h

- *SHINE* (for nine- to fourteen-year-olds) and *Sparkle* (up to age ten). http://tinyurl.com/b3v488q

Nicole Clark's DVD and workshops. http://tinyurl.com/nzc3rwy

Leah Darrow. http://tinyurl.com/asolcfd

Question 10: Should I go on a diet?

National Eating Disorders Association. http://tinyurl.com/b7h35h

BMI percentile calculator. http://tinyurl.com/4tazduc

Become TV-free:

- http://tinyurl.com/yqj9u5
- http://tinyurl.com/azsnzus
- http://tinyurl.com/b38z6sh

Question 11: What can I do if I'm overweight?

Learn to read nutritional labels. http://tinyurl.com/cw948

SuperSized Kids Test activity and nutrition assessment test. http://tinyurl.com/bjoz2ju

Eight-Week Family Fitness Plan. http://tinyurl.com/12b21b4

Meet Families who have used the eight-week plan. http://tinyurl.com/bklelw4

Level 2 (Advanced) Eight-Week Family Fitness Plan. http://tinyurl.com/bxabe94

SuperSized Kids: How to Rescue Your Child from the Obesity Threat. http://tinyurl.com/bgbosgh

Question 13: How do periods work, anyway?

Ovulation video. http://tinyurl.com/ye8rkco

Question 18: Can my moods be dangerous?

Eating disorders information:

- http://tinyurl.com/a9argd6
- http://tinyurl.com/6w3skv2

Question 20: Why do I sweat? It makes me feel like a boy.

"Tanning" Your Smelly Feet:

- The People's Pharmacy. http://tinyurl.com/ajttkee
- Dr. Oz. http://tinyurl.com/ak59qq7

Question 21: What's the big deal about modesty?

Pure Fashion. http://tinyurl.com/bz6qwcz

Question 22: Clothing, thoughts, and good choices — what's the connection?

The Modesty Survey. http://tinyurl.com/aames7x
Saige Hatch's Modesty Club. http://tinyurl.com/bcbqn8w
8 Great Dates for Moms and Daughters. http://tinyurl.com/ncbvh2k
Secret Keeper Girls' Truth or Bare Fashion Tests. http://tinyurl.com
  /krpt5hd

Question 23: Nails, makeup, and hair — how much should I care?

Curly Girl: The Handbook. http://tinyurl.com/cmwca6c
Hair Styling Tips and Tricks for Girls. http://tinyurl.com/bfsu5dl

Question 28: Social media is fun, but how much is too much?

What Would Jesus Text? WWJTXT? http://tinyurl.com/a87hc5x
Plugged In media reviews. http://tinyurl.com/as28qzv

Question 29: What if my friends want to try alcohol, drugs, or dangerous games?

The choking game:
  • http://tinyurl.com/arx6fs5
  • http://tinyurl.com/aczkemr

Question 30: Sex — part of God's plan? Are you serious?

It's Great to Wait. http://tinyurl.com/4zvbatd
Virgin by Grace. Find a counselor near you:
  • Heartbeat International's Option Line, (800) 712-HELP or
    http://tinyurl.com/alldskm
  • Focus on the Family, (800) A-FAMILY
True Pink. http://tinyurl.com/bbpfe96
TeenSTAR Program. http://tinyurl.com/b5462te
Abstinence Clearinghouse. http://tinyurl.com/l9nt7x
Best Friends Foundation. http://tinyurl.com/a5l3nfe
Legacy Institute. http://tinyurl.com/bbpfe96

Question 31: Talk to my parents about sex? Are you crazy?

Secret Keeper Girl. http://tinyurl.com/a7v36v3
Pure Freedom Live. http://tinyurl.com/9wunuuy
Family Life. http://tinyurl.com/b8oa85
Passport2Purity. http://tinyurl.com/acwllde
Biblical Blueprint for Sexual Integrity. http://tinyurl.com/abc5c63
Legacy Institute. http://tinyurl.com/ay3h48g
Relationships With Integrity. http://tinyurl.com/b5mqqp8
Theology of the Body for Teens. http://tinyurl.com/b397pjh
Theology of the Body for Teens: Middle School Edition.
    http://tinyurl.com/6nn556w
True Beauty Bible study. http://tinyurl.com/bbpfe96

Question 32: Is there a monster in my computer?

The Drug of the New Millennium. http://tinyurl.com/bcx4x6q
Internet filters and accountability software:
• Bsecure Online. http://tinyurl.com/ya8vx64
• Netintelligence. http://tinyurl.com/bcktmtx
• Covenant Eyes. http://tinyurl.com/nrf8tc
• X3watch. http://tinyurl.com/c6avbrv

Final Word for Daughters and Parents

Richard Swenson, *Margin: Restoring Emotional, Physical, Financial,
    and Time Reserves to Overloaded Lives* (Colorado Springs:
    NavPress, 2004). http://tinyurl.com/ay7qjxs

Finding God in Tough Times

90 Devotions for Real Girls Facing Real Life

Kristi Holl

You Don't Have to Go It Alone

Every girl deals with hard situations at some time in her life, from stress, peer pressure, and perfectionism to divorce, bullying, and abuse. This 90-day devotional will help you find God and grace in the midst of your storms and struggles. Whether you are looking for help for yourself or for a hurting friend, this book provides wisdom from God's Word and advice from trusted Faithgirlz! author Kristi Holl. Through activities, journal prompts, and stories from real girls like you, you'll find comfort in God's presence—no matter what the circumstances.

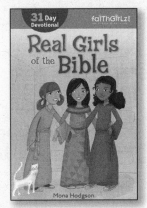

You! A Christian Girl's Guide to Growing Up

Nancy Rue

Knowledge is power, girlfriend.

One day you were an easy-going kid, and the next—wham! You're an emotional roller-coaster. Hair is growing in all-new places, and your best friend whispers the word "bra" in gym class.

Discover God's plan for the beautiful, confident, grown-up you!

Everybody Tells Me to Be Myself but I Don't Know Who I Am, Revised Edition

Nancy Rue

How many times have you heard grown-ups say, "Just be yourself"?

But how can you be yourself when that self always seems to be different—depending on where you are, who you're with, or what you're doing? This book will help you figure out who you really are deep down inside. You'll learn to be the young women God created you to be!

Girl Politics, Updated Edition

Nancy Rue

In this revised edition, bestselling author Nancy Rue provides a guide on how to deal with girl politics, God-style.

Girl Politics has all the info on friends, bullies, frenemies, and more, with real-life examples, conversation starters, Internet tactics, and tips to protect yourself—God style—Revised and updated with more examples from real girls, tackling more issues relevant in today's media-driven world.

Available in stores and online!

Every girl wants to know she's totally unique and special. These Bibles say that with Faithgirlz! sparkle. Through the many in-text features found only in the Faithgirlz! Bible, girls will grow closer to God as they discover the journey of a lifetime.

NIV Faithgirlz! Bible
Hardcover

Features include: ✶ Book introductions—Read about the who, when, where, and what of each book. ✶ Dream Girl—Use your imagination to put yourself in the story. ✶ Bring It On!—Take quizzes to really get to know yourself. ✶ Is There a Little (Eve, Ruth, Isaiah) in You?—See for yourself what you have in common. ✶ Words to Live By—Check out these Bible verses that are great for memorizing. ✶ What Happens Next?—Create a list of events to tell a Bible story in your own words. ✶ Oh, I Get It!—Find answers to Bible questions you've wondered about. ✶ The complete NIV translation ✶ Features written by bestselling author Nancy Rue

NIV Faithgirlz! Backpack Bible
Italian Pink Duo-Tone™

Small enough to fit into a backpack or bag, this Bible can go anywhere a girl does. Features include: ✶ Fun Italian Duo-Tone™ design ✶ Twelve full-color pages of Faithgirlz fun that helps girls learn the "Beauty of Believing!" ✶ Words of Christ in red ✶ Ribbon marker ✶ Complete text of the bestselling NIV translation

Available in stores and online!

Young Women of Faith Bible, NIV

Susie Shellenberger,
general editor

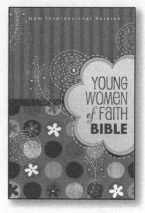

The study Bible that's just for girls!

This Bible is filled with engaging features that will help you learn more about yourself and your relationship with God. Designed to encourage you to develop a habit of studying God's Word, you'll discover how relevant the Bible can be to your everyday life. Weekly studies and many of the side notes are also linked to the women's study Bible, the NIV Women of Faith Study Bible, allowing you and your mom to share God's Word together.

Features include:
- Weekly Bible studies apply biblical truths to life
- Side notes address difficult passages and offer historical and cultural insights
- Journal captures other girls' experiences or struggles along with space for you to record your own
- "I Believe" statements of faith and foundational beliefs
- "Memory Challenges" are verses worth remembering
- "If I Were There . . ." include Bible stories that place you in the Bible character's situation

Available in stores and online!

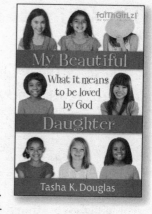

We want to hear from you. Please send your comments about this
book to us in care of zreview@zondervan.com. Thank you.